Reforming the Governance of the Financial Sector

Many financial institutions have in recent years failed – failed either completely, and gone into bankruptcy, or failed in the sense that they have not achieved what their owners or their customers expected them to deliver. This has had significant and adverse effects on customers, taxpayers, shareholders, and sometimes management. There has been much discussion of what should be done about this, and some action has been taken. But has it been the right kind of action?

Crises of the sort being experienced are low probability but high impact events. This volume, from an international group of scholars, deals with two main issues: first, how can the governance of the financial sector by the authorities be improved and, second, how can the governance of firms and institutions within the sector be improved to render the probability and cost of future crises lower?

Poor governance has been one of the major contributors to the global financial crisis. With better governance of and in the financial sector, the financial crisis might well have been avoided altogether and certainly could have been much milder in its impact. This is not simply a case of being wise after the event. These problems were widely discussed before the event, but little action was taken. This book explores not only what the contribution of poor governance was to the crisis and to its depth, but also why it is often difficult to improve governance. The volume offers a positive critique of the measures that are being put in place in the light of the experience of the crisis and suggests how they might plausibly be improved.

This book will be of particular interest to students and researchers of economics and international finance, but will also prove profitable reading for practitioners and the interested public.

David G. Mayes is BNZ Professor of Finance and Director of the New Zealand Governance Centre and the Europe Institute at the University of Auckland, New Zealand.

Geoffrey Wood is Professor Emeritus of Economics at Cass Business School, City University, UK and Professor Emeritus of Monetary Economics at the University of Buckingham, UK.

Routledge International Studies in Money and Banking

1 **Private Banking in Europe**
Lynn Bicker

2 **Bank Deregulation and Monetary Order**
George Selgin

3 **Money in Islam**
A study in Islamic political economy
Masudul Alam Choudhury

4 **The Future of European Financial Centres**
Kirsten Bindemann

5 **Payment Systems in Global Perspective**
Maxwell J. Fry, Isaak Kilato, Sandra Roger, Krzysztof Senderowicz, David Sheppard, Francisco Solis and John Trundle

6 **What is Money?**
John Smithin

7 **Finance**
A characteristics approach
Edited by David Blake

8 **Organisational Change and Retail Finance**
An ethnographic perspective
Richard Harper, Dave Randall and Mark Rouncefield

9 **The History of the Bundesbank**
Lessons for the European Central Bank
Jakob de Haan

10 **The Euro**
A challenge and opportunity for financial markets
Published on behalf of Société Universitaire Européenne de Recherches Financières (SUERF)
Edited by Michael Artis, Axel Weber and Elizabeth Hennessy

11 **Central Banking in Eastern Europe**
Edited by Nigel Healey and Barry Harrison

12 **Money, Credit and Prices Stability**
Paul Dalziel

13 **Monetary Policy, Capital Flows and Exchange Rates**
Essays in memory of Maxwell Fry
Edited by William Allen and David Dickinson

14 Adapting to Financial Globalisation
Published on behalf of Société Universitaire Européenne de Recherches Financières (SUERF)
Edited by Morten Balling, Eduard H. Hochreiter and Elizabeth Hennessy

15 Monetary Macroeconomics
A new approach
Alvaro Cencini

16 Monetary Stability in Europe
Stefan Collignon

17 Technology and Finance
Challenges for financial markets, business strategies and policy makers
Published on behalf of Société Universitaire Européenne de Recherches Financières (SUERF)
Edited by Morten Balling, Frank Lierman, and Andrew Mullineux

18 Monetary Unions
Theory, history, public choice
Edited by Forrest H. Capie and Geoffrey E. Wood

19 HRM and Occupational Health and Safety
Carol Boyd

20 Central Banking Systems Compared
The ECB, the pre-Euro Bundesbank and the Federal Reserve System
Emmanuel Apel

21 A History of Monetary Unions
John Chown

22 Dollarization
Lessons from Europe and the Americas
Edited by Louis-Philippe Rochon and Mario Seccareccia

23 Islamic Economics and Finance: A Glossary, 2nd Edition
Muhammad Akram Khan

24 Financial Market Risk
Measurement and analysis
Cornelis A. Los

25 Financial Geography
A banker's view
Risto Laulajainen

26 Money Doctors
The experience of international financial advising 1850–2000
Edited by Marc Flandreau

27 Exchange Rate Dynamics
A new open economy macroeconomics perspective
Edited by Jean-Oliver Hairault and Thepthida Sopraseuth

28 Fixing Financial Crises in the 21st Century
Edited by Andrew G. Haldane

29 Monetary Policy and Unemployment
The U.S., Euro-area and Japan
Edited by Willi Semmler

30 Exchange Rates, Capital Flows and Policy
Edited by Peter Sinclair, Rebecca Driver and Christoph Thoenissen

31 **Great Architects of International Finance**
The Bretton Woods era
Anthony M. Endres

32 **The Means to Prosperity**
Fiscal policy reconsidered
Edited by Per Gunnar Berglund and Matias Vernengo

33 **Competition and Profitability in European Financial Services**
Strategic, systemic and policy issues
Edited by Morten Balling, Frank Lierman and Andy Mullineux

34 **Tax Systems and Tax Reforms in South and East Asia**
Edited by Luigi Bernardi, Angela Fraschini and Parthasarathi Shome

35 **Institutional Change in the Payments System and Monetary Policy**
Edited by Stefan W. Schmitz and Geoffrey E. Wood

36 **The Lender of Last Resort**
Edited by F.H. Capie and G.E. Wood

37 **The Structure of Financial Regulation**
Edited by David G. Mayes and Geoffrey E. Wood

38 **Monetary Policy in Central Europe**
Miroslav Beblavý

39 **Money and Payments in Theory and Practice**
Sergio Rossi

40 **Open Market Operations and Financial Markets**
Edited by David G. Mayes and Jan Toporowski

41 **Banking in Central and Eastern Europe 1980–2006**
A comprehensive analysis of banking sector transformation in the former Soviet Union, Czechoslovakia, East Germany, Yugoslavia, Belarus, Bulgaria, Croatia, the Czech Republic, Hungary, Kazakhstan, Poland, Romania, the Russian Federation, Serbia and Montenegro, Slovakia, Ukraine and Uzbekistan
Stephan Barisitz

42 **Debt, Risk and Liquidity in Futures Markets**
Edited by Barry A. Goss

43 **The Future of Payment Systems**
Edited by Stephen Millard, Andrew G. Haldane and Victoria Saporta

44 **Credit and Collateral**
Vania Sena

45 **Tax Systems and Tax Reforms in Latin America**
Edited by Luigi Bernardi, Alberto Barreix, Anna Marenzi and Paola Profeta

46 **The Dynamics of Organizational Collapse**
The case of Barings Bank
Helga Drummond

47 International Financial Co-operation
Political economics of compliance with the 1988 Basel Accord
Bryce Quillin

48 Bank Performance
A theoretical and empirical framework for the analysis of profitability, competition and efficiency
Jacob Bikker and Jaap W.B. Bos

49 Monetary Growth Theory
Money, interest, prices, capital, knowledge and economic structure over time and space
Wei-Bin Zhang

50 Money, Uncertainty and Time
Giuseppe Fontana

51 Central Banking, Asset Prices and Financial Fragility
Éric Tymoigne

52 Financial Markets and the Macroeconomy
Willi Semmler, Peter Flaschel, Carl Chiarella and Reiner Franke

53 Inflation Theory in Economics
Welfare, velocity, growth and business cycles
Max Gillman

54 Monetary Policy Over Fifty Years
Heinz Herrman (Deutsche Bundesbank)

55 Designing Central Banks
David Mayes and Geoffrey Wood

56 Inflation Expectations
Peter J.N. Sinclair

57 The New International Monetary System
Essays in honour of Alexander Swoboda
Edited by Charles Wyplosz

58 Taxation and Gender Equity
A comparative analysis of direct and indirect taxes in developing and developed countries
Edited by Caren Grown and Imraan Valodia

59 Developing Alternative Frameworks for Explaining Tax Compliance
Edited by James Alm, Jorge Martinez-Vazquez and Benno Torgler

60 International Tax Coordination
An interdisciplinary perspective on virtues and pitfalls
Edited by Martin Zagler

61 The Capital Needs of Central Banks
Edited by Sue Milton and Peter Sinclair

62 Monetary and Banking History
Edited by Geoffrey E. Wood, Terence Mills and Nicholas Crafts

63 New Approaches to Monetary Economics and Theory
Interdisciplinary perspectives
Edited by Heiner Ganßmann

64 Social Banks and the Future of Sustainable Finance
Edited by Olaf Weber and Sven Remer

65 Policy Makers on Policy
The Mais lectures
Edited by Forrest H. Capie and Geoffrey E. Wood

66 Prediction Markets
Theory and applications
Edited by Leighton Vaughan Williams

67 Towards a Socioanalysis of Money, Finance and Capitalism
Beneath the surface of the financial industry
Edited by Susan Long and Burkard Sievers

68 Doing Money
Heiner Ganßmann

69 Banking Regulation and the Financial Crisis
Jin Cao

70 Banking Crises, Liquidity and Credit Lines
A macroeconomic perspective
Gurbachan Singh

71 New Paradigms in Financial Economics
How would Keynes reconstruct economics?
Kazem Falahati

72 Risk, Risk Management and Regulation in the Banking Industry
The risk to come
Peter Pelzer

73 Financial Systems in Troubled Waters
Information, strategies, and governance to enhance performances in risky times
Edited by Alessandro Carretta and Gianluca Mattarocci

74 Reforming the Governance of the Financial Sector
Edited by David G. Mayes and Geoffrey Wood

Reforming the Governance of the Financial Sector

Edited by David G. Mayes and Geoffrey Wood

Routledge
Taylor & Francis Group
LONDON AND NEW YORK

First published 2013
by Routledge
2 Park Square, Milton Park, Abingdon, Oxfordshire OX14 4RN

Simultaneously published in the USA and Canada
by Routledge
711 Third Avenue, New York, NY 10017

First issued in paperback 2014

Routledge is an imprint of the Taylor & Francis Group, an informa business

British Library Cataloguing in Publication Data
A catalogue record for this book is available from the British Library

Library of Congress Cataloging in Publication Data
Reforming the governance of the financial sector/edited by
David G. Mayes and Geoffrey Wood.
p. cm.
Includes bibliographical references and index.
1. Financial institutions–Management. 2. Financial institutions–State supervision. 3. Corporate governance. 4. Financial crises. I. Mayes, David G. II. Wood, Geoffrey Edward.
HG173.R393 2012
332.1–dc23

2012016012

ISBN 978-0-415-68684-6 (hbk)
ISBN 978-1-138-79947-9 (pbk)
ISBN 978-0-203-08454-0 (ebk)

Typeset in Times New Roman
by Wearset Ltd, Boldon, Tyne and Wear

This book is dedicated to the memory of Horace Alfred Mayes 1906–2010

Contents

Figures

Tables

Contributors

Christine Brown, Professor of Finance, Monash University.

Jeffrey M. Chwieroth, Reader in International Political Economy, London School of Economics.

Kevin Davis, Professor of Finance, University of Melbourne.

Jane Diplock, Chairman, New Zealand Securities Commission.

Gillian G.H. Garcia, President, Gillian G.H. Garcia Associates, Washington, DC.

Ali Kabiri, Cass Business School, London.

Charles Littrell, Executive Director, Australian Prudential Regulation Authority.

David G. Mayes, BNZ Professor of Finance, Director New Zealand Governance Centre and European Institute, University of Auckland.

Geof Mortlock, Australian Prudential Regulatory Authority.

John Pinfold, Associate Professor of Finance, Massey University.

Deborah Ralston, Professor of Finance, Director, Australian Centre for Financial Studies, Melbourne.

Lawrence C. Rose, Dean, College of Business and Public Administration, California State University, San Bernadino.

Bruce Sheppard, Partner, Gilligan Sheppard, Auckland.

Grant Spencer, Deputy Governor, Reserve Bank of New Zealand.

William Wilson, Lecturer in Finance, Massey University.

Geoffrey Wood, Professor Emeritus, Cass Business School and University of Buckingham.

Preface

This book is the fortunate outcome of a combination of wants. It was clear to the New Zealand Governance Centre that the governance of the financial sector was in urgent need of improvement in the light of both the problems in the global financial crisis and the demise of the finance company sector in New Zealand between 2005 and 2009. The Seelye Foundation awarded David Mayes and the Europe Institute the opportunity to bring out Geoffrey Wood from London as a Distinguished Visitor to give a public lecture and undertake further joint research with David Mayes. The Bank of New Zealand laid down only one objective for the chair of finance which it had endowed, and David Mayes holds, which was to improve the financial literacy of New Zealanders. The retired and other less informed investors and depositors had been heavily hit in New Zealand and, uniquely in the OECD, had been unprotected going into the financial crisis. The Research Centre for Business Law was keen to work on financial institutions and their regulation. Taken together, this enabled the organization of a conference on the topic of 'Reforming the Governance of the Financial Sector', which is the title of this book, in September of 2010.

We selected papers from a carefully mixed group of academics, practitioners, and regulators, with a similarly balanced group of discussants to ensure a good debate and the development of the ideas in the papers from early versions. We have chosen the best for publication following the refereeing process.

As is clear from the Introduction, we regard this topic as one of the key areas to be addressed if future financial regulation is going to stand a better chance of achieving stable financial markets and avoiding a repeat of the present crisis. Unless those running banks want to achieve stability for their own benefit and unless the regulatory framework deals with the financial system as a whole, it is unlikely that these objectives will be achieved, however detailed and intrusive the regulation becomes. That will merely hobble the institutions it covers and drive activity elsewhere. At the same time, the extensive losses endured by many households and unsophisticated investors shows that the idea that disclosure alone will protect them adequately is unrealistic. Financial education, while helpful, is unlikely to be enough and some level of protection, if only for bank deposits, is needed, otherwise distress such as that incurred by the collapse of the finance company sector in New Zealand may occur again.

D.G.M.
G.E.W.

Acknowledgements

We are grateful to John Farrar and Susan Watson, co-Director and Deputy Director of the NZ Governance Centre, for their help in putting the conference behind this book together and to the various staff in the Business School in the University of Auckland who managed to make the arrangements run smoothly. We are also grateful to Rick Bigwood, then Director of the Research Centre for Business Law, for his participation and help. We are grateful for funding to the Seelye Foundation, The Europe Institute, Buddle Findlay, and the BNZ Chair in Finance.

Several of the authors have their own acknowledgements and disclaimers, as the views expressed were, in the main, personal and did not reflect any which might have been held by the organizations for which they work.

Jeffrey Chwieroth is grateful for helpful comments from J. Corbett, H.K. Chey, Y.K. Kim, S.H. Lee, D. Mayes, and G.E. Wood.

Gillian Garcia thanks Chris Adam, George Blackford, Andrew Campbell, Robert Eisenbeis, Joseph Gunnel, George Kaufman, John Raymond LaBrosse, Joseph Mason, David Mayes, Maria Nieto, Dalvinder Singh, and Larry Wall for their help and/or their comments on earlier drafts of Chapter 10.

Geoffrey Wood is indebted to Forrest Capie, Andrew Colquhoon, Richard Epstein, and David Mayes for most helpful comments on Chapter 7.

Geoffrey Wood and Ali Kabiri thank Rae Balbach, Charles Goodhart, and Martin Ricketts for most helpful comments on Chapter 13.

We are particularly grateful to Janet Mayes for her key role in preparing the typescript.

Acknowledgements

1 Introduction

David G. Mayes and Geoffrey Wood

Poor governance has been one of the major contributors to the global financial crisis. With better governance of and in the financial sector, the financial crisis might well have been avoided altogether and certainly could have been much milder in its impact. This is not simply a case of being wise after the event. These problems were widely discussed before the event, including by the present authors, but little action was taken. In this book, we explore not just what the contribution of poor governance was to the crisis and to its depth but also why it is often difficult to improve governance. This enables us to offer a positive critique of the measures that are being put in place in the light of the experience of the crisis and to suggest how they might plausibly be improved. Crises of the sort being experienced are low-probability but high-impact events. Until they are a reality, it is very difficult to persuade people to take the actions necessary to provide the balance between good crisis avoidance and management preparation efforts, on the one hand, and greater risk taking, on the other, that people think appropriate once they have seen what a bad crisis can be like. The Nordic and Asian countries learnt a lot from their crises in the 1990s but others did not. Even so, the messages for better governance by and large did not get through.

In this book, we deal with two main issues: first, how can the governance of the financial sector by the authorities be improved and, second, how can the governance of firms and institutions within the sector be improved to render the probability and cost of future crises lower? However, such recommendations have to balance the cost of avoidance against the cost of occurrence. The costs of avoidance are incurred whether or not a crisis would have occurred. The costs of a crisis occur only when it does.

The institutional arrangements

The most obvious institutional failures in governance were:

- lack of responsibility for financial stability at the economy-wide level
- inability to resolve problems without the use of taxpayer funds – particularly the ability to permit smooth exit of inefficient banks
- neglect of the non-bank financial sector

- national regimes to handle cross-border problems and multinational financial groups
- regulatory capture of the international standard setting process.

Clearly there were others. One illustrated in the case of the failure of Northern Rock in the UK was the inability of different institutions to work together harmoniously in a crisis (Mayes and Wood, 2008). Furthermore, as also illustrated by Northern Rock and problems in several other countries, supervisors simply did a poor job of recognizing the normal signs of potential stress in financial institutions, from excessive growth, concentration on property, related-party exposures and simply excess leverage. We must ask whether there is something in the governance arrangements of supervisory authorities that leads to these deficiencies. In part, it was recognized 20 years earlier in the US, with the introduction of mandated prompt corrective action as part of FDICIA (the Federal Deposit Insurance Corporation Improvement Act of 1991). However, since these same failures were apparent this time in the US, as described by Garcia in Chapter 10, clearly the governance failure was more pervasive.

Lack of responsibility for financial stability at the economy-wide level

In the years running up to the crisis, there had been increasing emphasis on the need for financial stability to match the well-developed focus on price stability that had emerged in the 1990s, illustrated most famously by the formal adoption of inflation targeting in New Zealand in 1989. Financial stability, while undefined (Allen and Wood, 2006), was adopted as an objective unilaterally by many central banks, without it being written explicitly into their terms of reference. In many respects, it was viewed simply as an obvious necessity for maintaining price stability. Instability in the financial sector is likely to have real consequences and, while most other sources of shocks might be outside central banks' control, at least the financial system was an area where it could have considerable influence.

Since, on the whole, central banks did not have any powers in this regard, they resorted to publishing information and analysis on the stability of the financial sector in the hope that others would act. Thus regular Financial Stability Reviews began to be published following the experience with Monetary Policy Statements.[1] However, central banks had a problem with such publications as talking up problems to encourage others to act could of itself generate instability as market participants would also react – particularly if they felt the government or responsible regulator would not respond. Hence there was a tendency for real pressure to be covert and for the reviews to be generally reassuring. Indeed the first financial stability reviews in Finland were produced with the deliberate aim of showing that the difficulties in the economy following the Finnish financial crisis of 1992/3 were clearly over and the banking system was well capitalized and efficient, financial ratios strong and financial markets functioning well.[2]

On the whole, financial supervisors did not feel the same need to consider the stability of the financial system as a whole. Their work focused on the strength and stability of each individual institution within their sector. One exception was the Financial Services Authority (FSA) in the UK, which each year prepared a risk review, where it explored some major risks and suggested scenarios for the performance of the financial sectors should these adverse (or positive) scenarios eventuate. These scenarios of course fell far short of what might have been regarded as stress tests of the financial sector.

One major problem was a lack of appreciation of the degree of interconnectedness of the financial system and how financial markets could come to a halt if there was a general worry over who might be facing failure through major losses. The second was the extent of imbalances and the concentration of risks. In some respects, investigations into the direct connections in the financial system were very misleading. Continental Illinois had not been allowed to fail in 1984 because of fear that it would bring down several other large banks with it. Subsequent calculations suggested that the chances were small once the exposures were known. Similarly, de Bandt and Hartmann (2000) estimated that the degree of interconnectedness in the European markets was quite low. These calculations may have been correct, ignoring off balance sheet items, but not allowing for the indirect contagion gave a very false sense of security. People react to supposed problems, so they exit from healthy banks on rumour and will not lend to anyone they have any doubts about. This can bring about the failure of otherwise sound institutions.

As a result, the fact that nobody was given clear responsibility in most countries, or worse still any ability to act if they did feel responsibility, combined with a serious underestimate of the potential problem. Central banks only had tools to handle monetary policy and in most cases limited that to a short interest rate. Macro-prudential concerns might conflict with monetary policy and would hence need their own tools. Such tools did exist. The Hong Kong Monetary Authority used loan-to-value ratios to try to restrict the rapid growth in property prices. (It also tried to achieve stability on the downside in asset markets by purchasing shares when it felt the market was becoming seriously undervalued.) However, most authorities held back.

Worse still, an approach developed in the US, labelled by Blinder and Reis (2005) as the 'Greenspan standard', that increased instability in the system by arguing that it was difficult to decide whether an increase in asset prices was a bubble or a correct adjustment to a substantial improvement in longer term prospects. Hence, while the correct strategy was to lean against such supposed bubbles, the central bank would be unwise to prick them outright in case they were wrong and damaged everybody's living standards unnecessarily. The view was that it was possible to intervene fast enough once the bubble was deflating to be able to avoid a really serious recession. Experience since 1987 appeared to bear this out.

Thus it was a combination of governance and the exercise of policy which was at fault.

Inability to resolve problems without the use of taxpayer funds – particularly the ability to permit smooth exit of inefficient banks

In most industries, competitive pressures force out the inefficient and those with less desirable products or services over time and this in itself acts as a brake on inefficient and weak management. In banking, this is not the case, and in the crisis it became clear that it was not just large banks that would not be allowed to fail but in some cases smaller ones too. This had the potential for serious moral hazard in terms of encouraging risk taking because the downside costs were limited, with losses being picked up by future taxpayers. In combination with the procyclical force of the 'Greenspan standard', noted above, and the procyclicality of the Basel 2 risk-weighted capital adequacy requirements (Peura and Jokivuolle, 2004), this provided a serious threat to stability. The problem was not so much that countries did not want to allow poorly performing financial institutions to close but that they did not have the tools to allow them to close without causing substantial financial disruption and making the crisis worse rather than better.

This problem had been widely foreseen and solutions existed or could be implemented (Mayes *et al.*, 2001). The United States in particular but also Canada had put in place a system where early intervention was mandated and the authorities had the power to step into banks before they became insolvent to resolve them without the use of taxpayers' money. However, even there, some banks were so large that this method would be infeasible – the problem of 'Too Big To Fail' (Stern and Feldman, 2004).

Addressing smaller banks has proved relatively straightforward, with the UK, for example, introducing a comprehensive range of powers through its 2009 Banking Act. Dealing with the large banks has proved harder, with the intention of introducing the concept of 'living wills', whereby banks have to explain how their impending insolvency could be handled in a manner which keeps their vital functions operating without involving the spending of public funds, thereby ensuring the continuation of the financial system with minimum disruption. A large part of this solution is going to come from the appropriate structuring of large financial institutions, so that vital functions, such as retail banking, can be isolated and resolved. In the UK, assisted by the report of the Vickers' Commission, there is talk of separating retail banking within the banking group so that it is not open to the threats of instability that have occurred in investment banking.

New Zealand has come up with its own solution, previously labelled Bank Creditor Recapitalization but now simply Open Bank Resolution, whereby the Reserve Bank steps in as statutory manager and writes down shareholders and then junior creditors (including depositors) in order of priority until the point that the bank has become adequately capitalized again.[3] All this has to be completed, on the basis of summary valuation, within the transaction day so the bank does not cease to provide its main services. There are obvious problems with this, but the greatest is the anomalous treatment of depositors.

All other OECD countries feel that depositors need to be protected/insured as they cannot be expected to work out if a bank is running excessive risks.[4] Moreover, depositors without protection are more likely to run on a bank at the first hint of difficulty, thereby turning a problem into a full-blown crisis. It seems unlikely that any government would be prepared to let a large bank go under in this manner as it would alienate too many voters. However, since the four largest banks in New Zealand are Australian owned and the Australian authorities have made it clear that they will not be allowed to fail, then it is likely that the New Zealand subsidiaries will not fail either, as that would be too great a damage to the parent banks' reputations. However, the resulting pressure from Australia for the New Zealand taxpayer to contribute to the cost would not be trivial, to say the least.

Neglect of the non-bank financial sector

However, one of the key lessons that has been learnt in the crisis and indeed outside it is the importance of being able to regulate, supervise and resolve all financial institutions that might threaten financial stability, not just those that have the technical status of being a registered bank. The clearest example was the failure of Lehman Brothers in the US, which was the direct cause of the main part of the global financial crisis. Had Lehman Brothers been a registered bank in the US, the authorities could have stepped in and limited the costs to society, not just at home but abroad as well, at very limited cost to the taxpayer. As it was, they had to use normal insolvency procedures for non-bank companies, which involved a stop in most transactions and the transmission of the shock round the world through counterparties and the fear of dealing with others who might have been affected or could possibly be affected in the future. This effectively closed wholesale financial markets until central banks could substitute for them.

In the US, the problems extended into insurance, where AIG had to be bailed out, as it was such an important player in the credit default swaps market. However, even in New Zealand, the failure to have anything other than very light regulation for all but registered banks led to the disappearance of the finance company sector and with it much of the non-bank deposit-taking sector, even before the crisis took hold. As a result, the Reserve Bank has taken overall responsibility for the prudential regulation of the financial sector as a whole and a new Financial Markets Authority (FMA) has been set up to try to provide much closer regulation of non-bank finance.

The new head of the FMA has made it clear that governance lay at the heart of the previous problems:

> the finance company failures were largely a failure of corporate governance. That is, that many of the directors of these companies (and others closely involved in their operations) weren't doing their jobs adequately. Sentences such as [the] prison terms given to some … directors do send a message to our corporate community that they have clear responsibilities and a duty to

> act with diligence and care. But the failures also raise the bigger question of the role of regulation and the pros and cons of 'light touch' regulation. ... It would be fair to say that there is little faith remaining in the notion of 'light touch' regulation and inherently stable markets...
>
> (Hughes, 2012)

Thus, although it may have been corporate governance which was at fault, it was the deficiencies in the regulatory framework that let this happen. It was the governance of the financial sector which bears the primary blame and governance within the sector followed from that. In some cases, the lapses are understandable. Nobody understood the full extent of the exposure of insurance companies such as AIG, presumably including the directors of AIG itself. However, other areas such as limited regulation of deposit takers and a lack of deposit insurance were, along with the need for a special resolution regime, well known. These were calculated risks, which turned out to be expensive when they were realized.

Other aspects of the limits to the supervisory and regulatory net have also been highlighted, where the nature of the deficiencies vary. Explosive growth and little understood products in over-the-counter (OTC) derivatives markets were examples that contributed to the crisis. The natural reaction has been to try to limit innovation and commodify such products so that they can be traded on markets with central counterparties. This would increase information, improve standards and reduce risks, and would substantially change the governance of the system.

The other major issue has been conflict of interest. Already before the crisis, this had been thoroughly aired in the case of auditors. Auditors are supposed to provide objective information on the company for the benefit of current and potential shareholders. Yet in some of the most egregious examples – Enron, for instance – they had effectively connived in permitting companies to take major risks that were not clearly disclosed. Part of the alleged reason was that they could earn far more from consultancy work for the company than they could from auditing and hence there was a potential temptation to produce reports that were favourable to the management who could award them those contracts.

A similar risk is present for ratings agencies, although there is (as yet?) no evidence that they manipulated ratings for the benefits of issuers. In the case of the ratings agencies, although technically independent, they work for the issuer, not the buyer. However, it is the buyers who want to know more about the potential risks in the product. As there are many potential buyers, it is very difficult to think of a way in which the buyer could organize and pay for the rating to eliminate the potential conflict. The interest has occurred because of the substantial overrating, especially of some of the more exotic derivatives, that was revealed once the crisis broke. It is clear that the ratings agencies made major mistakes, perhaps justifiably given the lack of evidence on the new products and the initial strong performance, but it is not clear whether there was a governance failure, despite the less-than-ideal structure.

A simple means of addressing the problem is to make sure that the incentives for ratings agencies are more aligned with those of the buyers by paying them fees over the lifetime of the security, which reflect the accuracy of the rating, instead of paying them all up front. If the rating proves unsound, then the fees stop.

This misalignment of incentives is even more obvious for agents and advisors, where they get their fees up front, with no penalties for poor performance. Clearly if there are long-term relationships then any agent who does a poor job will not get repeat business. However, if the information about performance is weak, such agents could easily move on to other suppliers and collect commissions for a considerable period. Again the problem is partly whether the agent is working for the buyer or the seller and whether the buyer appreciates what the relationship actually is. Even with full disclosure, it is still the case that an investment company gets its income from fees and not from the performance of the securities it holds on behalf of clients. Hence there will always be an incentive to recommend fee-intensive products where this has little impact on performance. However, performance cannot be too poor or the firm will lose its clients to better performing competitors.

This lack of exposure distinguishes hedge and other funds aimed at more sophisticated investors. There it is essential that the fund managers are also investors in the funds so that they have just as much riding on their success as do their clients. Otherwise clients will not trust them enough to invest. Thus, although hedge funds may be little known and may in some cases have the potential for destabilizing markets, it is by no means clear that they face serious governance issues in the way that independent and tied advisors do. Indeed, it seems likely that hedge funds have helped in stabilizing the crisis, as they have been able to absorb losses rather than multiply them through the system through contagious failure.

The crisis has therefore renewed the old debate about how far out one should push the boundary of closer supervision and control. Some self-regulated groups appear to have remained unreproached – actuaries, for example. Although they work in the main for sellers rather than buyers, there has been little complaint that they have been tilting the statistics to favour that relationship. The further out the boundary is pushed, the greater the likelihood that the risky transactions will be pushed into areas where it is more difficult to find out what is going on or assess their risk to financial stability. The greater the restrictions on products then the more likely it will be that useful innovations that will help the development of the real economy will be inhibited. (Of course some, such as Paul Volcker, have doubted the ability of financial markets to provide anything much of such a contribution and hence would not be concerned by the restriction.)[5]

National regimes to handle cross-border problems and multinational financial groups

A governance issue at the global level was the fact that the regimes designed to handle financial stability were all national, even within the EU, while the problems they were designed to tackle were global and the more important institutions they were trying to regulate were also cross-border, if not global, themselves. As a result, there were major gaps in both coverage and coordination.

The simplest issue was that, even though the country in which a cross-border institution was headquartered might be responsible for the supervision of the whole group, it would nevertheless not have any jurisdiction outside its borders. Cooperation of host countries would therefore be required in the process of monitoring and ensuring compliance with regulations. In the event of a problem, the difficulty would be much greater, as not only was there no jurisdictional power but interests might well conflict as each country would be concerned to look after the interests of its own citizens and companies first.

The problem was greatest inside the EU as elsewhere authorities could control cross-border activities and make sure that they were conducted in a way that was compatible with financial stability. Thus New Zealand, for example, could insist that cross-border institutions that were of systemic importance were locally incorporated and also able to operate in completely free-standing mode within the transaction day, should there be a problem with the parent. In the EU, if a bank registered in one country wishes to set up a branch in another country, it can do so without the consent of the host country, and prudential regulation (and deposit insurance) will be the responsibility of the home country. Thus a host country could have systemically important financial activities going on within its own borders, which it could not control. By the same token, while the host country would be unable to control its own financial stability, the home country would not necessarily want to handle a problem in subsidiary elsewhere in the EU to the primary benefit of the host country if their interests conflicted.

Despite considerable concerns among the Nordic countries, where the major banks ran across borders (Mayes *et al.*, 2001; Mayes and Liuksila, 2004), these worries were treated as being largely theoretical by the EU authorities. However, with the collapse of the Icelandic banks, it became all too much a reality. Mayes and Liuksila (2004) had already used the phrase 'Too Big To Save' to cover the case of Iceland, and Hüpkes (2004) in the same volume explains how Switzerland had realized that the same applied to UBS and Credit Suisse and had acted upon it, limiting the size of the total payout that could be made from the deposit insurance fund.

When the Icelandic banks did collapse, there was no way that the Icelandic authorities could save them, nor could they afford to pay out their deposit insurance liabilities.

Since the crisis, there has been a lot of effort to try to organize the appropriate handling of the world's largest SIFIs (systemically important financial institutions) – which have been labelled G-SIFIs (global SIFIs). Here the concerns over living wills are writ even larger as it requires cooperation among different countries. Again it is clear that much of the effort will go into trying to structure these institutions in a way that they can be handled readily by the different authorities with a plausible level of cooperation. Rather, that is, than there being an agreement on how the burden should be shared out after the event, either where the home country acts or where the various countries struggle to cooperate. The case of Fortis provides the most realistic example of what is likely to happen, when the Dutch authorities chose to nationalize the part of the bank in their jurisdiction, rather than attempt to save the group as a whole in a joint effort with their Benelux partners, led by the home country, Belgium (Kudrna, 2010).

Regulatory capture of the international standard setting process

It is very difficult to understand how prudential standards were able to drop so far in the run-up to the global financial crisis. After international problems in the 1970s and 1980s, the Basel Committee on Banking Supervision had been set up and had produced two sets of regulatory standards – the second, Basel 2, not long before the crisis broke. Basel 2 in particular was highly detailed, had taken a long time to negotiate and had been 'trialled' in a series of quantitative impact studies. Rather than encouraging greater provisions against risk and a more stable system, the rules were associated with reductions in capital buffers and a system that was procyclical, amplifying rather than reducing the cycle in the real economy as was intended.

Clearly there were major collective errors, but with the benefit of hindsight an obvious candidate for the lowering of standards was capture of the system by the major international banks. There is a clear difficulty that all regulators face. They are not going to be completely up to date with the latest products and they will always be less informed about any individual institutions than those working in them. What they can offer is a much better appreciation of the impact of joint actions, where individual firms will tend to focus only on their own risks rather than the consequences of large numbers taking the same risk at the same time.

What is clear is that simply having a wide range of detailed rules is not per se a solution. Having a regulatory environment where firms pursue goals that are consistent with systemic stability while in pursuit of their own interests would be much more likely to succeed. Similarly, the disclosure-based system implemented in 1996 by New Zealand should in principle have a good chance of success. It focused on the measures that a bank would want to collect so that it could manage its own risks and on the disclosure of information that any informed investor would require – looking, for example, at maximum rather than end-of-period or average exposures. This, coupled with personal financial liability for misleading statements and prison terms for directors, might have been thought to align directors' interests with those of the supervisor and other stakeholders.

It is difficult to know how well this has worked. Clearly retail investors make no use of disclosure statements and somewhat surprisingly the market, in the form of informed journalism, seems to do relatively little. It had been assumed in designing the rules that the most important discipliners would have been competitors, who would pick on any weakness and ensure it was heavily publicized. In practice, the main banks have been strong and survived the crisis well. But they are all Australian owned and the Australian Prudential Regulatory

Authority (APRA) has followed a traditional approach of close supervision with extensive rules. No other country has followed the NZ example, so clearly the approach has not been persuasive.

This provides a dilemma in present circumstances as the main response has been more regulation, when a more appropriate one would have been smarter regulation that got banks to want to work with the authorities for their own benefit (Mayes *et al.*, 2009). There appears to be a danger already that the punch is being pulled and that the new regulatory environment, while much more burdensome in terms of compliance, will not actually tackle some of the underlying problems of how financial institutions tend to behave in what they perceive as their own interest. Part of this may be that they do not behave in the interests of their owners, which is the topic of the next section, but much still seems to be down to the difficulties in the governance of the sector by the authorities. Central banks in the past have been accused of being a trade association acting on behalf of the commercial banks. The nature of the response in many countries, with the extensive bail-outs by the taxpayer, might lead people to think that was still true.

The governance of individual firms and organizations

Most people tend to associate the concept of governance with corporate governance and, for that reason, we have spent most of our effort in this Introduction considering governance of the financial sector rather than corporate governance within it, as it is the less familiar. Problems in corporate governance, however, do indeed lie at the heart of the financial crisis. Shareholders in a financial institution are the first to bear losses when it gets into difficulty. On this occasion, their losses have been major, in several cases seeing the value of their shares fall to zero as banks fail or are nationalized on failure. Such drastic losses have included household names, such as Royal Bank of Scotland, Lloyds, Bank of America and Citibank, just to mention a few.

The question of interest here is whether financial institutions have been subject to unusual corporate governance problems or whether as the most exposed sector the results are more obvious. After all, General Motors also had to be bailed out in the US. It is not clear that their governance structures were particularly different from that of other firms but, as we have noted with the existence of deposit insurance and the expectation of bail-outs, the factors disciplining management may have been rather weaker than in non-financial firms. The existence of depositors in any case adds another stakeholder. Depositors are a combination of customers and junior creditors. Protecting depositors ranks above protecting shareholders to a much greater extent than it does other junior creditors compared to shareholders. Borrowers are also in an unusual position as they are also customers. Outside financial institutions, firms do not normally have a claim on their customers. Financial institutions are clearly more risky than their non-financial counterparts and are hence subject to a range of prudential controls. However, such controls should help protect the shareholder more than in non-financial companies, especially where any taxpayer intervention does not come in the form of common stock. The lack of competition in many countries also protects the shareholder, with a small group of large banks effectively running a cartel, although not normally breaking the anti-trust rules.

Banks have also featured highly on one of the other well-known governance problems, namely excessive remuneration. Banks seem to have typified the culture of greed that has characterized recent years. Not only were remuneration packages subject to the same design flaws that meant there was a lack of requirement to achieve any longer term value in awarding bonuses or other special payments, but much of the trading gains for which people were rewarded did not represent exceptional performance compared to the market, but simply a rise in value which was part of a general market movement.

Some changes are taking place but it is clear that the culture of expecting major bonuses and large salaries has not changed, despite political resentment and righteous indignation on the part of taxpayers, who have seen their own income diminished in order to support banks that have taken excess risks.

As noted earlier, those governance issues extend to other financial companies beyond banks. Clearly it extends to the investment banks in the US, which were outside the ordinary banking umbrella and close control – a situation which has now changed, both through legislation and the action of the investment banks themselves as they either became bank holding companies or were acquired by them. However, it also relates to agents and rating agencies.

We complete this Introduction by reviewing the papers in this volume, which deal with governance, first at the individual firm level and then more generally, and then move on to policy.

Governance

In his fascinating and vigorous analysis in Chapter 2, Bruce Sheppard deals primarily, though certainly not exclusively, with shareholders. He points to failures by regulators, an inadequate legal framework and, in detail, failure by shareholders to exercise their powers and indeed to live up to their responsibilities. His analysis essentially provides the analytical underpinnings for an organization he established in 2001, the New Zealand Shareholders' Association. Its aim is, to quote 'to help small shareholders understand and exercise their rights'.

The organization has 11 'fundamental beliefs' (listed on pp. 33–4), but our remarks focus on two issues which arise from them – the particular problem which occurred in the New Zealand finance sector, and chief executives' pay. Bruce Sheppard's discussion of these is wide ranging and shows just how complicated the governance problems in the sector are. Solving them will not be easy.

The finance sector in New Zealand is of special interest because the failure of it was so spectacular. It started with money illusion. When inflation fell and with it interest rates, many people, not distinguishing between real and nominal returns, unwittingly took on more risk in an effort to sustain high nominal returns on their deposits. These returns were in general offered not by banks, but by recently or newly established finance companies. The companies took on more risk to pay these returns, driving out investors (such as private equity groups) who knew they were bearing risks. To that problem was then added a series of misaligned – indeed, perverse – incentives. These affected the brokers who brought deals to the firms, the managers of the firms, financial advisors whose commissions did not depend on repayment of invested capital, auditors and directors and trustees appointed by and dependent on the firms. Focus was on dividend policy, 'and often dividends were necessary to provide cash to the owners to ensure that loans made to associates of these owners were serviced, thus continuing the illusion of solvency and security' (p. 37).

To this, there was added the absence of regulation, apart from that over prospectuses when the companies were launched. The outcome of all this was that 'moral hazard was abused by all'.

Sheppard then turns to management compensation. Here he remarks on the little-noted fact that the evidence for incentive-based contracts improving performance is weak, before addressing another neglected issue. When aligning with shareholder interests, do all shareholders actually have the same interests? Sheppard suggests there are different groups of shareholders ('punters', those simply seeking safety who hold the investment as part of a broadly diversified portfolio, and those who behave like owners). On this basis, he then considers various ways of incentivizing managers, recognizing it as a useful way of locking in key staff if the incentives are properly designed. There are also thoughts on the appropriate level of compensation, as well as those on its design.

Finally, there are shareholders. These have, in law, numerous powers, and they should use them (a point also made in Gardner and Wood, 2004, in a UK context). Then last he mentions a power not given by law: 'Finally, all shareholders have the power of thought and voice; the power to humiliate idiots is the most effective power any of us have and more of us need to use it' (p. 52). Although dealing with a particular sector of the finance sector in a small economy, Sheppard has opened up the issues that pervade discussion in this volume – in particular, and frequently forgotten when there is zeal to regulate, the role of incentives.

We come next to an appraisal of performance, and contributions to that performance, in the Australian superannuation system. Brown and Ralston set out briefly the development and performance of the sector, and then turn to considering how governance models affect 'agency and direct costs' (p. 54). The latter is important as direct costs are important determinants – sometimes overriding determinants – of a fund's performance. And the former is generally little discussed in this context.

Compulsory superannuation was introduced in Australia in 1992. The scheme required employers to make tax-deductible superannuation contributions from their employees' earnings. These are in effect forced savings by the employees.[6] How the funds have thus raised performed as investments, and how governance has affected this, are the questions of this chapter.

The first pages of the chapter provide data on performance, costs, and so forth, of the various funds. Next comes the analysis.

> The structure of pension funds gives rise to agency problems or conflicts of interest because those who own the pension fund assets … are not the same as those who operate the pension fund … Simply put, corporate governance deals with the ways in which members assure themselves that their entitlements are secure and … assures them of an appropriate return on their investments…
>
> (pp. 64–5)

There is, in sum, the well-known problem of separation of ownership and control. The authors review the various ways this is addressed across Australia's superannuation funds and explore how, and indeed if, there is any systematic connection between those methods and fund costs and performance. They note that the 'usual market mechanisms to mitigate the agency problem' (p. 76) are not available in pension funds. Here they do take for granted what Sheppard questions – the relevance of financial incentives for performance. They note also absence of a market in control and that members often have no representative among trustees. (Such a situation would actually be rare in, for example, comparable UK pension funds.)

Their analysis is, as they admit, exploratory, but on the basis of a wide-ranging review they find absence of market discipline has been a contributor to unsatisfactory performance. Here their results again link back to Sheppard. For they claim that attempts to 'promote efficiency through member choice have largely failed due to the apathy and disconnections of the public with the superannuation system' (p. 76). A differently put version of Sheppard's urging for the use of 'the power to humiliate idiots'. They also find that outcomes are highly sensitive to fund types and, unsurprisingly, that cost control is very important. They thus conclude that changes in governance designed to increase focus on that is greatly welcome and, although they do not say so explicitly, overdue.

Wilson, Rose and Pinfold, in the next chapter in the volume, consider corporate governance in an individual firm. An admirable summary of the paper is given in the following quotation:

> Instead regulations, which should have offered some protection to depositors, were used to obfuscate the true financial situation as the Securities Commission, trustees and auditors appeared to be more concerned with compliance rather than the substance of underlying transactions. This allowed substantial shareholders on the … board of directors the opportunity to entrench themselves and disregard the interests of depositors while paying lip service to best practice corporate governance.
>
> (p. 80)

How was this the case? The authors point to numerous failures by almost all parties involved. A system based on trust – very efficient and low cost if it works, and relied on for many years in New Zealand – was abused. Non-bank deposit takers (NBDTs) had to lodge a trust deed with a trust company. The purpose of this deed was to ensure that the trust company, which was supposed to act on the part of depositors, monitored financial statements issued by the company. But no body ensured that these statements were issued in a clear and useful form, and it appears that only about a fifth of depositors at such companies paid any heed to the statements. These companies usually raised deposits in the form of fixed-term debentures of one to three years' maturity from the general public. (There were a few exceptions to this – for example, GE Finance, which raised funds from its parent.) These companies grew rapidly from the late 1990s to around the middle of the next decade. The problems developed in companies concentrated on the finance of used cars; but the general view appeared to be that these were a special case, and after a brief hiatus deposits at other companies resumed their growth. Then in mid-2007 Bridgecorp, a company involved in property finance, failed, and this was rapidly followed by severe problems at numerous other firms. As the authors concede, the situation was exacerbated by the global financial crisis; but there were also significant specific factors: 'rather than being created by the GFC, a likely cause of subsequent failures and the inability of some earlier failures to recover was a crisis of confidence across the entire industry due to perceptions of poor management' (p. 82).

What allowed this crisis? A complete failure in the oversight of the sector is the answer given by the authors. The Reserve Bank was responsible for any macroeconomic impact it might have, but not for individual firms, and the Securities Commission had in practice few powers, a situation which the government, despite prompting, did not move to remedy. As a result, the finance sector displayed in abundance the problems resulting from asymmetric information and moral hazard.

The consequences of this oversight failure were severe for the individuals who lost wealth, and also for the New Zealand economy as the reduced opportunities for access to finance that many individuals and firms faced after the crisis in the sector impeded investment and growth.

The authors first review the literature which suggests how such failure of regulation can lead to problems, and then provide a detailed study of the Bridgecorp case.

Again the authors provide an admirable summary.

> Issues of concern are: extremely low levels of closely held equity, an overly complex organizational structure and a lack of management oversight. Effectively a *black box* was created with the purpose of circumventing New Zealand's limited prudential regulation, allowing dubious related party transactions to occur, which were ultimately to the detriment of retail depositors.
>
> (p. 90)

Another way of summarizing their analysis would simply be that, if anything could be done wrong, it was.

The details which follow are nothing less than startling. Anyone with an interest in seeing sailing close to the wind could do no better than read this part of the paper with beady attention. The story is truly extraordinary, and told in detail. What general principles emerge?

Really the key is what was noted at the start of the discussion of this paper. Trust and integrity make for an efficient and low-cost financial system. But they need to be backed up by effective supervision to stop the exploitation of this by less reliable participants. And, as the authors remark:

> More generally, responsibility for the systemic failure of New Zealand NBDTs rests with the New Zealand government. In 2003 and 2004, both the Reserve Bank and the Securities Commission made public statements regarding their concern about the sustainability of rapidly growing finance companies. However, neither of these government agencies had jurisdiction to address the rapidly developing crisis. At the end of 2005, the cabinet agreed in principle for consolidation of prudential supervision of NBDTs into a single regulator and for this regulator to be the Reserve Bank…
>
> However, before this legislation could be completed, the situation was overtaken by the Global Financial Crisis.… While citizens cannot be protected from every danger, governments have a duty to ensure a level playing field exists. In this regard, many would suggest the Government failed in its duty to protect vulnerable depositors.
>
> (p. 101)

Altogether, the story this chapter tells is not encouraging. There was failure which was pointed out repeatedly, but a response which could scarcely have been more sluggish.

The next chapter in this volume, by Kevin Davis, broadens the governance discussion from a special part of the finance sector in one country to banks in general, and essentially worldwide. This is essential, for, as Davis quotes Ard and Berg (2010), governance failures in the recent crisis occurred in what were generally supposed to be sophisticated banks operating in 'some of the most developed governance environments in the world'.

Sheppard in his chapter shows how better governance can be achieved in the sector he studies by better exertion of rights within the existing legal and regulatory framework. This chapter looks at the possibility of changes to firm structures and to legal rights, and to how such changes may improve performance.

As Davis notes, most proposals for such changes focus on the implications for financial stability – but the implications of them go much wider. A key point in his argument is that '[t]he discussion [of corporate governance] thus rarely addresses the important prior question of whether the institutional/organizational structures and allocations of legal rights which have emerged are indeed suitable for achieving good corporate governance' (p. 109).

Applying the voice–exit framework developed by Albert Hirschman in 1970, he observes two distinct anomalies in banking. Depositors are the main suppliers of funds to banks, but they have no voice. If dissatisfied, their only serious option is exit. This is in contrast to the suppliers of capital to almost any other kind of firm. Second, also anomalous, shareholders in banks can and often do exit, choosing that over voice. This is in contrast to what often happens in other kinds of firm, even when the option is also available there, because when things go wrong, or even appear to go wrong, in a bank they can accelerate from trivia to disaster very rapidly.

This is of great importance. To quote: 'Sarra argues that the traditional approach to corporate governance (and corporate law) assumes that control rights reflect incentives to monitor due to economic interest, and that without the latter control rights can involve moral hazard' (p. 123).

The chapter reviews ownership structures of banks worldwide, remarking how they can differ in major and possibly significant ways, and noting also the neglect of cooperative and mutual banks in most empirical work. Given these limitations, general findings are few and not particularly robust. Independent directors are beneficial for both performance and risk control. Concentration of ownership increases alignment with shareholder goals. And separation of the chairmanship and the CEO role may reduce risk taking. But the main conclusion is the cautious one that general conclusions are sparse and, in any event, based mainly on one data set, that of US bank holding companies.

All this leads naturally to an examination of the role of governance in the recent crisis. It is of course hard to separate governance effects from management effects. But that noted, there is little clear connection between governance arrangements and serious difficulties or failure in banks. How banks performed within their regulatory and governance arrangements appeared to depend more on how people behaved within the arrangements than on the structures themselves. A point with implications notably for the UK is that many regulators have 'fit and proper' requirements for directors, but these tend to focus on probity and reputation rather than knowledge. The first two are important, but so is the often neglected third. This is emphasized, for example, in Kaarlo Jännäri's report for the Icelandic Parliament and the IMF on the collapse of the Icelandic Banking system:

> For the most part, the new owners and the people behind them were not traditional commercial bankers; instead they had the rather innovative and somewhat adventurous mindset of investment bankers, which favoured a strategy of rapid growth and adventurous, highly leveraged deals.
>
> (Jännäri, 2009, p. 14)

And later:

> The banking culture in Iceland seems to have been rather immature in that the banks did not give much consideration to the underlying purpose of the regulations and sought ways to circumvent them as much as they could if it served their (or their owners' and customers') perceived interests.
>
> (p. 30)

He next turns to remuneration. His focus here is somewhat at odds with Sheppard, who expresses considerable doubts about the benefits accruing from linking ownership to some measure of performance, even in principle. Davis surveys a good range of evidence, drawn from several countries but, as with the previous section of the chapter, predominantly from the US. One point he makes is that made more recently by Haldane (2011) – that linking to equity returns is linking to a *leveraged* claim on bank assets. This, a point neglected by Haldane (unsurprisingly in his UK context), can be aggravated if there is a holding structure with remuneration linked to shares in a leveraged holding company.

But, as he admits, on the basis of the evidence, it is hard to go beyond straightforward recommendations, such as ensuring that bank management shares the downside as well as the upside. While much seems to be going on in the world of policymaking and discussing, there is little evidence that it is being informed by either the evidence or the theory. This is, as he admits, understandable, as the theory is not well supported (or rejected) by the sparse and somewhat contradictory evidence on the roles of governance and remuneration. Many questions on the role of governance remain unanswered, even though important.

David Mayes, and Geof Mortlock (the author of the extensive comment on his paper), both consider the desirability and consequences, as well as some of the practicalities, of the extension of deposit insurance in the wake of the crisis.

It is often forgotten that deposit insurance, when it first was introduced in the United States, was intended to prevent bank runs. The innovation was thought to be necessary because, in the wave of panics which started the Great Depression, the Federal Reserve had failed to act adequately as lender of last resort. (An overview of the lender of last resort role can be found in Wood, 2000: the classic discussion of the Federal Reserve's failure remains Chapter 7 of Friedman and Schwartz, 1963.)

It has been introduced in various countries at different times and for different reasons; but nowadays it is generally seen as a form of social protection, rather than as a way of stabilizing the banking system. In the UK, for example, this is made very clear in 'The Run on the Rock', the fifth report of the Treasury Select Committee, 2007–8,[7] into the bank failure which started the banking crisis in the UK (and see also Mayes and Wood, op. cit.).

More generally, the banking crisis, which became close to worldwide, had a major effect on deposit insurance. 'What has happened in the present crisis is that the implicit schemes have become explicit and hence the role of the limited schemes has disappeared' (Mayes, p. 134 in this volume).

This, Mayes suggests, is not a sustainable situation.

> This chapter explores the consequences of the general increase in deposit insurance coverage that has occurred in the present crisis for bank governance, moral hazard and the viability of deposit protection in the future once countries return to 'normal times'.
>
> (p. 135)

The situation is not sustainable because it gives rise to incentives which make bank failures more likely and also increase the scale of losses likely to be borne by taxpayers when such failures occur.

David Mayes explains why this is the case, and suggests what may be done about it.

Problems are increased by such insurance because depositors pay little heed to the risks associated with institutions; this applies even to fairly sophisticated depositors, who would be capable of seeing the risks. Further, as guarantees become implicit, they implicitly become open-ended. David Mayes argues that the only way to prevent this enormous potential drain on resources is to ensure that banks can be closed promptly, in an orderly fashion, and, most important, while ensuring essentially no break in the access depositors enjoy to their funds. If such plans are in place, then institutions can be closed before calls on deposit protection funds (if they exist – otherwise the calls are directly on the taxpayer) become more than very modest.

This of course is complicated for large banks and for cross-border banks. He suggests that, for the former, 'countries need to implement "going concern" resolution methods…, which involve the use of contingent capital so vital functions do not stop operating' (p. 133). Problems are also very substantial for cross-border banks. Here he points out that: 'while deposit insurance may not need to be coordinated, resolution and supervision most certainly do' (p. 133). The tasks he lists are in increasing order of complexity. Going concern resolution probably involves 'living wills', plainly sensible in principle but as yet untested in practice. And while international coordination of supervision is with a little goodwill easy, coordination of resolution faces difficulties, of which one of the most significant is that the definition of insolvency is not the same in every country. This chapter does not of course attempt to solve all these problems. Rather it highlights them and suggests approaches to their solution.

Geof Mortlock, in his comment on the paper, develops the suggestions made by David Mayes, listing requirements for orderly resolution in detail, based on developments in Australia.

He writes:

> The key elements required for an effective response to financial distress in a bank include:
>
> - clear and well thought-through policy objectives and public policy principles for financial distress resolution that are transparent and well understood by all relevant stakeholders;
> - robust legal powers that enable the resolution authority to implement a range of financial distress resolutions with legal certainty;
> - a government agency with clear responsibility for financial distress resolution;
> - a framework for coordinating the actions of all relevant government agencies;

- strategies for resolving bank distress that take into account the systemic impact of a failure, including options for closing a bank in ways that minimize disruption to depositors and other bank customers, and options that preserve core elements of a distressed bank, either in its existing form or in a restructured form;
- funding arrangements that provide credible, viable and sustainable resolutions, with minimal distortions to banking system efficiency and with minimum moral hazard risk; and
- a framework for resolving banks with cross-border operations in ways that minimize adverse systemic impacts in all the relevant jurisdictions in which the bank operates, and that facilitate a whole-of-group resolution.

(p. 153)

These he calls the 'key elements' for effective bank resolution. He then goes on to develop and illustrate these points, making clear which are relatively straightforward to achieve and which are more complex, and suggesting possible approaches to dealing with them. This comment admirably supplements the overview by David Mayes.

In the subsequent paper, Geoffrey Wood addresses the issue of defining 'governance' and 'regulation', and then considers, first by means of examples, what each may achieve and when each may be the better way of producing a particular result. There are, he writes, two ways for governments to get organizations to do what they think is in the public interest. One is telling them what to do. This can mean prescribing the outcome, prescribing the process or even both together. That he defines as regulation. The other is explicitly to recognize that organizations are run by people, not by automata. They therefore do not wait passively to be told what to do. That, he argues, suggests that as a substitute for issuing instructions one can organize incentive structures so that individuals, out of their own self-interest, do what the government wishes. The latter course is, he says, what is generally meant by governance. His chapter contrasts regulation and governance. Definitions of regulation and of governance are proposed. Then three examples, from different areas of finance, are considered, and it is suggested on the basis of these that in general governance is better than regulation in two ways. First, it is more likely to achieve the desired result. Second, it is likely to be effective for longer.

The examples which suggest that conclusion are followed by an analytical framework by which it is argued that the claim based on examples is likely to hold in general. The discussion is then briefly related to the distinction between common law and civil law.

Wood quotes the definition of regulation provided by George Stigler in 1975. Regulation, he wrote, is 'the exercise of coercive government power'. It is, in other words, telling people what to do and punishing them in some way if they do not perform as instructed. He does acknowledge that there is a problem with this definition. It is somewhat too wide, in that it seems to imply that any legal rule is regulation; so that a libertarian who wants state enforcement of contracts would be said to be in favour of regulation. But it does help capture the difference which is at the heart of the argument of Wood's chapter. Regulation tells people what to do, while governance involves setting up structures, inside or outside organizations, so as to make it desirable for the organizations *in the best service of their own interests* to do what is thought also to be in the public interest.

His argument for the superior effectiveness of governance (at least in his sense of the word) is based on the theory of contract design. This theory, Wood observes, has a long history in economics, being discussed by Hume and Smith, as well as numerous subsequent writers. The extensive and often complex literature which has examined contract design problems faces such difficulties and sometimes reaches impasses because of three main types of information problem – adverse selection, moral hazard and non-verifiability. Wood argues that none of these is likely to be a problem in financial services and that accordingly 'governance' should be the first approach tried, and may well, because it is successful, be the last one needed to be tried, thus making regulation largely otiose in this sector.

Chapter 8, which moves us from individual firms or sectors to the overall perspective, is by a policymaker, Grant Spencer, who reviews the problems and responses to them in New Zealand in the wake of the crisis. He reiterates the importance of a price stability focus for monetary policy, emphasizing that though not sufficient for financial stability it is absolutely necessary. (On this, see also Schwartz, 2007.)

Moving on to consequences of the crisis, he notes a most interesting one – at least in New Zealand the crisis appears to have increased sensitivity to monetary policy by easing, due to the resulting steepening of the yield curve, shifting mortgage borrowing to the short end of the curve, the end most immediately affected by monetary policy changes.

But there were implications not just for the private sector. The authorities too learned useful lessons. In particular, they learned more on how to implement 'key requirements for central bank (liquidity) facilities'. These are that 'their pricing encourages a return to normal market trading; they are targeted at system liquidity not individual institutions; and they are fully collateralized'. It is perhaps surprising that these had to be learned – after all, they are the principles laid out by Walter Bagehot in *Lombard Street* and in numerous other writings. But learning is welcome, as these principles were so important in the many years of financial stability that the British economy enjoyed from the last quarter of the nineteenth century. Welcome, too, is the widening of collateral, again a return to nineteenth-century practice.

There is also reflection on accounting standards and how they contributed to the crisis. Mark-to-market valuation is noted as a problem, for example. This of course prompts the question of what might replace it. Mark-to-model led many astray, as of course did historic cost valuation, that well established way of hiding mistakes. There should be reflection, though, on how mark-to-market can collapse to 'mark-to-last trade' in a thin and stressed trading environment, and modification, with the inevitable associated complication, of the rules accordingly. In the context of rule setting, there is also a reminder that rules on capital and on 'macro-prudential tools' have to be useful without unduly impeding the functioning of the banking system. But the chapter concludes with reiterated emphasis on liquidity. As Grant Spencer notes in his concluding sentence, the dominant channel of international transmission in the crisis was 'an unprecedented reduction in global financial system liquidity'. That is a most useful conclusion, shifting focus as it does from the need for the inevitably long, drawn-out international discussions over capital and so forth to things that can be done rapidly by central banks.

Jeffrey Chwieroth, in Chapter 9, continues with the overall perspective, but from a most unusual, at least in economics, angle. He explores the role of stigmas in economic policy. Immediate definition is essential. He writes:

> A policy stigma is severe social disapproval of a particular course of action that is perceived to be against prevailing standards of behaviour. Within the field of international political economy, policy stigmas are understood to result from constitutive and regulative systems.
>
> (p. 188)

The chapter discusses views on exchange controls as an example. But before that, there is a general analytical discussion of their role, which can be 'paralytic' or 'catalytic', at least in the context of IMF action. The former restricts access to market funds if the IMF disapproves of a country's policies, the latter encourages such funds if the IMF approves. (The evidence, Chwieroth observes, is stronger for the former than for the latter.) Stigma thus restrict policy choice. There is nothing wrong with this if the stigma are rational and justified by evidence. But Chwieroth argues from an analysis of the attitude of the IMF to exchange controls that stigma are not invariably so justified. His claim is that views were always dependent on a particular subsection, albeit a large one, of economists; and, more important, that the views of that subsection for many years paid no effective heed to the importance of uncertainty (as distinct from risk) in everyday life and particularly in finance. Because stigma constrain policy, it is, as he says, important to understand their shortcomings. Even if they are well-founded, this may be undesirable, for while well-founded they may not be universally applicable.

These criticisms are supported by way of his detailed discussion of the IMF's attitude to capital controls. This attitude was affected not only by economic analysis but also by changing attitudes of policymakers in the USA, the dominant member of the IMF for much of the post-Second World War period. (What caused these views to change he does not examine.) An important factor in recent changes in IMF views, and in views on regulation more generally, was, he suggests, that '[a]cademic economists began to devote greater attention to factors intrinsic to operation of capital markets that could trigger herding behaviour and market panic' (p. 207).

This seemed to spill over from the international domain to that of domestic policy in the wake of the financial crisis. There was more willingness to at least consider controls. (This was of course far from universal – recollect Grant Spencer's contribution.)

But that they have not yet been enthusiastically embraced does not vitiate the importance of Chwieroth's arguments. Policy stigma do appear to have affected policy choices. Thus if organizations – Chwieroth cites the IMF as an example – get locked into a particular view, reconsideration of it may itself be stigmatized and any desirable changes slow to come about. As he asks in his conclusion, 'how can we avoid group-think in policy?'. That is an important question which this chapter does not answer, but it is one that is seldom raised and highlighting it is in itself a valuable contribution to debate on governance and regulation.

Gillian Garcia, in Chapter 10, reinforces the criticisms of regulation so far made in this book. She reminds the reader that the 111 banks and thrifts that failed in the United States with material losses to the Federal Deposit Insurance corporation (FDIC)'s Deposit Insurance Fund during the period 2007–9 failed 'for reasons long recognized to be causes of bank failure: weak management, fast growth, reliance on volatile sources of funding, inaccurate accounting that exaggerated earnings and capital, concentrated assets, particularly assets involving commercial real estate and construction, acquisition, and development loans.' The 'red flags' had been missed.

She also considers why prompt corrective action did not achieve its goals and why supervisors did not adequately implement the prompt corrective action provisions of the FDIC Improvement Act. The chapter concludes by asking why prompt corrective action (PCA) failed to achieve its goals and suggesting changes, including macro-prudential oversight that might improve supervisory achievements in the future. There are in the USA both 'capital' and 'non-capital' actions regulators can take. The latter exist because capital shows what banks have done, not what they are likely to do (although of course in this area of finance at least the past is to an extent a guide to the future).

Garcia argues that use of the (in fact rarely used) non-capital provisions would have helped considerably and at the least reduced the losses the failure of these institutions imposed on the FDIC.

She writes, 'the non-capital provisions would have allowed regulators to take action against almost all of the failure-causing problems…'. Why, she asks, were the risks ignored?

> It is possible to understand that it was hard for an individual examiner to lean against the prevailing profitable wind. But I wonder why no senior supervisory manager or agency leader questioned whether it was possible for so many of the banks to continue to be profitable in what was clearly perceived at the time, as I have been informed in conversations with supervisory staff, to have been a bubble situation.
>
> (p. 232)

She produces an interesting range of answers, based on discussions with regulatory office staff, to the question she raises. They are of sufficient importance to be well worth quoting at length.

> ...examiner personalities make them loners. They conduct their inspections and file their reports away, without discussing their work with their fellow examiners ... Second, examiners individually knew that there was a real estate bubble. Third, examiners did not make strong representations about the bubble to their managers because they knew they would not get a sympathetic hearing. Fourth, some agency heads did not wish to address the bubble problem because they were being influenced by the politicians to whose committees they reported ... they knew that both the Democratic and the Republican Administrations wanted to encourage economic growth, favoured housing as a target of national policy and wanted to extend home-ownership to lower-income households. But ... many of the failures reviewed were caused by commercial, not residential, real estate...
>
> Consequently, the fifth explanation becomes important for explaining what went wrong. It asserts that the politicians, to whom the regulatory agencies report, were being advised by the powerful finance and real estate industries to let the country ride the then-profitable real estate wave. Sixth, politicians were sympathetic to these industries' concerns because they were dependent on their contributions to their re-election campaigns. Sadly, that is the analysis presented by staff from the regulatory agencies whose opinion I sought. This interpretation is consistent with the findings in the special report on backdating capital contributions by the United States Department of Treasury's Inspector General (2009a).... Such backdating allowed the thrifts to maintain their well-capitalized status and thus continue to avoid PCA discipline and in particular to remain liquid by relying on brokered deposits for funding, without risking the rejection of their request to the FDIC for a waiver from this FDICIA provision. In some instances, the Treasury's special backdating report states that the OTS actually required thrifts to backdate the receipt of capital from their holding company, thus thwarting PCA discipline.
>
> There is perhaps another reason why the country's and the regulatory agencies' leaders did not take stronger measures to restrain the risky behaviour that they observed. Maybe they truly believed that 'this time is different' (Reinhart and Rogoff, 2009). Maybe they did not restrain bank risk taking because doing so would have meant pricking the bubble, which was contrary to Federal Reserve policy at the time.... Maybe policymakers really believed that increasing productivity and greater prosperity meant that real estate valuations were based on fundamentals and did not reflect a bubble. Maybe they judged that during 'the Great Moderation' they had conquered financial crises and could successfully prevent/combat future recessions. Maybe such hubris prevented needed restraint.
>
> (pp. 234–5)

Even one of these would be a significant barrier to effective prompt corrective action. How can these barriers be reduced or removed? She suggests several 'fixes' – including less reliance on peer review analysis, maintaining intensive supervision of new institutions for ten years rather than six or seven and more use of the non-capital provisions available. But Garcia is not optimistic. At the root of the problems was what was in fact close to politically mandated failure. Unless political interference is greatly eliminated and international cooperation increased (another major task), Garcia implies that crises such as we have experienced, with substantial costs falling on the taxpayer, are likely to recur.

Jane Diplock, as her very ambitious chapter shows, does to an extent share that pessimism. But the chapter starts optimistically.

> I begin by sketching my perspective on the crisis, its causes and lessons and go on to explain the new thinking replacing the old orthodoxy, and what the implications of this new thinking are – not just on a world-scale but for individual boards and their directors, shareholders and the wider community at home.
>
> I begin and end, however, with the importance of corporate governance.
>
> (p. 238)

She defines governance as 'the codification of sound ethical standards' – a more subjective definition than that advanced by Wood in Chapter 7 of this book. But in practice her definition is not so far from that offered by Wood, as she goes on to describe how governance is a way of influencing behaviour. So her definition really differs from his in that it embodies the kind of behavioural outcomes she wishes to produce. What are they? 'The purpose of corporate governance standards is to influence the drivers of market players' behaviour, to encourage greater transparency, reduction of conflicts of interest and a focus on the interests of investors and other stakeholders' (p. 238). Few would differ with these recommendations.

Her chapter of course looks more widely. She notes that markets – the connections between individual firms – matter, as well as the firms themselves, and that these markets are linked internationally. Neither of these observations is new, but having them embedded in a chapter which also considers the contribution that governance can make to financial stability and reviews the experience of a very open economy, New Zealand, in the recent financial crisis is most useful. There are also thought-provoking discussions of the role and accountability of directors and of the composition of boards of directors. All in all, this is a lively chapter from a perspective somewhat different from others in the book, and it gives a welcome emphasis to the importance of individual integrity to the efficiency and stability of the financial system.

The perspective of Charles Littrell's fascinating chapter is also unusual, in that it considers 'several cultural characteristics that are relevant to prudential supervision'. Littrell goes on:

> I define 'culture' mainly on two axes:
>
> 1 What is most important to a given group; and
> 2 How priorities have changed in the past 30 or so years.
>
> The different industries within the financial services sector view the world through somewhat different perspectives. Understanding (while not necessarily agreeing with) these perspectives helps prudential supervisors become more effective.
>
> (p. 248)

This approach makes for a readable chapter with many insights. An important and overarching one is that risks emerge from 'cultural blind spots'. Littrell therefore starts by identifying the main cultural characteristics of the subdivisions of the financial sector he examines. These parts are: banking, investment banking, life insurance, general insurance and superannuation.

Banking, he writes, 'has been characterized and often damaged by four cultural characteristics: size mania, dislike of the core business, changing views on the value of capital soundness and changing definitions of what is moral' (p. 248).

Banking is a risky business which, Littrell says, often thinks of itself as a stable one. Its losses, and failures, stem very often from poor lending quality, which is in turn associated with rapid balance sheet growth. Until recently, banks were enthusiastic about growth, becoming the biggest bank sometimes being a goal of management. This enthusiasm has waned, as bankers learned from what Littrell calls 'horrid example' (p. 249).

Another example they could learn from is that trying to move from their unloved – perhaps because unglamorous – core business is a mistake. Diversifying into investment banking or insurance has damaged many banks. '[T]he lesson seems reasonably clear: worry when a banker loves non-bank businesses more than the core lending and deposit-taking business' (p. 249).

Views on capital, too, changed; it became desirable not to have lots of it but to be 'efficient' with it – which, as Littrell observes, often in practice meant 'minimizing equity and maximizing leverage' (p. 251). And as for morality, the self-imposed moral duty to depositors faded; that in itself induced more risk taking.

Littrell carries out a similar analysis for every part of the finance sector he examines. Investment banking was driven by the urge to get bigger, so risks were run and margins shaved. Expertise acquired on behalf of clients was used to manage the bank's own funds, and risks were run in consequence. But also, as attention moved away from dealing on the part of clients, conflicts of interest were no longer self-policed for the sake of the firm's long-term prosperity. Clients became less important relative to the firm's own trading.

> A wise prudential supervisor, faced with an investment bank heavy with proprietary trading and investment, will realize that it is up against a difficult

> supervisory proposition. Culturally, investment bankers are very intelligent but not necessarily very wise. An abundance of intelligence tends to lead to an abundance of profits in good times. But a paucity of wisdom means that greed and hubris can overwhelm caution, in an environment changing so rapidly that regulators will have difficulty keeping up.
>
> (p. 253)

Life insurers tend, he suggests, to be schizophrenic, the consequence of comprising two groups: actuaries and salesmen. This schizophrenia tends to produce safe, but poor value, products. However, '[i]t would be fair to observe that the typical sales manager personality differs greatly from the typical actuarial personality' (p. 254). Accordingly, 'a wise prudential supervisor will pay close attention to the balance of power in a life company between actuaries and sales managers' (p. 254).

General insurance, in contrast, is mainly salesman driven. When this was combined with the availability of reinsurance and the somewhat elastic morality many individuals develop when making insurance claims, these companies tended to be perhaps more buccaneering than a prudential supervisor could wish. In Australia at least, the resulting underwriting cycle, combined with failures, led to both tighter regulation and more cautious companies. 'There is more actuarial and professional risk manager input to balance the industry's sales-driven tendencies' (p. 257). His discussion of superannuation largely confirms, from his different perspective, the conclusions set out by Brown and Ralston in Chapter 3.

Turning next to professions, he considers first auditing. For various reasons, audit opinions are, he suggests, taken less seriously than they once were. 'We consider an audit opinion valuable on strictly objective matters, such as statistical return accuracy' (p. 258). But on matters of opinion, where error can through litigation bring catastrophic consequences for the auditor, caution rules and the opinion becomes of little value.

Actuaries, he suggests, are much less constrained by 'extreme risk avoidance' (p. 259) and their opinions more valued by regulators than are those of auditors. Whether this can last he is unsure, but, at least in Australia where the profession is small, 'an actuary must guard his or her personal reputation in a consequently smaller and better informed field' (p. 259).

He concludes his chapter by briefly discussing how regulators should respond to the different cultures of different sectors: 'the cultural look and feel of each industry and supporting profession differs. Prudential supervisors can improve their performance by understanding and responding appropriately to these differences' (p. 260).

The novel approach of this chapter both makes it a most engaging read and produces most useful insights.

Geoffrey Wood's chapter (written with Ali Kabiri) shifts the focus completely. It argues that concern on the part of regulators with individual firms is, so far as financial stability goes, misconceived. He argues this by suggesting that economists and the regulators who have followed them have often, implicitly or explicitly, used a definition of competition which is unhelpful in this area. Competition is often understood to be atomistic competition, when many firms are in an industry – the Walrasian notion of competition. Wood directs attention to another version, the Marshallian version, of competition. That version focuses not on the number of existing firms in an industry but on how easy it is for potential entrants to threaten incumbents and to enter if an opportunity emerges.

> When the regulators examine the grocery business in the UK they are invariably concerned with competition ... is the industry competitive is always, in one form or another, the question that is being asked.... A question that is never asked is how robust a particular individual firm is.
>
> To anyone familiar with regulation in the financial sector, that is distinctly odd. A question always in regulators' minds there is how stable is the firm. Why is that not asked of firms in the grocery sector? Banking services are important but so, after all, is the supply of food...
>
> Why is that question not asked? The answer is surely in two parts. First, and very important for the failing firm's suppliers and employees, there is for such firms a well-established and well-tested insolvency regime.... Second, there is no fear that a vacuum would be left by such insolvency ... [the] main competitors would be fighting vigorously over this new market opportunity.
>
> (p. 261)

The argument of the chapter therefore is that, if barriers to entry and exit are removed, financial sectors need worry about individual firms only for consumer protection reasons.

The argument is advanced by considering first the notion of barriers to entry to be found in the standard industrial economics literature, and then the insolvency code. Wood argues that the somewhat different notions of barriers to entry suffer from two limitations in this context – they neglect speed of entry, and they are of questionable use when discussing regulated industries. Various proposals to facilitate entry are set out. But, as Wood notes, all these are of little importance unless exit from the industry by failing incumbents is easy. If failing firms are propped up, there will be no new entrants. Firms have been propped up recently – the example of Northern Rock in the UK is cited. Why did this happen, and how can it be prevented from happening in the future?

The support of Northern Rock is examined, and while it is maintained that there were a range of reasons for it, the absence of an insolvency regime which would allow orderly closure for a bank was crucial. Various proposals are made to achieve this – some have already been implemented, and others, such as 'living wills', are both discussed elsewhere in this book and are in many countries in the process of implementation.

The chapter moves on to discussion of consumer protection in a regime where banks are allowed to fail, and then concludes by placing the concept of competition which underlies the recommendations in the history of economic thought, noting a lineage which runs certainly from Alfred Marshall through Schumpeter to, in the present day, Eugene Fama and William Baumol.

The chapter's final sentence sets the chapter's conclusion out boldly: 'The key point of this chapter is that industry stability matters for banking and firm stability does not' (p. 271).

In the book's final chapter, David Mayes discusses how to survive the next financial crisis. As he acknowledges, '[t]his implies that I regard the occasional occurrence of financial crises as inevitable and I explain why I think that is the case' (p. 274).

Why does he consider crises inevitable? His conclusion is based on work done by the Bank of Finland in the aftermath of the Nordic crises. Seven factors are enumerated:

1 a major regulatory change that opens both buyers and sellers to new opportunities and risks of which they have little experience
2 a period of rapid economic growth
3 a rapid rise in asset prices
4 a weak framework for supervision
5 a tax regime that encourages borrowing
6 unsustainable macroeconomic policies
7 a substantial adverse shock.

(p. 276)

His reason for expecting the persistence of crises is that every crisis since the Nordic crisis occurred, and lessons were drawn from it, was caused by some combination of these factors. Little appears to have been learned.

Bearing in mind that crises can sometimes cost more to prevent than they are worth, what can be done to help economies absorb their impact? He lists three factors which in the recent crisis increased the size of losses – slow action, absence to tools to resolve problems without recourse to the taxpayer and an inadequate safety net. The chapter lists proposals for all of these.

Under the first heading he writes, after listing various suggestions, that 'the major lesson we have learnt is that traditional supervisory schemes that concentrate on making sure that each individual financial institution is run prudentially are not enough. We need to look at system-wide problems as well' (pp. 277–8). He also recognizes the great difficulty of ensuring speedy action. 'Ending a period of rapid growth that turns out to have been sustainable will be a career-ending move. There is hence a tendency to forebear' (pp. 278–9). He argues, therefore, that there should be triggers which compel action unless a case is made against it – the 'default case' is action.

What about the tools? Prompt action is necessary, but so is having the tools with which to act. The authorities must be able to effect a quick transition to a new institution and ensure that individuals do not lose access to their funds. Unless this can be done in hours, and preferably while depositors are asleep (he cites [p. 281] the example of the closure of the Dunfermline Building Society in the UK, in the course of which deposits were switched to the Nationwide Building Society over two hours in the middle of the night), then deposit insurance is necessary.

However, he writes, 'unfortunately, one of the major changes to emerge from the crisis is the attitude to deposit insurance' (p. 282). Originally intended to help stabilize banking systems, and in addition to protect the 'widow and orphan', its coverage has widened and in some cases, including, one suspects, those cases where it is implicit, has become unlimited.

He also notes problems over large banks. In principle, the same resolution procedures apply to them as to small ones, but as he observes, preparation is particularly important here; and he endorses living will for this purpose. Of course, market discipline preventing such problems from occurring would be even better.

> If markets work well then banks that are being poorly managed should either be restructured through shareholder pressure or be taken over by others who believe they can run them more efficiently. Unfortunately the second mechanism does not work well, which means that one of the main forces for market discipline is impaired.
>
> (p. 283)

The reasons he adduces are fear of concentration in some cases and in general the difficulty we observe in one bank taking over another. There is often overpaying – Mayes cites the examples the Royal Bank of Scotland-led takeover of ABN-AMRO and of Lloyd's takeover of HBOS.

Some have proposed breaking up banks. Mayes does not evince great sympathy for this, but rather focuses on how to make bank resolution 'less costly and disruptive' (p. 284). He favours automatic triggers for action and, with some qualifications, one of the actions being conversion of debt to equity.

He then turns to the importance of the safety net.

> To handle a crisis, one needs a balance between what people can be realistically expected to do for themselves in the way of insurance and what society needs to provide in order to spread the shock sufficiently over the country as a whole and over time.
>
> (p. 286)

His discussion extends beyond deposit insurance, taking in both the welfare system and compulsory savings schemes. It is unusual to see such a rounded consideration of safety net issues, and this will surely be followed up in future work, by other scholars as well as Mayes himself.

The chapter concludes with a discussion of why the recent crisis was not foreseen. As he observes, in fact it was. But many of the warnings and suggestions were ignored, and in some small countries (such as Finland) where they were acted on the consequence was that large banks moved out of local control.

The final pages of the chapter comprise a summary of the chapter's eight main points. But the chapter's final observation is perhaps the most important point of all.

> It is inherent in crises that the warning signals are for some reason ignored or explained away or that significant activities lie outside control, as in the case of the investment banks in the US. Carmen Reinhart and Ken Rogoff (2009) have written an excellent book called *This Time is Different....* Watch out for those words – they are accompanied by a flashing sign which reads 'Fasten Your Seatbelt'.
>
> (p. 294)

Conclusion

It is impossible to summarize all that has gone before – an already terse summary cannot usefully be summarized further. Rather we conclude simply by observing that the chapters in this book cover a wide range of issues and use evidence from a wide range of countries, including some that are often not studied outside their own shores. There is much to be learned from these studies, including in particular that there is not just much to be done, but also a lot more that needs to be studied.

Notes

1 Liedorp *et al.* (2011) provide an assessment of how well central banks manage to communicate on the topic of financial stability.
2 Wilkinson *et al.* (2010) provide an analysis of how much the Financial Stability Reviews in the Nordic countries may have contributed to reducing the impact of the global financial crisis. They suggest that, while the reviews were quite good at identifying the potential threats, it is not clear that this led to much in the way of preventative actions.
3 A simple exposition is given in www.rbnz.govt.nz/finstab/banking/4368385.html.
4 Some countries, Australia included, also offer depositor priority, so that depositors (or insurance funds that have succeeded to their claims on paying out) get paid out first in any insolvency, thereby offering an extra level of protection.
5 Paul Volcker's William Taylor Memorial Lecture in Washington, DC on 23 September 2011, on the subject of 'Three Years On: Unfinished Business in Financial Reform', is a recent case in point.
6 Brown and Ralston say these do not involve higher labour costs for employers. Whether or not this is correct of course depends on supply-and-demand elasticities for labour, an area unexamined in this chapter.
7 HC 56-I, London: HM Stationery Office.

References

Allen, W. and Wood, G.E. (2006) 'Defining and achieving financial stability', *Journal of Financial Stability*, 2(2): 152–72.

Ard, L. and Berg, A. (2010) 'Bank governance: lessons from the financial crisis', *Crisis Response Note 13*, World Bank, available at http://rru.worldbank.org/documents/CrisisResponse/Note13.pdf.

Blinder, A.S. and Reis, R. (2005) *Understanding the Greenspan Standard*, Jackson Hole Conference, Federal Reserve Bank of Kansas City.

De Bandt, O. and Hartmann, P. (2000) 'Systemic risk: a survey', *ECB Working Paper*, No. 35, available at SSRN: http://ssrn.com/abstract=258430.

Friedman, M. and Schwartz, A. (1963) *A Monetary History of the United States 1867–1960*, Princeton: Princeton University Press.

Gardner, P. and Wood, G.E. (2004) 'The regulatory response', in T. Adams, *The Split Capital Investment Trust Crisis*, pp. 117–27, Chichester: Wiley.

Haldane, A. (2011) *Control Rights (and Wrongs)*, Wincott Annual Memorial Lecture, Westminster, 24 October, available at www.bankofengland.co.uk/publications/speeches/2011/speech525.pdf.

Hirschman, A.O. (1970) *Exit, Voice, and Loyalty: Responses to Decline in Firms, Organizations, and States*, Cambridge, MA: Harvard University Press.

Hughes, S. (2012) 'Finance firm debacle shows light touch failed', *The New Zealand Herald*, January 2, B14.

Hüpkes, E. (2004) 'Learning lessons and implementing a new approach to bank insolvency resolution in Switzerland', in D.G. Mayes and A. Liuksila, *Who Pays for Bank Insolvency?*, pp. 242–71, Basingstoke: Palgrave Macmillan.

Jännäri, K. (2009) *Report on Banking Regulation and Supervision in 'Iceland: Past, Present and Future*, Reykjavik: Prime Minister's Office, available at http://eng.forsaetisraduneyti.is/media/frettir/KaarloJannari_2009.pdf.

Kudrna, Z. (2010) 'Cross-border resolution of failed banks in the EU: a search for the second-best policies', *Working Paper no. 08/2010*, Institute for European Integration Research, Austrian Academy of Sciences, Social Sciences Research Centre.

Liedorp, F., Mosch, R., van der Cruijsen, C. and de Haan, J. (2011) 'Transparency of banking supervisors', *Working Paper no. 297*, De Nederlandsche Bank.

Mayes, D.G. and Liuksila, A. (2004) *Who Pays for Bank Insolvency?*, Basingstoke: Palgrave Macmillan.

Mayes, D.G. and Wood, G.E. (2008) 'Lessons from the Northern Rock episode', *Economie Internationale*, 114: 5–27.

Mayes, D.G., Halme, L. and Liuksila, A. (2001) *Improving Banking Supervision*, Basingstoke: Palgrave.

Mayes, D.G., Pringle, R. and Taylor, M. (2009) *Towards a New Framework for Financial Stability*, London: Central Banking.

Peura, S. and Jokivuolle, E. (2004) 'Simulation based stress tests of banks' regulatory capital adequacy', *Journal of Banking and Finance*, 18(8): 1801–24.

Schwartz, A. (2007) 'Why financial stability depends on price stability', in G.E. Wood, *Money, Prices and the Real Economy*, pp. 34–40, Cheltenham: Edward Elgar.

Stern, G. and Feldman, R. (2004) *Too Big To Fail: The Hazards of Bank Bailouts*, Washington, DC: Brookings Institution Press.

Stigler, G.J. (1975) *The Citizen and the State*, Chicago: University of Chicago Press.

Wilkinson, J., Spong, K. and Christensson, J. (2010) 'Financial stability reports: how useful during a crisis?, *Federal Reserve Bank of Kansas City Economic Review*, 1: 41–70.

Wood, G.E. (2000) 'The lender of last resort reconsidered', *Journal of Financial Services*, 18(2): 203–27.

2 Fundamental problems with the governance of the financial sector

Bruce Sheppard

There are aspects of the governance of the financial sector and other corporates in New Zealand over the last 20 years which have frankly been appalling. Directors have not only not looked after shareholders' interests but they have impoverished some small shareholders for their own gain. People have seen their life savings wiped out. Some of the worst offenders have been convicted, but for many it has not been possible to compile a convincing case. Other cases are still before the courts. Even where the actions have not been illegal, there has been a widespread lack of regard for ethics. While it is a well-known joke that 'business ethics' is a paranym, actual behaviour has been far from a joke. I feel so strongly about these issues that I have tried to do something about it.

There were three obvious failings in the system. The first was that the legal framework protecting the rights of small shareholders, creditors and even customers was inadequate. Second that the framework of regulation, with several regulators all with limited powers, meant that poor behaviour was not addressed and even that the outright illegal went unpunished. However, the third failing was rather different in character – even given all these disadvantages, shareholders had failed to exercise the rights which they did have. With careful scrutiny and exercise of their powers, they could do a lot to improve company performance.

Legislation is now being introduced, with a new Securities Act, and the regulatory structure has been improved with the creation of the Financial Markets Authority (FMA) as a single agency with enhanced powers and the assignment to the Reserve Bank of prudential responsibility for most of the non-bank financial sector. All this is to be welcomed and I like to think that my actions have contributed to making these changes possible. Nevertheless, it is all too late for the large majority of the finance company sector, which has failed or is at least under moratorium. The small investors have lost their money, as indeed has the taxpayer, with the demise of South Canterbury Finance while under a temporary retail deposit guarantee.

My major step was to set up the New Zealand Shareholders' Association (NZSA) in 2001, after taking direct action in General Meetings of companies in which I was a shareholder. The point of the organization is to help small shareholders understand and exercise their rights. By having an organization, it helps overcome some of the problems where each individual shareholder has not the time, the resources nor the information to promote their case. The organization has blossomed since then and I particularly hope that its work in shareholder education will be of widespread benefit.

The exploitation of small shareholders is one of the reasons why share ownership is poorly developed in New Zealand among the advanced countries, particularly in comparison with our near-neighbour Australia. This contributes to the difficulty firms have in raising funds for investment and the consequent lagging of economic performance behind potential. It also contributes to New Zealand's love affair with housing, where most people put their assets into a house and beyond that into rental properties, rather than investing in productive activity. The savings rate in New Zealand is very low, despite the advent of Kiwisaver as an encouragement. This contributes not just to the balance-of-payments deficit but it emphasizes the practice of entrepreneurs in developing innovative ideas but then selling out to foreign investors once the idea really gets going.

There is not the space here to deal with all the issues in governance of the finance sector that need attention so I deal in the main with just two of them: the nature of the problem with the finance company sector and the question of chief executive pay. A final section draws some of the threads together. However, I start with some of the NZSA's fundamental beliefs:

- All business, corporate or otherwise, is about teams of people that come together to do or provide something for reward.
- Companies are just a form of partnership between capital and labour providers.
- Companies have no soul or values, and are incapable of being ethical or otherwise; such is the prerogative of the people who operate in those companies.
- People have integrity based on what they do and whom they associate with. If people do bad things or associate with bad people then words do not make up for it.
- An organization's purpose or its strategy is best measured by what it does rather than what is says.
- Shareholders are the only parties in the corporate business landscape that have the power to fire management; therefore, inevitably, managers are accountable only to shareholders and therefore it is to be expected that business will be run for the benefit of shareholders. Therefore, shareholder values are of ultimate importance.
- All shareholders have different values but collectively all shareholders want to maximize long-term business value.
- It is the job of shareholders to behave as good business owners and as responsible stewards over the resources committed to such business.
- A company's share price is the result of shareholders trading with one another based on information provided by management. It is therefore irrelevant to the company's management, except in situations where the

company is raising or redeeming equity on market. Management should focus on running the business not the share price. If management does the former with distinction, the share price will eventually look after itself.
- The best associations come from those who associate based on free will, and do so for a commonly shared purpose, carried into effect with common values that are respected with integrity.

Finance companies: how did it happen?

In simple terms, the ingredients are:

- greed and stupidity
- misaligned incentives
- governance failure
- regulatory failure.

Investor greed and stupidity

The seeds of the finance company fiasco occurred in the mid-to-late 1980s when coupon interest rates with banks were in the 20 to 30 per cent range. At the time, tax rates were 33 per cent and inflation was up to 20 per cent, so, in short, interest rates reflected the environment and investors became used to high coupons. Then it all changed in the late 1980s when, in nominal terms, interest rates collapsed but, in real terms, they rose. Investors did not notice this and instead looked for the higher rates they were used to in nominal dollars.

A number of finance companies were born in this market, who then offered a higher rate of return than the banks. As the cash rolled in, in quite exceptional volumes, the finance companies had to do something with it. Prime bank interest rates continued to fall and finance companies continued to attract more money at relatively low-risk spreads.

Finance company owner/manager greed and stupidity

When you have a dollar in the bank that you have borrowed at 9 per cent and it is on deposit at 5 per cent, your cost of liquidity is the difference and this was enormous for finance companies. Lazy cash is a serious driver of losses. Thus the money had to work. There was a ready market. In the early 1990s, cash strapped property developers sought finance in effect from the private equity markets and paid appropriately high returns for very high risks.

Thus the first round of activity was taking on more risk for less return. The private equity players were driven out of the development market and the finance companies entered, at relatively low interest rates relative to the risk, but certainly at a considerable margin on the buy cost of money. This growth in part fuelled the property bubble in the inner cities around New Zealand, as projects that should never have been built on any reasonable assessment of risk were built on mispriced money.

As even more money came in than the finance companies could lend out to reasonable parties representing reasonable credit risks, the temptation to lower the credit bar and take more risk became insurmountable. They faced a certain loss of a 4 per cent holding cost or a probable margin of 8 per cent. As it became harder to lend, the temptation to finance your own projects became an inevitable consequence and related-party loans became a strong feature of each issuer; the separation of decision making between borrower and lender became a point not only of disclosure but potentially of conflict and moral hazard. As more money came in, more was lent out on projects started by in effect the lenders themselves. If growth is good, anything that promotes growth is good, fuelling the bubble mantra of property lending in finance companies.

Misaligned incentives

The food chain of finance companies is as follows:

- Someone (investor) puts money in, sometimes encouraged by an advisor, and the advisors get paid commissions.
- Once the money is in, someone has to lend it out and there has to be deal flow to get the money working. Thus there are also finance brokers, who get paid to put deals before the finance company.
- The management team have incentives mostly based on profit. Profit is driven by interest income, fee income, low bad debts and controlled costs.
- The auditors check the manager and are appointed by the board and, as far as the auditor is concerned, the clients are the company and its managers/directors. Their fees are fixed and are competitively priced, sometimes on tender. But lucrative consulting contracts from the company itself or the shareholders or their associates make the amounts involved too much to lose.
- The trustees are appointed by the company and paid by the company but owe a duty of care to the investors, who they do not know and who do not pay them, again on a simple fixed-cost basis, and usually tendered, but with no consulting fee upside.
- The emergence of rating agencies increased the moral hazard, where these agencies were paid by the finance companies to provide ratings that were deceptive. An A rating indicates high risk; the public did not realize that – an A is an A, and understanding the difference between an A and AAA was beyond them.

Financial advisors

Financial advisors have always been required to disclose commissions, but the omission (which is still an omission) is that there was no requirement to disclose the commission on alternative investments. The commissions paid were not contingent on repayment of the capital to the investors. Some commissions were as high as 5 per cent; sometimes the advisors were further corrupted by trail commissions inducing them to leave cash in situ, rather than considering redemption. Others withdrew and re-invested to maximize commission income and deliberately churned investments. Flat and recurring commissions corrupted the advisors' independence and ultimately their judgment.

Brokers

Once upon a time, a broker was paid a commission on a deal on the basis that, if the referred deal went sour, the broker indemnified the company. Progressively, this arrangement retreated, to a situation where an up-front fee was paid with no recourse to the broker for a deal that fell over, either for the capital or even the fee. Thus the brokers were paid on volume not quality. Progressively, the credit application files were also prepared by the brokers and the finance executives reduced the work done in house, particularly so with the consumer finance companies.

Auditors and trustees

Both auditors and trustees were underpaid and, in the case of auditors, who wanted to retain the fee for the next year without having to confront a tender and sometimes even were awarded plum consulting work either for the audited entity or a related party, were tempted to sign unqualified reports when they should not have. The level of fees paid to auditors to turn a blind eye resulted in the eyes being blinded. Auditors relied on property valuations in the lending files of the finance company to determine if loans were impaired, and those valuations were usually supplied by the borrowers; there is an equally depressing story to be told about the incentives for valuers. The trustees were not paid enough to spend any time looking at anything, so they did not.

Managers, owners and directors

The managers, owners and directors had an incentive to keep the profits going up. This allowed them to book profits and pull out cash dividends and incentives. Thus it was good to write more business with front-end fees and they got substantially reported as income up front, and if interest could not be paid, new loans could be made to pay the interest. Furthermore, bad debts do not look good, so there was a strong incentive to avoid recognizing them. Thus they also had an incentive to confuse the auditors.

Governance failure

The boards of finance companies were often the owners, or were certainly appointed by the owners. The so-called independent directors were usually long-term appointments and thus over time, if not from the beginning, the objectivity of these independents was at best questionable. Sometimes the fees paid entrenched the capture of some directors. In any case, despite the existence of independent directors, boards were dominated by the owners. Thus the robustness of credit decisions on related-party transactions was not all it could have been.

The audit committees of these boards, to the extent that they existed at all, rarely picked up the obvious audit failures and, in particular, failed to provide realistic judgment on the quality of 'assets' and the necessary impairment testing. Dividend policy to the owners was the prerogative of the board, which was dominated by owners. Hence the prudence of dividend policies was rarely tested and often dividends were necessary to provide cash to the owners to ensure that loans made to associates of these owners were serviced, thus continuing the illusion of solvency and security.

Regulatory failure

For most of the time that these finance companies took deposits, there was no effective prudential regulation. Thus the regulation of equity cover to total assets, which ultimately was the security for the depositors, was unregulated, and this aspect of the finance companies was left to the trustees and the terms of the covenants included in the trust deed.

The Companies Office was left to approve the prospectuses and had limited grounds for refusing registration or compelling the withdrawal of a prospectus. The Securities Commission's role was largely limited to breaches of disclosure in these prospectuses after the failure was evident, and the Serious Fraud offices was limited in jurisdiction to matters of fraud. In short, regulation was disjointed, with each pointing the finger at the other, and collectively the powers available to be brought to bear were only usable after collapse, if at all.

The outcome

The combination of investors' naivety and lower interest rates on cash deposits, coupled with a governance and regulation void, created an environment when moral hazard could be abused by all.

The government's response has been as follows:

- Prudential regulation has been introduced and is supervised by the Reserve Bank. Most of the marginal finance companies no longer comply and as such have been forced out of business, some cataclysmically.
- The non-prudential regulatory functions have been consolidated into one body, the FMA, under new legislation, which includes additional powers to deal with matters not covered in the Companies Act, the Securities Act, the Security Markets Act and other less important Acts. The FMA began operating in May 2011.

- A Crown Guarantee Scheme, introduced at the height of the crisis to avoid a run on funds from those finance companies still left standing, created further moral hazards, where some finance companies had a sea of cash come in, which simply extended the lending hazard, and also created a moral hazard for the investing public in that they could get a higher return for the same risk. South Canterbury Finance's failure has underlined this starkly at a huge cost.

While there is no perfect solution to this, clearly the spreading out of the failure over the whole community through taxpayer subsidy has at least smoothed out what could have been a failure of devastating proportions, and the regulatory response over time will have an impact on investor confidence provided the FMA judiciously uses its powers and attempts to provide a fence at the top of the cliff, but nothing will change unless two additional things occur:

- first, that all information available to managers and those taking funds off others is made available to the market in a timely fashion, in an understandable format and with complete honesty; and
- second, the investing public must significantly increase their financial literacy so that they understand what is being disclosed.

CEO remuneration

Executive reward is the front line on the battlefield between shareholders and management. Executive remuneration has become a hot topic and has become a common ground for shareholder disquiet. When the debate is at its worst, shareholders allege that executives are greedy and executives allege that shareholders are envious. The topic is set to become even more hotly contested over the coming decades due to the simple issue of demographics. In the West, the population is aging, resulting in fewer workers and more retirement-aged citizens. There is already a growing trend to later retirement, paralleling longer life. Simple supply and demand will push up the cost of labour and reduce the cost of capital. Those not working will rely on either the state or investment income to sustain themselves in their retirement. Either way, management will be under pressure to pay higher taxes and/or higher dividends or returns to shareholders. In the absence of higher returns, retirement-aged citizens will have no choice but to liquidate their capital partially, which in turn will reduce share prices and/or make it harder for business to raise capital.

In addition, there is the social issue. If returns on investment capital decline, then more will seek state support, and then taxes go up, returns go down and so the cycle continues. If we are to encourage self-reliance, it must be based on enterprising and profitable business carried on between willing partners where management accepts willingly the social responsibility to provide decent returns. The issue of social trends and demographics will affect all players in share markets and as a result the interface between managers and owners will become more not less tense.

Research indicates that no incentive is best!

When it comes to executive reward, there are as many approaches as there are boards to think about the issue, with the full spectrum from flat pay with no incentive to highly incentivized structures being in evidence internationally. Interestingly, research to date, admittedly largely out of the US, indicates that there is no correlation between incentive-based reward and shareholder-value performance. Such research as is available indicates the contrary view that better shareholder rewards are derived when executives are not strongly incentivized. Of course that research is historical and is based on incentive structures that were poorly designed and based on lack of symmetry of information, which in effect put executives in competition with owners rather than the alignment sought.

The case for no incentive

The case for a flat salary with no incentive rests on the premise that a person should be recruited for the job who has the utmost integrity and who completes the job for which they have been engaged for the joy of the job itself. Certainly intelligent and industrious people exist who also have integrity and will do what is required of them without the need for incentive regimes. The difficulty for any board engaging a new CEO is that intelligence and work ethic are relatively easy to judge but integrity is almost impossible to judge with foresight and easily judged with hindsight. Then of course it is too late.

The fundamental premise behind performance remuneration

The case for incentive-based reward has historically been made on the basis that alignment with shareholder values will produce the best performance from executives who have been assumed to strive to maximize their own self-interest. While this may well be true for some or even many, it is not true for all.

Human empowerment, an alternative case for performance-based rewards

A further case can be made for performance-based reward based on employee empowerment. When executives are paid high base salaries, performance expectations are in turn heightened. More is expected from someone paid $1 million than someone paid $100,000. As executive rewards grow higher so too do performance expectations. The result is that executives are overworked and overstressed. Employers that encourage such work practices are hardly responsible employers and, further, might have statutory liability to boot. Lower base salaries and sensible performance-based pay regimes allow executives to design their job around their willingness to work and, if they choose to work less, they then also earn less, reducing the risk for the employer. In essence, the work place becomes a work place of partners that associate with each other based on levels of choice that effectively can empower all participants in the process.

Managing the conflict: believable transparency is the best disinfectant

When performance-based reward programmes are extensively used for CEO and other management, who have control over both performance and the information arising out of that performance, the situation arguably puts such executives in conflict with the organization's owners. It is this conflict that gives rise to the most significant governance threats. Interestingly, it is this situation that has given rise to the largest corporate collapses, particularly where incentives have been short term and options based.

This 'conflict' can simply be avoided through absolute transparency, an absolute commitment to independent audit in substance form and appearance, and clear strategies of aligning shareholder interest with executive reward.

Alignment with shareholder value: which shareholders, which values?

A further difficulty most boards face is understanding shareholder value. Without an understanding of this, it is not possible to achieve alignment. All shareholders are different and have different values and investment horizons; some are short-term-focused on share price and others are long-term-focused on business development and growth. Often the short term and the long term are in conflict. For example, do we cut research and improve this quarter's or year's profits and cut projected new product launches in year five?

Who are the shareholders and what do they want?

Generally, shareholders fall into three broad categories and the objectives of each category are different. From time to time, share registers will be dominated by one group or another and this in turn drives board strategy, and the challenge is to move the CEO's thinking and reward packages as these competing objectives evolve.

Punters

These are the share market, share price-focused investors, including momentum traders, day traders and hedge funds. These shareholders get their rewards out of short-term share price movement, either way if short trading is included. They want short-term news that will move the share price. They are punters, not proprietors. Attempting to align CEO rewards with the objectives of this class of shareholder is always dangerous. The executives control the flow of information and, regardless of continuous disclosure, boards can only disclose what they know and it is what you do not know that can hurt. Selective reporting should never be encouraged. It was the abundance of these shareholders in capital markets in the late 1990s that drove Enron, at least in part, when the performance-based remuneration consultants provided CEOs with excessive rewards based on share price movement.

Bank term deposit holders

This group of shareholders falls into the 'I want a broad portfolio to mitigate business risk' category. The balance diversified portfolio holder, including passive funds, super funds and diversified individuals, falls into this category. These shareholders want stable returns that beat fixed interest and, regardless of what they say, they are loss averse. This group's time horizon depends largely on demographics and the need for cash at defined times, intermittency theory in the extreme. Aligning executive rewards with the objectives of this group will stifle innovation and risk taking, which is what business is about. When these types of holders dominate a share register, the CEO in essence has to become a custodian on a flat salary, and the company has to focus on consistent yields.

Business owners

The final group of shareholders is those that behave like owners. These shareholders want boards to take risks and get it right more than they get it wrong. They want the CEO to build long-term business value through sustainable growth. They want to understand the business and the CEO. These shareholders want to see rising long-term earnings and cash flows, clear understandable strategy and honest execution of that strategy. These shareholders want a balance between short- and long-term performance and they want the CEO to share in these rewards. The challenge is how.

Transparency

As a matter of principle, the NZSA seeks disclosure of the full details of the CEO's package, including base pay, sign-on handshakes, golden parachutes, pension arrangements, option plans, share purchase schemes, fringe benefits and any other benefits provided to the CEO. It is not important how an executive chooses to take his or her pay, just how much in total is paid in one form or another. Disclosure can be made on the basis of Total Employment Cost (TEC). Clearly what employees choose to do with their reward package is to a degree their private business. Full disclosure of performance-based payments and incentives, including the amounts paid, the basis of computation and the performance criteria for each payment, is also required, as is clear and consistent descriptions of short- and long-term incentives.

The counter argument to this is that the CEO is entitled to some privacy and the basis of payment may be commercially sensitive intellectual property of the company. However, if a CEO chooses to work for a publicly accountable body, he is implicitly becoming a public figure and, in respect of the TEC level, privacy has long gone. Commercial sensitivity also goes if everyone discloses. At that point, how a company pays ceases to be a basis of competitive advantage as the playing field is levelled (if it ever was a basis for commercial advantage).

The advantages of full disclosure are these.

- The greed/envy debate ceases, provided proper alignment is achieved, as everyone has a full belly, and the basis of what appears excessive is then understood by all.
- Shareholders can get a true feel for a company's strategy, as how the CEO is paid should be closely aligned with strategy. Mission statements, vision statements, etc. are just cheap PR words if not backed by a chequebook.
- If shareholders understand a company's strategy and its business and, through transparent disclosure on issues upon which there might be a conflict, begin to understand the people with whom they are investing, rational investment decisions can be made more effectively, improving capital allocation and reducing resource wastage.

This leads to the following position on executive remuneration: strong support for performance-based rewards for CEOs and, for that matter, all workers within the company, for the following reasons:

- Flat pay discourages risk taking and encourages flat performance. Such regimes rely on integrity to obtain value and this is almost impossible to judge with foresight.
- Performance-based pay allows executives to design their job around the other priorities within their life and ensures that the financial cost of these life trade-offs are shared.
- Performance-based pay, if managed well, reduces stress in the work place through allowing employees to perform at a level that they are comfortable with and be rewarded for that level of performance and no more. High base salaries drive high base demands.
- Performance-based rewards if well-constructed should drive shareholder value and increase business efficiency.

Basis for CEO reward

The overriding principles should be believable transparency, simplicity and consistency. Participants must have clear objectives and deliverables that they can monitor and against which their superiors can judge their performance. These objectives must be consistent with long-term shareholder value. For each employee, critical key performance indicators (KPIs) should be developed. For the CEO, all of these diverse KPIs should come together to arrive at a basis for measuring performance in terms of the organization's delivery of long-term shareholder value.

If performance-based pay is to be used in an organization, it must be based on alignment of long-term shareholder values, therefore inevitably a balance between long- and short-term reward must be achieved. Each organization is different and the KPIs that are developed for each business will be different.

However, no short-term executive reward structure should be based on share price activity, in whole or in part. For the CEOs, the KPIs that should be used are those that transparently relate to shareholder value. In our view, shareholder value is achieved through predictable earnings per share growth.

Appropriate KPIs?

Various aspects of KPIs are relevant to monitoring a company's long-term economic performance. I have divided KPIs into the following categories:

- earnings
- growth
- predictability.

Broadly, each KPI can be looked at as a hard number in isolation or can be looked at as a trend over time; both of course are relevant at different times.

Earnings

Common indicators are reported profit, earnings before interest and tax (EBIT), earnings before interest, tax, depreciation and amortization (EBITDA), profit before abnormals, dividends, all measured on a per share basis, return on equity (ROE), return on total assets, economic value added (EVA), cash flow per share, or sales or revenue per share. In isolation, none of these is truly reflective of earnings and can even be misleading. Clearly profit on its own is a meaningless number, however computed, if it is not related to the capital deployed to earn that profit.

For example, earnings per share can be manipulated by simply retaining earnings and not paying dividends, so if earnings per share are to be used as the KPI, it obviously needs to be subject to maintaining return on equity, or EVA. Further either of these indicators can be manipulated by changing the debt equity ratio of the business to use 'cheaper' debt funding. Obviously increasing the financial leverage of the business can increase the return on equity, but it also comes with an increase in the risk associated with the enterprise. So regardless of the earnings number per share that is used, further KPIs should be in place around dividend and financial leverage to ensure that the short-term earning number is not materially affected by financial engineering.

Profit and even operating cash flows can be manipulated by the assumptions made on what is an expense versus what is capital. A further option is to look at the operating cash flow relative to capital deployed. Use of this measure by the firm provides an incentive to increase operating cash flows and reduce capital expenditure or funds deployed. When commencing a regime of this nature, a starting value for capital needs to be established. If you are using equity earnings, then book equity is as good as any other measure. If you are using EBITDA, then gross assets is an appropriate measure. Going forward, however, complexity sets in when the CEO is selling down assets. Do you then reduce the funds deployed by the book value of the asset sold or by the amount realized? You should reduce the capital by the book value of the asset sold and treat the excess as income. This then begs the question of what you should do with lock-in goodwill at the commencement of the arrangement. These points illustrate that there is no one golden bullet.

Another option is to ignore reported profit entirely and take profit to mean the improvement in the shareholders' equity from one reporting period to the next and add to this improvement the dividends paid and deduct any capital raised. On this basis, shareholders have either had their return in cash or improved the net asset backing per share. This would be fine if we did not have to deal with share buybacks on market. Pro rata buybacks of course can be treated as dividends for the purpose of this calculation. Again such a simple formula of asset improvement plus dividends is also not a golden bullet but at least it picks up the things that go directly to reserves, which are easily ignored (e.g. exchange reserves).

One thing is certain, however, and that is dividends. It is cash, it is paid out and it is hard to manipulate. When a CEO joins a company, an existing dividend policy will be in place. If under a CEO's stewardship, dividends are increased, then the increase is a good indicator of performance, so long as earnings per share is also increasing and financial leverage is not increasing and return on equity is being maintained.

EVA is also not a bad measure, but it does require some assumptions about cost of capital, which, if applied in the pure way in which it has been designed, will reference cost of capital back to share price volatility. Thus it is not my preference, as it assumes that share markets price risk efficiently in real time, and I do not believe that this base assumption holds true in New Zealand, if anywhere. Be that as it may, EVA on its own is no worse than any other measure on its own. In summary, a mixture of ROE, or EVA when related to earnings per share and dividends, cross-checked to financial leverage will provide a reasonably robust measure of earnings performance. Before leaving this point, it is worth mentioning off-balance-sheet leverage. Financial leverage should also include an analysis of operating lease commitments perhaps to revenue.

Growth

When we look at growth, shareholders are in essence looking at the long-term trend in the ratios identified above. The historic five-year trend in key ratios is a good guide to historic performance; the future likely growth is far more subjective. Certainly, improvement in key ratios over time is what shareholders are looking for. One overriding factor, however, is growth in total revenue. If profit is rising over time and sales are not, there is only so much that can be achieved through margin improvement. Obviously profit growth without sales growth is not sustainable going forward. The issue is then how sales are being grown, as clearly sales revenue can grow organically or through acquisition. If it is through acquisition, either financial leverage will increase or more equity will be raised. So in addition to other indicators, sales revenue per share is important in assessing long-term growth prospects, subject of course to the financial leverage trend within the business.

Predictability

Predictability is about historic earnings volatility but it is also about sustainability. While Triple Bottom Line as it is currently reported does not add much to the sustainability argument, at least from a shareholder's perspective, there are some key ratios that can be extracted from this process which are useful. A good guide to financial stability is the audit cost relative to either gross assets or equity. Ignoring rising audit costs due to market circumstances, if the cost of audit is rising relative to assets or equity, it is an indicator that the auditors are finding it increasingly difficult to audit the enterprise. This will be due either to the auditors finding more risks in the business on which they have to satisfy themselves or to inadequate reporting or internal risk management systems. This ratio and the trend should be monitored. Audit costs in this respect include associated consultancy whether completed by the auditors or others, and internal audit costs should be factored into this ratio.

If it is accepted that people are a company's most important asset, then ratios and trends in staff turnover and absenteeism are also useful. To be really meaningful, however, such a ratio should be calculated in meaningful bands. Motivated and loyal people are a company's most valuable asset. If it is also accepted that all businesses are in the business of selling, customers are just as important as the internal team. For this reason, trends in market share and customer turnover are important. Customer concentration and turnover in key accounts may also be a significant KPI, if not for the CEO then certainly for appropriate team members. If shareholders have a feel for staff and customer retention and market share, they will have a better feel for the sustainability of the enterprise.

The final matter out of Triple Bottom Line is the issue of environmental concerns. The number of prosecutions under environmental law may also be a KPI and again the trend in this would be useful.

Share price as a key performance indicator

Share price is not an appropriate short-term performance indicator for the following reasons:

- Share price is a function of willing buyers and willing sellers (shareholders not managers) trading their positions based on their own needs and information provided by management.
- Despite academic beliefs, share markets are not efficient arbiters of a company's risk, in real time. To a significant degree, share markets reflect

human emotion at least as much as the efficient pricing of risk. Interestingly, alternative research from human science departments is now beginning to emerge to dispute efficient market theory.

- Even if efficient market theory could be established to be operative, it requires full information and high liquidity. With continuous disclosure, it is hoped that we might get close to the former, but the latter is beyond all but a small group of NZX listed companies.
- In any event, information is under the control of management and, if management are incentivized based on share price, an implicit conflict of interest is created whereby management can attempt to manage the share price through the selective control of information.
- Share price for listed companies is an instantaneous barometer. Shareholders and managers alike can look up the share price of a company in real time all the time. It is hard enough to get shareholders to focus on the business rather than the share price. If managers can see the result of their decisions and the communication of them in real time, the natural instinct is to look for short-term gratification, particularly where a significant portion of a manager's reward is based on share price. Such short-termism creates the environment in which situations like Enron and WorldCom can occur.
- In the absence of deliberate manipulation by management, share price is beyond the control of management, unless they are also significant shareholders. A fundamental of any successful performance-based pay regime is that the KPIs selected must be simple, transparent and within the control or responsibility of the person being monitored.

Long-term incentives

Inevitably, short-term rewards are usually based on annual results. Business is a continuous activity broken into accounting periods for administrative and reporting convenience. There is always the risk when executives are overly rewarded based on short-term results that executives will manage the information flows to maximize their own position. Clearly in preparing Financial Statements on a period-by-period basis, assumptions are required to be made in valuing assets and calculating liabilities. New Zealand's regime is a descriptive regime. This allows flexibility to management to present data in a way which describes the business in a true and fair way. Equally it allows manipulation. The alternative of a more prescriptive regime also has its problems in that compliance with a prescriptive standard is a defence for management at the expense of owners if the result is still misleading. Where one party controls information and the way in which it is conveyed, and is rewarded significantly for positive results, we have a classic moral hazard situation. This is one of the significant arguments against performance-based rewards.

The old saying that you can fool some of the people some of the time and all of the people none of the time is the basis for providing a mixture of short- and long-term incentives. There are a number of ways in which this can be achieved.

Long-term KPIs

One common mechanism is to have short-term rewards paid on long-term KPIs on the basis that these are harder to manipulate than short-term indicators. While this is true, there is always the problem that each time leadership changes in an organization, or within a business unit, the accountability and responsibility for long-term indicators gets blurred – that is, long-term indicators are only a useful incentive for long-term employees.

Another variation on this theme is the high watermark approach. What this says is that a portion of an executive's reward comes from beating the company's previous best. High watermarks only really work in conjunction with other long-term incentive arrangements but are again prone to manipulation.

Long-term KPIs cannot be readily set that are fair to incoming and outgoing management. Be that as it may, long-term trends should be part of the reward structure for any CEO.

Bonus banking

Another method is to calculate reward based on short-term KPIs and only pay out a portion of the earned incentive, retaining the balance in an internal bonus bank. In subsequent years, the bank gets further credits or perhaps gets debited as well when there is under-performance. Bonus banking provides companies with the means of holding back short-term incentives until they have seen if the performance that has occurred is a sustainable improvement or is otherwise the subject of management managing information. The negative with bonus banking is that, unless each employee maintains a separate account in the bonus bank, you can have arguments from current performers about covering past shortfalls or from historic performers having their performance docked by the work of others. Again it is the same problem as the long-term KPI issue. To some degree, this can be dealt with by team members having their own 'account' within the bonus bank.

A further useful by-product of bonus banking is that it can be used as a tool to assist in locking in key staff. Taking executive remuneration captive is not an appropriate way to achieve lock-in. Teams do not function well if they include members who would prefer to leave but are locked in financially and whom the balance of the team wants to be rid of. While there is a role for using reward as part of a lock-in strategy, value and objective alignment will achieve the same outcome in a more positive manner. The prime purpose of bonus banking is to ensure that the information upon which short-term rewards are paid is reliable and to share the consequences when this is not the case.

Issuing shares

Another mechanism is to use shares as part of the reward package. Historically, option grants with long exercise periods and medium-term vesting periods were used, on the premise that share price growth responded to positive short-term performance indicators and that the resultant improvement was an appropriate basis for reward. This premise is false.

Of late, in New Zealand at least, options have become less common and a practice is emerging whereby executives are issued with restricted shares. Every scheme is different but common features include the following:

- An element of base reward or at-risk reward is forfeited and then paid net of tax with shares.
- The vesting of the shares is contingent on performance hurdles and sometimes longer-term hurdles. In other instances, there are no performance hurdles.
- Once the shares are vested, their ability to be traded is restricted for a period of time, either as a lock-in or to ensure that the performance hurdles are met on a sustainable basis.

While there are rare circumstances in which options are an acceptable form of reward due to the inordinate emphasis of that reward on share price action, these arguments are less compelling with restricted shares due to the lesser leverage.

With options, the incentive is share price improvement and nothing else. If the share price does not improve, there is no reward and the options can then become a disincentive. With restricted shares, so long as the employee lasts the distance, there should always be at least some element of recovery.

A workable model

While one size does not fit all, the following model is robust for many companies.

- All executives should have a portion of their base remuneration at risk.
- There should be a comprehensive reward programme based on sensible KPIs, which each executive is measured against. Those KPIs should be within the executive's control. In the case of the CEO, those KPIs should be publicly reported and perhaps even the Continuous Disclosure Regime should dovetail into those KPIs. If the KPIs are met, the 'at risk' portion of the base reward should be paid out in cash. In addition, if the KPIs are exceeded, there should be a bonus plan over and above base reward that has no limit. Bonus rewards should be paid out entirely in company shares. Obviously the KPIs should be devised around long-term shareholder value, as discussed in this chapter.
- The shares issued on account of the bonus component should be blocked from trading but not otherwise for a minimum period of, say, three years. If the executive leaves, the restriction should still apply and should rarely be waived. This ensures that the executive's short-term reward is paid in a manner that puts that reward at the same risk that shareholders suffer if the

KPI achievement was not sustainable or was otherwise manipulated. If audit raises issues of manipulation, all shares subject to restriction should be subject to forfeiture. In the meantime, the executives should have full voting rights over the stock and should receive all dividends and the right to participate in all rights issues and bonus issues available to shareholders. In effect, the executives should be shareholders like any other with restrictions on trading only.

- It is unacceptable for CEOs to resign and then exercise all of their options or sell all of their restricted shares and leave the mess for the next person to clean up. Sure, the retiring CEO might think that the next CEO will do badly and may want to sell for that reason. This is a valid concern; however, the greater risk is that the CEO has milked the cow dry to maximize his KPIs and then passed an empty parcel to his successor. Thus it will be rare for a CEO's restricted shares to be released early.

If rewards are to be paid in shares, there are clearly two options:

- the company issues new shares; or
- the company buys shares on market.

On market buyback

Shareholders, particularly large shareholders, will be concerned about dilution and therefore our preference, wherever possible, is that the shares be bought on market by an independent trustee in a nominated period within the unrestricted envelope available to insiders.

The key constraints regarding a buyback option are as follows:

- The need to obtain shareholder approval. However, under both the Companies Act 1993 and the NZX Listing Rules, the only requirement is that of an ordinary resolution, which, subject to full disclosure of the purpose and intent of the proposal, should not create any shareholder issues. Issuing shares, however, does not require such approval, subject of course to the Company's Constitution. Generally up to 20 per cent of the company's issued stock can be created in any 12-month period by the board and issued without shareholder approval; that, however, is another issue of concern to shareholders.
- The company's cash flow and its ability to meet the cash payments for executive rewards. It is, however, fair to say that if rewards are payable and there is insufficient cash or borrowing capacity, then it is likely that the KPIs upon which the rewards are calculated are flawed. Be that as it may, it is a constraint. However, taxes must be paid on the reward programme and only the net can be converted to shares. So if cash is a real problem, it may well be that there is no alternative to using options that avoid tax until the options are exercised. An alternative is now available to deal with the cash problem

of the tax payments at the time of the bonus payment. Employee share option trusts are worth exploring in detail, for this issue alone, but such structures also have other benefits.

- The liquidity of the company's share is also a fundamental issue. If the level of buying is likely to move the company's share price and/or reduce the freely tradable float to any significant degree, on market buybacks are not appropriate. While the determination of this issue is not a precise science, if the buyback programme in any 12-month period is likely to reduce the free float by more than 2.5 per cent or is likely to account for more than 10 per cent of the average daily volume over the nominated period in which the buying activity will occur, then the company's stock is not sufficiently liquid to sustain an on market buyback.

Issuing stock

Where it is not feasible to buy back stock on market, it is considered acceptable for the company to issue new stock. An added advantage of this option is that over time such a programme will increase the free float and liquidity of the company's shares, which is of benefit to all non-strategic shareholders. Major shareholders who hold, say, 50.1 per cent are unlikely to be happy losing their majority.

The key issues under this alternative are dilution, pricing and timing. Timing should be at a nominated time each year following the announcement of results and the determination of the KPIs giving rise to the reward payment. The pricing should be referenced to the current share price as quoted on the NZX. However, if a stock is illiquid, this might not give a true measure of the company's worth either way. Therefore, some flexibility will be required to enable the board to price the stock in a manner that is fair to the employees and to the existing shareholders. Regardless, there must be full disclosure of the pricing regime used for the issuance of stock. If a price other than the current market price or the weighted average of the stock price since the date of the announcement of the result and the date of issue is used, the board should fully disclose its rationale and have this verified by an independent expert. If the price is more than a 20 per cent discount to the prevailing market price at the date of issue, the matter should be submitted to shareholders for approval. In the event that shareholder approval is not forthcoming, the executive reward would then be payable in cash but subject to an appropriate bonus banking arrangement.

Team cohesion

A further valid criticism of performance-based rewards when spread through an organization is that it encourages individual performance at the expense of team cohesion. In some organizations, it is not possible to separate individuals. For example, in a steel mill, the whole production line is effectively one operating unit. Therefore, team performance hurdles are also important and team reward programmes should be entrenched as part of a firm's reward structure. If well done, this can over time provide shared ownership through the whole organization.

How much is enough?

Once upon a time, a promise to pay someone his or her weight in gold would have been beyond even the wildest of expectations. Now even if an executive was seriously obese, it would be hard for an executive to walk out with much more than $10 million. How times have changed.

The amount of a CEO's bonus should not matter so long as it is transparently disclosed and it is seen to be fair. Shareholders will not care too much who gets the incentive so long as it is a portion of shareholder value added, up to a point. It is, however, fundamentally important that the rewards of success are perceived by all those who earned it to have been fairly distributed. If it is not, team cohesion and motivation will be adversely affected, as will long-term shareholder rewards as a result.

The CEO's base pay must have some reference point to the economic reality of the company in which they work and the team with which they serve. Twenty years ago, a CEO's salary on average was about ten times the average for the company as a whole. Now it is nearer 30. Have the risks gone up that much? How much is one person worth relative to another? These are fundamental questions of social justice and sadly shareholders are at the front line on this issue. If rewards for the CEO are perceived to be at the expense of the team, the team will fall apart and long-term shareholder value will be destroyed. Therefore, when shareholders are considering CEO reward, they should consider the reward structure for the company as a whole to ensure that long-term interests are served.

Often when seeking a pay increase, boards will trundle out 'experts' who inevitably report that an executive is paid below average. Never do they compare the reward structure for the company as a whole with the rewards proposed for the CEO. They then usually suggest that the CEO is an above-average performer and recommend that he should be paid an above-average pay. Have you ever seen a report that tells shareholders that a CEO is a below-average performer? Then of course the new salary is factored into the averages, which of course perpetually rise, and then another report is generated recommending yet another increase and so the cycle goes on.

Other experts suggest that high differentials are desirable based on 'Trophy Theory'. This theory basically surmises that if CEOs are paid excessively it provides an incentive for the next level to work harder in the hope that they will be the one to win the Trophy of succession. Is it fair to expect second-level managers to bet their life in a lottery? This theory could only ever have a modestly sustainable position if most companies promoted from within. In NZ, this is not the usual model.

Executive overall reward has to have some common-sense correlations to the rewards of shareholders and the rewards of other members of the CEO's team to be socially and or economically sustainable. Hence, the CEO's base reward, including the at-risk portion of that base reward, should not be higher than twice the base reward paid to the highest paid team member reporting directly to the CEO. Also the at-risk portion of the CEO's base pay should be approximately 50 per cent of the total base reward, and for second-tier management the level should be about one third at risk, reducing in sensible steps as we move down through the organization.

Role of shareholders

There has been some debate over the role of shareholders on the issue of executive reward. All business is a partnership between owners and workers and therefore the reward structures of workers is as much the prerogative of owners as it is of workers. Directors are the agents of the owners and are charged with carrying into effect the wishes of and representing the interests of owners. It therefore behoves directors to understand the position of shareholders on this matter.

The power of shareholders

Shareholders have only limited power but in the main small shareholders do not bother to use even those powers they do have. Although small shareholders have been treated very badly, both by directors in the examples from the finance company sector and by major shareholders, some of that treatment is their own fault; first, through not paying enough attention before purchasing the shares in the first place and, second, through not trying to change behaviour, even through exit. They should recall that:

- shareholders have the right to vote at AGMs on major transactions, transactions with related parties, including remuneration issues and on changes to the company's constitution;
- shareholders can nominate directors, vote on the appointment of directors and the remuneration of directors;
- shareholders can vote on the appointment and remuneration of auditors;
- shareholders can attend or requisition AGMs or EGMs and are entitled to speak or question management at any such meeting;
- shareholders, like everyone, can inspect the company statutory records, including the share register, the directors' register of interest and charges register and the minutes of meetings of shareholders;
- the most important power and the one so infrequently used is any shareholder can propose business on notice, and the company must circulate it to all of its shareholders with notice of meeting together with up to 1,000 words of explanatory material – this is an enormous power and one that should be used sparingly but sadly it is almost never used;
- finally, all shareholders have the power of thought and voice; the power to humiliate idiots is the most effective power any of us have and more of us need to use it.

All of these powers are low cost and can be delivered with massive impact.

Shareholders also have further powers but for most they are utterly impractical. They can exercise minority buyout, they can launch derivative actions in the name of the company at the company's expense and they can apply to the court to have a company liquidated on just and equitable grounds. All involve lawyers and the court so, unless you are a major shareholder, entirely impractical. In all cases, it makes sense for small shareholders to coordinate so that their voice is loud enough for the management to hear and take notice. The New Zealand Shareholders' Association is an example, which exists to fill the ownership vacuum. The consequence for society from shareholders acting together in this way to promote their interests as owners rather than punters (or effectively bondholders) can only be good.

3 The poor performance of compulsory saving in Australia

Superannuation and corporate governance

Christine Brown and Deborah Ralston

> Corporate governance is 'the framework of rules, relationships, systems and processes within and by which authority is exercised and controlled in corporations'. It encompasses the mechanisms by which companies, and those in control, are held to account. Corporate governance influences how the objectives of the company are set and achieved, how risk is monitored and assessed, and how performance is optimised.
>
> (ASX Corporate Governance Principles and Recommendations, 2nd edition, 2010, p. 3)

As at June 2010, superannuation funds under management in Australia totalled $1.23 trillion. This figure includes a large pool of compulsory savings contributed by the 85 per cent of the adult population now covered by the Superannuation Guarantee Contribution (SGC). While this pool of savings is only one pillar of the retirement system, which also includes the age pension, voluntary superannuation savings and personal savings, including home ownership, it is a critical pillar. An emerging theme in the recent Cooper Review (2009c), which was charged with examining the equity, simplicity and efficiency of the system, has been that, given the dependence of the Australian retirement system on compulsory superannuation saving, the heavy emphasis on defined contribution funds and the wide range of choices available, individuals tend to bear a higher level of investment and other financial risks than is the case in many other pension systems worldwide. Consequently, the need to maximize the safety and efficiency of the superannuation system takes on particular importance. In the final report, Cooper (2010) stated that *improving governance practices and structures is the key to improving member outcomes*. In this chapter, we focus on exploring potential factors behind the low returns on superannuation funds, such as differences in the structure of funds and the governance issues that can lead to higher costs and consequently lower subsequent rates of return to members. We develop a framework to explore possible links between governance models and their impact on agency and direct costs.

Compulsory superannuation has been a feature of retirement savings in Australia since 1992 when the superannuation guarantee was introduced, requiring employers to make tax-deductible superannuation contributions on behalf of their employees. While compulsory superannuation contributions are made by employers, in the longer run it is better to think of them as 'forced savings' of employees out of wages rather than as involving higher labour costs for employers. From a base of 3 per cent, higher levels of compulsory contributions were phased in over a ten-year period, reaching the maximum of 9 per cent in 2002–3.

As a result of this mandatory saving over the last decade, superannuation assets have trebled and, since 1994, the managed fund industry has enjoyed a compound growth rate of over 10 per cent per annum. Consequently, Australia now has almost $1.03 trillion invested in superannuation assets (Cooper Review, 2009a). As a consequence, Australia has the fourth largest funds management industry in the world and the largest in the Asia Pacific region. Apart from the depth of the savings pool, another key strength of the Australian system is its breadth of coverage. While the superannuation guarantee provides exemptions for some categories of employees,[1] the current Australian superannuation system stands up well under international comparisons, with around 85 per cent of the working population having superannuation accounts (OECD, 2008).

But despite the relatively broad coverage of superannuation and the large amount of funds invested, the adequacy of the Australian retirement system is not particularly strong.[2] Indeed, in the Melbourne Mercer Global Pension Index (Melbourne Centre for Financial Studies, 2009), which provides an international comparison of the adequacy of benefits in 11 countries around the globe, Australia was ranked fourth behind the Netherlands, Canada and Sweden. Interestingly, all of these countries have a much larger average fund size and structures which are primarily defined benefit.

In the recent *Review into the Governance, Efficiency, Structure and Operation of Australia's Superannuation System* (Cooper Review), which reported in June 2010, a number of areas of weakness that have impacted on the performance of superannuation funds and, consequently, on the net returns of compulsory savings were identified. These include lack of scale, poor operational efficiency in manual back-office processes, fees that are too high, excessive complexity, poor reporting and disclosure, and a number of issues related to governance of superannuation funds. The Super System Review Final Report (hereafter Cooper, 2010)[3] points out that system design and regulatory settings have not adequately ensured that member interests have remained paramount in a system that is compulsory and fully outsourced to the private sector.

In terms of governance, the Cooper Review has identified a number of agency and structural issues which constrain the opportunity for member vigilance and give rise to a lack of incentive for agency vigilance. Cooper states (p. 2) that 'improving governance practices and structures is the key to improving member outcomes'. Superannuation governance has been complicated over recent years by the move in funds from defined benefit (DB) to a defined contribution (DC) structure.[4] In making this change, funds have exchanged the complexities of DB liabilities for complexities in the design and management of DC assets (Clark and Urwin, 2010). This is especially true for smaller DC funds which lack a depth of in-house expertise and therefore develop a complex web of outsourcing relationships to manage their portfolios.

This chapter's central focus is an examination of the governance structure of superannuation funds in Australia and how it relates to their performance. The remainder of the chapter is structured as follows. The development and performance of the Australian superannuation industry is outlined first. Then we investigate the governance problem and review the relevant literature, before considering the recent performance of Australian superannuation funds. Throughout, key recommendations from the Cooper Review inform the analysis.

The superannuation industry in Australia

The superannuation industry in Australia has developed considerably over the past decade. We first describe the rationale and development of the industry as a tool for establishing a pool of compulsory saving, before reviewing recent rates of return of superannuation funds, their expense ratios and their investment strategies in order to build a picture of relative performance of the different types of funds and the different benefit structures.

Background to compulsory savings through superannuation

According to the Australian Prudential Regulatory Authority (APRA), the rationale behind the introduction of mandated superannuation was three-fold. First, the aim of compulsory saving through superannuation is to assist individuals to provide for their retirement and to ensure a better standard of living in post-retirement years. Second, increasing the level of private savings in the economy assists economic growth and creates jobs by providing a pool of funds for investment. And third, private saving for retirement reduces the burden on the public purse in terms of the age pension and support for the older community, thereby allowing public spending to be directed towards other policy demands (APRA, 2007).

Since July 1992, when employers were required to provide most employees with a minimum SGC of 3 per cent of earnings, compulsory saving under the 'superannuation guarantee' has become the central plank of Australia's retirement system. The contribution rate increased to reach 9 per cent by July 2002, thereby leading to a rapid expansion in the percentage of employees with superannuation and their balances in the system. By 2007, 11.6 million people over the age of 15 had superannuation accounts and 4.8 million did not. Of those with superannuation, 10.8 million had accounts in the accumulation phase, another 0.4 million were accumulating and drawing on their superannuation and 1.2 million were drawing on their superannuation (Allen Consulting Group, 2009). Since then the superannuation industry has continued to develop so that at June 2009 the industry accounted for over $1.03 trillion in assets. Superannuation funds therefore are responsible for the compulsory savings of a large proportion of the Australian population.

As Table 3.1 shows, superannuation contributions comprised only around 20 per cent of household assets for 55 to 65-year-olds in 2005–6. Retirees in this age group might be expected to rely more on the age pension safety net, other financial assets and home equity. Given that compulsory superannuation was not introduced until 1992, however, that proportion might be expected to increase substantially for this age group when the system matures by the mid-2030s, as they will have contributed over their whole working lives.

The management of these savings is undertaken by four major types of superannuation funds (outlined in Table 3.2). Public sector and corporate funds are those established by an employer for employees and were traditionally – but increasingly less so – defined benefit schemes. Retail funds are those offered by 'for-profit' financial institutions to the general public (open or public offer) and are generally accumulation schemes. Industry funds emerged with the introduction of compulsory superannuation in the early 1990s and were initially focused on providing accumulation schemes for employees within a specified industry group. Employees initially had no choice of fund but freedom of choice was introduced under the *Superannuation Legislation Amendment (Choice of Superannuation Fund) Act 2004* and many industry funds have since become public offer, while most offer a range of investment options to members. Self-Managed

Table 3.1 Household assets and liabilities, 2005–6[a]

	AU$000
Accounts with financial institutions	42.4
Shares	29.6
Trusts	23.4
Debentures and bonds	2.3
Own business interests (fin. assets)	56.6
Superannuation	202.7
Total financial assets	359.3
Owner-occupied dwelling	399.0
Other property	150.9
Total property assets	549.9
Own business interests (other assets)	29.5
Contents of dwelling	69.6
Vehicles	29.3
Other assets	1.4
Total other assets	129.8
Total household assets	1,039.1

Source: adapted from the Australian Bureau of Statistics (2007) *Household Wealth and Wealth Distribution Australia 2005–2006*, No. 6554.0, Table 20, p. 32.

Note

a Figures in thousands of dollars applied to couples aged from 55 to 65 years old. Those 65 years or older had assets of $884,500. This lower figure may reflect debt repayment as well as expenditure on retirement as the superannuation balance drops from $202,700 to $107,200. Total liabilities drop from $62,500 to $16,900 with the major drop in property loan liabilities. Errors in totals are due to rounding.

Superannuation Funds (SMSF) are funds catering to four or fewer members and administered by one (or more) of those members, all of whom are trustees (usually outsourcing most administration to an accounting or other financial services firm). We return to the issue of the relative importance of each type of fund later.

The question of adequacy of the system

Overall, returns on superannuation funds have been positive, at an average since 1994–5 of 6.9 per cent for growth funds, which is 4.2 per cent above the average inflation rate over that period. It could be contended that, given that most superannuation funds aim to realize returns of 4 per cent above the inflation rate, superannuation funds have performed well over the medium term (Allen Consulting Group, 2009). But as the rationale for the establishment of the superannuation system indicated, sound performance is not only important with respect to maximizing the return on the savings of individuals but also to stimulating investment and reducing the impact on the public purse of an aging population.

By the mid-2030s, when the system matures, projections from the Intergenerational Report indicate that the proportion of individuals being entirely reliant on the age pension will fall, and the proportion of self-funded retirees will increase from around 17 per cent in 2008–9 to 23 per cent in 2034–5 (Treasury, 2010), as shown in Figure 3.1.

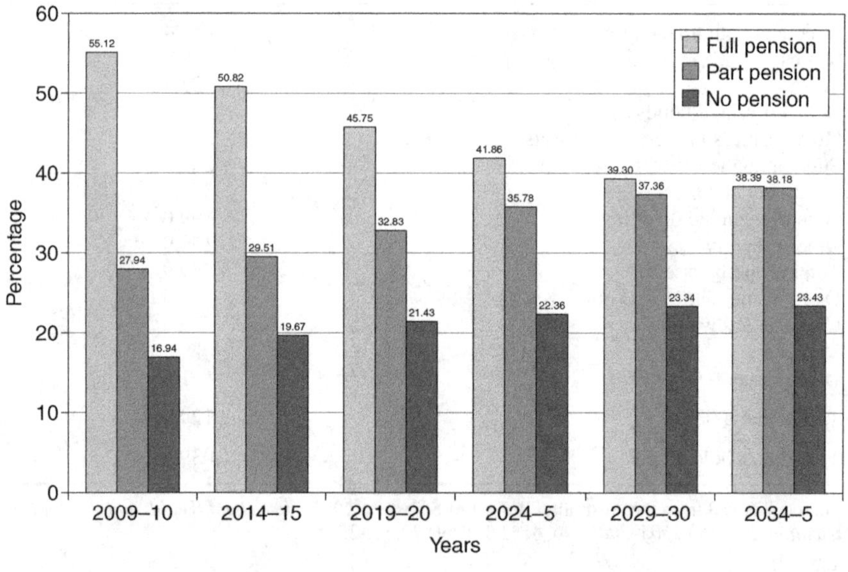

Figure 3.1 Projected percentage composition of age pensioners (source: The 2007 Intergenerational Report, Australian Treasury).

Note
www.archive.treasury.gov.au/documents/1239/PDF/IGR_2007_final_report.pdf.

While the superannuation system is clearly having an impact on the financial well-being of retirees, it is not evident that the reduction in pension costs to the public purse is commensurate with the costs of the system. Indeed, the total cost of the retirement system policy in 2010 is around $50 billion, or 5 per cent of GDP, including age pension outlays, the co-contribution, and labour and capital income tax concessions. Pender (2010) suggests a more direct and efficient means of assisting retirees may be to disband the present system and double the age pension!

Another measure of the adequacy of the current system is the retirement savings gap. Rice Warner (2010) calculations show that current funding for superannuation is still insufficient to provide the population with a comfortable living standard in retirement. Based on the target replacement rate of 62.5 per cent of average earnings, they estimate a deficit of some $695 billion at 30 June 2008, or approximately $73,000 per person. They estimate that the savings gap has actually increased by about $26,000 per person since their previous estimate in 2004, partly due to investment losses through the GFC.

As at June 2009, the individual average member account balance across a wide range of super funds was below $25,000, with retail and industry fund accounts having average balances of $18,400 and $16,600, respectively, as shown in Table 3.2 (Panel A). Members of small funds held the largest average account balance of $429,400. Corporate fund members held $81,200 on average, followed by members of public sector funds, with an average account balance of $49,400 (Cooper, 2010). Individuals often have more than one superannuation account however. With this in mind, Rice Warner estimate the June 2008 average balance per member (not per account) at $32,895 for industry funds, $46,710 for retail, $100,302 for public sector and $133,492 for corporate funds, with roughly 80 per cent of members in the default strategy.

Table 3.2 also shows the distribution of entities by benefit scheme type as at June 2009 in Panel B, where it can be seen that DC funds dominate DB funds, in terms of both the number of entities and the value of assets under management.

Over the past five years, SMSFs have enjoyed an annualized growth rate of 20 per cent, compared with 8 per cent annualized growth rate for APRA funds over the same period. By March 2010, SMSFs accounted for the largest portion of superannuation assets, holding 31.8 per cent of total superannuation assets. It should be noted, however, that despite their popularity, SMSFs are only well-suited to higher-income individuals who can afford to establish a personal fund of sufficient size to achieve the necessary economies of scale required for efficient operation.

Concerns about the performance of superannuation funds have prompted a number of recent inquiries. The Henry Review[5] of *Australia's Future Tax System* examined taxation issues impacting on superannuation and its adequacy, while the Cooper Review[6] examined the simplicity, efficiency and equity of the system. The Henry Review endorsed the three-pillar structure of the Australian retirement system of the age pension, compulsory saving through the superannuation guarantee and voluntary savings. With respect to adequacy, the review

Table 3.2 Distribution of superannuation entities

Type of fund	*Number of entities*	*Number of member accounts ('000)*	*Assets ($bill)*	*Average account balance ('$000)*
Panel A				
Corporate	190	665	54.0	81.2
Industry	67	11,551	191.8	16.6
Public sector	40	3,095	153.0	49.4
Retail	166	16,591	304.7	18.4
Small[a]	414,707	779	334.3	429.4
Pooled super. trusts	82		69.7	
Total	415,252	32,680	1,073.3	
Panel B				
DC	414,982	19,550	655.4	33.5
DB	36	660	53.4	80.9
Hybrid[b]	152	12,471	329.0	26.4
Total	415,170	32,680	1,037.9	

Source: APRA Quarterly Statistics, June 2010.

Notes

a Small superannuation funds listed in Panel A above include SMSFs, single-member approved deposit funds and small APRA-regulated funds which have fewer than five members, but are not an SMSF.

b Hybrid funds are superannuation entities that have a combination of both accumulation and defined benefit members.

recommended an increase in age pension eligibility to 67 years to improve sustainability but also recommended that there be no change in the 9 per cent SGC. The latter recommendation was not accepted, however, and in the 2010–11 Commonwealth Budget a staged increase in the compulsory contribution rate was announced, starting in 2013–14 to reach 12 per cent by 2019–20.

As Figure 3.2 demonstrates, the average net retirement income fell marginally in the period June to December 2009 but an additional 3 per cent SGC would increase average net retirement incomes by $1,574 to $45,710. However, the full benefit of an increase in the SGC will not be felt till today's young people retire. Factoring in an increase to 12 per cent reveals 20- to 24-year-olds will benefit the most, with an increase in their retirement adequacy expected to be around 75 per cent of their income – 10 per cent more than the current 65 per cent benchmark – and they are expected to have an extra $107,535 in assets in today's dollars when they retire (AMP, 2009).

While the Henry Review addressed the adequacy of the system, it is the Cooper Review that is likely to have the greatest impact on the future of superannuation and compulsory savings in Australia. The review was conducted in three phases, addressing *Governance*, *Operation and Efficiency* and *Structure* and reported in June 2010. Early in the review, a number of themes emerged, including that the social policy objectives of the superannuation system mean that it cannot be treated as just another financial product, that market forces have not always been effective in delivering the best outcome for individuals and that different models of governance are required to fit the varied operational and structural aspects of funds. It was also noted that, given the dependence of the

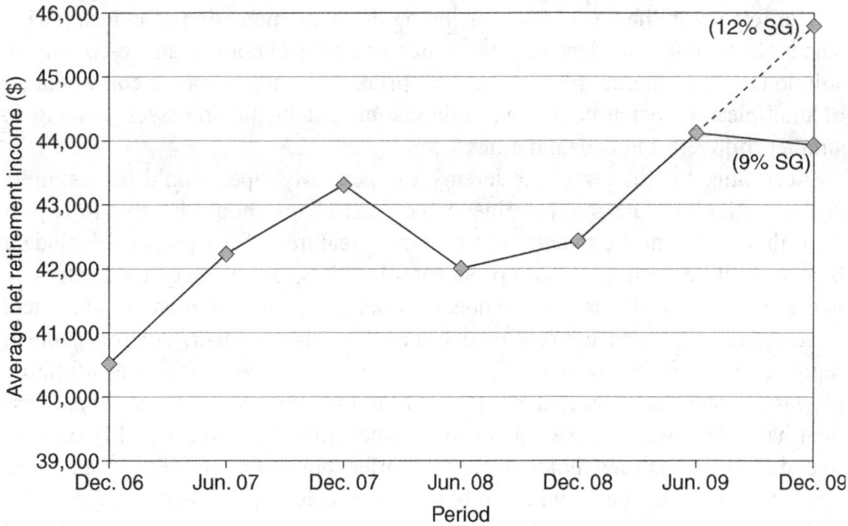

Figure 3.2 The impact of an increase in the SG from 9 per cent to 12 per cent on average net retirement income (source: AMP Retirement Adequacy Index, Summary of Trends, July–December 2009).

Australian retirement system on the second pillar of compulsory saving through superannuation, the heavy emphasis on DC funds and the wide range of choices available, individuals tend to bear a higher level of investment and other financial risks than is the case in many other pension systems, hence the need to maximize the safety and efficiency of the superannuation system (Cooper, 2009c).

Another aspect of the system which preoccupied the review in its second phase on *Operations and Governance* was the issue of economies of scale. While there was little evidence of size benefits within the Australian environment, which has an average fund size of $2.38 billion in assets, international evidence suggests that investment costs will decrease by about half from 0.33 per cent for funds under US$1 billion to 0.16 per cent for funds over US$50 billion (Cooper, 2009b, p. 33). A major change in the cost base occurs when funds achieve a sufficient size to allow for funds management to occur internally and thereby dispense with the need to offer a range of expensive outsourced funds management contracts.[7] According to the Report of the Ontario Expert Commission on Pensions (2008), funds in Canada, Sweden and the Netherlands of US$20 to US$40 billion may still be considered too small to deliver the quality and depth of governance, investments skills and risk management needed for optimal performance.

Recommendations from the review strongly emphasize the need for improved governance of funds. It recommends clarifying some of the ambiguity surrounding the trustees' role and proposes a Code of Trustee Governance. The review also resulted in the MySuper and SuperStream proposals, which are estimated to reduce member fees by about 40 per cent, leading to a subsequent increase in superannuation balances of around $40,000, or 7 per cent, after 37 years in the workforce. 'SuperStream' proposes a package of measures to address problems of inefficiency in the back office, including the implementation of industry-wide standards to improve data quality, better use of technology and e-commerce solutions, use of the tax file number as a primary identifier, easier consolidation of multiple member accounts and eliminating redundant processes, leading to simpler rollovers and consolidations.[8]

According to Review Chair Jeremy Cooper, 'MySuper would be a simple, cost-effective product that redefines what Australians should be able to expect from their super in the twenty-first century.' Features of the proposal include a ban on trailing commissions, no contribution fees, a new duty on trustees to manage the overall cost to members, a default post-retirement product and trustee duties focused entirely on looking after the member. An independent report commissioned by the review from Deloitte shows that, if the MySuper proposals were introduced, some default fund members could expect to pay less than half what they are paying for their super now. The proposed MySuper is intended to be just one choice of fund on offer, but some features – such as the trailing commission ban – will also be recommended to apply across the board.[9]

It is worth noting that much greater benefits can be obtained by reducing administrative costs and fees, which apply to the whole account balance and reduce the rate of return received by members, than by reducing up-front fees on contributions. Table 3.3 illustrates the effect on the future accumulated value in

Table 3.3 Real future value of a regular contribution stream

	Real rate of return[a]	
Net monthly contribution	0.04	0.03
100	$118,196	$92,606
99	$117,014	$91,680

Source: Australian Centre for Financial Studies (2010) *Financial Wellbeing in Retirement*, Finsia.

Note

a The future value is calculated for monthly contributions over 40 years, which accumulate at the real rate of return shown.

a fund arising from a 1 per cent fee applied to each contribution and from a 1 per cent fee per annum applied to the account balance. Up-front fees of 1 per cent on each contribution, which reduce the net contribution from $100 to $99 reduce the future accumulated amount by around 1 per cent. In contrast, a 1 per cent fee on the current account balance which reduces the real rate of return from 4 to 3 per cent per annum reduces the accumulated amount by around 21 per cent.

Taking this comparison one step further, AIST (2010) find that an asset-based fee resulted in 80 per cent higher cost to members than a fixed dollar cost fee, on a realistic Australian equity index fund.

The governance problem

Superannuation funds operate under a trustee model derived from the general law of equity. Tax concessions can only be granted to funds which the Commonwealth is able to regulate directly under its corporations or pensions powers (in addition to its taxation power). Consequently, the trustee of the superannuation fund needs to be a corporation, or the fund has to have as its substantial or dominant purpose the provision of age pensions, within the meaning of the Constitution. In Australia, most superannuation funds are companies. The corporate trustee, or a group of individual trustees, controls the fund's assets and operates them solely for the benefit of its members and beneficiaries. Each trustee has a fiduciary obligation to the members and beneficiaries, which involves taking ultimate responsibility for the entity, and an obligation to manage the assets of the entity with competence, diligence, prudence and honesty. The Superannuation Industry (Supervision) Act 1993 (SIS Act) also specifies obligations of trustees that automatically form part of the governing rules of all superannuation funds. Many of the obligations in the SIS Act embody duties already imposed on trustees by trust law.

Closely tied to governance is prudential regulation. Prudential regulation helps ensure that funds deliver on their long-term financial promises. Important features of the superannuation fund prudential framework include the 'sole purpose test', which is designed to ensure superannuation funds are maintained solely for retirement income purposes (and a limited range of ancillary purposes, including the provision of death and disability insurance) and licensing of participants through the registrable superannuation entities (RSE) concept. APRA has enforcement powers, including powers to investigate trustees and funds, issue directions and disqualify trustees, and provide financial assistance to compensate APRA-regulated funds where the fund has suffered loss as a result of fraudulent conduct or theft.

APRA is responsible for the prudential regulation of all regulated superannuation funds other than SMSFs, which the Australian Tax Office supervises. APRA licenses superannuation trustees and can impose penalties on trustees that breach their responsibilities under the SIS Act. APRA requires that trustees operating APRA-regulated superannuation funds demonstrate that they meet minimum standards of fitness and propriety and have in place appropriate risk management mechanisms to identify, measure and manage risks to the trustee and to the fund.

Among the issues examined by the Cooper Review were the governance problems which can arise due to the complexity of the superannuation system and the extent to which these problems impede the ability of the fund to deliver the best outcome for members. Important elements in this regard are the nature and extent of the trustees' duties, the reliance that most funds have on outsourcing to third parties for essential services and the conflicts that trustees may have in balancing member interests when dealing with an associated service provider. The review also examined the governance of investments and the extent to which trustees are required to consider the net return to members after taxes and costs. Recommendations contained in Cooper (2010) strongly emphasize the need for improved governance of funds. The report recommends clarifying some of the ambiguity surrounding the trustees' role and proposes a Code of Trustee Governance to be developed to assist in identifying best practice principles (Recommendation 2.18, Cooper, 2010).

A useful way of framing the governance problem is given in Figure 3.3, which simplifies the complex relationships involved in most superannuation fund structures to illustrate the nature of the corporate governance and agency costs. First, the structure of the fund is depicted with separation of the roles and responsibilities of the trustee and the individual directors of the board of the trustee company (Cooper, 2010). Second, the operating environment in the top left-hand corner illustrates the regulatory environment in which superannuation funds exist, including the SIS Act, the Corporations Law, APRA oversight, etc. The top right-hand corner of Figure 3.3 is where explicit requirements of trustee-directors under the SIS Act, such as 'fit and proper', are illustrated with the development of best practice principles, as recommended by Cooper.

Moving down through Figure 3.3 to the level of the superannuation fund itself, the complexity of the relationships between the superannuation fund, its members, external asset consultants, external fund managers and any firms to which the fund outsources operations is highlighted. It is in this set of interrelationships that governance problems arise.

The goal of corporate governance is to ameliorate the agency problems or conflicts of interest that arise because those who own the pension fund assets or benefit from their investment (the pension plan members and their beneficiaries)

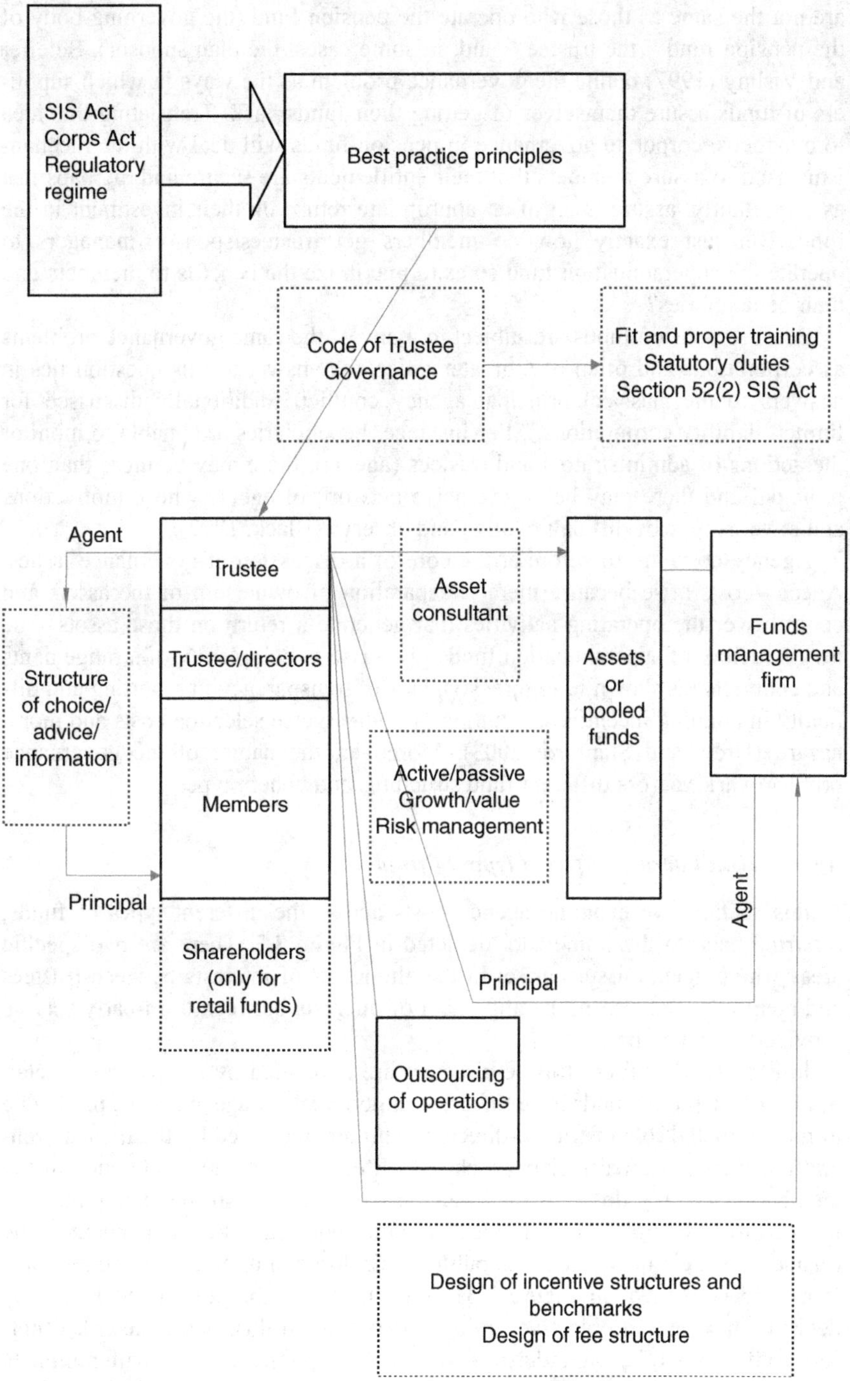

Figure 3.3 Stylized depiction of the corporate governance structure

are not the same as those who operate the pension fund (the governing body of the pension fund – the trustee – and, in some cases, the plan sponsor). Shleifer and Vishny (1997) define the governance problem as the ways in which suppliers of funds assure themselves of getting their funds back. Translating this idea to our focus, corporate governance in pension funds will deal with the mechanisms used to assure members that their entitlements are secure and, perhaps just as importantly, assure them of an appropriate return on their investment in the fund. But just exactly how do members get trustees/sponsors/managers to operate the superannuation fund so as to maximize the benefits to members and their beneficiaries?

Because pension funds are subject to many of the same governance problems as corporations and often of a greater order, the answer to this question lies in answers to the classical principal agency conflict, traditionally discussed for limited liability corporations.[10] For instance, beneficiaries are unable to monitor the actions of administrators and trustees (agents), there may be more than one principal and there may be an extensive network of agents whose motivations and rewards may be difficult to align and observe (Black, 1992).

Agency costs are therefore at the core of a discussion of governance issues. Agency costs arise because there is separation of ownership of the assets and control over the operating activities that generate a return on those assets. The trust structure of superannuation funds gives rise to complexity of arrangements and contracts (as shown in Figure 3.3), lack of transparency in reporting and difficulty in aligning incentives, resulting in both adverse selection costs and moral hazard (Drew and Stanford, 2003). Moreover, the nature of the governance problem varies across different fund structures and benefit types.

Agency issues across different types of funds

In this section, we examine agency costs across the different types of funds, referring back to the framework depicted in Figure 3.3. There are two specific areas where agency issues arise: in the alignment of interests between trustees and members, and also in the alignment of interests between third-party service providers and members.

In each type of fund, trustee-directors are appointed by the trustee.[11] Retail funds or 'for-profit' funds have the greatest potential for agency costs, partly due to the conflicted role of trustee-directors who are appointed by the trustee (generally a financial intermediary, such as a life-office), without reference to the members. Not only do retail fund members have no say in the appointment of trustee-directors, but these individuals are not required to be independent of the trustee and their names are not publicly disclosed. Further, retail funds have shareholders (shown in Figure 3.3), who must also be considered in trustee decision making and objective setting. In contrast to this, the trustee of a 'not-for-profit' – that is, an industry, corporate or public fund – will nominate members as trustee-directors and will normally seek some form of input from members on the selection of employee representatives. Trustee-directors in not-for-profits are therefore more likely to align with member interest.[12] The SMSF sector is least likely to experience this first type of agency cost, as members are also the trustees.

The second area which presents a potential for agency issues is in outsourcing, which *has been a hallmark of the Australian superannuation industry* (Cooper, 2010). Most funds undertake outsourcing to a greater or lesser extent. In the early days of superannuation funds, when there was a preponderance of corporate funds, employers often made their administrative resources available to assist the trustee and contain costs to employees. In other contexts, related parties were often used (or established) to provide services to a particular fund or to a group of funds. Even now, despite the growth of the industry as a whole, funds often lack the scale to provide the skills or resources necessary to perform all the required services cost effectively. Consequently, funds often outsource some or all of their back-office operations and investment decision making to third parties, as shown to the right of Figure 3.3 in the box labelled 'outsourcing' and the box labelled 'funds management firm'. This practice gives rise to potential conflicts of interest and higher agency costs. In retail funds especially, Coleman *et al.* (2006) contend that misaligned incentives and higher agency costs have produced lower rates of return, a matter to which we return.

The issue of small size, lack of expertise and the consequent need for outsourcing is a recurring theme in the pension governance literature. Clark (2004) argues that one solution to overcoming problems of governance and lack of expertise within pension funds is to increase internal resources sufficient to employ professional managers and advisors, a solution that it is only feasible, however, for large-size funds or if governments promote the formation of larger multi-employer pension funds. Similarly, interviews with a selected group of pension funds executives (Clark and Urwin, 2008a) emphasize the need to treat governance as a long-term investment rather than a short-term cost. In the better governed entities, the governance budget was treated as part of the management of risk and return. Once again, Clark recognizes difficulties in widespread adoption of best practice governance principles in smaller funds which do not have size and structure advantages. Clark further suggests that leadership may be another important ingredient towards high-quality governance, which is then discussed in Clark and Urwin (2008b).

Clark and Urwin (2008b) identify three types of investment governance in DC funds. In Type 1 funds, investment decisions are less formalized and the board delegates the decision making to a committee which acts with the support of a consultant and external service providers. Type 2 funds have a more sophisticated structure that utilizes an investment sub-committee, subject to the final approval of the board, and relies on collective decision making according to regular meetings. Type 3 funds have in-house investment expertise and decision making is implemented by the executive and an appointed CIO, identified as a key factor to drive real-time decision making. In the latter, the formal structure of decision making is strengthened by having an internal executive and a 'core' group. The authors believe that, at each level, formal procedures can compensate to a certain extent for the lack of scale and expertise and mention this as an avenue for further research, especially the consequences of such structures for investment performance. Stewart and Yermo (2008) also imply some support towards the more formalized Type 3 as they assert that key topics receive the required level of consideration by using an investment committee and the appointment of a top executive who is responsible for investment management.

The nature of the principal agent conflicts is argued to be more severe in DC schemes (Drew and Stanford, 2003; Clarke and Urwin, 2010), giving added cause for concern as the superannuation system in Australia is now predominantly defined contribution in nature (see Table 3.2, Panel B). DB schemes align the interests of the members with the objectives of trustees in managing the liabilities of the fund. In contrast, DC schemes swap this liability problem with a rather more complex problem of managing multiple assets and accounts and member objectives of a DC fund (Clark and Urwin, 2010). Moreover, members in DC schemes bear the full risk of investment outcomes and often have little choice of trustees. An important focus of governance in Cooper (2010) concerns the trustees' investment decisions, which encompass (*inter alia*) asset selection and allocation, how much of the decision making in this arena to outsource and whether to assign asset management to active or passive fund managers. In this regard, the pertinent questions are whether fund managers can actually beat the market after costs and taxes and, if there are such managers, can trustees pick those managers.[13] Therefore, given the complexity of the decision making in DC schemes, and the arguably greater agency costs, it is even more important to manage the direct costs involved in outsourcing operations and investment decision making.

Cooper (2010, Part 2) recommends the restructuring of the governance of superannuation funds to more clearly delineate the roles and responsibilities of the trustee from the trustee-directors. Figure 3.3 illustrates that, with regard to the member/trustee relation, the trustee acts as agent for the member, whereas when the trustee delegates investment management, the fund managers act as agent for the trustee as principal. The corporate governance principles governing the trustee investment management decision include consideration of the expected costs of the decision, the taxation consequences of the decision and 'performance fee standards', which are proposed as a benchmark for costs (Cooper, 2010). Agency costs also arise in the outsourcing of operations. Costs in these areas can have a large impact on member benefits at retirement, as shown in Table 3.3. Therefore, understanding and effectively aligning the complex incentive structures and interactions between principal and agent in superannuation funds is essential for driving greater efficiency and generating a better net return to members. AIST (2010) has recently reviewed fee structures within the superannuation industry and recommends that trustee-directors not only focus on risk and return, but turn their attention also to fees and taxes. In the next section, we undertake an examination of costs across the different fund types.

In addition, as part of the mitigation of agency costs that arise from the principal/agent relationship between the trustee-directors and the funds management firm, trustees will be required to have a proxy voting policy. Issues that require careful consideration include whether superfund trustee-directors have the ability to secure the interests of members in their dealings with the funds management industry, and the alignment of interests between trustee-directors and fund managers. In complex, multi-layered relationships, the diffusion of accountability must be carefully managed to engender good governance.

Recent performance of Australian superannuation funds

Reflecting the fall in equity markets globally as a consequence of the global financial crisis (GFC), total superannuation assets decreased by 5.8 per cent during the year to 30 June 2009 to just over $1 trillion.[14] Of this June 2009 total, $613.9 billion is held by APRA-regulated superannuation entities and $332.3 billion is held by self-managed superannuation funds (SMSFs), which are regulated by the ATO. The remaining $127.2 billion comprises exempt public sector superannuation schemes ($91.7 billion) and the balance of life office statutory funds ($35.5 billion). Small funds, which include SMSFs, single-member approved deposit funds and small APRA funds, showed the largest growth during the year to June 2009, with assets increasing by 0.5 per cent. Industry funds' assets declined by 4.7 per cent during the year, corporate funds' by 9.5 per cent, retail funds' by 9.6 per cent and public sector funds' by 10.3 per cent.

While SMSFs, single-member ADFs and small APRA-regulated funds appear to have weathered the GFC more successfully than other funds, of more interest are the long-run trends in superannuation fund performance. It is difficult to make direct comparisons of the SMSF sector (which reports to the ATO) with the APRA-regulated sector because data and reporting methods differ systematically between the two groups. Differences are also compounded by the fact that APRA-regulated funds are required to report asset values at market value, while SMSFs do so only under special circumstances.[15] Nevertheless, we attempt to draw some conclusions about differences in performance across the two sectors in the following discussion.

Prior to June 2009, the performance of superannuation funds was reported using the ROA measure but since that date APRA has used a rate-of-return measure, arguing that it is a better measure than ROA for calculating compound returns.[16] The rate of return (ROR) measures the combined earnings of a superannuation fund's assets across all its products and investment options, and is calculated as net earnings after tax divided by cash flow adjusted net assets.

$$ROR = \frac{\text{Net earnings after tax}}{\text{Cash flow adjusted net assets}}$$

The Superannuation Industry (Supervision) Act 1993 (SIS Act) requires that superannuation trustees formulate and give effect to an investment strategy that has regard to the whole of the circumstances of the superannuation fund and is in the best interest of its members.[17] Whole-of-fund ROR gauges the relative performance of trustees at generating long-term returns for fund members' retirement benefits (APRA, 2009a).

The ROR statistics as reported at March 2010 are given in Table 3.4 for APRA-regulated entities with at least $50 million in assets. Over the year to March 2010, the returns remained volatile but returned to positive figures for the year ended March 2010 with an ROR of 18.7 per cent as compared to –17 per cent for the year ended March 2009.

We are interested in the performance of DC schemes as a separate group, as they now dominate DB schemes in terms of assets under management and number of members, as shown in the figures in Table 3.2. Data from APRA enable calculation of the RORs for DC schemes amongst the top 200 (by asset size) and a comparison of the RORs against DB and hybrid schemes (APRA, 2009a). Table 3.5 contains the results of this analysis over the period 2004–9, illustrating that pure DC schemes performed the worst out of the three types of funds, with a rate of return over the five-year period more than 100 basis points lower than hybrid schemes and 91 basis points lower than DB schemes. These calculations do not account for the different risk characteristics of the funds.[18]

In Table 3.6, we classify the DC schemes amongst the top 200 APRA-regulated funds by type and recalculate the ROR statistics. Over the seven-year period ending 2002, Coleman *et al.* (2006) show that on average after adjusting for risk, the returns (ROA) on corporate, public sector and industry funds were each significantly higher than the returns on retail funds. Their analysis was performed on 225 funds that submitted complete data over the period 1995 to 2002. The results in Table 3.6 suggest that, among DC schemes, on average retail funds underperform industry funds. The numbers of corporate and public sector funds in this sample are too small to draw comparisons for these types. Our finding for DC schemes is consistent with the findings more generally that, independent of the benefit structure type, retail funds underperform the not-for-profit funds on average (Coleman *et al.*, 2006).

Given the economic importance of the SMSF sector, it is of interest to gauge how the SMSF sector fared in comparison to the APRA-regulated sector. According to ATO estimates for financial years 2006, 2007 and 2008, the return on assets (ROA) for the SMSF sector was 12.6 per cent, 16.9 per cent and –6.1 per cent, respectively. By comparison, at a whole of industry level, APRA-regulated funds with more than four members returned 12.2 per cent, 13.3 per cent and –7.8 per cent, respectively.[19] However, direct comparisons are difficult because of the data issues identified earlier. It is important to recognize that, whilst the ATO attempted to replicate the same method of calculating ROA as that used by APRA for the data period presented, the results may nevertheless not be directly comparable.[20]

Operating expenses are an important determinant of the trustee's ability to deliver the objective of prudently maximizing long-term returns. There are two key components to operating expenses: administration and investment management expenses. The latter includes expenses associated with generating a return on the portfolio of assets and includes the cost of investment management, asset consultants, brokerage and custodial services. Table 3.7 presents trends in operating expenses for funds which were not subject to any structural change over

Table 3.4 Rates of return for APRA-regulated entities with at least $50 million in assets

	Mar. 2009	*Jun. 2009*	*Sep. 2009*	*Dec. 2009*	*Mar. 2010*	*Year-end Mar. 2009*	*Year-end Mar. 2010*
Net investment income ($m)	–22,547	30,397	68,996	18,796	13,638	–139,396	131,827
Other income ($m)	69	90	63	93	97	508	343
Total operating expense ($m)	890	976	958	1,035	1,024	3,806	3,993
Tax expense on earnings ($m)	–1,439	430	2,924	218	352	–11,158	3,924
Net earnings after tax ($m)	–21,929	29,080	65,177	17,636	12,359	–131,536	124,253
Cash flow adjusted net assets	671,582	657,260	694,208	765,189	788,742		
Rate of Return (%)	*–3.3%*	*4.4%*	*9.4%*	*2.3%*	*1.6%*	*–17.0%*	*18.7%*
Number of entities	291	290	278	277	271	291	271

Source: APRA Quarterly Statistics, March 2010.

Table 3.5 RORs for different benefit structure types, June 2004 to June 2009

Type of fund	*One-year ROR (%)*						*Three-year p.a. ROR (%)*	*Five-year p.a. ROR (%)*	*No. of funds*
	Jun. 2004	*Jun. 2005*	*Jun. 2006*	*Jun. 2007*	*Jun. 2008*	*Jun. 2009*	*2007–9*	*2005–9*	
DC	11.06	11.16	12.62	13.39	–8.25	–10.87	–2.58	2.93	120
DB	13.93	13.37	15.71	16.11	–5.87	–15.47	–2.62	3.84	5
Hybrid	13.12	12.66	14.71	15.11	–7.25	–11.69	–1.96	4.02	75

Source: APRA Superannuation Fund-level Rates of Return (2009a).

Table 3.6 RORs for DC schemes (amongst top 200 APRA-regulated funds)

Type of fund	*One-year ROR (%)*						*Three-year p.a. ROR (%)*	*Five-year p.a. ROR (%)*	*No of funds*
	Jun. 2004	*Jun. 2005*	*Jun. 2006*	*Jun. 2007*	*Jun. 2008*	*Jun. 2009*	*2007–9*	*2005–9*	
Corporate	12.7	12.1	14.7	14.0	–7.7	–12.2	–2.6	3.5	2
Industry	12.7	12.7	14.3	15.7	–6.9	–12.8	–2.1	3.8	36
Public sector	10.8	11.5	12.6	13.1	–5.4	–12.0	–2.0	2.7	5
Retail	10.4	10.6	12.1	12.7	–9.8	–10.3	–3.1	2.4	71
Retail-ERF	6.5	7.1	7.7	7.7	–1.5	–4.8	0.2	2.6	6

Source: APRA Superannuation Fund-level Rates of Return (2009a).

Table 3.7 Trends in funds' operating expenses, June 2004 to June 2006

	June 2004	*June 2005*	*June 2006*	*June 2007*	*June 2008*	*June 2009*
Number of funds	348	358	368	372	376	322
Total assets at end of period ($m)	345,506	421,859	539,603	672,041	640,951	574,867
Total member accounts ('000)	21,873	23,249	25,704	27,023	28,878	27,156
Total operating expenses ($m)	2,028	2,293	2,801	3,315	3,638	3,581
Cash flow adjusted net assets ($m)[a]	293,834	356,731	443,411	549,342	671,981	627,009
Average fund size ($m)	993	1,178	1,466	1,807	1,705	1,785
Average number of member accounts ('000)	63	65	70	73	77	84
Average account balance ($)	15,796	18,145	20,993	24,869	22,195	21,169
Average operating expense ratio (%)	0.69	0.64	0.63	0.60	0.54	0.57
Average operating expenses per member account ($)	93	99	109	123	126	132

Source: APRA (June 2009) Annual Superannuation Bulletin.

Note

a Cash flow adjusted net assets is the sum of net assets at the beginning of the period and half of net flows.

the period June 2004 to June 2009 (all funds in the sample still existed as at June 2009).[21]

As Table 3.7 shows, the average operating expense ratio consistently fell over the period June 2004 to June 2009 from 0.69 to 0.57 per cent. At the same time, however, average operating expenses per member account increased from $93 to $132. Table 3.8 shows the breakdown of estimated administration and investment management expenses by industry sector. While total operating costs average 1.21 per cent across the industry, there is a wide range from 0.67 per cent for public sector funds to 1.81 per cent for retail funds. It should be noted, however, that such cost comparisons can be confounded by in-kind support from employers that often assists corporate and public funds, who enjoy the lowest administrative costs of 0.21 per cent in each case. It is also notable from this analysis that, with the exception of retail funds, investment costs are the major cost component.

An insight into the key cost drivers in supperannuation funds, scale and the complexity of the investment portfolio, is provided in the total cost estimates for a standardized MySuper product, shown in Table 3.9. As the scale of the fund increases from $2 billion to $20 billion, total costs decline from 0.6 to 0.32 per cent for a passive balanced or conservative fund and from 1.04 to 0.66 per cent for an active balanced portfolio with alternative assets. Similarly, total costs

Table 3.8 Estimate of super fees by segment (2008) – percentage of funds under management

Sector	*Administration (%) (1)*	*Investment management (%) (2)*	*(1) + (2)*	*Cost of advice*	*Total expenses (%)*
Corporate	0.21	0.47	0.68		0.68
Industry	0.38	0.67	1.05		1.05
Public	0.21	0.46	0.67		0.67
Retail	0.69	0.69	1.37	0.44	1.81
SMSF	0.31	0.52	0.83	0.15	0.98
Total	0.42	0.59	1.02	0.19	1.21

Source: Bank of America Securities – Merrill Lynch estimates based on Rice Warner 2008 fee analysis.

Table 3.9 Estimated total annual percentage costs for MySuper products of varying sizes and portfolio composition

MySuper fund size/investment strategy	*$2bn*	*$5bn*	*$10bn*	*$20bn*
Passive balanced (%)	0.60	0.46	0.38	0.32
Passive conservative (%)	0.58	0.45	0.37	0.32
Active balanced (%)	0.94	0.83	0.70	0.60
Active conservative (%)	0.80	0.70	0.59	0.49
Active balanced (with alternatives) (%)	1.04	0.89	0.77	0.66
Active conservative (with alternatives) (%)	0.89	0.76	0.64	0.54

Source: Cooper (2010, Part 1, page 19).

can be seen to rise for increased complexity of the portolio. A $2 billion fund comprised of a simple passive balanced portfolio will have estimated costs of 0.58 per cent but the same size fund with a more complex active balanced portfolio with alternative investments will have total costs of 1.04 per cent.

Given that costs increase with smaller scale and complexity of the portolio, it can be seen that smaller DC funds will bear the greatest costs, all things being equal. Further, not only are direct costs greater but Klumpes and McCrae (1999) find evidence to support the hypothesis that agency costs are greater in DC funds than in DB schemes because of higher intermediary costs. Indeed, there would appear to be a strong association between costs, complexity and governance issues in superannuation funds.

Conclusions

Australia has experienced a similar trend to other countries in the increased adoption of DC schemes. Pension funds generally have yet to accommodate the governance issues endemic in DC schemes fully in terms of the multiple layers of devolved decision making and consequent lack of transparency and direct accountability. Given the heavy reliance of individuals in Australia on superannuation as their main form of retirement saving, the economic significance of DC funds and the wide range of choices available, Australians are more exposed to financial and other risks impacting on their retirement savings than is the case in many other pension systems.

Despite the growth in the compulsory savings pool and the widespread coverage of superannuation, the retirement system, which is costing around $50 billion per year, has generally failed to provide an adequate retirement income for the majority of individuals or a reasonable return to taxpayers for the costs involved.

Part of the explanation behind this poor performance lies in a lack of the usual market discipline mechanisms which mitigate agency problems and thereby improve governance in the corporate sector, such as compensation plans that align pay and performance, beneficiaries which can normally participate in a market for corporate control and representation of stakeholders on the governing body. Policy attempts to introduce market forces to promote greater efficiency through member choice have largely failed due to the apathy and disconnection of the public with the superannuation system. Consequently, there is a strong argument for regulatory intervention, such as that proposed by Cooper (2010), to ensure better outcomes.

As we show in this exploratory analysis, performance varies across fund types and benefit structures. Outcomes for individuals are highly sensitive to these factors and especially higher returns produced by greater efficiency through cost control. Recent and proposed initiatives to focus the industry and fund managers on post-cost, post-tax and risk-adjusted net returns, such as APRA's ROR measure and proposed changes to trustee-director duties in the SIS Act, should greatly assist in dealing with the maze of governance and agency cost issues.

Notes

1 Among people not included are employees earning less than $450 per month, part-time employees under 18 and employees aged 65 and over.
2 For an early paper that questions the adequacy of the Australian superannuation system, see Scheiwe (1999).
3 The final reports are available at www.supersystemreview.gov.au and are in two parts. Part 1 consists of the Overview and Recommendations and Part 2 consists of the Recommendation Packages.
4 A defined benefit (DB) fund is one where contributions are pooled and are not allocated to particular members. Under the SIS Act, if a fund has even one member with a defined benefit, it is treated as a defined benefit fund. A defined contribution (DC), also known as an accumulation fund, is one where the value of the final retirement benefit payable to members is the member's account balance at the relevant time (Cooper, 2010, p. 111).
5 http://taxreview.treasury.gov.au/Content/Content.aspx?doc=html/home.htm.
6 www.supersystemreview.gov.au.
7 See Figure 3.3.
8 Super System Review, 2010, *SuperStream – bringing the back office of super into the 21st century*, Media Release No. 001/2010, 22 March, www.supersystemreview.gov.au/content/content.aspx?doc=html/media_releases/2010/001.htm.
9 Super System Review, 2010, *Super System Review releases latest preliminary report: MySuper A super option designed just for members*, Media Release No. 002/2010, 20 April, www.supersystemreview.gov.au/content/content.aspx?doc=html/media_releases/2010/002.htm.
10 For an excellent review of the corporate governance literature in this context, see Shleifer and Vishny (1997).
11 While each fund nominates a number of 'trustees' effectively to serve as directors of the fund, the trustee itself is usually a corporation. To avoid confusion on this point, Cooper (2010) has recommended that trustees appointed by a corporate trustee should be referred to as 'trustee-directors', a convention that will be adhered to here.
12 Normally employee representatives form around half of the trustee board, the other half being comprised of employer representatives. The selection of employee representative trustee-directors varies widely from fund to fund. Employee input may be sought via union nominations (industry funds), an election of members or through nomination of staff representatives.
13 Cooper (2010), Part 2, Chapter 3.
14 By March 2010, assets had increased to $1.26 trillion.
15 Review into the governance, efficiency, structure and operation of Australia's superannuation system: www.supersystemreview.gov.au/content/downloads/statistical_summary_smsf/SMSF_statistical_summary_report.pdf.
16 It is a closer approximation to the Global Investment Performance Standards (GIPS) total return, as published by the Chartered Financial Analyst Institute as stated in APRA (2009b).
17 The SIS Act is currently the major point of reference to guide the duties of superannuation fund trustees. Statutory duties applying to trustees are specified in Section 52(2) of the Act.
18 Coleman *et al.* (2006) do not find that differences in benefit structure account for differences in performance across fund types, but over their sample period they find ROA for DC schemes to be insignificantly greater than that for DB schemes. We find the opposite but have not tested for statistical significance. Differences in fund selection, data period and return measure may account for the different results.
19 December 2009, www.supersystemreview.gov.au.

20 Some possible reasons that the ROAs may not be directly comparable are as follows: valuation and accounting practices, tax treatment differences, under or overstatement of costs, establishment costs of new SMSFs, and MERs of public offer funds not being directly comparable to expense ratios of SMSFs.

21 See Malhotra *et al.* (2004), who explore the determinants of expense ratios.

References

Allen Consulting Group (2009) *Better Living Standards and a Stronger Economy: The Role of Superannuation in Australia*, report to The Association of Superannuation Funds of Australia, available at www.superannuation.asn.au/Reports/default.aspx.

AMP (2009) *AMP Retirement Adequacy Index, Summary of Trends*, July–December 2009, December.

APRA (2007) 'A recent history of superannuation in Australia', *APRA Insight*, Issue Two, 2007, Special Edition, pp. 3–10.

APRA (2009a) *Superannuation Fund-level Rates of Return*, June 2009 (reissued 30 March 2010).

APRA (2009b) *Response to Submissions: Fund-Level Disclosure from the APRA Superannuation Statistics Collection*, available at www.apra.gov.au/Statistics/upload/Response-to-Submissions-Fund-level-disclosure-of-APRA-Super-statistics-collection.pdf.

Australian Centre for Financial Studies (2010) *Financial Wellbeing in Retirement*, an exposition paper prepared for Finsia.

Australian Institute of Superannuation Trustees (2010) *Investment Management Fee Research*, available at www.aist.asn.au/media/43411/aist_research_report_webv.pdf.

Black, B.S. (1992) 'Agents watching agents: the promise of institutional investor voice', *UCLA Law Review*, 39: 811–93.

Clark, G.L. (2004) 'Pension fund governance: expertise and organisational form', *Journal of Pension Economics and Finance*, 3: 233–53.

Clark, G.L. and Urwin, R. (2008a) 'Best-practice pension funds governance', *Journal of Asset Management*, 9(1): 2–21.

Clark, G.L. and Urwin, R. (2008b) 'Making pension boards work: the critical role of leadership', *Rotman International Journal of Pension Management*, 1(1): 38–45.

Clark, G.L. and Urwin, R. (2010) 'DC pension fund best-practice design and governance', *Working Paper*, in draft, available at http://economics.ouls.ox.ac.uk/15019/1/wp10-09.pdf.

Coleman, A., Esho, N. and Wong, M. (2006) 'The impact of agency costs on the investment performance of Australian pension funds', *Journal of Pension Economics and Finance*, 5: 299–324.

Cooper Review (2009a) *The Scope of the Review: A Three Phase Consultation*, August 25.

Cooper Review (2009b) *Phase Two: Operation and Efficiency*, Issues paper, 16 October.

Cooper Review (2009c) *Clearer Super Choices: Matching Governance Solutions*, Phase One preliminary report, 14 December.

Cooper Review Final Report (2010) *Review into the Governance, Efficiency, Structure and Operation of Australia's Superannuation System*, Final Report, Commonwealth of Australia, June.

Drew, M. and Stanford, J. (2003) 'Principal and agent problems in superannuation funds', *The Australian Economic Review*, 36: 98–107.

Klumpes, P.J.M. and McCrae, M. (1999) 'Evaluating the financial performance of pension funds: an individual investor's perspective', *Journal of Business, Finance and Accounting*, 26(3) and (4): 261–81.

Malhotra D., Martin, R. and Marisetty, V. (2004) 'An empirical analysis of Australian superannuation fund expenses', *Review of Pacific Basin Financial Markets and Policies*, 7: 451–69.

Melbourne Centre for Financial Studies (2009) *Melbourne Mercer Global Pension Index*, available at www.novatv.nl/data/media/db_download/167_6490fc.pdf.

OECD (2008) *OECD Private Pensions Outlook*, Secretary General of the OECD.

Ontario Expert Commission on Pensions (2008) *Expert Commission on Pensions, A Fine Balance: Safe Pensions, Affordable Plans, Fair Rules (the Report)*, Government of Ontario, 21 November.

Pender, H. (2010) *Reviewing Cooper*, 15th Melbourne Money and Finance Conference, Melbourne Centre for Financial Studies, June 1.

Rice Warner (2010) *Superannuation Savings Gap 2008*, prepared for IFSA, January.

Scheiwe, D. (1999) 'Why Australia's pension system is not a good international model', *Discussion Paper PI-9912*, The Pensions Institute, available at www.pensions-institute.org/workingpapers/wp9912.pdf.

Shleifer, A. and Vishny, R.W. (1997) 'A review of corporate governance', *Journal of Finance*, 52: 737–83.

Stewart, F. and Yermo, J. (2008) 'Pension fund governance: challenges and potential solutions', *OECD Working Papers on Insurance and Private Pensions*, No. 18, OECD Publishing.

Treasury (2010) *Australia to 2050: Future Challenges*, Commonwealth of Australia: Barton ACT, available at: http://archive.treasury.gov.au/igr/igr2010/Overview/pdf/IGR_2010_Overview.pdf.

4 Best practice corporate governance?

The failure of Bridgecorp Finance Ltd

William Wilson, Lawrence C. Rose and John Pinfold

Corporate governance, especially by financial institutions, has increasingly come under the spotlight as economies and governments have struggled to come to grips with the recent financial crisis. While predating the financial crisis, it is argued that limitations in regulatory structure and corporate governance contributed to the recent collapse of the finance company industry in New Zealand. This is illustrated by the Bridgecorp Finance Ltd failure. Bridgecorp was, by some measures, a successful company as it maximized the wealth of its owners; however, this was at the expense of depositors, who may have believed they were protected by New Zealand prudential regulation. Instead regulations, which should have offered some protection to depositors, were used to obfuscate the true financial situation as the Securities Commission, trustees and auditors appeared to be more concerned with compliance rather than the substance of underlying transactions. This allowed substantial shareholders on the Bridgecorp board of directors the opportunity to entrench themselves and disregard the interests of depositors while paying lip service to best practice corporate governance. Tragically, warnings given as early as 2003 of possible non-bank deposit taker (NBDT) failures such as Bridgecorp went unheeded. The costs of failures were ultimately borne by depositors, taxpayers and the New Zealand economy as a whole. New Zealand has a venerable tradition of using trust and transparency to regulate its financial markets. The benefits of such an approach include the empowerment and individual accountability of institutions, who then can act on shared beliefs to obtain optimal benefits for the society at large. The social contract that underlies the principal of trust and ethical behaviour can and has added value beyond expectations. It can also reduce compliance costs. But, a regulatory system based on trust, ethical behaviour and transparency will have few oversight mechanisms in place to regulate behaviour. If trust and transparency principles are violated, sub-optimal outcomes can and will occur. This was the case in the New Zealand finance company industry.

Prior to October 2008,[1] depositors in finance companies in New Zealand were solely responsible for the safety and soundness of their investment decisions. There was no direct supervision of New Zealand NBDTs by government agencies, as the prevailing government approach was to use market-discipline instead of prudential regulation. While the Reserve Bank monitored registered banks, all other deposit-taking institutions fell under the Securities Act of 1978 and its subsequent regulations. So, New Zealand depositors were reliant on the management of NBDTs, trusting they would respect their interests and follow accepted corporate governance principles. However, there is a growing body of literature which suggests corporate governance with its emphasis on shareholder rights may not be a sufficient safeguard in financial institutions where the bulk of funding comes from depositors. This chapter employs the failure of Bridgecorp Finance Ltd (BCL) to illustrate a number of deficiencies in the management of New Zealand finance companies.

Under New Zealand legislation, NBDTs are required to negotiate a trust deed with a trustee company which acts on behalf of all depositors. Before taking deposits from the public, NBDTs must register a prospectus containing relevant financial information which is available to depositors. Prospectuses are required to be updated on an annual basis or sooner if the information becomes misleading. The trustee monitors the NBDT on an on-going basis to ensure compliance with the trust deed. The Securities Commission, also established under the Securities Act 1978, was charged only with ensuring NBDTs complied with provisions of the Securities Act. Expectations were that New Zealand investors would make use of the information disclosed to make appropriate investment decisions. It now appears that, while finance companies in the main appeared compliant with the Securities Act, no one had responsibility actually to examine disclosure statements to ensure they were useful to investors. Not surprisingly, Wilson (2009) found only 20 per cent of survey respondents relied on investment statements and prospectuses when assessing finance company risk.

In New Zealand, NBDTs were more numerous, but considerably smaller, than banks, with over 200 finance companies making up the bulk of NBDTs (Bollard, 2006). Other NBDTs are building societies and credit unions. Finance companies played a valuable role in the New Zealand economy, providing much of the funding for consumer credit, small and medium enterprises and development projects, as banks were often unwilling or unsuited to service these sectors. New Zealand finance companies were typically unlisted, private and closely held limited liability companies who raised around 90 per cent[2] of their funding from the public, in the form of fixed-term debentures, secured by a general charge over the assets of the firm. Debenture terms were commonly one to three years with most debenture holders rolling their investments over at maturity. Exceptions to the debenture model are two of the largest New Zealand finance companies: GE Finance Ltd, which obtained funds from its international parent, and UDC, who received a significant portion of its funding from its owner, the ANZ Bank Group. For simplicity, future reference to deposits and depositors includes debentures and debenture-holders.

In general, New Zealand finance companies prospered and grew rapidly in the first half of this decade, as New Zealand experienced full employment, increasing real-estate prices, favourable agricultural prices and cheap imports as a result of higher exchange rates. The total deposits of large finance companies (with assets over $100 million[3]) rose from less than $2 billion in 1998 (RBNZ Staff, 2009a) to $9 billion in 2007 (RBNZ Staff, 2009b). Finance companies projected an air of respectability and many investors may have seen them as an easy way to earn 1 or 2 per cent over bank term deposits.

In mid-2006, problems surfaced in three firms active in the financing of used cars and, over a short period of time, receivers were appointed at National Finance 2000 Ltd (NF2K), which had total assets of NZ$25 million,[4] Provincial Finance Ltd (PF), which had total assets of NZ$346 million, and Western Bay Finance Ltd (WBF), whose assets were NZ$55 million. These actions initially dampened the flow of new funds into NBDTs and total assets fell slightly in the second quarter of 2006. However, it is likely that many investors thought problems were restricted to companies involved in the financing of used cars, as finance companies' total assets began to increase again, reaching a peak of $8.979 billion in the middle of 2007. At this point, property financier Bridgecorp Finance Ltd (BCL), with total assets of NZ$620 million and deposits of $570 million, was forced into receivership.

The Bridgecorp failure was followed rapidly by further failures. When the retail deposit guarantee was introduced in October 2008, 48 firms with over $6 billion of depositor funds were at risk. An unknown number of other firms were under immense liquidity strain as they attempted to match their deposits and loans maturities. No doubt the situation was aggravated by the 2008 global financial crisis (GFC) but our research suggests investors would have difficulty differentiating between finance companies during this period. Therefore, rather than being created by the GFC, a likely cause of subsequent failures and the inability of some earlier failures to recover was a crisis of confidence across the entire industry due to perceptions of poor management.

The collapse of the finance company industry will have a profound impact on New Zealand for a number of years to come. Tragically, many investors were retirees who lost their entire life savings and will have a dramatically lower standard of living in retirement as a consequence. Industries which were dependent on financing from NBDTs, such as used-vehicle dealers, large ticket consumer product retailers and property developers, will face an extended period of business stagnation if they are unable to source alternative funding. Ultimately, New Zealand's economy, which is reliant to a large extent on SMEs, could grow more slowly in the future. The government, facing criticism for allowing the situation to develop, now has a financial interest in the crisis after it moved to guarantee deposits held in firms in October 2008 for two years. The direct cost to the state could be significant as nine institutions triggered the original deposit guarantee[5] in its first two years of operation. Estimates are that the liability to the Crown could exceed $2 billion (Treasury, 2010).

However, the Crown's exposure under the retail deposit guarantee was limited as it restricted pleas to make the guarantee retrospective. While the guarantee must be honoured for those which have failed since October 2008, some of this cost will be covered by the premiums paid[6] into the scheme. The greater urgency facing the government is to create an environment to ensure such widespread failures do not occur again without adversely affecting prudent risk taking by institutions, borrowers and depositors.

Clearly the disclosure-based system in place since the late 1970s was no longer working. Earlier empirical research examining the risk–return relationship in New Zealand deposit takers (both banks and non-banks) for evidence of market discipline identified deficiencies[7] in the disclosures of NBDTs (Wilson, 2009). As a result, no relationship was found between disclosure risk indicators and observed risk premiums in NBDTs, with Wilson (2009) concluding that disclosure statements provided little, if any, value to investors.

Furthermore, the regulatory system formulated in the late 1970s offers little in the way of regulatory discipline, as no government agency was responsible for oversight of NBDTs. Finance companies were treated much like any other New Zealand company, apart from requirements for investment statements, prospectuses and trustees. The Reserve Bank was responsible for the prudential oversight of registered banks, while the role of the Securities Commission was to ensure all other deposit takers complied with the then disclosure requirements of the Securities Act and its regulations in areas such as advertising, investment statements, prospectuses and trust deeds. In its April 2005 report on disclosure by finance companies, the Securities Commission categorically states: 'the Commission does not have a role in relation to the prudential supervision of finance companies and does not comment on this' (Securities Commission Staff, 2004b, p. 1). Thus, there was no official prudential oversight of the industry. Consequently, depositors in NBDTs relied on the honesty and integrity of management and directors, in short the firm's corporate governance, to ensure capital and interest payments were received when due.

Regulation of New Zealand non-bank deposit takers

In New Zealand, there was a clear demarcation between banks and all other deposit takers. Banks are the responsibility of the Reserve Bank, with all banks registered by the Reserve Bank and subject to the provisions of the 1996 bank disclosure regime. Finance companies and other NBDTs were subject to the Securities Act 1978 and its accompanying regulations, which were developed in response to the collapse of significant financial institutions in the 1970s.[8] The Reserve Bank's only interest in NBDTs was limited to the contribution they make to the maintenance of a sound and efficient financial system and the impact on the Reserve Bank's other area of responsibility, the implementation of monetary policy. No NBDT was considered *systemically important*[9] by the Reserve Bank. The Reserve Bank has in the past, however, issued general warnings about the vulnerability of NBDTs to a slowing economy, first, in its Financial Stability Report of October 2004, where it stated: 'some investors may find, after the fact, that the risks inherent in their investments have not been adequately compensated' (Bollard, 2004, p. 21), and then in later reports.

In general, for a non-bank to issue debt securities to the public they were required to find a registered trustee company prepared to represent investors and a trust deed was negotiated. While the trustee has a fiduciary duty to act on behalf of depositors, their role was limited to ensuring compliance with the relevant trust deed. Potential investors must be supplied with an investment statement before any money was paid and a prospectus must be supplied to investors within five days on request. Requirements of the investment statement and prospectus are set out in the 1983 securities regulations, with Schedule 2 setting out the requirements of the prospectus and Schedule 3d specifying the information required in the investment statement.[10] One concern was that the investment statement did not require financial statements to be produced and most retail investments were made without investors having seen the financial statements of the issuing firm. Requirements of the prospectus were more detailed, the basic provisions of the trust deed were outlined and more detailed financial information given in annual, independently audited financial statements and notes. New prospectuses had to be registered annually with the Companies Office and were generally required immediately after the annual audit was completed. Section 44 of the Securities Act 1978 requires, however, that if a prospectus becomes false or misleading, during the course of the year it may be suspended,[11] or cancelled, by the Securities Commission. This normally occurred only after the Securities Commission had been advised by the trustee/s that the prospectus was false or misleading. The institution was then required to refuse all deposits until such time as a new prospectus was registered.

The Securities Commission has in the past had concerns about compliance by NBDTs and in September 2004, following a review of a number of finance companies, issued a discussion document on compliance in the sector. The introduction stated:

> The Commission is of the view that some finance companies are not meeting the minimum requirements of the legislation. The Commission considers that these finance companies need to consider the disclosures that they are making, and make changes where necessary to their disclosure documents to ensure future compliance with the legal requirements of the act and regulations.
>
> (Securities Commission Staff, 2004b, p. 2)

But even when the Securities Commission had concerns about the viability of specific institutions, there was little it could do, stating in a news release following the failure of Bridgecorp Ltd:

> The Commission cannot step in to stop a finance company failing, or take action against a finance company that fails, or help investors recover their money. The Commission can intervene only if a finance company does not provide the required information for investors to make a decision on whether or not to invest.
>
> (Securities Commission Staff, 2007a)

When intervening, the Commission was only able to suspend a firm's prospectus[12] for up to 14 days and was not even able to inform the public of the suspension unless it subsequently cancelled the prospectus.

In summary, it can be concluded there was no prudential oversight of NBDTs in New Zealand. Although warnings were raised by both the Securities Commission and Reserve Bank regarding disclosure and the adequacy of returns prior to the first collapse, the government assigned little urgency to addressing the regulatory deficiencies apparent in the industry. As a result, depositors were left with no explicit protections and were expected to apply market discipline facilitated by limited disclosure. In 2006 and 2007, many NBDTs investors, who also failed to heed the warnings of the Securities Commission and Reserve Bank, found their investment decisions had been sub-optimal and a threat to their future economic well-being. Critically, as this source of financing disappeared, the New Zealand economy was damaged when many small and medium enterprises found they were without access to capital.

The government's role in prudential regulation of deposit takers

The important role played by banks and other financial institutions in the economy has led to governments taking on the role of supervisor and regulator of financial institutions. Governments consider supervision and regulation necessary to ensure the managers of financial institutions do not take excessive risks, thus putting the funds of depositors at risk. While a loss of funds is devastating to individual depositors in a financial institution failure, significant damage to the economy as a whole can result in the failure of unrelated institutions. There are two main reasons for the contagious nature of a financial institution failure: first, the inability of depositors to assess the risk due to the presence of asymmetric information results in their withdrawing funds from otherwise healthy financial institutions; and second, the interrelatedness of the financial system means all banks have significant exposures to one another.

Excessive risk taking by banks has led to financial crises in many developing countries. Mishkin (1999) argues that costly crises in Chile in 1982, Mexico in 1994 and 1995 and several Asian countries beginning in 1997 were the result of bank liberalizations and inflows of funds which led to unsustainable lending booms. Due to the asymmetric nature of banking contracts, depositors and other investors were unaware of the deterioration in bank loan asset values until it was too late. This is not unlike the current global credit crisis, with banks and other financial institutions failing in many developed countries as a result of their investments in financial assets incorrectly valued. Governments are facing the direct costs of bailing out banks and other financial institutions as a result of unwise investment and loan decisions. The greater cost, however, is the loss of economic activity as credit is curtailed throughout the economy, forcing those with profitable and productive ventures to limit growth due to a reduced supply of capital.

Governments attempt, through the application of regulations, to moderate excessive risk taking. This is necessary because few governments are prepared to risk the destabilizing effects of the failure of a significantly large financial institution. These effects could include not only the loss of the savings of individual citizens but also the collapse of other financial institutions. Mishkin (2001) further argues that the role of banks in directing funds from savers to those with the most productive investment opportunities for a given level of risk (financial intermediation) is critical to economic growth; however, a significant impediment to this process is the asymmetric information present in banking contracts. Asymmetric information simply means one party to a financial contract (the borrower) has better risk information than the other party (the lender). Similarly, depositors must also overcome asymmetric information in directing their savings to the most productive banks (for a given level of risk). Just as banks assess competing investment opportunities, savers must assess the risk–return characteristics of competing banks, a task made more difficult if the public has low levels of financial literacy, as indicated in surveys undertaken by the government's Retirement Commission (Colmar Brunton, 2006) and Reserve Bank (Widdowson and Hailwood, 2007).

Asymmetric information also gives rise to two related problems: adverse selection and moral hazard. If a lender is unable to determine the true risk of a borrower, a solution is to accept an average rate of interest, which would apply to all borrowers. However, if low-risk borrowers are not prepared to borrow at an average interest rate, lenders are left with only higher-risk borrowers in the market, so the average interest rate is no longer appropriate. Moral hazard occurs after a loan has been made, when a borrower changes their behaviour and engages in a high-risk activity. Asymmetric information, adverse selection and moral hazard are problematic when financial institutions are lending to households and businesses, but are even more difficult to address when it is households and businesses lending to financial institutions. Depositors often do not have the required financial expertise to challenge institutions which occupy a respected position in the economy. If the lender (or depositor) is an individual or small business, they do not have the same advantages as a financial institution; typically, they are a non-expert engaging in a one-off transaction representing a considerable portion of their wealth. Banks have a dominant position in the relationship with customers. Stiglitz and Weiss (1983) argue that banks are able to use the threat of cutting off credit to a customer as a means of moderating risk taking by borrowers. As a result of the imbalance, customers are price-takers rather than price-setters in banking transactions. Due to the importance of financial institutions to economic development and in an attempt to overcome the unbalanced relationship between financial institutions and their depositors, governments have over time developed prudential regulations with the aim of enhancing the safety and soundness of the banking system.

However, the regulatory regime applying to New Zealand NBDTs was less restrictive than that applying to banks. Unlike banks[13] there was no official prudential oversight and little in the way of a licensing process, with NBDTs only needing to supply the New Zealand Companies Office with a trust deed negotiated with a registered trustee company and prospectus for the firm to be registered. Oversight was then provided, at least on an annual basis, by independent auditors and trustees to ensure the NBDT complies with the terms of their trust deed. This leaves depositors reliant on market discipline, the honesty and integrity of the management – that is, the corporate governance policies and procedures in use for each NBDT.

Corporate governance in financial institutions

Corporate governance as defined by La Porta *et al.* (2000) 'is to a large extent, a set of mechanisms through which outside investors protect themselves against expropriation by the insiders' (p. 4). At the forefront of corporate governance, as a guiding principle, is the duty of care directors and managers of the firm have to shareholders. Early research by Jensen and Meckling (1976) identified situations where the management of the firm used the profits of the firm to benefit themselves rather than return funds to outside investors. The agency problem identified by Jensen and Meckling (1976), in which management consume *perks*, is part of the expropriation talked about by La Porta *et al.* (2000), but also includes the simple theft of profits or asset stripping, where assets of the firm are transferred to related parties at less than true value. The consequence of widespread expropriation of investor funds is a natural reluctance by those with surplus funds to invest in ventures outside of their control, resulting in an undermining of the financial system and economic development.

Over time, rules and regulations have been developed in many countries designed to protect the interests of both shareholders and creditors. In countries with corporate governance codes in place, well enforced by regulators and courts, the financing of firms by outside investors works well. An alternative system has been developed in some economies where business is funded by banks, who take both equity and debt stakes in the firm. Shleifer and Vishny (1997) point to the developed economies of the US, Germany, Japan and the UK as having some of the best corporate governance codes, though La Porta *et al.* (1998) later find common-law countries have stronger corporate governance protections when they compare legal systems. Despite having one of the better corporate governance codes in place, the US business community was shaken in 2001 by the failure of Enron and the after-shocks of Tyco and WorldCom. In response, US legislators moved to strengthen corporate governance, passing the Sarbanes–Oxley Act of 2002. Provisions of the act were aimed at improved corporate disclosure, increased management responsibility and tighter board oversight (Spong and Sullivan, 2007).

Effective corporate governance of an organization ultimately rests with the board of directors, who have a fiduciary duty of care to the owners of the firm and are responsible for monitoring and provision of strategic advice to the CEO. To this end, most codes of corporate governance recommend the inclusion of *independent* directors. However, Adams and Ferreira (2007) suggests the two roles of monitoring and strategizing can give rise to conflict when the CEO and executive directors are reluctant to supply information necessary for developing strategy, where the same information can be used to monitor and discipline.

De Andres and Vallelado (2008) argue that, in order to avoid conflicts of interest, independent directors should be in the majority. In New Zealand, Guideline 2.1 of the Securities Commission Principles and Guidelines only says 'every issuer's board should have an appropriate balance of executive and non-executive directors, and should include directors who meet formal criteria for "independent directors"' (Securities Commission Staff, 2004a, p. 15). The power of the CEO also may affect board composition. Boone *et al.* (2007) point out that powerful CEOs will try to appoint fewer independent directors, while Westphal and Zajac (1997) indicate they try to appoint directors with close ties to management. Angbazo and Narayanan (1997) find the reputation of directors also matters to future outcomes, as outside directors with quality reputations are more effective in assuring positive outcomes for commercial banks. So, consistent with Anderson *et al.* (2011), there are definitely strong arguments for seeking board heterogeneity. However, they and Erickson *et al.* (2005) find that there are costs to heterogeneity, which, in certain circumstances, could outweigh the benefits. Regardless of the number of independent directors on a board, governance will be ineffective if the board does not receive appropriate information from management. Similarly, corporate governance codes will have little impact if boards only pay lip service to them, as we are about to see.

Corporate governance codes can also provide great benefit where there are a large number of investors in the firm. However, due to the firms' existing fiduciary duty to shareholders and possibly to the prevalence of equity investing, there appears to be an emphasis on the interests of equity investors over depositors. Key differences exist between equity investors and depositors around control, cash flows and bankruptcy or liquidation. Depositors have no say in the running of the company, whereas equity holders are at least entitled to vote for directors. While equity holders are generally asked to approve dividends, the payment of a dividend is at the discretion of the firm. On the other hand, the firm has a contractual obligation to pay interest and principal to depositors when due. If depositors do not receive payments when due, they are able to force the winding up of the firm and receive repayment of outstanding interest and principal prior to any payments being made to equity holders.

Financial institutions such as banks and other deposit takers, with their high levels of debt, are fundamentally different from other corporations. Benston and Kaufman (1996) claim they are inherently unstable, due to their low ratios of cash reserves to assets and capital to assets. Macey and O'Hara (2003) argue the fiduciary duty of bank directors and managers should be broadened to include all providers of funds, to ensure the safety and soundness of the institution. Levine (2004) suggests two key factors single financial institutions out for special treatment: they are more opaque than other industries and they face a greater regulatory burden. The fragility of financial institutions, derived from their high leverage, is a reason for the other regulation and government oversight faced by banks. Bank debt levels are so high it is difficult to conceive of any other industry where they would be sustainable. Finance companies in New Zealand did not face significant regulation or oversight; as a result, they were beset with asymmetric information and moral hazard problems.

Much of the existing academic research dealing with corporate governance in banking institutions focuses on the areas of risk taking and improved efficiency or performance derived from sound corporate governance. For example, Glassman and Rhoades (1980) show owner-controlled banks tend to have a higher profit rate than manager-controlled banks. Spong and Sullivan (2007) confirm this, finding when managers and directors have an ownership stake, performance is improved due to a reduction in the agency problems identified by Jensen and Meckling (1976). Important differences in risk attitudes are pointed to by Spong and Sullivan (2007) when insiders have an equity stake in the firm. They suggest non-owning managers are risk adverse, due to receiving no direct benefit from a risky venture, while putting their jobs at risk if the venture has a negative outcome. An ownership interest in the firm allows managers and directors to share in the upside. Attitudes to risk are tempered by wealth concentration, with Spong and Sullivan (2007) revealing an effect, where banks in which managers, directors or owners have a significant portion of their own wealth invested in the business have a lower level of risk and less chance of default. In contrast to Spong and Sullivan (2007), Laeven and Levine (2009) show it is the power wielded by owners which is crucial, with banks with more powerful owners taking greater risks. Gropp and Köhler (2010) show owner-controlled banks, in the 2008 GFC, had higher profits preceding the crisis but incurred greater loses during the crisis and were more likely to require government assistance. They suggest, from a societal viewpoint, contracts which simply align the interests of management and shareholder may be socially sub-optimal in banks.

Corporate governance was very much at the forefront of the collective public's mind during the 2008 GFC as several respected financial institutions failed. These failures were similar to the earlier failures of non-financial firms such as Enron and WorldCom; simply one group of managers/investors were able to misappropriate large amounts of capital from another, largely uniformed, group of investors. The situation is concisely summarized by Ireland (2010), when he says:

> The no-obligation, no-responsibility, no-liability nature of corporate shares permits their owners – or their institutional representatives – to enjoy income rights without needing to worry about how the dividends are generated. They are not legally responsible for corporate malfeasance, and in the event of failure only their initial investments are at risk.
>
> (p. 845)

The Bridgecorp example, reported in the next section, is of a deposit-taking financial institution operating in New Zealand until June 2006. In many respects, it was not unique as there were a number of other similar finance companies operating in New Zealand. What was unique was they were all primarily funded (90 per cent of total tangible assets) by fixed-term retail debt and the holders of this debt proved incapable of effective monitoring of management. These institutions were privately owned, with managers/directors holding the majority, if not all, of the equity. Further aggravating the situation, unlike other countries, there was no official oversight or effective enforcement of what regulation existed.

Bridgecorp clinical study

The Bridgecorp group of companies in New Zealand is used to illustrate a lack of effective governance in New Zealand finance companies. While the examples of poor corporate governance provided here occurred in Bridgecorp, similar examples could be found in other New Zealand finance companies. Issues of concern are: extremely low levels of closely held equity, an overly complex organizational structure and a lack of management oversight. Effectively, a *black box* was created with the purpose of circumventing New Zealand's limited prudential regulation, allowing dubious related-party transactions to occur which were ultimately to the detriment of retail depositors.

Background

Bridgecorp Ltd (BCL) was a prominent New Zealand finance company established by Rod Petricevic. Rod Petricevic was well known in New Zealand investment circles and had a chequered business career. He was originally employed by Securitibank in the 1970s, which he left just before its collapse to join Fay and Richwhite to set up the merchant bank Magnum Investments. The threesome split in 1980 and Petricevic established the EuroNational investment bank in the mid-1980s. EuroNational was listed on the New Zealand Exchange in 1985 and initially its share price surged from \$1.90 to \$8.26. However, following the 1987 stock market crash and EuroNational's involvement with Judge Corp, Kupe and Renouf Corp, its share price fell to \$0.08 (Gaynor, 2007). Petricevic's wealth was decimated by the 1987 market crash and he was fortunate to avoid bankruptcy as he had borrowed from NZI Bank to purchase his EuroNational shares. When NZI Bank pursued Petricevic for loan repayment, Justice Robertson found the original contract to be void and unenforceable (Robertson, 1992).

Petricevic's next move was to take over the previously NZX listed Bridgecorp Holding after it was delisted and re-develop it as a finance company. Although Petricevic was successful in growing the business in New Zealand, he was unable to regain the NZX listing. Consequently, in 2002, Bridgecorp Holdings was deregistered in New Zealand and the firm shifted its head office to Australia. However, its activities in Australia were curtailed when in February 2006 the Australian Securities and Investments Commission (ASIC) stopped it from raising new funds or rolling over existing funds as the regulator had concerns as to the accuracy of the firm's Australian prospectus.

In response, the board of BCL decided to fund the Australian operation in New Zealand via a series of related-party transactions with its parent and the parent's subsidiaries. This allowed the firm to continue until the end of June 2007 when BCL defaulted on New Zealand obligations. As a consequence of this default, BCL's trustee Covenant Trust Ltd, on 2 July, appointed Waller and McCloy of PwC as receivers (Waller and McCloy, 2007a). Secured creditors on receivership were reported by BCL management to be $458.738 million (Waller and McCloy, 2007e).

Ownership

BCL was primarily a property financier with reported assets at June 2006 of NZ$595 million in New Zealand, Australia and Fiji. It was owned by the Australian firm Bridgecorp Holdings Ltd (78.24 per cent) and Bridgecorp Investments Ltd (21.76 per cent). Bridgecorp Investments Ltd, who also held $35 million of BCL preference shares, was solely owned by Bridgecorp Holdings Ltd. Bridgecorp Holdings Ltd was owned by Petricevic Capital (53.34 per cent), Urwin Fernandez (NZ) Ltd (25.18 per cent) and the remaining 21.48 per cent owned by a number of parties. The only shareholder of Petricevic Capital was Rodney Michael Petricevic (managing Director of BCL). Urwin Fernandez (NZ) Ltd was owned by Australians Gary Urwin (non-executive director of BCL) and John Fernandez. Along with Petricevic and Urwin, the board of BCL included: chairman and non-executive director Bruce Davidson, a high-profile lawyer, Robert Roest, a chartered accountant who acted as finance director, and Peter Steigrad, a non-executive director (Bridgecorp Ltd, 2007b).

Organizational structure

The BCL charging group included eight subsidiaries, five in New Zealand and three in Australia (Figure 4.1). Neither Bridgecorp Holdings Ltd nor Bridgecorp Investments Ltd[14] were members of the charging group.

The management of BCL itself was contracted out to Bridgecorp Management Services Ltd (BMSL), a New Zealand company, wholly owned by Bridgecorp Holdings Ltd. The BCL monthly management fee charge, in the six months to December 2006, amounted to $1.196 million (Bridgecorp Ltd, 2007b). BMSL was not party to the Bridgecorp trustee and therefore not subject to trustee oversight. The Australian-domiciled subsidiaries of BCL paid management fees to Bridgecorp Holdings Australia Ltd, a subsidiary of Bridgecorp Holdings Ltd. The owners of BMSL were Bridgecorp Holdings Ltd and directors were Davidson, Petricevic, Roest and Urwin. Steigrad resigned from the BMSL board in December 2006. Despite being a separate company, BSML occupied the same premises as BCL.

Additionally, Bridgecorp Holdings Ltd had a number of subsidiaries, apart from Bridgecorp Investments Ltd, which were not part of the BCL charging group; including in New Zealand, Poseidon Ltd, whose primary asset was the motor launch Medici (Waller and McCloy, 2007d), and Goodman Ltd (liquidator appointed 9 August 2007), a property management company (Waller and McCloy, 2007c). Again, companies outside the charging group were not parties to the Bridgecorp trust deed and not subject to trustee oversight.

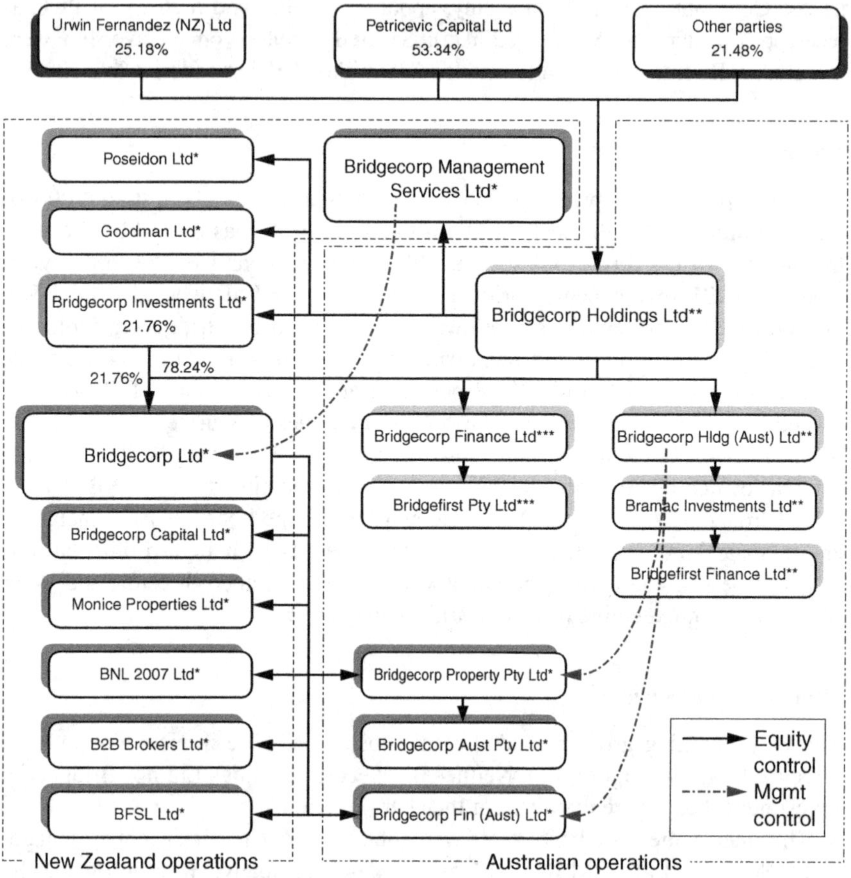

Figure 4.1 Bridgecorp group structure

Notes
* PWC NZ Receiver, ** PWC Aust. Administrator, *** Ferrier Receiver.

Equity capital

Unlike banks, New Zealand NBDTs have no legally prescribed minimum equity level: instead this was specified in the issuer's trust deed. In BCL's case, their trust deed with the Covenant Trustee Company Ltd (Covenant) sets minimum equity at $5 million in clause 4.1(a)(i). Clause 4.1(a)(ii) further specifies the charging group's total liabilities plus contingent liabilities could not exceed 90 per cent of the total tangible assets of the charging group[15] (Bridgecorp Ltd, 2003, p. 31). This effectively required BCL to maintain equity greater than 10 per cent of total tangible assets. The last financial statements published by BCL were in March 2007. It reported total assets[16] at the December 2006 balance date of $620.439 million against total liabilities of $533.220 million, to give equity of

$87.219 million, or 14 per cent. Of this $87.219 million of equity, reserves were $0.435 million, retained earnings were $40.005 million, ordinary shares were $14.177 million and preference shares were $32.602 million (Table 4.1). All BCL equity was held by the Australian parent firm, Bridgecorp Holdings Ltd.

However, while BCL appeared to have a surplus of $25 million equity over the trust deed mandated minimum of $62 million, it also had significant related-party transactions outside the charging group. Foremost was an amount of $14.020 million advanced to BCL's immediate parent, Bridgecorp Holdings Ltd. This was not defined as a related-party loan, rather it was designated a *permitted* loan under the BCL trust deed. Additional loans of $60.478 million (or 9.75 per cent) were disclosed as having been made to other subsidiaries of Bridgecorp Holdings Ltd, outside of the BCL charging group. These included a series of loans to Real Estate Assets Limited Group, a 50:50 joint venture between BCL and the Urwin Fernadez Group (a shareholder of Bridgecorp Holdings Ltd, whose principal, Gary Urwin, was also a director of BCL and Bridgecorp Holdings Ltd). In December 2005, $40.506 million (7.03 per cent) of BCL total assets was

Table 4.1 Bridgecorp Ltd – selected balance sheet data (figures in thousands)

	Account balance date			
	Dec. 2006	*Jun. 2006*	*Dec. 2005*	*Jun. 2005*
BCL balance sheet				
Total assets	$620,439	$652,287	$576,439	$558,972
Total liabilities	$533,220	$565,803	$490,456	$480,828
% total assets	86	87	85	86
Total equity	$87,219	$86,484	$85,963	$78,144
% total assets	14	13	15	14
Related-party loans				
Permitted loans to parent	$14,020	$18,935		
% total assets	2.26	2.90		
Subsidiaries of parent	$60,478	$54,501	$51,415	$40,519
% total assets	9.75	8.36	8.92	7.25
Other related party			$40,506	$20,497
% total assets			7.03	3.67
Total related-party loans	*$74,498*	*$73,436*	*$91,921*	*$61,016*
% total assets	12.01	10.26	15.95	10.92
Barcroft Holdings Acc Rec[a]	$47,685	$76,759		
% total BCL assets	7.69	11.77		
Compass Capital Ltd[b]	$5,770			
% total BCL assets	0.93			

Source: Bridgecorp Ltd, 2007a.

Notes

a The Barcroft Acc Rec arose when the 'other related-party loans' in December 2005 were sold to Barcroft.

b Source for CCL data: Compass Capital Ltd (2007).

outstanding (Bridgecorp Ltd, 2007a). By June 2006, these loans had been sold to Barcroft Holdings Ltd (Barcroft) for $76.759 million (11.77 per cent of total assets) and appeared as an account receivable in the BCL June 2006 accounts.

The loan to the parent of BCL combined with loans to various subsidiaries totalled $74.498 million, representing 12.01 per cent of total assets and, if offset against BCL's equity, BCL would only have 1.9 per cent equity. Further, if the Barcroft account receivable was classified as related-party lending, as suggested by the Ministry of Economic Development (MED) National Enforcement Unit (2010a para. 62), BCL's equity position would deteriorate further.

While BCL had little equity to absorb unexpected losses, ultimately its failure was caused by poor board decision making. The ability of the board to formulate strategy and monitor the performance of management was compromised by the inclusion of substantial shareholders Petricevic and Urwin at the table, as the next section demonstrates.

Management oversight

BCL prospectuses detail a number of mechanisms in place which should supposedly provide effective oversight of management. Foremost, BCL was '*committed to ensuring that best practice corporate governance structures and principles are maintained at all times and that the highest ethical standards are adhered to*' (Bridgecorp Ltd, 2007a, p. 4, emphasis added). To this end, BCL put in place a *Corporate Governance Charter* based on principles developed by the New Zealand Securities Commission. Under this charter, the board included three non-executive directors, Davidson, Steigrad and Urwin, though Urwin was a shareholder and not independent. To further enhance the board's effectiveness, BCL used three sub-committees: audit, credit, and remuneration and nomination (Bridgecorp Board, 2006). The board, board committees and board members all had either a code of conduct or charter in place to foster the highest ethical standards.

Despite their code of conduct or charter, these standards were not always met. The remainder of this section details examples of when the code or charter was ignored. These were the Barcroft transactions, the establishment of Compass Capital Ltd and unauthorized payments to CEO Petricevic. All appear to have benefitted substantial shareholders at the expense of debenture investors.

Barcroft transactions

An area of major concern was BCL's exposure to a resort development in Fiji. BCL financed a development at Moni Bay, involving a 250-bed resort and a 400-lot residential subdivision. However, the development was delayed due to political uncertainty surrounding the most recent Fijian coup. Through a complex arrangement, BCL's loan was transformed into an accounts receivable. This involved BCL selling the loan to Barcroft Holdings, which issued a promissory note to BCL, due in 2008 or 2009. Barcroft then sold the loan back to BCL at a

2 per cent premium (McNabb, 2007a). BCL in their amended prospectus stated that Barcroft was an unrelated party to BCL (Bridgecorp Ltd, 2007a) as it was not owned by BCL.

Barcroft Holdings was owned in July 2006 by Corporate Trustee Services Ltd with Anthony John McCullagh, a charted accountant, as sole director (NZ Companies Office, 2010). The ultimate beneficial owner of Barcroft was unknown but Bridgecorp interest was suspected as Barcroft's director, McCullagh, had previously been employed by BCL as a consultant (McNabb, 2007b). The *NZ Herald* reported the transaction also raised some suspicion at the Ministry of Economic Development (MED), although the MED still registered the prospectus (Gregor, 2010). In an appeal by BCL's chair, Bruce Davidson, of the court's decision to ban him as a director, while Justice Miller (2010, para. 117) did not rule if the Barcroft transaction was or was not a related-party loan, he noted it exceeded the 5 per cent threshold for single-borrower lending specified in the prospectus. Interestingly, Justice Miller went on to say that the loan increased to $90 million by 30 November 2006 and $122 million by 30 April 2007 with some of the additional funds used to pay a salary to BCL director Gary Urwin and to the son of BCL's CEO, Rod Petricevic (Justice Forrest Miller, 2010, para. 117). Further, correspondence between BCL's internal audit and risk manager, Mr Kumar, and finance director, Robert Roest, on the 2 May 2007 (cited in the MED NEU report, 2010a, para. 55) argues the transaction was a related-party loan as Gary Urwin has a beneficial ownership and was also the person who provided all information on the loan. Gary Urwin's attendance at BCL board and audit committee meetings was a clear violation of the BCL corporate governance code, which simply states 'directors have a duty to avoid conflicts of interest between the best interests of Bridgecorp and their own personal or commercial interests' (Bridgecorp Board, 2006, part 7).

Regardless of the question as to the related-party nature of the Barcroft transaction, the transaction highlights deficiencies in the BCL board. Despite the internal auditor for BCL raising serious concerns to the BCL audit committee regarding the Barcroft transaction and subsequent loan extensions, there were serious failings in the documentation and risk evaluation (Justice Forrest Miller, 2010, para. 125). Critically though, board chair Bruce Davidson failed to require Gary Urwin to play no part in the board's decision making (NZ Companies Office, 2010, para. 126) when such a significant loan (at times 20 per cent of the BCL asset value) to a company owned by Urwin was considered.

The establishment of Compass Capital Ltd

In mid-2006, after the ASIC ban in Australia, an attempt was made to raise additional funds in New Zealand with the establishment of Compass Capital Ltd (CCL). CCL was set up to issue NZ$100 million of secured bonds to the public, the proceeds of which were to be used to purchase better-quality[17] BCL loans. The sale of loans to CCL were not reported as related-party transactions in the BCL prospectus as CCL was owned by Compass Capital Trust Ltd, the trustee of which was NZ Guardian Trust Ltd, which was also trustee of the secured bonds. The beneficiary of the trust was Bridgecorp Holdings Ltd and it was managed by Compass Management Ltd (CMgmt), which was owned by Bridgecorp Holdings Ltd. As a result of this structure, CCL was not considered a related party by BCL, despite CCL being administered and promoted[18] by BCL. BCL finance director Robert Roest was also a director of CCL CMgmt (Compass Capital Ltd, 2006). But the purchase of loans from BCL was disclosed as a related-party transaction by CCL (Compass Capital Ltd, 2006).

The view of the MED (2010a, para 72) was that risks and rewards to BCL had not been transferred when the loans were sold. Therefore, CCL should have been consolidated into the BCL charging group. Although funds from CCL improved the liquidity position of BCL, the sale of loans to CCL would have lowered the overall asset quality of BCL if lower quality loans than those sold were made with the proceeds.

Unauthorized payments to Petricevic

The judgment of Justice Miller, in the appeal by BCL chair Bruce Davidson of the decision to ban him as a company director (Justice Forrest Miller, 2010), highlighted a number of unauthorized payments made over an extended period of time. These payments serve to illustrate what little control the board had over the actions of its CEO. These include the purchase by Petricevic of the Medici yacht, payments to Janita Wright (with whom he may have been in a relationship) and salary and tax payments made to and on behalf of Petricevic.

Medici

In the evidence of Bruce Davidson (cited in Justice Forrest Miller, 2010, para. 60), Rod Petricevic, without authority, entered into a 2002 transaction to purchase the Medici yacht. After failing to gain support of other directors, Petricevic put a proposal before the board, which was rejected on 21 May 2002. Petricevic then announced he would purchase the vessel himself and requested a bridging loan. When this loan was not approved, he entered into an alternative funding mechanism.

The NEU report on Petricevic details the mechanics of the transaction for $1.65 million (MED National Enforcement Unit, 2010b, para. 132) to acquire the Medici yacht. The yacht was owned by Poseidon Ltd of which Petricevic was the sole owner and director. The funding mechanism involved a loan of $1.65 million from Dominion Finance and a reciprocal loan to Dominion Finance, with an undertaking that the loan to Dominion would not be withdrawn (MED National Enforcement Unit, 2010b, para. 132). Petricevic also drew up a sponsorship agreement between BCL and Poseidon Ltd for $350,000 giving BCL clients use of the vessel during the 2003 America's Cup competition. The NEU report acknowledges these actions were without board approval but notes all board members visited the yacht for business purposes (Justice Forrest Miller, 2010, para. 46).

Mr Davidson claims Petricevic acted dishonestly in the purchase of Medici and subsequent transactions with Dominion. At the September 2004 board meeting, they made known their 'grave concern' and decided to acquire the vessel in order to resell it (MED National Enforcement Unit, 2010b, para. 61). On 6 September 2005, on Mr Roest's instruction, the debenture stock deal with Dominion Finance Group was broken and offset against the Poseidon loan. On 14 October 2005,[19] Petricevic's shares were transferred to Bridgecorp Holdings Ltd (MED National Enforcement Unit, 2010b, paras 136 and 137). The Medici was not subsequently sold. Justice Miller highlights the significance of the Medici purchase as illustrating the dishonesty of Petricevic and the inaction of the board to take disciplinary action, who only 'made known its grave concern' (Justice Forrest Miller, 2010, para. 122).

ABb group invoices

From February 2004 until June 2007, 41 payments totalling $1,083,434 were made by BCL to the entity ABb. The invoices were detailed as covering consultancy, database creation, call centre services, marketing consulting and other charges (MED National Enforcement Unit, 2010b, paras 122 and 123). The receivers investigated the work Ms Wright did for BCL, finding the call centre work to be on weekends and minimal. BCL staff were not aware of any data entry work and no evidence of marketing consultancy was found (MED National Enforcement Unit, 2010b, para. 126). Petricevic personally authorized 35 of the 41 invoices rendered for payment. During at least part of the period in which Petricevic was authorizing payments to Ms Wright, they were in a personal relationship (MED National Enforcement Unit, 2010b, para. 128). The personal relationship was not disclosed to the BCL board and no independent review of the services was undertaken to ensure they represented 'fair value' to BCL (MED National Enforcement Unit, 2010b, para. 129).

Remuneration committee

As per the BCL corporate governance code, a remuneration committee was in place to decide the salaries and appointments of senior executives. Salaries were paid via Bridgecorp Management Services Ltd (BMSL) and, as CEO, Petricevic received his annual salary, performance bonus, vehicle costs and other payments, such as back pay and a management fee (MED National Enforcement Unit, 2010b, para. 110). The BCL receivers claimed Petricevic was paid $4,249,347 for the three years prior to the collapse of BCL (MED National Enforcement Unit, 2010b, paras 111–14). The receivers contended these payments were excessive and in June 2008 obtained judgment in the Auckland High Court against Petricevic for excess remuneration of $3,912,612 plus costs (MED National Enforcement Unit, 2010b, para. 114).

There was no formal employment agreement in place between BCL and Petricevic. A draft unsigned agreement produced in court by Petricevic did not show any amounts for salary, vehicle expenses or other benefits and had no job specification or position description (MED National Enforcement Unit, 2010b, para. 115). Additionally, receivers were unable to locate minutes of meetings of the remuneration committee, where Petricevic's salary had been considered or approved (MED National Enforcement Unit, 2010b, para. 115). Davidson refutes the receivers' interpretation that an employment contract did not exist, indicating Petricevic was entitled to an annual salary of $500,000 with a further annual performance profit payment of $500,000, but this was not concluded as Petricevic would not agree (Justice Forrest Miller, 2010, para. 57).

Discussion

Bridgecorp chairman Bruce Davidson, in defending his actions as chairman, blamed the failure of BCL 'on a combination of factors, including anxiety about finance companies following the failures of several, political problems in Fiji, liquidity concerns in Australasia, and the dishonest and unauthorized actions of two executive directors' (Justice Forrest Miller, 2010, para. 50). The board was unaware of the actual remuneration paid to Petricevic, did not know about the payments made to ABb or Ms Wright until June 2007 and Petricevic acted without authority in the purchase and subsequent financing of the Medici. Mr Davidson argued that, as chairman and non-executive director, he had little ability to control Petricevic as Petricevic owned over 50 per cent of the company (Justice Forrest Miller, 2010, para. 50).

However, problems at BCL predate the collapse of any other finance companies in New Zealand as evidenced by the ASIC interim stop order on the Bridgecorp Australian prospectus issued on 17 February 2006, and the final order issued on 3 April 2006 (ASIC Staff, 2006). The ASIC action was reported in the New Zealand press by *NZ Herald* property reporter Anne Gibson (2006), who linked the ASIC stop order to Bridgecorp's involvement in Melbourne's ill-fated Westpoint development. Subsequently, the *NZ Herald* reported Bridgecorp's decision to continue funding its international operations from New Zealand, with Adam Bennett's headline '*NZ cash bails out Aussie investors*' (2006).

The first recent finance companies to fail in New Zealand were National Finance 2000 Ltd (15 May 2006), Provincial Finance Ltd (2 June 2006) and Western Bay Finance Ltd (4 August 2006). While these failures would have affected re-investment rates, these failures appeared to be restricted to problems with used-car financing. Reserve Bank data suggests that, while finance company deposits fell from a peak in the June 2006 quarter, deposits began to recover from September 2006. The peak in deposits occurred immediately before the collapse of BCL in June 2007 (Wilson, 2009).

Further, political problems in Fiji should not have come as a surprise to BCL, as the company had been involved in a joint venture with Urwin Fernandez Ltd since 2003 (Bridgecorp Ltd, 2007a). Fiji has a history of political instability since independence, with racially motivated coups in 1987 and 2000 followed by several years of unrest leading up to the 2006 coup. BCL had a duty to manage risk by investing prudently; to this end, the board placed limits on connected lending at 5 per cent. Yet, BCL's exposure in Fiji was at times considerably greater than this amount. The April 2007 prospectus (Bridgecorp Ltd, 2007a), under 'Other Material Matters', disclosed the Barcroft/Fiji exposure to be $49.1 million relating to stage 1 of the Momi Bay development, of which there were pre-sale contracts of $85 million. BCL receivers (McCloy, 2010) detail the Moni Bay exposure to be $106 million and report the first mortgagee held an unsuccessful auction in August 2009. The land in question has now been given to the first mortgagee by the Fijian government, precluding further legal claim by BCL receivers (McCloy, 2010). The BCL board appeared to allow risky investment in Fiji, which if successful would have paid substantial dividends to individual BCL board members.

Professional external oversight of BCL was provided by Covenant Trustee Company Ltd as trustees, PKF Chartered Accountants and Business Advisors (Sydney) as auditor, Property Investment Research Pty Ltd, who provided an independent rating of BCL securities, and Lloyds Insurers, who provided insurance on some *qualifying* loans. It seems puzzling that the unauthorized payment involving Petricevic did not come to light when due diligence of the company was completed by these parties. As Bridgecorp Holdings Ltd and Bridgecorp Management Services Ltd were outside the charging group, effective control of BCL rested in these two entities, neither of which was answerable to the BCL trustee or responsible to New Zealand depositors. This complex management structure may explain why transactions were opaque.

Investors were able to monitor their investments through prospectuses, which were issued on an annual basis with audited accounts, though amended prospectuses were produced as necessary throughout the year. Independent valuations were obtained from professional valuers for significant property and equity assets held by BCL. However, prospectuses were only made available to investors and other stakeholders on request.

Conclusion

Corporate governance was certainly an illusion as recently practised within parts of the finance company industry in New Zealand. Using Bridgecorp Ltd to illustrate the existing governance structure, it is clear that if people behave ethically then corporate governance oversight based on trust can work. If market participants are not ethical, no code of conduct can ever work and alternative prescriptive actions become necessary. Ultimately, while directors have a primary fiduciary duty to shareholders, this does not negate their duty of care to other stakeholders. Many of the abuses highlighted were linked to the use of trust and transparency instead of active regulatory oversight. Instances of CEOs controlling appointments to boards, inadequate oversight of compensation and inappropriate linkages to related parties were more the rule than exception. Interestingly though, the absence of trust is a short-term strategy, as eventually markets do work and, as we have seen, entire industries can be affected.

Sadly, the interests of depositors, who supplied considerably more capital than shareholders, received scant regard by the board of BCL. It seems obvious with hindsight; the board of Bridgecorp used their code of corporate governance as a marketing tool rather than as a guide to their ethical behaviour. Depositors should also be entitled to rely on a degree of oversight from external professionals, such as valuers, accountants, lawyers, rating agencies, auditors and trustees. Though the value of any oversight was limited, as these overseers were simply selected by Bridgecorp, to verify information supplied by Bridgecorp.

Although many BCL investors can take some pleasure in seeing directors being called to account, it has not resulted in any financial benefit to them. In their seventh receivers' report, issued in September 2010, McCloy (2010) warned secured investors that the potential payout may be less than ten cents on the dollar. Justice is a long process; criminal proceedings against directors were not completed until early 2011, with the principal directors receiving terms of imprisonment. In the meantime, BCL directors are free to enjoy their retirement.

Blame for the failure of Bridgecorp must rest with Davidson and BCL's board. Their inability to rein in the excesses of executive directors Petricevic and Roest and non-executive director Urwin are a graphic example of ineffective corporate governance. However, the failure of Bridgecorp was not unique; it was just one failure of what has developed into a systemic failure of the entire non-bank deposit-taking industry in New Zealand. Three factors which feature in the Bridgecorp failure were also present in most other failures: very low levels of equity, which were insufficient to absorb shocks, no prudential supervision from government agents and little from trustees or auditors, and finally limited market discipline applied by depositors. Ultimately, this was a system failure.

The equity reported on Bridgecorp's balance sheet was nothing more than a mirage once related party and lending to parties with close connections to Bridgecorp were considered. It can be argued that Bridgecorp's equity was effectively –6 per cent, which should have triggered a response from BCL's trustees, who had a fiduciary duty to depositors to supervise BCL. The apparent lack of a response from the BCL trustee may have been due to BCL's complex organizational structure, placing key functional areas outside of the trustee's reach. Additionally, no government agency had a duty to supervise, with the Reserve Bank's role limited to registered banks and the Securities Commission only charged with ensuring provisions of the Securities Act 1978 were met. Consequently, depositors were left to make their own investment decisions. However, investors in NBDTs were in the main unsophisticated retail investors with limited financial literacy. While the Securities Act 1978 required risk return information to be made available to depositors, its value was severely limited as information was not timely, published generally six months after balance date and up to 18 months old when the investment decision was being made. Once the decision to invest was made, no further market discipline could be applied as investment terms were commonly one to five years, with little possibility to break the investment mid-term.

More generally, responsibility for the systemic failure of New Zealand NBDTs rests with the New Zealand government. In 2003 and 2004, both the Reserve Bank and the Securities Commission made public statements regarding their concern about the sustainability of rapidly growing finance companies. However, neither of these government agencies had jurisdiction to address the rapidly developing crisis. At the end of 2005, the cabinet agreed in principle for consolidation of prudential supervision of NBDTs into a single regulator and for this regulator to be the Reserve Bank. Following work by the Reserve Bank, a proposed regulatory regime for NBDTs was announced in late 2007 by the Minister of Finance, with enabling legislation expected to modify the Reserve Bank of New Zealand Act in March or April 2008 (Cabinet Economic Development Committee, 2007).

However, before this legislation could be completed, the situation was overtaken by the global financial crisis. Then in October 2008, in the last weeks of an election campaign, the Labour government acted by introducing a poorly specified retail deposit guarantee. In New Zealand, 48 NBDTs had failed and over $6 billion of depositors' funds placed in jeopardy. While citizens cannot be protected from every danger, governments have a duty to ensure a level playing field exists. In this regard, many would suggest the government failed in its duty to protect vulnerable depositors.

The Reserve Bank, during the early 1990s, recognized deficiencies in the regulation of registered banks, leading to the 1996 regulatory reforms (Wilson, 2009). Following these reforms, the government should have addressed deficiencies in the prudential regulation of NBDTs. Inaction proved very costly to depositors, taxpayers and the economy. The Reserve Bank has now been given responsibility for NBDTs. While maintaining disclosure principles and a supervisory role for trustees, prudential regulations already introduced include requirements for NBDTs to have: credit ratings, independent governance, risk management plans, minimum capital ratios of 8 per cent (10 per cent for those without a credit rating), limits on related-party exposures and appropriate quantitative liquidity measures. A second round of proposals is expected to include Reserve Bank licensing of NBDTs, a *fit and proper* test of directors, and management and ownership controls.

The government has also recognized the need to update the Securities Commission and in 2011 replaced the Securities Commission with the Financial Markets Authority[20] (FMA). The *twin peaks* of the New Zealand financial markets regulatory system are now the Reserve Bank and the FMA. The Reserve Bank has responsibility for registered banks and other deposit takers such as finance companies. The FMA monitors, licenses and supervises other financial market participants. The monitoring of NBDTs is still the responsibility of trustees; however, trustees will now be licensed and supervised by the FMA. The FMA also has a role in monitoring prospectuses, under which it may review the prospectus to ensure it complies with the Securities Act 1978 and Securities Regulations, does not contain errors and is not false or misleading. The FMA has wider responsibilities and greater enforcement powers than the Securities Commission.

It remains to be seen if responsibilities now given to the Reserve Bank and the Financial Markets Authority to reform NBDTs will be successful. If successful, NBDTs will behave ethically and once again be part of New Zealand's fair, efficient and transparent financial markets. Investors will consider risk as well as return when making investment decisions as ultimately the state cannot and should not regulate against risk. The state can only ensure its citizens are able to make informed decisions, thus allowing markets to operate freely and efficiently.

Notes

1 After October 2008, the NZ government introduced a temporary deposit guarantee. This was not primarily designed to protect depositors but was justified by the perceived difficulty for NZ financial institutions to raise capital on international credit markets. The NZ government felt it was necessary to introduce the temporary deposit guarantee as the Australian government had announced a similar guarantee.

2 Finance company trust deeds typically set a requirement for owners' equity to be a minimum of 10 per cent of total tangible assets, though this level can vary from firm to firm, with smaller firms often required to hold a greater level of equity.

3 The Reserve Bank only collects these data from institutions with assets greater than $100 million. It is estimated that if the assets of smaller finance companies were included, the additional total assets for the industry would be less than $1 billion in 2006.

4 Total assets as reported in the last registered prospectus.

5 The government announced on 25 August 2009 that it would extend the retail deposit guarantee until 31 December 2011. Membership of the extended scheme is not automatic, with only firms with a recognized credit rating of BB accepted. Premiums were paid on all deposits guaranteed and were based on the firm's credit rating ranging from 15bp at AA to 150bp at BB.

6 Initially premiums were set at 10 basis points but were limited to institutions with deposits greater than $5 billion, effectively the large, Australian-owned banks. From October 2010, premiums were based on S&P credit ratings and ranged from 15 basis points to 150 basis points; deposit takers unable to obtain a credit rating of BB or better by October 2010 were ineligible for deposit cover under the extended scheme.

7 Deficiencies identified in disclosure statements included: data which were 6–18 months old not being timely, inconsistent trust deeds leading to a lack of comparability, prospectuses which were overly long with critical data obscured by less important material, and statements produced using accrual accounting methods were not designed for providing information to potential investors.

8 JBL (1972), Cornish Lamphouse (1974) and Securitibank (1976).

9 Systemically important banks are defined as those having liabilities, net of amounts due to related parties, in excess of NZ$10 billion; this status is limited to the four largest RBs – ANZ/National, ASB, BNZ and Westpac (Chetwin, 2006).

10 The Securities Commission set out these requirements for the information of investors in a brochure entitled 'Your right to know: Get informed about investing', which is available on its website (Securities Commission Staff, 2007b).

11 If the Securities Commission suspended an issuer's prospectus, it was not able to publicize the suspension unless it subsequently cancelled the prospectus.

12 If a prospectus was suspended, any new investments had to be held in trust until a new one was registered. If the prospectus was subsequently cancelled, any such new investments had to be returned to the investors.

13 Banks are required to have minimum capital and show they have necessary procedures and policies in place before being registered by the Reserve Bank. Bank directors and senior management are also required to pass a fit and proper test.
14 Assets $35 million, liquidator appointed 6 July 2007 (Waller and McCloy, 2007b).
15 The charging group was allowed to exceed this level if such borrowing were to be used within three months to repay liabilities specified to the trustee.
16 The 2003 trust deed definition of total tangible assets reduces total assets by adjusting for tangible assets held outside NZ, 80 per cent of market value of listed investments, 85 per cent of market value of real property, market value of all approved investments and unlisted shares, permitted loans to BCL parent are valued at 2.5 per cent of total tangible assets rather than the 5 per cent allowed and deferred tax assets (Bridgecorp Ltd, 2003).
17 Defined as loans qualifying for Lloyd's insurance cover.
18 All directors of BCL signed the CCL prospectus as the promoters of the issue (Compass Capital Ltd, 2006).
19 The transaction was recorded as happening on 1 July 2004.
20 The FMA was established by the Financial Markets Authority Act 2011, which also disestablished the Securities Commission.

References

Adams, R.B. and Ferreira, D. (2007) 'A theory of friendly boards', *Journal of Finance*, 62(1): 217–50.

Anderson, R.C., Reeb, D.M., Upadhyay, A. and Zhao, W. (2011) 'The economics of director heterogeneity', *Financial Management*, 40(1): 5–38.

Angbazo, L. and Narayanan, R. (1997) 'Top management compensation and the structure of the board of directors in commercial banks', *European Finance Review*, 1(2): 239–59.

ASIC Staff (2006) 'ASIC obtains consent orders from Bridgecorp Finance to protect interests of noteholders', *vol. 06–287*, Australian Securities and Investments Commission.

Bennett, A. (2006) 'NZ cash bails out Aussie investors', *New Zealand Herald*, 23 August.

Benston, G. and Kaufman, G. (1996) 'The appropriate role of bank regulation', *Economic Journal*, 106(436): 688–97.

Bollard, A. (2004) *Financial Stability Report*, Wellington: Reserve Bank of New Zealand.

Bollard, A. (2006) *Financial Stability Report*, Wellington: Reserve Bank of New Zealand.

Boone, A.L., Casares Field, L., Karpoff, J.M. and Raheja, C.G. (2007) 'The determinants of corporate board size and composition: an empirical analysis', *Journal of Financial Economics*, 85(1): 66–101.

Bridgecorp Board (2006) *Bridgecorp Corporate Governance Charter*, Auckland: Bridgecorp Group of Companies.

Bridgecorp Ltd (2003) *Trust Deed between Bridgecorp Ltd and Covenant Trust Ltd*, Auckland: Companies Office.

Bridgecorp Ltd (2007a) *Memorandum of Amendment to a Registered Prospectus*, Auckland: Companies Office.

Bridgecorp Ltd (2007b) *Prospectus Extension and Financial Statements to 31/12/06 (unaudited)*, Auckland: Companies Office, available at www.companies.govt.nz/cms/banner_template/CNAME.

Cabinet Economic Development Committee (2007) *Review of Financial Products and Providers: Regulation of Non-bank Deposit-takers*, Wellington: Office of Minister of Finance.

Chetwin, W. (2006) 'The Reserve Bank's local incorporation policy', *Reserve Bank of New Zealand Bulletin*, 69(4): 12–21.

Colmar Brunton (2006) *ANZ-Retirement Commission Financial Knowledge Survey*, Wellington: New Zealand Retirement Commission.

Compass Capital Ltd (2006) *Prospectus Compass Capital Ltd Secured Bonds*, available at www.companies.govt.nz/cms/banner_template/CNAME.

Compass Capital Ltd (2007) *Compass Capital Ltd Unaudited Financial Statements*, available at www.companies.govt.nz/cms/banner_template/CNAME.

de Andres, P. and Vallelado, E. (2008) 'Corporate governance in banking: the role of the board of directors', *Journal of Banking & Finance*, 32(12): 2570–80.

Erickson, J., Park, Y.W., Reising, J. and Shin, H.-H. (2005) 'Board composition and firm value under concentrated ownership: the Canadian evidence', *Pacific-Basin Finance Journal*, 13(4): 387–410.

Gaynor, B. (2007) 'Read the small print or get burned', *Milford Asset Management*, 7 July.

Gibson, A. (2006) 'Bridgecorp funding halted after developer collapses', *New Zealand Herald*, 9 March.

Glassman, C.A. and Rhoades, S.A. (1980) 'Owner vs. manager control effects on bank performance', *The Review of Economics and Statistics*, 62(2): 263–70.

Gregor, K. (2010) 'Bridgecorp prospectus labelled "Enronish"', *The New Zealand Herald*, 7 May.

Gropp, R. and Köhler, M. (2010) 'Bank owners or bank managers: who is keen on risk? Evidence from the financial crisis', *SSRN eLibrary*, available at http://ssrn.com/paper=1555663.

Ireland, P. (2010) 'Limited liability, shareholder rights and the problem of corporate irresponsibility', *Cambridge Journal of Economics*, 34(5): 837–56.

Jensen, M.C. and Meckling, W.H. (1976) 'Theory of the firm: managerial behavior, agency costs and ownership structure', *Journal of Financial Economics*, 3(4): 305–60.

Justice Forrest Miller (2010) *Bruce Nelson Davidson v. Registrar of Companies*, Wellington: High Court.

La Porta, R., Lopez-de-Silanes, F., Shleifer, A. and Vishny, R.W. (1998) 'Law and finance', *The Journal of Political Economy*, 106(6): 1113–55.

La Porta, R., Lopez-de-Silanes, F., Shleifer, A. and Vishny, R. (2000) 'Investor protection and corporate governance', *Journal of Financial Economics*, 58(1–2): 3–27.

Laeven, L. and Levine, R. (2009) 'Bank governance, regulation and risk taking', *Journal of Financial Economics*, 93(2): 259–75.

Levine, R. (2004) 'The corporate governance of banks: a concise discussion of concepts and evidence', *World Bank Policy Research Working Paper*, No. 3404.

Macey, J.R. and O'Hara, M. (2003) 'The corporate governance of banks. Part 2: the governance of banks', *Federal Reserve Bank of New York Economic Policy Review*, 9(1): 91(17).

McCloy, C. (2010) *Receivers' Seventh Report on the State of Affairs of Bridgecorp Group of Companies*, Auckland: PricewaterhouseCoopers Limited.

McNabb, D. (2007a) 'Debt vehicle for Bridgecorp exposed', *The Independent Financial Review*, 9 May.

McNabb, D. (2007b) 'Watchdogs close on Bridgecorp directors', *The Independent Financial Review*, 8 August.

MED National Enforcement Unit (2010a) *Report to the Registrar of Companies for the Prohibition of Bruce Nelson Davidson*, Wellington: Ministry of Economic Development.

MED National Enforcement Unit (2010b) *Report to the Registrar of Companies for the Prohibition of Rodney Michael Petricevic*, Wellington: Ministry of Economic Development.

Mishkin, F.S. (1999) 'Lessons from the Asian crisis', *Journal of International Money & Finance*, 18(4): 709.

Mishkin, F.S. (2001) 'Prudential supervision: why is it important and what are the issues?', in F.S. Mishkin (ed.), *Prudential Supervision: What Works and What Doesn't*, pp. 1–30, Chicago: University of Chicago Press.

NZ Companies Office (2010) *Barcroft Holdings Ltd*, retrieved 1 October 2010, from www.business.govt.nz/companies/app/ui/pages/companies/1836528/documents.

RBNZ Staff (2009a) *Household Financial Assets and Liabilities: Annual Series 1978 to 2008*, available at www.rbnz.govt.nz/statistics/monfin/c18/hc18.xls.

RBNZ Staff (2009b) *Non-bank Financial Institutions (NBFI) SSR survey*, retrieved 2 March 2009, from www.rbnz.govt.nz/statistics/monfin/nblissr/download.hmtl.

Robertson, J. (1992) *Euro-National Corp Ltd v. NZI Bank Ltd*, Auckland: High Court (vol. reported at [1992] 2 NZLR 739; (1992) 6 NZCLC 67,453).

Securities Commission Staff (2004a) *Corporate Governance in New Zealand: Principles and Guidelines*, Wellington: Securities Commission.

Securities Commission Staff (2004b) *Discussion paper on disclosure by finance companies*, Wellington: Securities Commission.

Securities Commission Staff (2007a) *News Release*, Bridgecorp prospectuses.

Securities Commission Staff (2007b) *Your Right to Know*, brochure, retrieved on 17 March 2007.

Shleifer, A. and Vishny, R.W. (1997) 'A survey of corporate governance', *The Journal of Finance*, 52(2): 737–83.

Spong, K. and Sullivan, R.J. (2007) 'Corporate governance and bank performance', *SSRN eLibrary*, available at http://ssrn.com/paper=1011068.

Stiglitz, J.E. and Weiss, A. (1983) 'Incentive effects of terminations: applications to the credit and labor markets', *American Economic Review*, 73(5): 912.

Treasury (2010) *Retail Deposit Guarantee Scheme*, 21 September, retrieved in December 2010, from www.treasury.govt.nz/economy/guarantee/retail.

Waller, J. and McCloy, C. (2007a) *Bridgecorp Limited and Subsidiaries Placed in Receivership*, Auckland: PricewaterhouseCoopers Limited.

Waller, J. and McCloy, C. (2007b) *Liquidators' First Report: Bridgecorp Investments Ltd*, Auckland: PricewaterhouseCoopers Limited.

Waller, J. and McCloy, C. (2007c) *Liquidators' First Report: Goodman Limited*, Auckland: PricewaterhouseCoopers Limited.

Waller, J. and McCloy, C. (2007d) *Liquidators' First Report: Poseidon Ltd*, Auckland: PricewaterhouseCoopers Limited.

Waller, J. and McCloy, C. (2007e) *Receiver's First Report: Bridgecorp Limited and Subsidiaries*, Auckland: PricewaterhouseCoopers Limited.

Westphal, J.D. and Zajac, E.J. (1997) 'Defections from the inner circle: social exchange, reciprocity, and the diffusion of board independence in U.S. corporations', *Administrative Science Quarterly*, 42(1): 161–83.

Widdowson, D. and Hailwood, K. (2007) 'Financial literacy and its role in promoting a sound financial system', *Reserve Bank of New Zealand Bulletin*, 70(2): 37–47.

Wilson, W.R. (2009) *New Zealand's Experiment with Prudential Regulation: Can Disclosure Discipline Moderate Excessive Risk Taking in New Zealand Deposit Taking Institutions*? Ph.D. dissertation, Massey University, North Shore City.

5 Bank governance

What do we know, what should we do?

Kevin Davis

This chapter addresses the issues of whether available empirical evidence supports the hypothesis that bad corporate governance in banks was a principal cause of the global financial crisis and the types of regulatory responses regarding bank governance which have resulted. It reviews what we know about bank governance, assesses key features of regulatory (and other) initiatives suggested, and concludes by considering whether contemporary approaches to thinking about bank governance are suitable.

Various definitions of corporate governance can be found in the literature but most share a common theme of specifying it as the set of relationships between stakeholders and decision makers in the organization designed to facilitate the achievement of the goals of the organization. In one of the most widely cited articles on corporate governance, Shleifer and Vishny (1997) commence by asserting that it 'deals with the ways in which suppliers of finance to corporations assure themselves of getting a return on their investment', thus focusing purely on agency problems. Because, as Macey and O'Hara (2003) note, complete contracts to cover every possible future contingency cannot be written, decision-making responsibilities, incentive structures, and monitoring arrangements are put in place to deal with the agency problems which result. Since then, broader, multi-disciplinary perspectives have come to the fore, as outlined by Filatotchev and Boyd (2009), reflecting recognition of a wider range of stakeholders and the role of internal organizational arrangements, processes, and cultures.[1]

Although corporate governance has been a dominant theme for the last two decades for academic research, business, and policymakers, there was relatively little explicit attention paid by researchers to corporate governance in banks prior to the global financial crisis (GFC). Macey and O'Hara (2003) noted that, despite the increasing attention being paid to corporate governance generally, 'very little attention has been paid to the corporate governance of banks'.

There had also been a relatively limited regulatory focus on bank corporate governance by regulators. In the Australian context, Davis (1999) notes that the 'Wallis Inquiry … paid relatively little explicit attention to governance issues, although several of its recommendations … have implications for governance mechanisms and structures'. APRA, however, released a draft prudential standard on board composition for ADIs in November 2001 and the subsequent draft of prudential standard APS 510 *ADI Governance* in May 2005. The focus of this standard was primarily upon board characteristics and structure. This was also the principal focus of the guidance note produced by the Basel Committee (1999) and updated subsequently (Basel Committee, 2006). In New Zealand, attention to bank governance also included significant directors' liabilities for misleading disclosures (Bollard, 2004), consistent with a perceived need for stronger governance in a less prescriptive regulatory environment.

The GFC has spawned extensive regulatory interest in bank corporate governance, although Mülbert (2010) reviews official studies of the GFC and argues that bank corporate governance failures did not feature as an explanation for the crisis for a year or more after its onset – following which this became a key issue for regulators. The current conventional wisdom is summarized as follows by researchers from the World Bank:

> If there is one lesson from the current crisis – a lesson consistent with the Asian financial crisis – it is that corporate governance matters. The central irony of the governance failures in this crisis is that many took place in some of the most sophisticated banks operating in some of the most developed governance environments in the world.
>
> (Ard and Berg, 2010)

This has led to a regulatory and supervisory focus upon improving governance in financial institutions reflected in the G20 Leaders' Statement that '[m]ore work is required to restore the soundness and enhance the transparency of banks' balance sheets and markets; and improve the corporate governance and risk management of financial firms…' (G20, 2010). There has been a range of initiatives and suggestions forthcoming relating to risk governance, remuneration, board arrangements, and shareholder rights and duties.

This chapter asks the questions of whether available empirical evidence supports the hypothesis that bad corporate governance in banks was a principal cause of the GFC and whether that evidence provides a foundation for the types of regulatory initiatives in train. It also asks the question of whether contemporary approaches to thinking about corporate governance in banks are well founded.

The first section briefly reviews why bank corporate governance may be special, and considers whether bank ownership and organizational structures conform to the model which underpins much current thinking. The second section reviews empirical studies which have addressed features of bank corporate governance and the following section focuses upon studies of banker remuneration, which has been a particular topic of interest and study. The fourth section looks at empirical work and official views on whether bad corporate governance in banks was a principal contributor to the GFC. The fifth section looks at the various changes to corporate governance requirements proposed and their merits. The final section considers whether contemporary approaches to bank corporate governance are appropriate given the characteristics of modern financial sectors and banks. In particular, the disjuncture between legal control rights and economic interests, high allowed leverage and financial safety nets, inherent complexity and opacity (both internally and externally), and limited liability arrangements suggest that an alternative perspective may be appropriate.

Is bank corporate governance different?

The European Commission (2010, p. 4) argues that 'the rules of corporate governance within financial institutions must be adapted to take account of the specific nature of these companies', specifically mentioning the role played by supervisory authorities as implicit representatives of stakeholders, such as depositors and (in the event of failure) taxpayers. This is well recognized, as are the special features of banks which create specific governance issues and prompt regulation. Davis (1999) notes difficulties posed for external monitoring by bank opacity, the increasing level of internal delegation of decision-making responsibility (and risk taking) within modern banks, and the free rider problem induced in private sector monitoring by official regulation and supervision. Levine (2004) also emphasizes the relevance of opacity, including the complications it creates in trying to design incentive structures to align management interests with those of shareholders (or other stakeholders). He also notes the adverse effect which government regulation of bank takeovers and concentrated ownership may have on pressure for improved governance – in addition to the effects of the 'safety net'. Macey and O'Hara (2003) argue that a Franco-German approach to corporate governance should be taken in the case of banks, which extends fiduciary duty of bank directors and management to a broader range of stakeholders (particularly depositors) as opposed to the US approach, which focuses on obligations to shareholder/owners. Similarly, the European Commission (2010) argues that corporate governance in financial institutions should involve directors, shareholders, and management assuming a greater level of responsibility.

Much of the analysis of bank corporate governance is addressed from a perspective of banks as limited liability, profit-maximizing, stock-market listed companies with diffuse owners and relates to the agency problems generated by the division between owners and managers, ameliorated by shareholder-elected boards of directors and the market for corporate control. This is a narrow perspective which, while possibly applicable to large banks in a number of major countries, ignores significant historical and contemporary geographic characteristics of banking. Fashioning governance requirements based on that perspective avoids the prior question of whether that organizational structure is the most appropriate for good bank governance.

There is a diversity of bank ownership structures around the world. They range from publicly listed companies (which may have widely held or concentrated ownership), to private, family-owned companies, to mutual or cooperative structures, to government ownership. Moreover, legal structures may involve banks as subsidiaries of holding companies or as parent companies in their own right with other financial or non-financial subsidiaries. In the US, for example, bank (or financial) holding companies have become the norm for large banks – on which most of the bank governance literature has been based. Partnership structures were also common in investment banking until recently, as, historically, was double or unlimited liability of bank shareholders.

Caprio *et al.* (2007) provide information on ownership structures of publicly traded banks for a sample of 244 large banks from 44 countries as at December 2001. Notably, widely held ownership structures are not common, with only Australia, Canada, Ireland, Norway, the UK, the US, and (to a lesser degree) Japan having widespread ownership predominating. A situation of a controlling family holding was more common internationally than widespread ownership, while state control was also frequently observed.

Because Caprio *et al.* restrict their sample to the ten largest publicly traded banks in each country, they exclude fully government owned banks and mutual or cooperative banks, which are also significant. Moreover, as Taboada (2008) notes, there has been a substantial wave of bank privatizations around the world in recent decades. He finds, for a sample of around 800 banks, that there is no significant difference between common law versus civil law countries in terms of ownership concentration (domestic, government, foreign blockholders) but that there is greater domestic blockholder and less government blockholder concentration in developed versus emerging markets (using data for 1995, 2000 and 2005).

In the Asian region, Fan and Wiwatanakantang (2006) provide information on ownership of 59 leading banks in Indonesia, Korea, Malaysia, and Thailand. Around 70 per cent of banks have a controlling shareholder and, while the relative importance varies across the countries, around one third are government controlled, one third foreign controlled and 10 per cent family controlled.

Governance arrangements also differ across countries. In some countries, banks have a dual-board structure, involving a supervisory board and an executive board. Ferreira *et al.* (2010) examine characteristics of boards of 740 large banks from 41 countries. They find that the importance of independent directors increased in the years prior to the GFC but that, for many countries outside the US, the extent of director independence is less. Countries with two-tier boards and those in which courts have powers to remove directors have fewer independent directors.

Partly missing from the mainstream literature on ownership and governance structures in banks is recognition of the importance of cooperative and mutual institutions in the sector, and the particular characteristics of these institutions. In Europe, for example, cooperative banks are a significant part of banking markets, as Table 5.1 shows. Fonteyne (2007) notes that the voting rights structure and the intergenerational wealth transfer implicit in such cooperative (or mutual) structures raises particular problems for governance – in particular, opportunities for management empire building and for attempts at expropriation. He notes that, while these organizational forms may have worked well for small community-based institutions for which they were designed, they may be subject to shortcomings when those institutions become large and complex, and that the

Table 5.1 Cooperative banking in Europe

Selected European countries: cooperative bank sector share (%)		
Country	*Banking assets (2003)*	*Retail deposits*
Austria	35.6	20–50
Finland	15.9	20–50
France	24.1	50–100
Germany	10.3	5–20
Greece	0.6	0–5
Italy	14.9	20–50
Netherlands	26.7	20–50
Portugal	3.5	5–20
Spain	3.9	5–20

Source: Fonteyne (2007).

absence of a market for corporate control for such entities also weakens governance incentives. The absence of owner-depositor agency conflicts is also relevant for potentially reducing incentives for excessive risk taking.

Studies of bank governance

Empirical studies of bank governance prior to the GFC are relatively few, although there are numerous studies not focusing on governance but still based on an agency perspective which examine 'bank' incentives for risk taking due to the financial safety net. Simpson and Gleason (1999) is one of the early empirical governance studies examining whether board attributes are relevant for performance. In this case, for a sample of approximately 300 US banks, the only characteristic (measured in 1989) found to be related (negatively) to probability of subsequent financial distress (measured at 1993) was CEO–chairman duality. It is suggested by the authors that a CEO who is also chairman is better able to withstand shareholder incentives for higher risk taking, which is contrary to the CEO's private interests. This result is supported by Pathan (2009), who studies 212 large bank holding companies for the period 1997–2004. He finds that bank risk (measured using both stock price data and Z-scores) is negatively related to CEO–chairman duality and positively related to 'strong' boards, as defined by small boards and those with few restrictions on shareholder voting power. But having more independent directors appears to lead to lower risk taking. Pathan and Skully (2010) use the same sample to analyse determinants of board structure, such as size, composition (independent directors) and CEO–chairman duality. Larger, diversified, banks have larger boards, more external directors, and more likelihood of CEO–chairman duality. They conclude that 'to the extent that bank board structure adapts to its unique competitive environment, it suggests that uniform rules or guidelines to reform board governance could prove counter-productive'.

Offsetting the risk reduction benefits of CEO–chairman duality, Pi and Timme (1993) find (for a sample of 112 US banks in the late 1980s) that duality reduces performance as measured by return on assets and cost efficiency. Adams and Mehran (2003) examine 35 large US bank holding companies over the period 1986–99. They find that, compared to manufacturing firms, bank boards are larger, have more committees, make less use of stock options in CEO compensation, and that CEO ownership stakes are lower and institutional shareholdings are lower. They note, however, that their empirical work suggests relationships found between board characteristics and firm performance in other industries is not necessarily replicated in the case of banks.

De Andres and Vallelado (2008) undertake a cross-country study of the role of board characteristics using data on 69 banks from the US, the UK, Canada, Spain, France, and Italy for 1995 to 2005. Bank performance (measured by Tobin's Q, return on assets, or shareholder return) is found to have an inverted U relationship to board size (with the peak occurring at around 19 directors) while having more outside directors is also associated with improved performance. Caprio *et al.* (2007) also provide cross-country evidence. Based on the assumption that higher market valuation (proxied by Tobin's Q ratio) is an indicator of better governance, their empirical work leads to the conclusions that concentrated ownership is consistent with good governance, as is minority shareholder protection provisions, but that stronger regulation or supervisory powers does not improve governance once ownership concentration is controlled for. Laeven and Levine (2008) also find that concentrated ownership leads to higher risk taking, consistent with the standard agency problem perspective. They also note that bank risk taking depends upon the interaction of regulation and governance structures, such that the diversity of ownership arrangements around the world suggests that 'one size fits all' regulation is not appropriate. For example, deposit insurance does not appear to induce moral hazard in the form of higher risk taking unless there is a single large equity owner.

Crespí *et al.* (2004) is one of the few studies to compare governance for different types of banks. They find that cooperative savings banks (Cajas) in Spain perform on average no worse than commercial banks but that there is more evidence of governance reactions via CEO replacement in commercial banks (and more use of friendly mergers for savings banks) following poor performance (measured using ROA). DeYoung (2007) finds from an examination of US community banks that the link between financial performance and governance indicators varies depending on the organizational and ownership structure of the bank. For example, CEO cash bonus salary component and existence of a management succession plan were significant positive influences on performance in 'Subchapter S' banks (which are small, with few shareholders and tax incentives to have a high dividend payout ratio), but not at publicly traded community banks.

What, tentative, conclusions might be drawn from this literature? Independent directors appear to be beneficial (both for performance and for limiting risk taking); concentrated ownership leads to closer alignment with shareholder goals (although whether that is socially desirable is another matter); CEO–chair duality might reduce risk taking. But the evidence is mixed, suggests there is no unique best governance structure, and is largely based on US bank holding company data – which may limit its more general applicability.

Studies of banker remuneration

Banker remuneration has attracted considerable attention since the GFC and led to a range of regulatory proposals internationally (Douglas, 2010). It is of particular interest because aligning executive incentives via remuneration structures with those of particular stakeholders may influence bank risk taking and performance.

Studies of banker remuneration essentially fall into two categories. One group examines the determinants of remuneration (such as bank size, link to past performance) and the other its composition (role of incentive components, such as option grants etc.) The other looks at whether compensation arrangements affect risk taking by, or performance of, the bank.[2]

Ang *et al.* (2002) examine remuneration arrangements at 166 US banks from 1993–6 and find that CEOs have a larger performance-contingent pay component than less senior executives, and a higher sensitivity of remuneration to bank performance. Cornett *et al.* (2009) find for the largest 100 US bank holding companies that, during the period 1994–2002, greater pay–performance sensitivity of CEO compensation was associated with more earnings management, but also with more independent boards, which tended to moderate the extent of earnings management. Ang *et al.* (2001), in a theoretical study, argue that performance-related pay for top executives induces greater internal monitoring by them of subordinates (enhancing performance) as well as aligning their interests with owners but that regulation, such as minimum capital adequacy requirements, reduces the sensitivity of the performance–pay relationship. John *et al.* (2000) develop a model of bank management incentives which implies that the structure of banker remuneration should be incorporated into deposit insurance pricing (and supervisory actions) to offset incentives to undertake risk-shifting actions (higher leverage, more risky investments) to the detriment of depositors and/or the deposit insurance fund.

Bliss and Rosen (2001), examining a sample of large US banks over 1986–95, find no difference in the link between CEO remuneration and growth in bank size via merger or non-merger means, even though merger activity might be thought to be an easier path to growth. They also find that larger share ownership by bank CEOs tends to reduce the incidence of acquisition activity (consistent with adverse effects on CEO wealth from poor acquisitions reducing hubris). Anderson *et al.* (2004), examining 330 large bank mergers from 1990–7, conclude that the post-merger increase in CEO remuneration is related to expected gains from the merger (measured via announcement stock price effects) and involves a shift towards longer-term compensation, suggesting that mergers are not necessarily an easier path to growth for CEOs. The inference they draw, that the market for corporate control works effectively in banking, is consistent with the results of Becher (2000), which found that the 558 bank mergers studied over the period 1980–97 had, on average, positive wealth effects (although previous studies surveyed had mixed results).

John *et al.* (2010) argue that the sensitivity of the CEO performance–pay relationship should decline as leverage increases (to reduce incentives for risk shifting from equity to debt) and increase with the intensity of outside monitoring (which allows for closer alignment of interest with owners while limiting potential for risk shifting). Using an index of outside monitoring (based on subordinated debt and regulatory data), they find support for these hypotheses for a sample of US bank holding companies over the period 1993–2007.

A number of studies have examined whether bank executive compensation is linked to risk taking by those institutions. Cheng *et al.* (2010) use residual compensation in excess of that explained by institution size as a measure of CEO risk-taking incentive and find that it is a predictor of subsequent institutional risk taking. However, they do not find that their results can be explained by standard corporate governance indicators but are more related to measures of shareholder short-termism (stock turnover and institutional ownership), suggesting that characteristics of executive remuneration generating risk-taking behaviour may be more driven by shareholder clientele objectives.

Chen *et al.* (2006) examine compensation in US banks following deregulation of the early 1990s and argue that increasing use of executive stock options occurred and was associated with increased risk taking by banks. (In 1992, options accounted on average for around 17 per cent of total CEO remuneration for banks in their study and had increased to almost 50 per cent in 1999. In Europe, Nestor Advisors (2008) found that, on average, for the largest 25 banks, salary accounted for 24 per cent, annual bonuses for 37 per cent and long-term incentive rewards for 40 per cent of CEO remuneration.) Chen *et al.* (2006) used four stock price-related measures of risk (stock price volatility, idiosyncratic risk, beta, and stock price return sensitivity to short-term interest rates); other factors controlled for included bank size, leverage, and diversification. Accumulated option holdings appear to have a closer relationship with the measures of risk taking than the option share of annual remuneration.

Fahlenbrach and Stulz (2010) examine whether alignment of CEO incentives with those of shareholders, through remuneration arrangements, was relevant in explaining differential bank performance in the GFC. They find no evidence that better alignment led to better performance as measured by bank stock price movements and argue that CEOs apparently took risks which were *ex ante* in shareholder best interests, but turned out to be *ex post* value destroying – including of their own wealth.

However, Bebchuk *et al.* (2009) analyse the compensation of top executives at Lehmann and Bear Stearns and note that substantial amounts ($1 billion plus) of remuneration were cashed out over the eight years prior to failure. Hence, even though senior executives in those firms 'lost' substantial amounts at the time of failure, their net wealth gain relative to eight years earlier was still substantial. They argue that this is consistent with remuneration arrangements encouraging risk taking – despite the *ex post* losses which were incurred.

Bebchuk and Spamann (2009) analyse banker remuneration arrangements, arguing that the ability of executives to access short-term remuneration gives incentives to take risks which may involve longer-term effects. This is aggravated by the linking of remuneration to equity returns, which are a highly leveraged claim on bank assets, and thus not forcing enough attention of bank executives on the potential downside faced by depositors and other creditors. The leverage effect is further exaggerated if a holding company structure exists with bank executives having remuneration linked to shares in the holding company which itself is leveraged. They argue that regulatory requirements which attempt to align executive remuneration with that of bank shareholders is not necessarily socially optimal, given the incentives of bank shareholders to encourage risk taking in the presence of a financial safety net (or inability of other creditors to discipline excessive risk taking adequately). Rather, regulation of remuneration should be designed to affect risk-taking incentives of bank executives and, perhaps, is better linked to returns to all the bank stakeholders than to shareholders.

For the former six main US investment banks, Nestor Advisors (2009) found that remuneration was strongly aligned with long-term shareholder interest but questioned whether this was in fact appropriate for systemically important financial institutions (SIFIs).

Chaigneau (2010) develops a formal model of socially optimal bank CEO remuneration in circumstances where alternative risky strategies can be taken and where deposit insurance/guarantees protect depositors and creditors from loss, and finds that structuring remuneration to align CEO incentives with shareholders is not optimal. As he notes, 'to the extent that the preferred strategy of the bank's shareholders is not socially optimal, then it is generally not socially optimal to let them set the incentives of bank CEOs'.

From this review of (a relatively small part of) the literature on banker remuneration, the following conclusions can be drawn. First, there has been an increase in the role of performance-related pay in banking over past decades. Second, performance-related pay aligns management incentives with those of bank shareholders and may encourage greater risk taking. Third, such alignment is not necessarily socially optimal, particularly in the presence of a financial safety net, and this can provide a rationale for the setting of regulatory parameters, such as deposit insurance premiums or capital requirements, to take into account characteristics of bank management remuneration arrangements. But, it is worth noting, while some studies may control for board characteristics in examining the relationship between remuneration and bank risk taking, they do not generally cast much light on the important question of the relative roles of boards and executives in determining bank risk taking.

Bank governance and the GFC

Interest in bank governance has increased significantly in the wake of the global financial crisis (GFC), reflecting a prior comment by Levine (2004) that '[b]anking crises dramatically advertise the enormous consequences of poor governance of banks'. In the case of the GFC, those consequences were substantial, as illustrated by data presented by Ladipo and Nestor (2009), for the ratio of the share price at the trough (February 2009) to its peak (January 2008) for the 25 largest banks (by initial market capitalization) in Europe. The highest ratio is 48 per cent, for nine of the 25 banks the ratio is over 20 per cent, and there are eight banks with a ratio below 10 per cent.

But, as cautioned by Davies (2003), it is important to distinguish between failures of management and failures of governance. Financial institutions can get into difficulties because decisions which turn out to be poor ones are made by boards and executives operating within a good corporate governance structure.

Academic studies

Beltratti and Stulz (2009) consider differences in performance of 98 large banks internationally to ascertain whether they can be attributed to different regulation, governance, or balance sheet characteristics. They do not find that poor governance, as measured by the Corporate Governance Quotient (CGQ score), explains poor performance during the GFC, and instead attribute differences in performance to balance sheet structures – where banks with boards more aligned with shareholders took *ex ante* value adding positions, which with hindsight exposed the banks to significant losses.

Adams (2009) compares the governance structures of banks with those of non-banks, focusing on standard indicators of governance characteristics, such as board independence, board size, CEO remuneration, etc. The data are for large financial and non-financial companies in the US. While there are some differences in governance characteristics, there is no clear evidence that they indicate that governance is worse in banks. When Adams compares banks which received Troubled Asset Relief Program (TARP) funds with those that did not, she finds that TARP recipients had larger and 'busier' (more outside directorships) boards, and with more CEO incentive pay. The first two characteristics are generally thought to be consistent with poorer governance and consistent with the perception that TARP recipients, by virtue of requiring assistance, were less well governed. The latter characteristic is consistent with higher risk taking by CEOs. However, TARP recipients were also characterized by having more independent boards – which Adams suggests may, in this case, indicate poorer governance in that independent directors may not have had adequate financial sophistication to assess risk taking by banks. Lower remuneration of directors at banks may also support this conclusion. A conclusion is that independence (and absence of conflict of interest) requirements for directors may have adverse effects on bank governance, particularly if legal liability is onerous.

Erkens *et al.* (2009) examine the role of governance in the GFC using data for 296 of the largest financial firms from 30 countries. They find that financial firms with greater institutional ownership took more risks and that greater board independence appears to lead to quicker reaction to bad outcomes. These responses, possibly reflecting reputational concerns of independent directors, include CEO turnover and capital raisings, even though such raisings may be inconsistent with the best interests of current shareholders. While apparently at variance with the results of Adams (2009), both these studies highlight an important role for independent directors and the need for them to have adequate financial skills.

Official views

The view expressed in the Walker Report in the UK (Walker, 2009) appears to be widely accepted.

> The fact that different banks operating in the same geography, in the same financial and market environment and under the same regulatory arrangements generated such massively different outcomes can only be fully explained in terms of differences in the way they were run. Within the regulatory framework that is set, how banks are run is a matter for their boards, that is of corporate governance.

Ard and Berg (2010), from the World Bank, argue that many of the problems of the GFC can be traced to flawed implementation of good governance principles and excessive short-term remuneration, and note that these were most apparent in some of the largest and supposedly most sophisticated financial institutions globally. They suggest four key areas have been identified:

a risk governance (including information, assessment capacity, management and systems failings – including identifying and internally pricing risk taking appropriately);
b remuneration and incentive alignment;
c board professionalism; and
d shareholder engagement.

In its Green Paper, the European Commission (2010) argues that 'it is clear that boards of directors, like supervisory authorities, rarely comprehended either the nature or scale of the risks they were facing'. The OECD, concludes that 'the financial crisis can be to an important extent attributed to failures and weaknesses in corporate governance' (Kirkpatrick, 2009), emphasizing particularly failures in risk management systems and remuneration structures. The Basel Committee highlights 'insufficient board oversight of senior management, inadequate risk management and unduly complex or opaque bank organizational structures and activities' (BCBS, 2010).

Given these perspectives, it is particularly interesting to examine the results of Senior Supervisors Group (2009) November 2008 survey of 20 of the largest global financial firms, asking them to self-assess their practices to industry standards proposed by industry and supervisory reports during that year. Their self-evaluation against assessment topics saw all 20 grading themselves as fully aligned on governance roles and responsibilities, governance policies, governance internal coordination, and communication. Eighty per cent or more graded themselves similarly on governance practices involving risk committees and role of the chief risk officer, and on risk disclosure and transparency, liquidity risk monitoring, planning and funding, and reserve management. Where self-assessment indicated least alignment was in areas more related to internal risk management practices, including inclusion of liquidity risk in transfer pricing, monitoring, mitigation, and close-out practices for counterparty risk, stress testing, and dealing with new products.

Policies and proposals

Regulatory and supervisory interest in bank governance arrangements has been building for a decade or more. The Basel Committee (2006) provides a list of corporate governance principles for banks (updating an earlier, 1999, document) and guidance to supervisors in assessing bank corporate governance standards. This has been further supplemented by a Consultative Document released in 2010 (BCBS, 2010). Their approach to corporate governance draws on the OECD approach, which identifies a range of stakeholders but also emphasizes internal processes, including independent oversight, line management supervision, and independent risk, compliance, and audit functions. The 2006 Basel (eight) principles relate to board member qualities, determining strategy and corporate values, ensuring suitable accountability, management and oversight structures, use of audit and compliance resources, compensation policies consistent with long-term goals, transparency and disclosure, and knowledge of structure. It argues that supervisors should review governance arrangements, particularly that they give suitable acknowledgement to protection of depositors. As Mülbert (2010) notes, the notion of governance implicit in the Basel Committee Principles is a broad notion which incorporates internal organizational structures, rather than the narrower, shareholder-focused one which emphasizes relationships between senior management, boards of directors, and shareholders.

Comparison of Principles set out in the 2010 and 2006 Basel Committee documents (which are summarized and matched in the appendix to this chapter) provides some interesting insights. In its 2010 Consultative Document (BCBS, 2010), the number of principles for good bank corporate governance has been expanded from eight to 14. Of the eight 2006 principles, all can be found explicitly reflected (albeit with some changes in emphasis) in the 2010 document (although the references in principles 2 and 3 to communicating values and enforcing lines of responsibility etc. *throughout the organization* do not appear). There are three new principles relating to risk management responsibilities, structures, and processes, one new principle relating to the board's responsibility with regard to its own processes and practices, and two focusing on board responsibilities and arrangements within group structures and where special purpose vehicles or operations, in particular overseas jurisdictions, create particular risks. Notably, there is no mention of a board responsibility for the 'living wills' requirement that some supervisors are in favour of.

Notably, the number of entries under the role of supervisors has fallen from six to five, although there is an element of 'tougher language' involved. While it is possible to 'map' the 2006 items into corresponding elements of the 2010 set, there are some differences, such as a greater emphasis on coordination across jurisdictions. It is also asserted (item 4) that supervisors should require and enforce action when governance shortcomings are observed, rather than determining suitability of practices and advising. What is particularly noticeable, however, is the absence of the second item in the 2006 list that '[s]upervisors should consider corporate governance as one element of depositor protection'.

Regulatory responses have been proposed in each of the four areas of risk governance, remuneration, board professionalism, and shareholder engagement identified by Ard and Berg (2010). The recommendations of the UK Walker Review fall into these categories and provide a useful framework for identifying issues commonly addressed elsewhere.

Risk governance

The Walker Review proposed that banks should have specialized board risk committees and an empowered chief risk officer, use appropriate external specialists, ensure acquisitions are subject to detailed risk committee scrutiny, and provide detailed risk reports in annual reports. These suggestions are reflected in the Basel 2010 principles, while risk reporting has been required for several years under the required Basel 2 disclosures. But what is particularly striking about the importance attached to this area is that enhanced risk management systems have been the focus of regulatory and bank attention for a number of years, with large banks spending hundreds of millions of dollars in preparing for qualifying for the Advanced Internal Ratings Based Approach in Basel 2.

Remuneration

The Walker Review proposed that bank board remuneration committees should set an overarching structure for bank remuneration policies and be responsible for setting remuneration and performance objectives of 'high end' managerial employees. Disclosure of remuneration for high-end employees should occur and those employees should be expected to build up an appropriate shareholding in the bank. Deferral of incentive payments should be a primary risk adjustment mechanism and some form of shareholder vote on remuneration should be required. 'In order to increase awareness and attention, it can be considered good practice that remuneration policies and implementation measures are submitted to the annual meeting and that there are procedures that enable shareholders to express their opinions' (OECD, 2010, p. 12). The G20 endorsed 'the implementation standards of the FSB aimed at aligning compensation with long-term value creation, not excessive risk-taking' (G20, 2009). In March 2010, the Financial

Stability Board (2010) produced a report on progress internationally in implementing the principles on remuneration (which can be grouped under headings of governance of compensation, alignment with prudent risk taking, and effective oversight by supervisors and stakeholders), which its predecessor, the Financial Stability Forum, had previously developed.

In some countries, the authorities have taken specific action on banker remuneration, in response to public concerns about taxpayer support for troubled banks being used for bankers' bonuses. In the US, through the Dodd–Frank Wall Street Reform and Consumer Protection Act, passed in July 2010, bank shareholders are provided with a relatively weak 'say on pay' right through requirements for a three-yearly vote on remuneration. This followed legislation in 2009 to limit executive salaries at banks receiving assistance under the Troubled Assets Relief Program (TARP) – perhaps inducing more rapid exit of large banks from that programme. In the UK, the FSA introduced a remuneration code (reflecting the FSF principles) in August 2009 for banks, building societies, and broker dealers, following earlier government budgetary tax imposts on bonuses. The European Union issued the Capital Requirements Directive (CRD 3) in July 2010 involving deferral requirements for bonus pay, share-linked compensation requirements, and requirements to ensure that variable compensation is reduced when firm performance is poor.

Board professionalism

The Walker Review proposed that non-executive directors (NEDs) should be well briefed and supported, be able to devote adequate time (at least 30–36 days p.a. for NEDs of major banks and the chairman to spend two-thirds of his or her time on the role), provide an adequate spread and depth of expertise, and be subject to appropriate 'interrogation' by experts appointed by the supervisor prior to appointment. The chairman and senior independent directors have special responsibilities for ensuring challenge and leadership, and the board should have appropriate performance evaluation. The OECD (2010) argues that director shortcomings were particularly important in causing the GFC, with relevant issues including inadequate input from NEDs, insufficient diversity of directors, and incomplete understanding of risks taken.

Many prudential regulators have in place 'fit and proper' requirements for directors of financial institutions, but these focus primarily upon good standing etc., rather than expertise. The OECD (2010) suggests that 'such tests should extend to the technical and professional competence of board members, including general governance and risk management skills'.

Within this context, the OECD (2010) notes that market or stakeholder discipline to deal with conflicts of interest may be particularly significant for large financial institutions, reflecting their complexity and opaqueness. This was most apparent in the Goldman-Sachs 'Abacus' case, where structured products (CDOs) were manufactured to best fit the preferences of a particular client wishing to take a short position on mortgage-backed securities, and were then sold to other clients. This issue also was significant in the 'Volcker' proposal (incorporated in the Dodd–Frank Act in the US) to ban banks from engaging in proprietary trading, with both issues highlighting the difficulties of maintaining adequate 'Chinese Walls' within financial institutions.

Shareholder engagement

The Walker Review recommended that boards should be aware of the composition of shareholders and that institutional investors should be required to exercise their stewardship role.

An assessment

This chapter commenced by noting that the corporate governance problem arises from the agency problems faced by suppliers of funds to business enterprises and that organizational structures and various control rights and monitoring devices are developed because complete contracting is not possible. It also noted that much of the corporate governance literature and focus has moved onto other issues, such as board size, composition, and processes, which largely take as given the organizational structures and control rights in existence. The discussion thus rarely addresses the important prior question of whether the institutional/organizational structures and allocations of legal rights which have emerged are indeed suitable for achieving good governance.

Some part of the current discussion about regulatory change is related to inducing or forcing changes in institutional structures – but generally premised on concerns about financial stability rather than governance, even though various proposals can have significant governance implications. For example, suggestions for requiring separation of 'utility' (commercial) banking from 'casino' (investment) banking would have significant implications for governance arrangements. If nothing else, it would reduce the likelihood of remuneration structures perhaps suitable for one type of activity (such as the high-powered incentives in investment banking) being spread throughout the institution into other activities (commercial banking) where they are perhaps less suitable. More generally, such institutional separation (and different remuneration structures) may induce self-selection by managerial employees into institutions where their personal risk appetites better match those of the institution.

Another example of potentially fundamental change lies in proposals for requiring banks to issue 'contingent capital' in the form of hybrid debt instruments, which convert automatically into an equity stake should a set of prespecified adverse outcomes occur for the bank. Investors in those instruments will expect some control or decision rights, with implications for the power of ordinary shareholders. For example, a requirement that holders of contingent capital have the right to elect one or more board members could be envisaged.

But these changes, involving relatively minor modifications to control rights, miss an important implication of the agency problem for suppliers of funds relating to banks. Shareholders in banks are very much minority suppliers of funds to banks. Legislative and regulatory systems have allowed owners of these institutions to exploit limited liability (arguably excessively) through high leverage. Limited liability, one of the great capitalist system innovations, brings benefits by enabling entrepreneurs to undertake risky ventures without exposing their entire wealth to loss. But it also enables those same entrepreneurs to expose the wealth of other non-equity investors to loss, while protecting the non-invested part of their own wealth from loss. It was not always so, with numerous examples in banking history of bank shareholders having double or unlimited liability![3]

This ability for leverage and undertaking actions which expose funds provided by creditors to loss would be of little concern if those creditors were capable of assessing the risk involved and acquiring some decision or control rights which protected their position. Banks, themselves, do so when lending to companies. But this is hardly the situation applicable in the case of depositors, who are often poorly informed (and comforted by perceived government protection) and where further (equal priority, potentially diluting) deposits can be raised by the bank without prospectus or need for approval by existing depositors. Arguably, there is a fundamental flaw in the governance arrangements for banks, whereby the dominant providers of funds (depositors) have no control rights in the form of 'voice' and can exercise influence only by 'exit'. In this regard, the deletion from responsibilities of supervisors in the Basel Committee's 2010 document that '[s]upervisors should consider corporate governance as one element of depositor protection' seems a retrograde step.

But there is a potentially more significant flaw in the conventional analytical approach to corporate governance which envisages shareholders as long-term owners of banks and effective controllers of the organization. Modern stock markets have facilitated the use of 'exit' rather than 'voice' as a means for equity investors to exert influence and, with share-turnover rates often exceeding once per year, it is difficult to interpret shareholders as long-term owners exercising control rights. Here, with two exceptions, there is a disjunction with regulatory approaches, which seem to place no importance on shareholders having a role in corporate governance. The Basel Committee's suggested 14 principles, for example, do not mention shareholders, except in principle 14, where they are treated equivalently with depositors and other stakeholders. Boards are treated as effectively self-perpetuating entities with composition determined by use of nominating committees, perhaps influenced by regulators (through fit and proper requirements), but with limited scope for effective shareholder influence.

The two exceptions mentioned are worth noting. One relates to the common use of maximum shareholding limits, which reduces the potential for a dominant shareholder, which some studies (Caprio *et al.*, 2007) find is associated with better performance (but also higher risk taking). The second is the attempts to get institutional investors, such as fund managers, to exercise a 'stewardship' role on behalf of their clients as the ultimate shareholders in the bank. But as the European Commission (2010) notes, short-termism of institutional investors, the free-rider problem for shareholder activism, lack of effective shareholder power, and inadequate disclosure to enable informed decision making are all factors which create complications.

Whether these issues should lead to an empowerment of depositors in governance arrangements (such as having a right to representation on the board), or whether director's obligations should be legally respecified to place a fiduciary duty to depositors ahead of shareholders (as occurs in the case of Australian life insurance companies and their policyholders), are questions which have not been seriously addressed.

Also potentially relevant is the argument advanced by Sarra (2009) that the growth of financial derivatives has weakened the correspondence between stakeholders' legal control rights and economic interests on which traditional approaches to corporate governance are based. Shareholders and creditors can hedge their economic exposures using (respectively) equity and credit derivatives with third parties taking on such exposures but with no control rights. Alternatively, third parties may have contracts with stakeholders which effectively give them control rights in some circumstances, meaning that directors and managers may not know who the ultimate stakeholders are for whom they are operating. Where derivative transactions change incentive structures, monitoring by large creditors or shareholders which provides externalities in governance arrangements to other 'free rider' stakeholders may no longer exist. Sarra argues that the traditional approach to corporate governance (and corporate law) assumes control rights reflect incentives to monitor due to economic interest and that, without the latter, control rights can involve moral hazard. He suggests that responses to these developments should include disclosure of economic interests acquired in derivative transactions.

Whether we know enough about how to design banker remuneration arrangements is also unclear – particularly since it is not clear what types of incentives they should be aiming to generate. Alignment with (even long-term) shareholder interest is not obviously socially optimal in the presence of a financial safety net. Attempting to 'cap' bankers' pay in response to populist demands is a forlorn task and perhaps there is merit in investigating imposing some form of 'downside' risk, whereby individual wealth is at risk, so as to induce appropriate risk aversion and prudence. (Requiring remuneration to be taken in deferred, partly paid shares could be one option.) Ideally, such incentive structures might also lead to decisions to divest particular activities into institutions which operate outside the financial safety net.

A global approach to implementing internationally common regulatory arrangements and governance principles and standards, such as has been adopted through the Basel Committee and the Financial Stability Forum, may also be missing an important perspective. Quite significant differences occur in ownership structures around the world. The impact of regulation will depend upon its interaction with private governance arrangements, and different governance arrangements may be appropriate for different types of ownership arrangements, such that a 'one size fits all approach' is not appropriate. More generally, much of the empirical research evidence on bank governance stems from the US, where studies are typically conducted on bank holding companies (BHCs), raising the question of whether this particular organizational structure involves idiosyncratic governance characteristics. As Adams and Mehran (2004) note, BHCs 'often have a complicated hierarchical structure through their ownership or control of banks, lower level BHCs and other subsidiaries. Each of these subsidiaries is separately chartered and therefore has its own board.' They conclude that 'the role of the board may be different in holding companies'. In this regard, if pronouncements by multinational agencies lead to uniform international governance principles and practices, the general approach to corporate governance regulation of 'comply or explain' may be more appropriate than a 'comply or else' approach, such as suggested regarding higher capital requirements for banks with governance arrangements not preferred by regulators.

BHCs have become the dominant form for banking organizational structure in the US, reflecting growth of interstate activities and an increasing range of activities. This prompts an important question: have large, modern, financial institutions become too complex and large to be adequately governed? Risk management is particularly critical[4] and, as Davis (1999) noted:

> [t]he changing nature of employee and management activities within financial firms, away from traditional activities such as transaction processing and toward decision oriented activities in a deregulated environment, gives rise to greater potential for risk and outcomes not expected or desired by other stakeholders in those firms.

This has been aggravated by complex corporate structures. As noted by Senior Supervisors Group (2009), '[a] key lesson of the crisis, drawn by both firms and supervisors, was that complex corporate structures hindered effective contingency funding'.

In this regard, Blundell-Wignall *et al.* (2009) advance the view that banks should be required to adopt a non-operating holding company (NOHC) structure in order to achieve a separation of commercial banking from investment banking, which still allows economies in use of common shared services. Dedicated subsidiary governance arrangements, together with separate capitalization, may improve governance and ease some of the difficulties in supervising and dealing with resolution of systemically important financial institutions (SIFIs). In Australia, Macquarie Bank restructured in 2007 into a NOHC structure, providing an interesting potential case study to assess the merits of such a structure.

A further issue worth examining is whether the joint-stock form is preferable to mutual or collective style structures for operation and governance of particular banking activities. These latter institutions remove the depositor–owner agency problem (since they are one and the same) but potentially involve greater management–owner agency problems, with this incentive structure consistent with lesser risk taking, as Esty (1997) finds in a study of the US savings and loan sector. While it may be argued that their decline in importance in recent decades is a reflection of market forces weeding out inferior, non-competitive, organizational structures, their demise can also be traced to other, less sanguine, factors. Regulators have tended to be antipathetic towards them, and regulatory requirements to build capital reserves has made them ripe for expropriation via demutualization.

Conclusion

There is much on-going research and regulatory action on bank governance. But there is relatively limited evidence that knowledge gained from empirical studies, or from theory, has underpinned regulatory proposals and approaches. That perhaps reflects a lack of clear guidance from empirical work and the focus of regulators on boards and internal arrangements, rather than a focus on the nature of the underlying agency problems which the organizational structures found in modern financial institutions generate.

Theoretical studies, which recognize the interaction of the financial safety net and governance, suggest that some more fundamental issues involving organizational structure warrant addressing. These issues have assumed even greater importance following government responses to the GFC which have undermined whatever perceptions previously existed about absence of implicit government guarantees of important financial institutions. How should control and decision rights be allocated amongst providers of finance in highly levered, implicitly government-supported, financial institutions? What restrictions on the range and mix of financial activities in such institutions might generate socially optimal governance arrangements? To whom should boards of directors have primary fiduciary duties? What contingent liabilities should stakeholders in failed financial institutions have? How should regulatory requirements (capital adequacy, deposit insurance premiums, etc.) be amended to take into account differences in 'governance' characteristics across financial institutions? These are the sorts of questions warranting further attention.

Appendix

The Basel Bank Corporate Governance Principles

BCBS 122 February 2006

PRINCIPLE 1

Board members should be qualified for their positions, have a clear understanding of their role in corporate governance, and be able to exercise sound judgment about the affairs of the bank.

PRINCIPLE 2

The board of directors should approve and oversee the bank's strategic objectives and corporate values that are communicated throughout the banking organization.

PRINCIPLE 3

The board of directors should set and enforce clear lines of responsibility and accountability throughout the organization.

PRINCIPLE 4

The board should ensure that there is appropriate oversight by senior management consistent with board policy.

PRINCIPLE 5

The board and senior management should effectively utilize the work conducted by the internal audit function, external auditors, and internal control functions.

PRINCIPLE 6

The board should ensure that compensation policies and practices are consistent with the bank's corporate culture, long-term objectives and strategy, and control environment.

PRINCIPLE 7

The bank should be governed in a transparent manner.

PRINCIPLE 8

The board and senior management should understand the bank's operational structure, including where the bank operates in jurisdictions, or through structures, that impede transparency (i.e. 'know-your-structure').

BCBS 168 May 2010

PRINCIPLE 1

The board has overall responsibility for the bank, including approving and overseeing the implementation of the bank's strategic objectives, risk strategy, corporate governance, and corporate values. The board is also responsible for providing oversight of senior management. (BCBS 122 #2)

PRINCIPLE 2

Board members should be and remain qualified, including through training, for their positions. They should have a clear understanding of their role in corporate governance and be able to exercise sound and objective judgment about the affairs of the bank. (BCBS 122 #1)

PRINCIPLE 3

The board should define appropriate governance practices for its own work and have in place the means to ensure such practices are followed and periodically reviewed for improvement.

PRINCIPLE 4

In a group structure, the board of the parent company has the overall responsibility for adequate corporate governance across the group and ensuring that there are governance policies and mechanisms appropriate to the structure, business, and risks of the group and its entities.

PRINCIPLE 5

Under the direction of the board, senior management should ensure that the bank's activities are consistent with the business strategy, risk tolerance/appetite, and policies approved by the board. (BCBS122 #4)

PRINCIPLE 6

Banks should have an independent risk management function (including a chief risk officer or equivalent) with sufficient authority, stature, independence, resources, and access to the board.

PRINCIPLE 7

Risks should be identified and monitored on an on-going, firm-wide and individual entity basis, and the sophistication of the bank's risk management and internal control infrastructures should keep pace with any changes to the bank's risk profile (including its growth), and to the external risk landscape.

PRINCIPLE 8

Effective risk management requires robust internal communication within the bank about risk, both across the organization and through reporting to the board and senior management.

PRINCIPLE 9

The board and senior management should effectively utilize the work conducted by internal audit functions, external auditors, and internal control functions. (BCBS 122 #5)

PRINCIPLE 10

The board should actively oversee the compensation system's design and operation, and should monitor and review the compensation system to ensure that it operates as intended. (BCBS 122 #6)

PRINCIPLE 11

An employee's compensation should be effectively aligned with prudent risk taking: compensation should be adjusted for all types of risk; compensation outcomes should be symmetric with risk outcomes; compensation payout schedules should be sensitive to the time horizon of risks; and the mix of cash, equity, and other forms of compensation should be consistent with risk alignment. (BCBS 122 #6)

PRINCIPLE 12

The board and senior management should know and understand the bank's operational structure and the risks that it poses (i.e. 'know-your-structure'). (BCBS 122 #8)

PRINCIPLE 13

Where a bank operates through special-purpose or related structures or in jurisdictions that impede transparency or do not meet international banking standards, its board and senior management should understand the purpose, structure, and unique risks of these operations. They should also seek to mitigate the risks identified (i.e. 'understand-your-structure').

PRINCIPLE 14

The governance of the bank should be adequately transparent to its shareholders, depositors, other relevant stakeholders, and market participants. (BCBS 122 #7)

The role of supervisors

BCBS 122 Feb. 2006

1 *Supervisors should provide guidance to banks on sound corporate governance and the pro-active practices that should be in place.*
2 *Supervisors should consider corporate governance as one element of depositor protection.*
3 *Supervisors should determine whether the bank has adopted and effectively implemented sound corporate governance policies and practices.*
4 *Supervisors should assess the quality of banks' audit and control functions.*

5 *Supervisors should evaluate the effects of the bank's group structure.*
6 *Supervisors should bring to the board of directors' and management's attention problems that they detect through their supervisory efforts.*

BCBS 168 May 2010

1 *Supervisors should provide guidance to banks on expectations for sound corporate governance. (BCBS 122 #1)*
2 *Supervisors should regularly perform a comprehensive evaluation of a bank's overall corporate governance policies and practices and evaluate the bank's implementation of the principles. (BCBS 122 #3)*
3 *Supervisors should supplement their regular evaluation of a bank's corporate governance policies and practices by monitoring a combination of internal reports and prudential reports. (BCBS 122 #4)*
4 *Supervisors should require effective and timely remedial action by a bank to address material deficiencies in its corporate governance policies and practices, and should have the appropriate tools for this. (BCBS 122 #2)*
5 *Supervisors should cooperate with other relevant supervisors in other jurisdictions regarding the supervision of corporate governance policies and practices. The tools for cooperation can include memorandum of understanding, supervisory colleges, and periodic meetings among supervisors. (BCBS 122 #5)*

Notes

1 This is reflected in a focus on board characteristics in supervisory approaches and in much recent empirical literature in contrast to the Shleifer and Vishney survey, which pays scant attention to boards of directors and emphasizes legal protections and concentrated interests of financier stakeholders (owners, creditors) as mechanisms for resolving the agency problem between financiers and managers.
2 Several earlier studies of (primarily US) banker remuneration are discussed in Fahlenbrach and Stulz (2010). Significant changes in the structure and level of banker remuneration following financial deregulation (a phenomenon of interest in its own right) make these studies of less current relevance.
3 Esty (1998) finds, in a study of US banks between 1900 and 1915, that stricter liability rules reduce bank risk taking.
4 Surprisingly, given that risk taking and management is one of the key economic functions of banking, Nestor Advisors (2008) found that only 44 per cent of the boards of the 25 largest European banks by market capitalization had a specialized risk committee.

References

Adams, R.B. (2009) 'Governance and the financial crisis', *SSRN eLibrary*, available at http://ssrn.com/paper=1398583.

Adams, R.B. and Mehran, H. (2003) 'Is corporate governance different for bank holding companies?', *Economic Policy Review*, 9: 123.

Adams, R.B. and Mehran, H. (2004) *Board Structure, Banking Firm Performance and the Bank Holding Company Organizational Form*, Federal Reserve Bank of Chicago Bank Structure Conference, Chicago.

Anderson, C.W., Becher, D.A., Terry, L., and Campbell, T.L. (2004) 'Bank mergers, the market for bank CEOs, and managerial incentives', *Journal of Financial Intermediation*, 13: 6–27.

Ang, J.S., Lauterbach, B., and Schreiber, B.Z. (2001) 'Internal monitoring, regulation, and compensation of top executives in banks', *International Review of Economics & Finance*, 10: 325–35.

Ang, J.S., Lauterbach, B., and Schreiber, B.Z. (2002) 'Pay at the executive suite: how do US banks compensate their top management teams?', *Journal of Banking and Finance*, 26: 1143–63.

Ard, L. and Berg, A. (2010) *Bank Governance, Lessons from the Financial Crisis, Crisis Response, Public Policy for the Private Sector*, Washington: World Bank.

Basel Committee (1999) *Enhancing Corporate Governance for Banking Organisations*, Switzerland: Bank for International Settlements.

Basel Committee (2006) *Enhancing Corporate Governance for Banking Organisations*, BCBS 122, Switzerland: Bank for International Settlements.

BCBS (2010) *Principles for Enhancing Corporate Governance*, Consultative Document, Basel Committee on Banking Supervision.

Bebchuk, L.A. and Spamann, H. (2009) 'Regulating bankers' pay', *Georgetown Law Journal*, 98(2): 247–87 (2010).

Bebchuk, L.A., Cohen, A., and Spamann, H. (2009) 'The wages of failure: executive compensation at Bear Stearns and Lehman 2000–2008', *Yale Journal on Regulation*, 27: 257–82 (2010).

Becher, D.A. (2000) 'The valuation effects of bank mergers', *Journal of Corporate Finance*, 6: 189–214.

Beltratti, A. and Stulz, R.M. (2009) 'Why did some banks perform better during the credit crisis? A cross-country study of the impact of governance and regulation', *SSRN eLibrary*, available at http://ssrn.com/paper=1433502.

Bliss, R.T. and Rosen, R.J. (2001) 'CEO compensation and bank mergers', *Journal of Financial Economics*, 61: 107–38.

Blundell-Wignall, A., Wehinger, G., and Slovik, P. (2009) 'The elephant in the room: the need to deal with what banks do', *OECD Financial Market Trends*, 2009: 1–27.

Bollard, A. (2004) 'Promoting strong corporate governance in New Zealand banks', *Reserve Bank of New Zealand Bulletin*, 67.

Caprio, G., Laeven, L. and Levine, R. (2007) 'Governance and bank valuation', *Journal of Financial Intermediation*, 16: 584–617.

Chaigneau, P. (2010) 'Risk-shifting and the regulation of bank CEOs' compensation', *SSRN eLibrary*, available at http://ssrn.com/paper=1663923.

Chen, C.R., Steiner, T.L., and Whyte, A.M. (2006) 'Does stock option-based executive compensation induce risk-taking? An analysis of the banking industry', *Journal of Banking and Finance*, 30: 915–45.

Cheng, I.H., Hong, H., and Scheinkman, J. (2010) 'Yesterday's heroes: compensation and creative risk-taking', *ECGI Finance Working Paper*, no. 285/2010, European Corporate Governance Institute.

Cornett, M.M., McNutt, J.J., and Tehranian, H. (2009) 'Corporate governance and earnings management at large U.S. bank holding companies', *Journal of Corporate Finance*, 15: 412–30.

Crespí, R., García-Cestona, M.A., and Salas, V. (2004) 'Governance mechanisms in Spanish banks. Does ownership matter?', *Journal of Banking & Finance*, 28: 2311–30.
Davies, H. (2003) *Corporate Governance in Financial Institutions*, International Monetary Conference, Financial Services Authority, Berlin.
Davis, K, (1999) 'Governance and Australian financial institutions', *Pacific Economic Papers*, 294.
de Andres, P. and Vallelado, E. (2008) 'Corporate governance in banking: the role of the board of directors', *Journal of Banking & Finance*, 32: 2570–80.
DeYoung, R. (2007) 'Corporate governance at community banks: one size does not fit all', in B Gup (ed.), *Corporate Governance in Banking*, Cheltenham: Edward Elgar.
Douglas, J. (2010) *Bank Remuneration Rules – a Case Study of Post-GFC Regulation Reform*, 15th Melbourne Money and Finance Conference, Brighton, Victoria.
Erkens, D., Hung, M., and Matos, P. (2009) 'Corporate governance in the 2007–2008 financial crisis: evidence from financial institutions worldwide', *SSRN eLibrary*, available at http://ssrn.com/paper=1397685.
Esty, B. (1997) 'Organizational form and risk shifting in the savings and loan industry', *Journal of Financial Economics*, 44: 25–56.
Esty, B. (1998) 'The impact of contingent liability on commercial bank risk taking', *Journal of Financial Economics*, 47: 189–212.
European Commission (2010) *Corporate Governance in Financial Institutions and Remuneration Policies*, Green Paper.
Fahlenbrach, R. and. Stulz, R.M. (2010) 'Bank CEO incentives and the credit crisis', *Journal of Financial Economics*, 99: 11–26.
Fan, J.P.H. and Wiwatanakantang, Y. (2006) 'Bank ownership and governance quality in four post-crisis Asian economies', in S.-W. Nam and Chee Soon Lum (eds), *Corporate Governance of Banks in Asia – Volume 2*, Asian Development Bank Institute.
Ferreira, D., Kirchmaier, T., and Metzger, D. (2010) 'Boards of banks', *ECGI Finance Working Paper*, no. 289, European Corporate Governance Institute.
Filatotchev, I. and Boyd, B.K. (2009) 'Taking stock of corporate governance research while looking to the future', *Corporate Governance: An International Review*, 17: 257–65.
Financial Stability Board (2010) *Thematic Review on Compensation*, Peer Review Report.
Fonteyne, W. (2007) 'Cooperative banks in Europe – policy issues', *IMF Working Papers*, WP 07/159.
G20 (2009) *Leaders' Statement*, the Pittsburgh Summit, 24–25 September 2009.
G20 (2010) *The G20 Toronto Summit Declaration*, 26–27 June 2010.
John, K., Mehran, H., and Qian, Y. (2010) 'Outside monitoring and CEO compensation in the banking industry', *Journal of Corporate Finance*, 16: 383–99.
John, K., Saunders, A., and Senbet, L. (2000) 'A theory of bank regulation and management compensation', *Review of Financial Studies*, 13: 95–112.
Kirkpatrick, G. (2009) 'The corporate governance lessons from the financial crisis, *Financial Markets Trends*, 2009: 1.
Ladipo, D. and Nestor, S. (2009) *Bank Boards and the Financial Crisis: A Corporate Governance Study of the 25 Largest European Banks*, London: Nestor Advisors.
Laeven, L. and Levine, R. (2008) 'Bank governance, regulation, and risk-taking', *Journal of Financial Economics*, 93: 259–75.
Levine, R. (2004) 'The corporate governance of banks: a concise discussion of concepts and evidence', *Policy Research Working Paper 3404*, World Bank.

Macey, J.R. and O'Hara, M. (2003) 'The corporate governance of banks', *Economic Policy Review*, April: 91–107.

Mülbert, P.O. (2010) 'Corporate governance of banks after the financial crisis – theory, evidence, reforms', *SSRN eLibrary*, http://ssrn.com/paper=1448118.

Nestor Advisors (2008) *Board Profile, Structure and Practice in Large European Banks: a Comparative Corporate Governance Study*, Institute for Corporate Governance and Strategy.

Nestor Advisors (2009) 'Governance in crisis: a comparative case study of six US investment banks', *NeAd Research Note 0109*, April.

OECD (2010) *Corporate Governance and the Financial Crisis Conclusions and Emerging Good Practices to Enhance Implementation of the Principles*, OECD Directorate for Financial and Enterprise Affairs, OECD Steering Group on Corporate Governance, available at www.oecd.org/dataoecd/53/62/44679170.pdf.

Pathan, S. (2009) 'Strong boards, CEO power and bank risk-taking', *Journal of Banking and Finance*, 33: 1340–50.

Pathan, S. and Skully, M. (2010) 'Endogenously structured boards of directors in banks', *Journal of Banking and Finance*, 34: 1590–606.

Pi, L. and Timme, S.G. (1993) 'Corporate control and bank efficiency', *Journal of Banking and Finance*, 17: 515–30.

Sarra, J. (2009) 'Dancing the derivative deux pas, the financial crisis and lessons for corporate governance', *University of NSW Law Journal*, 32: 447–87.

Senior Supervisors Group (2009) *Senior Supervisors Group Report on Risk Management: Lessons from the Global Banking Crisis of 2008*, Financial Stability Board.

Shleifer, A. and Vishny, R. (1997) 'A survey of corporate governance', *The Journal of Finance*, 52: 737–83.

Simpson, W.G. and Gleason, A.E. (1999) 'Board structure, ownership, and financial distress in banking firms', *International Review of Economics and Finance*, 8: 281–92.

Taboada, A.G. (2008) *The Impact of Changes in Bank Ownership Structure around the World*, Graduate Program in Business Administration, Ohio State University.

Walker, D. (2009) *A Review of Corporate Governance in UK Banks and Other Financial Industry Entities: Final Recommendations*, HM Treasury, UK Government.

6 Moral hazard, bank governance and the protection of depositors

David G. Mayes

This chapter explores the consequences of the general increase in deposit insurance coverage that has occurred in the present crisis for bank governance, moral hazard and the viability of deposit protection in the future once countries return to 'normal times'. It argues that deposit insurance needs to be explicit but limited, that countries need to implement resolution regimes that can cut in rapidly and resolve banks without any loss of access to their funds by depositors. Furthermore, it suggests that countries need to implement 'going concern' resolution methods for larger banks, which involve the use of contingent capital so vital functions do not stop operating. Lastly, it addresses the problem of cross-border banks, suggesting that while deposit insurance may not need to be coordinated, resolution and supervision most certainly do.

The moral hazard associated with deposit insurance has come to the fore again in New Zealand with the collapse of the second largest finance company, South Canterbury Finance (SFC), at the end of August 2010 and the resulting payout by the government of nearly $2 billion under the temporary deposit guarantee scheme implemented in October 2008 at the height of the global financial crisis. Most of the impaired loans were already on the books by that date but the company was able to expand its balance sheet still further after that date as investors took comfort from the scheme and the high rates of interest being offered. Eligibility for the government scheme depended on the credit rating, a condition SFC met at the time. However, since there was no permanent deposit insurance scheme in place with matching close supervision of institutions on behalf of the insurer, the government could only find out the detailed state of the company after offering the guarantee. There is therefore a prima facie case for suggesting that New Zealand should join the rest of the OECD in having a permanent limited explicit deposit insurance scheme with its associated close supervision to provide a balance of protection for ordinary people and a curb on the moral hazard that the insurance offers. At least New Zealand has increased the level of supervision of its few remaining finance companies in the light of the near extinction of the industry.[1]

Depositor protection is normally organized through one of two schemes. It can take the form of insurance, provided by contributions by the banking system either before or after a bank failure according to rules laid down by the authorities, which normally include compulsory membership.[2] In other cases, particularly in Europe, it is provided in the form of a guarantee through a government agency, where the cost is either borne by the taxpayer or recovered from the surviving banks at a later date. In many countries, even under insurance, the scheme is also run by a government agency and, even where it is not, it is usually a government agency that determines when deposit insurance is triggered even if they have to apply to the courts to get the finding implemented. In the present crisis, however, governments have taken a much stronger role in protecting deposits and many have offered blanket guarantees. Even where such guarantees have not been offered, the coverage of insurance schemes has been raised substantially (IADI, 2010).

Previously (IADI-BIS, 2008), deposit insurance was thought to have two main objectives.[3] The first was to protect those in society who could not really be expected to assess the risk of their banks and for whom the loss of their deposit would cause serious hardship. The second was to help ensure financial stability. With the rise in coverage, it is the second reason that has become dominant and few ordinary depositors can expect to lose anything. However, this reflects a further widely held view that, in the event of crisis, depositors will not lose, irrespective of what the terms of the deposit insurance/guarantee scheme actually say. There is thus implicit systemic deposit insurance to add to the explicit schemes. While the explicit schemes may not have existed before the crisis – Australia and New Zealand, for example – the implicit schemes did (LaBrosse and Mayes, 2008) and the behaviour of the authorities in providing guarantees has borne this out in practice. Two schemes have thus been in place side by side in most countries: a limited explicit insurance directed at coping with the failure of the occasional small bank and an implicit complete guarantee that will cut in if a major bank gets into difficulty or an important segment of the market is approaching failure.[4]

What has happened in the present crisis is that the implicit schemes have become explicit and hence the role of the limited schemes has disappeared. We are now at the phase in the crisis when authorities are looking ahead to the post-crisis 'normal' world and trying to sort out what the insurance/guarantee scheme should look like. In Australia, an explicit decision had to be made in October 2011 when its scheme came up for review and it opted to continue but with a reduced coverage of $250,000 (AU$).[5] New Zealand's scheme only lasted for two years, with a transition final year for smaller institutions, and, uniquely among the OECD countries, New Zealand has opted to have no deposit insurance at all in future. This decision runs against the trend which is not simply for insurance but for a considerable expansion of insurance. In many countries, including the US and the EU, it looks as if they intend to continue in normal times with the special regime introduced for the crisis. This will not only make such insurance expensive but will tend to increase the associated moral hazard, thereby possibly increasing future financial instability. Deposit insurance is part of a comprehensive safety net and makes little sense on its own. The old system in most countries was balanced. Prima facie any new scheme needs similar balance and coherence within the regulatory framework for the banking sector as a whole. In this chapter, therefore, I discuss the factors that should affect the review of what a deposit insurance regime should look like for normal times in the light of the experience from the crisis.

Deposit insurance has always led to worries about the moral hazard it might cause, as on the one hand banks may be prepared to take more risks if they think the depositor will be saved and on the other funding will become more certain for banks as depositors will have less to fear from a bank failing and will hence have little incentive to monitor their activities.[6] Now with the change in the coverage of deposits, these problems are potentially enhanced; this chapter explores the consequences and suggests a way forward. That way forward is to return to the previous concept of suitable coverage as soon as the crisis is clearly past. However, despite all the discussion about moral hazard, it is difficult to provide estimates of the contribution the safety net and explicit parts of it make to increasing the risk propensity of banks. We have been able to observe the extensive risks that many banks took in the run-up to the crisis, which threatened their solvency, but there is usually quite a long list of contributory causes and moral hazard from the structure of deposit guarantees is only one of them. It is important to stress that it is not necessarily just that banks took increasing risks but that the authorities also relaxed their vigilance (see Demyanyk and van Hemert, 2008, and Garcia, Chapter 10 in this volume, for an analysis of both trends in the US). Furthermore, market discipline through debt markets seems to have played little role until the crisis itself when markets largely closed to the sector as a whole.

Even so, at present, most countries have two classes of banks: those that can go through ordinary resolution processes and those which have to be maintained as a going concern because, to use the traditional phraseology, they are 'too big to fail' (TBTF). There has long been pressure to end TBTF (Stern and Feldman, 2004; Mayes *et al.*, 2001) but until recently there has been little enthusiasm for seeing it through. Now it seems to be becoming the accepted way forward for handling systemically important financial institutions (SIFIs) (Herring, 2011; Hüpkes, 2011). Following new interest, particularly in the UK (Tucker, 2010, at the Bank of England; Huertas, 2010, at the FSA, for example), the aim is to achieve 'going concern resolution' for at least the parts of these institutions whose continuing operation is thought essential for the maintenance of financial stability. Such continuity may be necessary because the institution is a key market maker, or the knock-on to counterparties may be too severe or just because the direct effect on people and real activity is too large to contemplate.

New instruments for automatic recapitalization are being proposed (see Wall, 2009, for a summary, Basel Committee, 2010b, for a recent discussion paper on the issue and Claessens *et al.*, 2010 for a proposal for how this can be applied to cross-border banks) and, as in the case of CoCo bonds for the Lloyds Banking Group, actually being implemented.[7] This chapter explores these ideas in some detail as part of the basis for advocating a return to the traditional model of deposit insurance, where it is a rarely used instrument that deals with the occasional small bank failure – clearly in a world where the moral hazard is not exploited. Except in crises, the normal experience among OECD countries outside the US is that bank failures are rare. There is no reason to expect that this experience will change, especially given the strong determination by the authorities to make banks safer, through the new Basel 3 proposals, for example.

There is a further aspect of guarantees revealed by the experience in Iceland: a bank or a group of banks may be Too Big to Save in the sense that the authorities do not have the resources to mount an orderly resolution (Mayes and Liuksila, 2004). Thus, in the Icelandic case, the borrowing power of the government was insufficient to recapitalize the banks that got into difficulty. Similarly the country could not afford to pay for all the insured deposits and transfer them to another provider while waiting to be repaid from the insolvency estate. The impact of this might not have mattered had it not been the case that the Icelandic banks were vigorously seeking deposits from overseas. Where these funds were raised through branches (in the EU), the Icelandic authorities were still required to provide deposit insurance by EU regulation (Iceland being a member of the EEA [European Economic Area] where EU law also applies). Even though Iceland did not have the fiscal capacity to honour its obligations to foreign depositors, retail depositors have in the main been paid out in full by the authorities in the host countries, who have thereby succeeded to their claims against the insolvent banks.[8]

The structure of the rest of the chapter is therefore as follows: the next section considers the routes that are available for going concern resolution, and is followed by a consideration of what would need to change in the structure of the system to achieve it. The next section focuses on the key issue for depositors: how a resolution can be achieved with no material break in their access to their deposits. The following section expands the discussion to examine what problems cross-border banks pose for these developments and then the chapter moves on to consider how countries can exit from the current special arrangements for deposit guarantees and near total insurance coverage. The last section sets out in the light of this what a new framework for deposit insurance might look like.

Routes to going concern resolution

The ideal outcome from the point of view of the authorities for resolving a troubled systemic bank is that the private sector recapitalizes it without the losses being absorbed by the taxpayer and that this process, while involving losses, does not lead to any loss of confidence in the financial system as a whole.[9] The current problem when a large bank runs out of capital, especially at a time of general difficulty, when the private sector cannot find – or is unwilling to find – the necessary funds, is that governments are then faced with a choice over whether to step in and use taxpayers' money or whether to let the bank fail and risk a serious threat to confidence and hence major contraction both in the financial system in and the real economy.

The result in the present crisis has tended to be 'open bank assistance' – that is, the government has provided capital for the bank and/or purchased distressed assets from the existing shareholders. Clearly this is only one example of going concern resolution and, as in the Nordic crises, the existing shareholders may be written down to zero if the losses are sufficiently large that their capital has been exhausted. Going concern resolution only requires that the parts of the business that are vital to financial stability continue operating uninterrupted, not that their ownership remains unchanged (Hüpkes, 2004b).

Effective going concern resolution is not just a fiscal matter but also a legal one. Various events, such as being taken into administration, may generate close-out clauses in financial markets, allowing counterparties to liquidate their positions rather than get drawn into the insolvency. If this happens, it is no longer a going concern resolution. Normal business has stopped. In the US, the law provides for a short stay, so that the contracts can be transferred or maintained after recapitalization. In other jurisdictions, this is not possible and hence the method of resolution has to keep the existing legal structure – possibly by issuing new shares that dilute the value of existing shareholders to trivial proportions.

With a small bank, it is relatively straightforward to achieve this ideal outcome, providing a bank is resolved early before losses mount, simply by applying the sorts of special resolution regimes that exist in many countries. The regime, pioneered in the US, is perhaps most straightforwardly set out in the Banking Act 2009 in the UK. This was prepared after extensive consultation to correct the serious difficulties the UK encountered in the present crisis. It is therefore something like current best practice. In such a regime, there are three straightforward solutions:

- the bank is placed in insolvency and the insured depositors paid out through the deposit insurer, the insurer succeeding to the claims of the depositors;
- the deposits and other viable parts of the bank are transferred to another provider, with any unsaleable parts being left in the insolvency estate; the deposit insurer may have to contribute to any shortfall in financing and the authorities will select the acquirer on the basis of least cost to the insurer and the best chance of a viable future (all the normal conditions for registering a new bank would need to apply to the merged institution, including 'fit and proper persons' etc.);
- the parts of the bank that the authorities think can best be saved, in the sense of minimizing the loss to creditors, are placed in one or more bridge banks, run by the authorities, temporarily until they can be sold on to another provider.

The middle of these is the normal choice, while a bridge bank is used if the authorities do not have enough time. The first is likely to apply only in the case of very small institutions. (Only a handful of the 300 or so banks that were resolved in the US in the period after the Lehman Brothers' failure until mid-2011 used either a direct payout or a bridge.)[10] Only if none of these three resolution techniques can be applied does the UK system offer the option of nationalization and a move to taxpayer funding.[11]

The problem of size comes either when the deposit insurance fund cannot afford to transfer the deposits or where the bank is so complicated that organizing the split into what must be continued in the interests of the stability of the system and what can be placed in the insolvency estate cannot be done in time. In the crisis, the state stepped in. Some method has to be found in future to substitute private funds for public funds in these cases so that the bank can continue to function as a going concern. Clearly increasing the size of the insurance funds will help and the US, for example, is putting such a process in place (Murton, 2011). Changing ex post funding to ex ante funding will also be essential. The EU is intending to get member states to set up resolution funds in addition to normal insurance funds to cover the costs involved in the resolution of SIFIs (systematically important financial institutions). Such funds can be contributed by the banking sector and do not necessarily represent a state back-up for the private system. In the US, the FDIC already has powers to use its funds to facilitate a least-cost resolution and not simply to pay out the depositors.

Simply raising the funds on the market at the time of a bank's difficulty is ruled out as that will already have been tried or contemplated, possibly even with a government guarantee. Indeed failure to raise such funds is normally the source of the failure.[12] Similarly ex post capital raising is not possible as the inability (or unwillingness) of the state to provide the bridging finance is the reason for the discussion. The choice therefore is between having some sort of private guarantee or insurance that can be drawn on, probably using foreign as well as domestic sources, or deriving the capital from the creditors.[13] The advantage of the creditor recapitalization is that the funds have already been paid and there is no need for an organization to have to pay out at a stage when markets are distressed. Furthermore, there is always the danger that several banks have used the same insurer and if one or two large banks get into difficulty at the same time the insurer itself will fail (Rajan, 2009). However, as Goodhart (2010) points out, the capital to be used needs to come from outside the banking system or the banks that are the creditors may themselves get into difficulty if their assets decline in value in this manner.

Creditor recapitalization can be effectively a debt for equity swap. It could be at two levels. A simple one would be to write down a set of junior creditors to the point that the bank returns to solvency. This would be the same position that they would be in in the event of insolvency, so they would not lose further by this action.[14] A second possibility is to write them down far enough that the bank becomes adequately recapitalized. In return for this further write down, the creditors would effectively become the equity holders of the recapitalized bank. The original shareholders would be written down to zero if the bank is insolvent.[15]

However, such a scheme could also be applied even if shareholder capital had not reached zero but the bank had become undercapitalized. In this case, junior debt could be turned into equity. There is some debate about whether this should be common equity or preference shares. The existing shareholders would have their holding diluted (Huertas, 2010, provides a numerical illustration).

The key question is then what the trigger point should be and who would decide when the trigger should be pulled. The common assumption is that it should be the supervisory or regulatory authority who should decide (Brunnermeier *et al.*, 2009). However, if it were a clearly objective measure then a bank could, for example, apply to the court for the trigger to be exercised rather in the same way that a commercial firm can make an application under Chapter 11 in the US code. Since this is a capital injection, it seems appropriate that the trigger should also be a capital ratio.[16] Clearly this approach could be used more than once while there is sufficient debt available if the extent of the losses turns out to be underestimated.[17] Banks are inherently likely to take an optimistic view of the value of their own assets and accounting measures are bound to be difficult to pin down in such turbulent times.

It would appear sensible to suggest that any such recapitalization should only be undertaken with debt which was sold with this option built in. It is already the case that subordinated debt holders can be written down in this manner in Denmark and it was used in the case of Roskilde Bank in August 2008 when Danmarks Nationalbank intervened. Similarly, the new CoCo bonds that have been issued by the Lloyds Banking Group have the contingency for conversion into equity written in.[18]

One of the key issues in making such a recapitalization work is that financial markets need to accept it. If it simply generates a series of close-out clauses and effectively excludes the bank from the payments system, then clearly it will not work. The requirement at the heart of this discussion is that the resolution be performed in such a way that the bank remains a going concern. This worry that the resolution process may not permit the existing bank to continue has been raised in the context of the Norwegian legal framework (Mayes, 2009). The recapitalization needs to avoid generating any default. In other cases, it may need to avoid generating a credit rating downgrade. If the authorities offer a guarantee for the recapitalized bank, this may be avoided.

The only country that has seriously contemplated using creditors to recapitalize the bank as part of the normal insolvency process is New Zealand (Harrison *et al.*, 2007). This is now the preferred scheme and its name has been changed from Bank Creditor Recapitalization to Open Bank Resolution (RBNZ, 2011).

Hüpkes (2004b) pointed out that when a large bank gets into difficulty it is only certain parts or functions of the bank that need to be saved in order to promote continuing stability in the financial system as a whole. However, confidence is difficult to predict and the authorities are likely to be cautious and hence veer towards continuing more of the activities of the bank. Shrinking a banking group can result in a fear that other subsidiaries may be closed with further losses. While continuing the normal retail banking activity is likely to be essential, other aspects of the bank's activities may also be of systemic importance, for example, as a market maker in some aspects of derivatives.

However, tackling an institution in this way on a going concern basis implies that it can readily be divided. This I deal with in the next section and again later for cross-border banks

Changing the structure of the system

In the present crisis, the initial response of the Bank of England (Tucker, 2009) to the problem of TBTF or perhaps 'too complex or too interconnected to fail' (Knight, 2009) was that the organization should be required to restructure itself in such a way that this was no longer true. Stern and Feldman (2004) suggest a similar condition that no merger should be permitted in the banking industry unless the authorities can see how to resolve it in the case of a crisis. The initial Bank of England position was that the onus should be on the bank itself to explain how it can be restructured in some form of 'living will'. The idea initially received limited support, largely because of issues of practicality, in the sense that one cannot be sure about whether the difficulties can be overcome until the particular nature of the crisis is clear. Huertas (2010) provides a range of suggestions as to how these difficulties can be overcome.[19] Now the approach is receiving general support in the Basel negotiations (Herring, 2011), although it is a long way off implementation. However, the idea that systems should become more robust with respect to the failure of a single institution has been widely endorsed (Brunnermeier *et al.*, 2009).

One immediate concern for ease of resolution of a complex institution is the degree of separability of the various parts of the bank. With the holding company structure in the US, constituent banks are often separable. Insurance arms are often also free-standing but, where the bank runs an integrated operation, it may be very difficult to carve out parts, even if they are not separately capitalized subsidiaries. The Hüpkes approach is therefore more like a set of rules for a traditional resolution, separating out those parts of the bank that must be kept operating from those that can go into the insolvency estate. If that approach can be applied and there are no close-out concerns, then the problem is much simpler (Hüpkes, 2009).

In present circumstances, therefore, extensive restructuring may be required, especially for cross-border banks (Claessens *et al.*, 2010) before a banking group can be of a form that it can be resolved satisfactorily should a crisis loom.[20] The most important aspect of that restructuring is that the group needs to be of a form where it is capable of being managed by the various authorities using the tools which they have to hand, such as the special resolution regime. In the case of cross-border entities, such as the main banks in Australia and New Zealand, this also entails that the relevant entities can be handled by the different legal regimes in each country. Given that some countries apply universality – taking all parts of the institution into common proceedings – while others, including the US, apply territoriality – dealing with the parts separately in each jurisdiction – some explicit compromise will be required beforehand if the system is to be operable in a crisis. Claessens *et al.* (2010) offer such a solution, which they label modified universality. They regard universality as being the better of the two approaches but acknowledge that, without an agreement on it, a more pragmatic modification is required to make it tractable in present circumstances. Hüpkes (2011) is suggesting a variation of this theme, whereby the authorities agree in advance to recognize the proceedings in other jurisdictions, such that an orderly resolution can occur. The major obstacle in this process is that each country will want the resolution to be organized in a way which protects its own financial stability at minimum cost. While this can be agreed as a principle in advance, it would require very considerable confidence in the other authorities at the time to pursue it in practice in a crisis. The clear temptation will be to try to limit in advance the degree to which any outcome could be disadvantageous – what the Basel Committee (2010a) describes as 'ex ante ring fencing'. The need to renege and separate out the local operations at the time of failure 'ex post ring fencing' will then be more limited. Ex post approaches are inherently likely to be more conflictual and result in uneven treatment of creditors at the same level of priority.

A further feature of going concern resolution that is going to be needed in all resolutions and not just those of the systemically important institutions is that depositors should not have a material break in the access to their funds. Where they think that may be likely, they will run on a bank even though they may be ultimately repaid in full. Thus resolution methods need to incorporate this provision, which may well be provided most readily through a deposit insurer or guarantor. I therefore turn to this facet in the next section.

No material break in access

A major lesson from the present crisis is that people are more inclined and much more able to run on a bank than was previously thought to be the case.[21] It is no longer true that there is a break between closing time fairly early on Friday afternoon and opening time on Monday morning, during which period depositors cannot get at their accounts and during which a resolution can be performed without inconveniencing them. Now internet access and EFTPOS makes it possible to access one's account at any time of day or night and it is only a small proportion of customers who need to visit the bank personally in order to make a substantial withdrawal. However, closing a fairly substantial account, even up to the previous EU coverage ceiling of €20,000, would require a physical presence, even if the transaction is then electronic and not a payout in cash.

Traditional deposit protection focuses on removing the credit risk but, in the modern environment, loss of liquidity could also have significant effects on people after only a few days (Kaufman, 2007). Hence people will run on the bank even if there is no prospect of a loss of their funds and they only fear a problem in access. Such a problem only needs to be possible to generate the run; it might not occur in practice. In the EU, until recently, they would have every reason for such a run, as the time allowed for a deposit payout was 90 days and this could be renewed twice in the face of difficulty. Deposit insurers are therefore now trying to make sure that there is no material break in service should a bank fail. There is no accepted definition of what a material break is. In New Zealand, operation is supposed to resume in the 'value day' and other countries aim to resolve the problem either overnight or over a weekend. In the EU, it has now been reduced to 20 days, although there is pressure to move to five days (European Commission, 2010). In the US, it is realistic to be confident of a swift solution because there is considerable experience of rapid access in the case of smaller banks. Other administrations have no such track record and so depositors could prove more sceptical unless a very convincing procedure is put in place for handling such problems in the future.

This need for speed has considerable implications for the nature of the resolution process for banks. Insured deposits need to be identifiable at the end of any day so that accounts can be divided (where necessary) into insured and uninsured portions, any aggregation across accounts for a single holder performed, etc.[22] Similarly the means of transferring deposits must be clearly established so that it can take place smoothly at the appointed time. This requires considerable prepositioning in the sense of the nature of bank computer systems. Small issues, such as whether, if account numbers change, payments into the previous number will still be picked up and rerouted without delay, all have to be addressed. Since these changes cannot be implemented only if the bank gets into difficulty, they have to be continuing characteristics of all banks' systems. The period of 2–3 months that the authorities hope they will have in preparing a resolution relate to establishing the problem, valuing the bank and finding suitable providers to take on the deposits and other parts of the bank and not to trying to establish the facility for making a resolution itself. Even hoping to complete due diligence in such a period is a tough ambition and almost certainly acquirers will be in for some surprises after the event when it is accomplished so rapidly. If such smooth transitions cannot be made, the political attractiveness of open bank assistance or nationalization increases, with its associated moral hazard.

Cross-border concerns

The systems of deposit insurance and the associated resolution and regulatory frameworks are national and are not well designed to handle financial institutions that run across borders unless the component parts are effectively separate legal organizations that can operate on their own and can be resolved largely independently. Where foreign operations are small, the fact that there are considerable difficulties in getting resolution regimes to work together can be coped with, albeit with various legal counterclaims after the event or the home country participants absorbing the claims. However, if the institutions are of significance in more than one country, then the problems become serious. Each country needs to be able to manage the concerns for its domestic financial stability which stem from these organizations (Brunnermeier *et al.*, 2009, set out the issues very clearly).

Deposit insurance is thus part of a wider concern. It is the problems with trying to organize a resolution that present the difficulty, rather than that of trying to coordinate the deposit insurance funds. While in the case of Fortis in October 2008, the Dutch and Belgian authorities did not agree on the best way forward, the fact that the Dutch authorities could step in and purchase the operations in their jurisdiction solved the crisis. They could manage this not simply because the Dutch operations were subsidiaries but because they were distinct free-standing operations. ABN-AMRO, for example, which had been purchased by Fortis as part of a consortium purchase led by the Royal Bank of Scotland only the year before, had not been integrated into the rest of the group. Nationalization of course removed the need to use deposit insurance as the whole bank was acquired but deposit insurance would not have been a problem in this regard as the insurance did not run across borders. It was ownership of the bank that ran across borders, rather than bank operations.

The problem with the Icelandic banks was that it was the operations that ran across borders. The Icelandic banks, particularly Landsbanki through Icesave, were soliciting deposits from foreign countries, not to run matching lending activities in those countries but to finance their general operations. There was thus no self-sufficient operating entity that could readily be acquired even if this had been legally possible. In the case of Heritable Bank, a Landsbanki subsidiary, and Kaupthing, Singer and Friedlander's Edge business (both in the UK), however, the banking operations could be transferred to ING Direct because they were free-standing. As internet banking operations, they were somewhat easier to transfer and the deposit insurer (the Financial Services Compensation Scheme) could finance the transfer of insured deposits. The UK government decided that it would protect all deposits (i.e. those above the £50,000 coverage limit) to preserve financial stability and hence there was no need to institute any complex splitting of accounts and to treat the various categories of depositors differently.

The EU is in a special position with deposit insurance because it wishes to encourage financial integration and hence allows branches of banks registered elsewhere in the EU/EEA to operate under the prudential supervision and deposit insurance of their home country (with the option of topping up to the level of the host country through the deposit insurer (Ayadi and Lastra, 2010). Other jurisdictions insist that all significant operations are locally incorporated and normally supervise branches as well as subsidiaries.[23] In the New Zealand case mentioned earlier, not only must all banks of systemic importance be locally incorporated and capitalized but they must be capable of operating on their own within the value day, should the need arise (RBNZ, 2006).[24]

It is really the experience in Iceland that has shown the weakness of the EU system. The Icelandic banks were able to operate on a scale completely inconsistent with any possibility that their insurance fund could pay out in the event of a correlated shock – given the size, interconnection and leverage of the three main banks, the chances were that a shock to any one of them would have brought the whole system into question. Furthermore, the country was too small relative to the banks to be able to offer any other going concern resolution to the three banks. What they were able to do was keep the domestic banking system in being by transferring domestic deposits and matching performing domestic assets into new banks and leaving foreign deposits and the remaining assets and liabilities in the insolvency estates. However, in order to cover for the inability to deliver the insurance to foreign depositors that had been taken out, they instituted depositor preference. Thereby depositors ranked above other creditors in the resolution and the chances are that this will enable the depositors to be paid in full – eventually.[25] In the meantime, the governments in the two countries most affected (the Netherlands and the UK) have paid out the retail depositors from their own funds and have succeeded to the claims of the insured depositors in the insolvency proceedings in Iceland.

In the circumstances, this is a rather ingenious 'solution' and will confirm in retail depositors' minds that effectively all deposits are insured in a crisis. Iceland was also a little unusual in that large-scale depositors formed about two thirds of total domestic deposits – in part perhaps because, as a small country, Iceland offered little other liquid domestic opportunity for such funds. The deposit guarantees/depositor preferences therefore apply to these depositors as well. Indeed such an arrangement would be clearly necessary, otherwise the business sector might have come to a halt if all such deposits were caught up in the insolvency. The belief in who is likely to be rescued in these extreme circumstances is therefore likely to stretch widely.

Exiting the special arrangements

Neither Australia nor New Zealand had deposit insurance in place at the start of the present crisis, although there were active plans in Australia. As a result, when the crisis struck, much more extensive guarantees were thought necessary to instil the necessary confidence in the financial system. These took two forms: guarantees for new wholesale borrowing and deposit guarantees. There were $1 million deposit guarantees in Australia and New Zealand, both provided by the government, although this had to be paid for by the larger banks in New Zealand, as was the case for deposits and wholesale funding over $1 million in Australia. These schemes were temporary in character and needed to be changed if a longer-term scheme were required. The New Zealand scheme was only offered to institutions with a credit rating of BB or above.

Exit clearly has to be timed carefully as it needs to occur when the crisis is past and no one thinks the banks are under threat, although deposit guarantees can be brought back in very rapidly if confidence falls again. There is a clear problem for troubled banks. If deposit guarantees exist, they can at least rely on those deposits and stand a better chance of raising other funding. Ending of the guarantees would simply result in the demise of the marginal banks just before the guarantee expired. The authorities therefore need to resolve any such marginal banks first. They either have to find sufficient capital that the ratings of the troubled banks rise and people believe them sound or they will have to close in an orderly manner, which could involve a merger or acquisition of the relevant deposits by another provider. The wholesale guarantees for new funds were ended in both countries after two years, although of course they continue for any covered funds for the term of the contracts. In New Zealand, the deposit insurance scheme was ended after two years for the banks but remains for a further year for the more lowly rated non-banks.

The decline of the finance companies, the increase in regulatory requirements and the ending of deposit insurance will mean that there will be very few institutions in New Zealand providing the riskier aspects of finance, such as secondary loans on property, as the deposit-taking finance company sector has largely disappeared through failure. Small institutions are singularly ill-suited to this sector as many of the higher-risk projects are quite large and problems in the property market tend to be correlated; hence ample capital cushions and diversification are required. In the US and some other jurisdictions, insurance premia for banks depend on the risk of the institution, so obtaining deposits becomes more expensive because of the higher premium that has to be paid. This may have relatively little impact on the cost of funds as such institutions have in any case to pay risk premia to depositors with such insurance (although it is sometimes argued that retail interest rates offered do not fully incorporate the risk or lenders would be frightened off).

There also has to be some degree of coordination in exit, especially where banks or deposits can run across borders. As the crisis winds down, confidence only returns slowly so people are likely to follow opportunities for greater safety, at least in the short run, even if there is a degree of interest cost to doing so. When there was little threat in Europe, then countries could operate with differing levels of insurance and little arbitrage as a result. Now it is less clear and in any case the agreement on minimum levels is EU-wide and any agreement to lower them would have to be EU-wide as well. Outside Europe, there is no particular need for the smaller countries to wait for the large ones to act if they have fairly independent financial markets.

A new framework for deposit insurance

Whereas most advanced countries could return to a system suitable for normal times outside crises simply by reverting to an improved version of their previous deposit insurance arrangements once the crisis is over, this does not apply to Australia and New Zealand, who had no such insurance. Insurance coverage does not have to be extensive for almost all depositors to be fully covered. Even with \$25,000 coverage per bank, a depositor could have \$100,000 covered by placing the funds in four banks. The big four banks in Australia already have what can be described as an implicit guarantee from the government. In those circumstances, an insurance scheme would have a different meaning.[26] The Australian guarantee would effectively apply to the New Zealand subsidiaries even though they might not be directly covered. Reputation risk would suggest that the parent bank could not let the subsidiaries fail if they are to survive themselves. If the Australian authorities decide to keep the parent going through ‘going concern resolution’ if the whole bank were in trouble, this would be likely to include the subsidiaries, especially since their structure has a strong element of ex ante ring fencing and hence they could be resolved separately.

In a sense, therefore, New Zealand is bound to be a free rider on the Australian system on the one hand or sufferer from Australian problems on the other. Currently the New Zealand regulatory and resolution system is rather different from that in Australia. While the New Zealand system has been geared towards avoiding providing any public finance for the financial system in the event of failure, it is not so clear what would be done in Australia, with the likelihood being that some such finance would be provided. This provides a prima facie basis for difficulty as the resolution of the New Zealand subsidiaries would be based on creditor recapitalization, while the Australian taxpayer would be keeping the parent in business.

If the large banks do not need deposit insurance because they will be 'bailed out' in a different manner, either through contingent capital or other forms of government intervention, then an insurance scheme would only apply to banks that are small enough that they could be allowed to enter insolvency or undergo transfers of deposits and other assets and liabilities through the resolution process. Both classes of bank need to pay for their protection in an equitable manner so that one class is not disadvantaged compared to the other. Where the contingent capital is provided through the market, this is automatic in the case of large banks[27] but if this comes through some form of government guarantee and requirement to hold more capital the correct pricing is less obvious. The government guarantee ensures that creditors will not lose in the case of a failure – which is certainly a prima facie moral hazard. That will also entail that large banks with the same risk in their business as a smaller bank will nevertheless have a lower cost of finance. In sum, this may be equitable by coincidence but the system is unlikely to have been designed with this in mind.

If only the small banks are in the insurance system, then there is a danger of underfunding of deposit insurance unless premia are to be quite high. In many funds, banks do not really pay a premium but have to build the fund up to a level that is expected to provide enough cover. Contributions will be in proportion to the deposits insured and there will be a contributions holiday, or at least contributions will be lowered to the level where they simply meet the deposit insurer's on-going costs, once the fund reaches the target level. In the US, despite the implicit guarantee for the largest banks, nevertheless all banks contribute to the scheme and this ensures its viability, even through the difficulties of the present crisis.[28]

If the large banks were excluded from a deposit insurance scheme in Australia, the effect would be considerable. (Kiwibank would presumably be excluded in New Zealand as well, as the government as owner would be expected to recapitalize the bank in the event of difficulty as that is likely to be the least-cost route. Insurance is therefore not relevant.) Interestingly enough, the guarantee implemented in the crisis in New Zealand was free for the small banks but the large banks had to pay for it on a basis that roughly covered the expected risk.[29]

In this new world, the attempt to reduce moral hazard by 'constructive' ambiguity largely disappears. It is clear what will happen to banks of all sizes if they face an idiosyncratic failure. The smaller banks will go through the normal resolution regime, shareholders will be wiped out, insured depositors made whole with the insurance fund succeeding to their claims and creditors will eventually be paid out according to the normal insolvency process. Systemic banks on the other hand will be allowed to continue their key operations, using either contingent capital or state support. What has become clear is that prudent use of deposit insurance funds to facilitate a resolution would be sensible to prevent even higher losses in the event of a disorderly resolution. Not only is the franchise value not lost and the receiver costs avoided but the potential much large spillovers to other institutions are avoided. If the threat to the system is general, then the reaction becomes more difficult to judge.

In the crisis, some countries issued blanket guarantees, some increased deposit insurance coverage markedly, while others simply bailed out the troubled banks. If there is no indication which of these routes will be followed next time, then the ambiguity returns. It even applies to individual institutions, as the chances are that the scale of a crisis may be mis-estimated. When the first small banks become insolvent, the insurance fund can cope and ordinary procedures can be followed. At some point, as the numbers mount, the authorities will become worried that there will be a systemic problem and more extensive guarantees will be issued. While shortly before the crisis it may be possible to rank banks in terms of when they might fail, this would not apply to any longer-term guarantees that are arranged.

The Swiss authorities (Hüpkes, 2004a) are among the only ones to recognize that the structure of their banking system, with two very large banks, Credit Suisse and UBS, might mean that the deposit insurer was unable to cope with the failure. Thus, while the system implemented in Switzerland in 2004 provided for the writing down of claims in the manner described above and advocated in Mayes *et al.* (2001), an absolute limit of CHF4 billion was placed on the payout. If this limit were reached, then a haircut would be placed on all insured deposits to limit the payout to the maximum. The limit has since been raised to CHF6 billion in the course of the crisis.

There is no reason why the Icelandic problems should recur in the EU if the countries were to set up a more Europe-wide system so as to eliminate the problem of large banks backed by small countries with limited ability to finance deposit insurance or deposit guarantee schemes. However, progress in this direction is slow. While more harmonization in the national systems is suggested (European Commission, 2010),[30] the idea that there should be EU-level insurance matched with EU-level supervision, still less EU-level regulation has received very little support. The Federal Deposit Insurance Corporation (FDIC) was set up in 1935 after the finding in the US that the previous state deposit insurance schemes could not cope. Even if there were some sort of reinsurance scheme, so that smaller schemes could lay off the risk across the rest of the area, the system might be viable. However, it would not solve the issue that a country could not guarantee its own financial stability as branches of foreign banks within its territory would still be regulated, supervised and resolved by the home country, whose interests might be very different.

The process of negotiating a new deposit guarantee directive is at a fairly advanced stage and may be completed by the end of 2011. The EU scheme (European Commission, 2010) is based on the idea that the member countries would cooperate but that there would be a funding cushion to handle large problems. There is no suggestion as yet that insurance coverage should return to pre-crisis levels, so the costs of important failures could be considerable. By offering a state back-up to deposit insurance funds in these circumstances, the EU is building in an incentive to take greater risks – given the much more comprehensive capital and liquidity buffers that are being planned for the EU's implementation of 'Basel 3'.

The problem with a non-credible insurance scheme in a small country is that, although it will work well in normal times with the occasional failure of a small bank, it is not going to be believable with much smaller banking problems than would be the case in a larger country. Thus the point at which state intervention and guarantees are required occurs much earlier. Ironically, this may increase the moral hazard as it removes the prospective resolution from a technical set of rules to be followed by the appropriate agency whose actions can be audited after the event for compliance with the rule. It also increases the chance that the problem will be allowed to mount and action will be delayed when the authorities realize their systems will not be able to cope.

The only difference to this outcome would occur if recapitalization methods are required that automatically write down the existing shareholders and implement a debt for equity swap for sufficient of the bondholders that the bank becomes healthy again. The interesting feature of such recapitalizations for cross-border banks (indeed as for any other bank) is that the bondholders will not necessarily be domestic and hence the recapitalization is likely to run across borders even without any attempt by governments to agree some burden sharing.

A future system would therefore seem to need at least seven ingredients.

- It would need to be explicit and limited in coverage so that there is a believable disincentive to risk taking, and manageable costs of failure.
- It would need to be funded up front and the size of the funds and any back-up arrangement through the state would need to be such that it could credibly cover the risks.
- It would relate to idiosyncratic failures in individual banks and not the looming failure of the whole banking system.
- It would cover a wide range of deposit takers.
- It would be accompanied by a special resolution regime that enabled speedy and smooth resolution of banks before losses mounted too far, using tools such as those set out in the UK Banking Act 2009 and avoiding close-outs.
- It would have a treatment of contingent capital such that going concern resolutions were possible for larger banks without using government funds.

- It would need careful prepositioning so that depositors do not have any material break in access to their funds and it would be implemented as soon as the crisis appeared to have passed and all existing troubled banks had been addressed.

For a deposit insurance system to work in normal times, even for large banks, the costs need to be manageable. This can be achieved by a combination of early intervention, contingent capital, adequate funding, limited coverage and depositor preference. Depositor preference ensures that the deposit insurance fund and the uninsured part of deposits will in most cases be paid out eventually from the insolvency estate. This seems likely even in the case of the failed Icelandic banks, where deposits were several times Iceland's GDP.

Notes

1 The non-bank deposit takers came under the supervision of the Reserve Bank as a result of the passing of the Reserve Bank Amendment Act on 3 September 2008. The regulations governing these institutions have come into force during 2009 and 2010 so the crisis measures came into effect before there was time to implement the new regime.

2 Risk-weighted contributions are rare and as a result there is an implicit subsidy from the less to the more risky banks, which might in itself encourage risk taking and act as a moral hazard. It is, therefore, probably not correct to view these contributions as premiums but simply as amounts designed to cumulate to a fund that will be large enough to cover the general run of claims without an immediate call for further funds, either from the banks or the taxpayer.

3 This is set out in the first of the Core Principles for best practice in deposit insurance developed jointly by IADI and the BIS.

4 Modern comprehensive deposit insurance stems from the creation of the Federal Deposit Insurance Corporation (FDIC) in the US in 1935 following the extent of the banking collapse in the Great Crash.

5 Australia was already addressing the issue before the crisis and a careful review of the pros and cons of guarantees across the whole of the financial sector had been undertaken in the Davis report (Davis, 2004).

6 There is in any case little evidence that retail depositors monitor banks even when there is an incentive to do so, as in New Zealand where there was no insurance (Wilson *et al.*, 2012) or the UK where there was coinsurance. (After the first £2,000, the next £33,000 was only 90 per cent covered, £35,000 being the coverage limit.) This was revealed clearly in the run on Northern Rock in August 2007 (Mayes and Wood, 2008) after which coinsurance has been abandoned, as the threat of a run undermines the financial stability objective of deposit insurance.

7 The conversion of these bonds is triggered when Tier 1 capital falls below 5 per cent.

8 Depositors have priority in the claims on the insolvency estate as a result of emergency legislation introduced in the crisis, so it is likely that all will be repaid in full – eventually.

9 Normally this is achieved using the priority ranking for insolvency, so that the shareholders bear the first loss, then the junior unsecured creditors, then the senior creditors and, so on.

10 There are other crucial aspects to such resolutions that do not lie at the heart of the present discussion but must be borne in mind. The most important of these is that deposits have to be transferred to a new provider as a working system. It may be

that all the information can be transferred from the failing bank's computer system to that of the acquirer and that the depositors can obtain access to their accounts but often it is not possible to dispense with either the failing bank's systems or many of its physical branches. This may mean that the residual bank has to run services for the transferred part of the bank until a final organization of such services can be achieved.

11 In the UK, as in many other countries, the deposit insurance is provided through the banks themselves and not through the government. Where government guarantee schemes are in place, there is an immediate call on the taxpayer as soon as any bank fails, although much of the payment may be recovered from the insolvency estate or the sale of assets in the resolution itself. Where the industry-backed insurer does not have prefunding or insufficient funding, then the taxpayer will also be called on initially, as in the UK.

12 It is of course a lack of liquidity that tends to put a sudden stop to a bank's activities but the exercise of the Lender of Last Resort Function of the central bank should normally mean that a bank that is solvent but illiquid can get access to the necessary funds to honour its payment obligations.

13 See Squam Lake Working Group (2009) and Wall (2009) for a recent exposition of the options.

14 This is by no means a new issue. Aghion *et al.* (1992) suggest it as the normal way to handle insolvency and Mayes *et al.* (2001) explore it as one of a number of ways to effect a bank resolution without involving public funds.

15 See Harrison *et al.* (2007) for a discussion of how this might be applied.

16 The drawback to using the capital ratio is that it is a lagging indicator of the trouble in the bank, especially since valuations are only periodic, and supervisors prefer to act earlier on a broader range of indicators, such as the US CAMELS (Mayes, 2009).

17 Mayes *et al.* (2001) assume that this form of recapitalization would be a routine option but others argue that it should only be used if financial stability is threatened (Squam Lake Working Group, 2009).

18 Tier 1 capital falls below 5 per cent.

19 In particular, he distinguishes between plans to turn a bank round before it reaches the point where regulators take its management over, which he labels 'recovery plans', and plans for when it is taken over, which he labels 'resolution plans'. The authorities need to be convinced that both are workable. If taking the institution into statutory management would generate a close-out and hence a disorderly resolution, only a recovery plan would meet the objective of maintaining financial stability.

20 Of the 30 largest international financial institutions considered by Claessens *et al.* (2010), all have over 100 subsidiaries, more than half have over 500 and three more than 2,000. Organizing them so that they can readily be handled in the event of difficulty clearly requires considerable simplification.

21 Pictures of the queues outside Northern Rock in the UK are frequently shown in the media.

22 In the UK, this is described as the 'single customer view'.

23 The EU also seeks to apply universality in resolution so that there is a single set of proceedings rather than the 'territoriality' applied in the US, which separates the proceedings in each jurisdiction.

24 New Zealand and Australia are heavily economically and financially integrated, in many respects more so than in the EU.

25 EU regulation requires that domestic and foreign depositors are treated equally (unlike the domestic depositor preference in Australia). Iceland therefore tried to ensure that domestic and foreign depositors would be paid out in full, although foreign depositors were likely to have a break in the access to their funds. Iceland pushed through emergency legislation on 6 October 2008, just before the banks failed, both to institute

depositor preference and to give the authorities the powers necessary to implement the sweeping resolutions.

26 Indeed it is not clear from the proposals in Australia whether the government sees the resolution of any of the large banks as being funded by the industry or the taxpayer.

27 Although we have seen persistent mispricing of risk in the run-up to the present crisis.

28 The FDIC's fund did become negative at the height of the crisis but is expected to become positive again in 2012, although it will take a number of years to return to full capitalization (Murton, 2011).

29 Some banks – Deutsche Bank, for example – do not need New Zealand deposit insurance as New Zealand depositors are covered by the home country insurance. Although one might realistically worry if the German scheme could cope with the failure of Deutsche Bank, more likely some other route would be found for saving such an icon.

30 The European Commission proposal suggests that the idea of funds at a European level could be pursued in 2014. However, in the meantime, the main purpose of the proposal is to suggest that each EU country should have to set up resolution funds that would be available in the event of a major failure. The implication is that such funds would be raised from banks and hence the full moral hazard would not be built into the design of the system.

References

Aghion, P., Hart, O. and Moore, J. (1992) 'The economics of bankruptcy reform', *Journal of Law, Economics and Organization*, 8: 523–46.

Ayadi, R. and Lastra, R. (2010) 'Proposals for reforming deposit guarantee schemes in Europe', *Journal of Banking Regulation*, 11(3): 210–22.

Basel Committee on Banking Supervision (2010a) *Report and Recommendations of the Cross-Border Bank Resolution Group*, Basel: Bank for International Settlements.

Basel Committee on Banking Supervision (2010b) *Proposal to Ensure the Loss Absorbency of Regulatory Capital at the Point of Non-Viability*, Consultative Document, August, Basel: Bank for International Settlements.

Brunnermeier, M., Crockett, A., Goodhart, C., Persaud, A. and Shin, H.S. (2009) *The Fundamental Principles of Financial Regulation*, 11th Geneva Papers on the World Economy, available at http://voxeu.org/index.Php?q=node/2796.

Claessens, S., Herring, R. and Schoenmaker, D. (2010) *A Safer World Financial System: Improving the Resolution of Systemic Institutions*, Geneva Report on the World Economy 14, London: CEPR.

Davis, K. (2004) *Study of Financial System Guarantees*, Canberra: The Treasury, available at http://fsgstudy.treasury.gov.au/content/davis_report.asp.

Demyanyk, Y. and van Hemert, O. (2008) *Understanding the Subprime Mortgage Crisis*, mimeo, Federal Reserve Bank of St Louis.

European Commission (2010) *Bank Resolution Funds*, Brussels, 26/5/2010, COM(2010) 254 final, available at http://ec.europa.eu/internal_market/bank/docs/crisis-management/funds/com 2010_254_en.pdf.

Goodhart, C.A.E. (2010) 'Are CoCos from cloud cuckoo-land?', *Central Banking*, 21(1): 29–33.

Harrison, I.G, Anderson, A. and Twaddle, J. (2007) 'Pre-positioning for effective resolution of bank failures', *Journal of Financial Stability*, 3(4): 324–41.

Herring, R.J. (2011) *The Central Role of Resolution in Dealing with Systemically Important Financial Institutions*, IADI Research Conference, BIS, 8–9 June.

Huertas, T. (2010) *The Road to Better Resolution: from Bail-out to Bail-in*, revised version of a paper delivered to the conference on 'The Euro Area and the Financial Crisis', National Bank of Slovakia, 6 September.

Hüpkes, E. (2004a) 'Learning lessons and implementing a new approach to bank insolvency resolution in Switzerland', in D. Mayes and A. Liuksila (eds), *Who Pays for Bank Insolvency*?, pp. 242–71, Basingstoke: Palgrave-Macmillan.

Hüpkes, E. (2004b) 'Protect functions, not institutions', *The Financial Regulator*, 9: 43–9.

Hüpkes, E. (2009) 'Resolving crises in global financial institutions: the functional approach revisited', in J.R. LaBrosse, R. Olivares-Caminal and D. Singh (eds), *Financial Crisis Management and Bank Resolution*, pp. 291–302, London: Informa.

Hüpkes, E. (2011) *The Role of Deposit Protection and Resolution Policy in Promoting Financial Stability*, IADI Research Conference, BIS, 8–9 June.

IADI (2010) *Discussion Paper on Cross Border Deposit Insurance Issues Raised by the Global Financial Crisis*, Basel: BIS.

IADI-BIS (2008) *Core Principles for Effective Deposit Insurance Systems*, Basel: BIS, available at www.iadi.org/NewsRelease/JWGDI%20CBRG%20core%20principles_18_June.pdf.

Kaufman, G. (2007) 'Using efficient bank insolvency resolution to solve the deposit insurance problem', in A. Campbell, R. LaBrosse, D. Mayes and D. Singh (eds), *Deposit Insurance*, pp. 198–211, Basingstoke: Palgrave-Macmillan.

Knight, M.D. (2009) 'Mitigating moral hazard in dealing with problem financial institutions: too big to fail? Too complex to fail? Too interconnected to fail?', in J.R. LaBrosse, R. Olivares-Caminal and D. Singh (eds), *Financial Crisis Management and Bank Resolution*, pp. 257–68, London: Informa.

LaBrosse, R. and Mayes, D.G. (2007) 'Promoting financial stability through effective depositor protection: the case for explicit limited deposit insurance', in A. Campbell, R. LaBrosse, D. Mayes and D. Singh (eds), *Deposit Insurance*, pp. 1–39, Basingstoke: Palgrave-Macmillan.

Mayes, D.G. (2009) 'Banking crisis resolution policy – lessons from recent experience – which elements are needed for robust and efficient crisis resolution?', *CESifo Working Paper 2823*, October.

Mayes, D. and Liuksila, A. (2004) *Who Pays for Bank Insolvency*?, Basingstoke: Palgrave-Macmillan.

Mayes, D.G. and Wood, G.E. (2008) 'Lessons from the Northern Rock episode', *Economie Internationale*, 114: 5–27.

Mayes, D.G., Halme, L. and Liuksila, A. (2001) *Improving Banking Supervision*, Basingstoke: Palgrave.

Murton, A. (2011) *Deposit Insurance and Bank Resolution Reforms Adopted in Response to the Crisis*, IADI Research Conference, BIS, 8–9 June.

Rajan, R. (2009) 'Cycle-proof regulation', *The Economist*, April 8, available at www.economist.com/businessfinance/displayStory.cfm?story_id=13446173.

Reserve Bank of New Zealand (2006) *Outsourcing Policy*, Financial Stability Department Document BS11.

Reserve Bank of New Zealand (2011) *Consultation Document: Pre-positioning for Open Bank Resolution (OBR)*, March, available at www.rbnz.govt.nz/finstab/banking/4335146.pdf.

Squam Lake Working Group (2009) *An Expedited Resolution Mechanism for Distressed Financial Firms: Regulatory Hybrid Securities*, Council on Foreign Relations

Press, April, available at www.cfr.org/content/publications/attachments/Squam_Lake_Working_Paper3.pdf.

Stern, G. and Feldman, R. (2004) *Too Big to Fail*, Washington, DC: Brookings Institution.

Tucker, P. (2009) *The Debate on Financial System Resilience: Macroprudential Instruments*, Barclays Annual Lecture, London.

Tucker, P. (2010) *Resolution of Large and Complex Financial Institutions: The Big Issues*, European Commission Conference on Crisis Management, Brussels, 19 March, available at www.bankofengland.co.uk/publications/speeches/2010/speech431.pdf.

Wall, L.D. (2009) *Prudential Discipline for Financial Firms: Micro, Macro, and Market Regimes*, paper presented at the Conference on Global Financial Crisis: Financial Sector Reform and Regulation, ADBI, Tokyo, 21–23 July.

Wilson, W.R., Rose, L.C. and Pinfold, J.F. (2012) 'Moderating risk in New Zealand retail banks: disclosure as an alternative regulatory regime', *Journal of Banking Regulation*, 13(1): 4–23.

COMMENTS BY GEOF MORTLOCK

In this chapter, David Mayes discusses a number of the elements required to respond to the distress of a bank or similar financial institution. In particular, he discusses deposit insurance arrangements, financial distress resolution frameworks for large or complex banks and cross-border financial distress resolution. My comments focus on a number of elements required for an effective response to distress in a financial institution. Many of these observations are similar to those identified in the chapter. I draw on the work under way in Australia and internationally.

Key elements required for effective bank resolution

The key elements required for an effective response to financial distress in a bank include:

- clear and well thought-through policy objectives and public policy principles for financial distress resolution that are transparent and well understood by all relevant stakeholders;
- robust legal powers that enable the resolution authority to implement a range of financial distress resolutions with legal certainty;
- a government agency with clear responsibility for financial distress resolution;
- a framework for coordinating the actions of all relevant government agencies;
- strategies for resolving bank distress that take into account the systemic impact of a failure, including options for closing a bank in ways that minimize disruption to depositors and other bank customers, and options that preserve core elements of a distressed bank, either in its existing form or in a restructured form;

- funding arrangements that provide credible, viable and sustainable resolutions, with minimal distortions to banking system efficiency and with minimum moral hazard risk; and
- a framework for resolving banks with cross-border operations in ways that minimize adverse systemic impacts in all the relevant jurisdictions in which the bank operates, and that facilitate a whole-of-group resolution.

I comment briefly on each of these elements.

Statutory objectives

The starting point for effective financial distress resolution is the need for clear and well-considered objectives. These should be transparent and desirably be included in the relevant legislation as an anchor for the use of resolution powers. Well-defined objectives are the foundation for a coherent and focused response to financial distress. They can also help to reduce the risk of subsequent legal challenge.

Financial distress resolution objectives would generally include:

- maintaining the stability of the financial system;
- protecting small depositors from loss;
- providing all depositors and those reliant on committed credit facilities with prompt access to at least a proportion of their funds;
- minimizing moral hazard risk and maintaining market discipline; and
- minimizing taxpayer risk.

While most of these objectives are complementary, there are potential or actual conflicts between some of them – such as minimizing losses for depositors and minimizing moral hazard. Striking an appropriate balance between these objectives is always challenging.

Legal powers

Robust legal powers are essential for effective bank distress resolution. There needs to be a high level of clarity and certainty around the powers, with clear specification of the purposes for which powers may be exercised and the grounds on which they may be exercised.

Legal powers may be required to implement financial distress resolution in respect of a bank, its holding company, its subsidiaries and the wider group of which it is part. This is particularly important in the case of complex banking groups, where essential functions and business lines are performed in a bank's holding company or subsidiaries, and where a group-wide resolution may be needed. Legal powers need to provide for early intervention, given that the earlier the intervention occurs the more likely it is that the resolution objectives will be achieved, and costs and losses minimized.

Legal powers will vary depending on the country in question, its institutional arrangements, and its legal and constitutional infrastructure. However, at a generic level, these are likely to include powers:

- to investigate a bank and its banking group, including through the appointment of specialist experts where appropriate;
- to give binding directions to the bank and its group, including in respect of potentially removing and replacing the board and/or management, suspending or discontinuing specified types of business, implementing holding actions to prevent further deterioration, measures to facilitate recapitalization where practicable, deferral of public disclosures for a short period pending the determination of the resolution and pre-positioning for restructuring measures;
- to place the bank and its group into statutory management or its equivalent to assume control of the bank and its group in order to implement a resolution – either closed or open. Statutory management needs to enable a range of actions to be taken, depending on the type of resolution being implemented, possibly including recapitalization, transfer of part or all of the business to another entity, and potentially the reduction of the amount payable under senior and subordinated debt and/or the conversion of debt to equity where estimated losses exceed capital; and
- to transfer some or all of the business undertaking (including assets, liabilities, data, systems and staff) from a distressed bank and any part of its group to another entity in such a manner that this does not provide the grounds for the termination of contracts, acceleration of debt or other similar measures.

As was seen in the UK in the Northern Rock bank distress episode and in other countries during the global financial crisis in 2007/8, inadequate legal powers proved a stumbling block to effective resolution. In particular, it was found that conventional insolvency regimes and court-based resolution processes are generally not adequate for addressing financial distress, given the need to move quickly and with certainty, and the need to maintain essential business functions on an uninterrupted basis.

Since the global financial crisis, many countries have taken steps to strengthen their legal powers to deal with financial distress situations, drawing on international guidance made available through the Financial Stability Board and the Basel Committee on Banking Supervision, including the recommendations issued in March 2010 by the Basel Committee's Cross-border Bank Resolution Group. Australia is also doing this, although it is fair to say that Australia started with a relatively robust set of legal powers for the most part in the first place.

Agency responsible for bank resolution

The legal and institutional framework should desirably provide for one agency to be responsible for implementing bank distress resolution, rather than this responsibility being split across different agencies. Where the allocation of responsibility is spread across different agencies, there is a need for close coordination between them.

Desirably, the same agency should also have responsibility for resolution of all prudentially regulated financial institutions (such as banks, insurance companies and superannuation), given that financial conglomerates may require a group-wide resolution. In such a situation, it is simpler if one agency has responsibility for resolving the entire group, rather than this being split across several agencies. Again, however, if the responsibilities are to be spread across more than one agency, then mechanisms to facilitate coordination are needed to deal with financial distress in a conglomerate comprising different categories of financial institution.

With the responsibility for financial distress resolution comes the need for transparency and accountability. There is therefore a need for the law to impose robust transparency and accountability measures on a resolution agency, including the capacity for judicial review of its actions. However, it is important that accountability frameworks do not impede the ability of the resolution agency to move quickly and decisively to respond to financial distress.

Coordination of financial distress resolution

Although there may be a single agency with responsibility for bank distress resolution, it will need to coordinate its actions closely with other relevant government agencies. In particular, there is a need for close coordination between the bank resolution agency, the supervisory authority (if different from the resolution agency), the central bank and the treasury department or finance ministry. Coordination with the securities market regulatory authority is also necessary, particularly where the bank in distress is listed on one or more securities markets.

Coordination can be facilitated through a number of mechanisms, including memoranda of understanding (MOUs), a council or committee that meets on a regular basis and other forms of bilateral and multilateral association. In Australia, the Council of Financial Regulators (the Council) provides a very effective means of coordinating between the four agencies responsible for financial sector regulation: APRA, the Reserve Bank of Australia, the Commonwealth Treasury and the Australian Securities and Investments Commission. In order to facilitate effective coordination further, the Council entered into a MOU on Financial Distress Management in 2008. It provides a helpful means of promoting coordination and cooperation, providing a clear identification of financial distress resolution objectives and principles, and a clear identification of responsibilities of each agency for each stage of financial distress.

As with any such arrangement, effective coordination requires the development and maintenance of sound working relationships at all times. No MOU will be sufficient if the working relationships between the agencies – at all levels – are not sufficiently sound. In this context, periodic financial distress simulation exercises to test distress resolution can be a helpful mechanism to promote effective coordination across the relevant agencies. Such exercises help to build and maintain working relationships between the agencies, to test communications and cooperation and to test crisis resolution decision-making processes.

Resolution options

Financial distress resolution for banks tends to fall into two broad categories:

- a 'closed resolution', in which depositors are paid out, generally in association with some form of deposit insurance or guarantee, and the bank is then liquidated; and
- an 'open resolution', where the bank is recapitalized to maintain at least its core operations, or where essential business undertaking of the bank (including deposits and credit facilities) are transferred to another bank or to a newly established bridge bank.

The choice of resolution will depend on the situation, including the size and complexity of the bank, whether it is a single or multiple bank failure situation, and the likely systemic and economic impact of the bank's failure.

A closed resolution is generally only a satisfactory option in the case of small banks, where the closure of the bank would not be expected to cause significant disruption to the financial system, trigger contagion or weaken confidence in the financial system. Even in such cases, an effective resolution requires depositors to be provided with prompt access to at least a proportion of their deposits, and desirably for the bank's customers, particularly businesses, which are reliant on committed credit facilities to have continued access to funding.

In the case of larger banks, resolution tends to take some form of open resolution, where depositors have uninterrupted access to at least a proportion of their funds and also continue to operate their transaction facilities with minimal disruption. Similarly, the resolution of a larger bank also tends to involve the maintenance of its lending capacity, given that many of the bank's customers, including businesses, may be reliant on credit facilities with that bank in order to meet their transaction and working capital needs. Many of these customers would have difficulty establishing credit facilities at short notice with other banks, particularly in a subdued banking market where other banks may be reluctant to extend credit to new customers. In these situations, the closure of the bank and payout of depositors would not provide a cost-effective response to the situation, given the likely adverse impact on market liquidity and confidence, the disruption to the financial system and economy, the risk of contagion and the potential to seriously undermine confidence in the banking system. In such situations, the better response is likely to involve a resolution that enables the bank or a successor entity to maintain core functions.

As discussed later, an open resolution may require a combination of measures, including the provision of liquidity support, recapitalization and potentially an interim government guarantee pending restoration of stability to the bank. In the absence of private equity, remedial measures can be funded by a number of mechanisms, including funding from the government, funding from the industry (pre-funded or post-funded) or funding from creditors, or any combination of these.

Deposit insurance or guarantees

Deposit insurance or guarantee schemes play an important part in bank resolution arrangements. A well-structured, explicit and transparent deposit insurance or guarantee scheme can facilitate the closure of small banks and reduce the temptations for government bail-outs by protecting small depositors and removing some of the 'noise', disruption and market friction associated with bank failures. To a degree, deposit insurance or guarantees can also reduce the risk of retail deposit runs and contagion via the retail deposit channel.

Although deposit insurance creates moral hazard risks and may reduce market discipline on banks, it can be justified on several grounds. In particular, it recognizes that many of those with small deposits are unlikely to have the information or skills in interpreting that information to identify and manage the risks associated with bank deposits. It also recognizes that, unlike the case with large deposits, where the risk of loss can be reduced by spreading deposits across several banks, this is not as readily practicable in the case of small deposits. Deposit insurance therefore provides a mechanism to protect deposits up to a defined level, particularly for those who are not readily able to protect their own funds.

If deposit insurance or guarantee arrangements are to be effective, they need to be explicit and well understood by depositors; a point well made by David Mayes. While there might be a place for 'constructive ambiguity' in the case of wholesale funding markets, there is little benefit in such ambiguity in the retail banking market. Indeed, a lack of transparency as to the extent and nature of deposit protection in the retail market creates a number of costs and risks, including a greater moral hazard (based on a presumption by depositors of complete bail-out by the government) and a higher risk of retail deposit runs. A lack of clarity of the deposit protection arrangements also impedes the incentive for, and ability of, depositors to manage their risks across the banking system.

Accordingly, the deposit insurance limit should be explicit and well publicized. The deposit protection scheme should be clearly disclosed to depositors at the time they place funds into a bank. When the scheme is invoked, depositors need to be provided with information quickly and efficiently as to when and how they will receive their protected funds and the position with respect to unprotected deposits.

If moral hazard risks are to be minimized, the scheme should desirably limit protection to relatively small retail deposits – sufficient to cover most households' and small businesses' transaction balances and some of their term deposits but not so great as to insulate larger deposits from loss. In most OECD countries, the deposit insurance coverage tends be in the range of two to four times per capita GDP.

An effective scheme also needs to provide depositors with prompt access to protected deposits – at least within a few days of the closure of the failed bank and if possible relatively uninterrupted access to transaction balances. This requires pre-positioned IT capacity in the banks and in the scheme administrator. It also requires banks to be able to calculate aggregated deposit balances on a single customer view so as to minimize the risk of payouts above the limit in the case of depositors with multiple accounts in a single bank. These requirements pose major IT challenges. A sensible balance needs to be struck between the potentially high compliance costs associated with IT pre-positioning and achieving policy outcomes.

As David Mayes notes in his chapter, there needs to be a sustainable funding mechanism for a deposit insurance or guarantee scheme to be effective and credible.

A scheme can either be pre-funded or post-funded. In a pre-funded scheme, banks are levied on their protected deposits to build up a fund sufficient to cover expected payouts over the long term. The establishment of a pre-funded scheme has the advantage of making funds available when the scheme is invoked and thereby reduces the need for the scheme to obtain funds from the government or central bank. However, a pre-funded scheme may still need to borrow in periods of greater-than-expected payouts.

In a post-funded scheme, the initial funding for deposit payouts or transfers is generally provided by the government and then reimbursed through the liquidation of the bank. If there is a shortfall in reimbursing the costs of the deposit payout, the scheme then applies a levy on the banking industry to reimburse the government.

Levies can be either risk-based, taking into account the risk profile of each bank, or applied at a uniform rate. Risk-based levies have the advantage – at least in theory – of reducing moral hazard and sharpening the incentives for prudent risk management. However, setting a risk-based fee is not without difficulties, including the inherent difficulty in assessing a bank's probability of default. An additional complication with pre-funded, risk-based schemes is the risk of adverse signalling arising from the disclosure of the risk premium applied to individual banks. In addition, pre-funded schemes tend to be more administratively expensive to operate than post-funded schemes.

Post-funded schemes avoid the costs and complexity of pre-funded schemes but arguably create greater moral hazard by applying a 'survivor pays' approach – that is, the banks that best manage their risks bear the costs of any shortfall in the liquidation process. Post-funded schemes also place a higher fiscal burden on central government, which could prove unsustainable in particularly acute periods of financial system distress. There is also a risk of pro-cyclicality with post-funded schemes, such that fees are raised in periods when the banking system is already under stress. However, that risk can be reduced by deferring the levying of fees until the banking system has returned to a sound condition.

Both options – pre-funded and post-funded – have advantages and disadvantages; there is no 'golden rule' to suggest that either approach is better than the other. However, the increasing tendency is for countries to implement pre-funded schemes, thereby reducing the fiscal burden on government and shifting the burden to banks.

Responding to larger bank distress situations

As noted in David Mayes's chapter, deposit insurance does not provide an effective resolution for the failure of a large, systemically important bank. In the case of a large or otherwise systemically important bank, the resolution needs to provide depositors – large and small – with uninterrupted access to most of their funds. It also needs to provide customers with committed credit facilities – such as businesses reliant on overdraft facilities for working capital purposes – with uninterrupted access to their funds under the facilities. The effective resolution of a systemically important bank also needs to avoid significant disruption to the derivatives markets – such as currency and interest rate swaps and options.

Given these imperatives, the resolution of a large or otherwise systemically important bank tends to require the bank to remain open or be re-opened after a very brief closure required to restore it to a sound financial condition. In the absence of a private sector solution, such as the sale of the bank to another bank or the injection of capital from existing or new shareholders, the resolution will generally require two or three key elements:

- the provision of liquidity support, generally by the central bank, and usually on a secured or asset repurchase basis, to enable the bank to continue to meet core functions;
- the restoration of capital sufficiency for at least that part of the bank that contains systemically important functions – such as deposit taking, payment functions and the provision of credit; and
- possibly the provision of a government guarantee on an interim basis pending a restoration of capital soundness, at least in respect of the bank's core functions. A temporary government guarantee may be needed to avoid events of default, to enable the directors of the bank to enable the bank to continue to trade and to enable the bank to continue to take in funds. A temporary guarantee may also reduce liquidity pressures on the bank by facilitating continued access to market liquidity and by reducing the rate of withdrawal of funds from the bank.

The dilemma in resolving large bank distress situations is whether this can be done in a manner that avoids a taxpayer-funded bail-out. In the global financial crisis, large and complex banks were essentially bailed out by government-funded rescues, usually involving a combination of capital injection and liquidity support, underpinned by explicit or implicit government guarantees. Since then, the international regulatory community and national jurisdictions have given a great deal of attention to alternative means of dealing with large and complex bank distress. This has involved three main streams of thought:

- Mechanisms to reduce the probability of default. This includes measures to strengthen capital and liquidity – the so-called Basel 3 reforms.
- Mechanisms to reduce the impact of the failure of a large or complex bank. This includes the so-called 'living will' proposal in which large banks are expected to establish plans to enable them to recover from a distress event and supervisors are expected to establish resolution plans to cater for a situation where a bank proves to be irrecoverable. Under the latter, consideration is being given to how a bank's functions and business lines could be pre-positioned to facilitate the separation of functions considered to be systemically important from those which are not. An option under such an arrangement is for the systemically important business units to be separated from the other parts of the bank and either to be provided with sufficient liquidity and capital to operate as a stand-alone entity (e.g. as a bridge bank) or to be transferred to another bank. The rest of the bank may then be liquidated or sold off. Living wills also involve measures to simplify banks and their groups, with a view to facilitating resolution better.
- Mechanisms to fund the resolution of a bank without recourse (or with only limited recourse) to taxpayer funding, including funding for recapitalization or to finance the transfer of core business functions to a bridge bank or another bank. Options being considered by the Financial Stability Board and the Basel Committee, and by some national authorities, include the establishment of a pre-funded 'financial stability fund' financed by levies on banks and the so-called 'bail-in' option.

  - A financial stability fund, such as the one established in Sweden and being considered in the European Union, involves the concept of using funds collected from the banks through ex ante fees to implement a resolution. In principle, such a fund could be used to recapitalize a bank, to capitalize a bridge bank or to finance the transfer of deposits and other liabilities to a bridge bank or other bank. However, depending on the size and scope of the fund, it may still be necessary to use taxpayer funds to implement a resolution, particularly if the bank in question is particularly large and/or splitting the bank into systemic and non-systemic parts is either not feasible in the timeframe required or uneconomic.
  - Bail-in involves the allocation of losses to bank debt holders where losses exceed capital. In principle, bail-in could be used to recapitalize all or part of a distressed bank by effectively converting bank debt (potentially including deposits above the level covered by deposit insurance) to equity. It can be applied either by contractual means (where bank debt includes clauses providing for the debt to be converted to equity upon specified triggers being reached) or by the exercise of forced conversion statutory powers.

These options are worthy of serious consideration and may have a place in the resolution toolkit. However, from a personal perspective, I have some reservations with aspects of them.

In the case of the living will concept, I see considerable merit in requiring banks to establish and maintain recovery plans, particularly where the board of directors is required to engage on these matters and satisfy themselves that their bank has well-developed plans to recapitalize, to obtain liquidity and to take other appropriate measures to resolve a distress event affecting their bank. I also see merit in measures to simplify banking groups, with a view to more easily separating systemically important functions from those which are more readily dispensable. Similarly, there may be merit in moving towards 'portable' deposit accounts and other mechanisms to enable the transfer of essential business functions to another bank as part of a resolution.

However, these kinds of measures need to be considered against the costs involved, including IT costs, on-going compliance costs and, importantly, the potential for severely reduced banking group efficiency. In particular, resolution plans that require banks and their groups to be split into self-contained units, separating systemic from non-systemic functions, may impose potentially large efficiency costs, thereby reducing the scope for banks to meet the needs of the economies in which they operate and raising the costs to consumers of banking services. As with all measures to promote a robust financial system, there needs to be a sensible balance between achieving a robust financial system, maintaining banking system efficiency and avoiding excessive compliance costs.

Bail-in also has potential merit, particularly in the case of subordinated debt or other bank debt where the debt was issued with explicit clauses that make it clear that it may be converted to equity or reduced in value upon specified trigger events. It is also important that bail-in is done in a manner consistent with the ranking of claims in a wind-up and where there is protection to ensure that creditors are not left worse off than they would have been had the bank been wound up. However, it remains to be seen how marketable such debt will be and what the likely cost of servicing the debt may be; the impact on banks' funding costs and access to funding could be considerable. It also remains to be seen what impact this may have on banking system stability – particularly if bail-in is applied to on-call or other short-term debt; it has the potential to trigger the very instability one seeks to avoid, including the potential for contagion.

Forced bail-in using statutory powers, and in the absence of contractual provisions, may have a place in bank crisis resolution but, in my view, also presents potentially serious risks of instability. This is particularly so if depositors become concerned in a period of market fragility that their deposits may be subject to a forced debt-to-equity conversion or debt reduction. Such concerns could easily lead to or exacerbate liquidity problems in the banking sector and trigger contagion across the banking sector. Bail-in could also have potentially severe impacts on wider market confidence, with consequences for continued access to funding, particularly if applied in economies reliant on offshore funding; it creates a heightened risk of foreign investors turning off the tap for a potentially long period of time, with attendant impacts on system-wide liquidity, interest rates, the exchange rate and the capacity of banks to maintain normal credit functions.

A bail-in approach may also increase the economic cost of recapitalizing a bank (or at least the systemic part of a bank) by reducing or eliminating its franchise value. For example, if a bank is severely under-capitalized but still has some positive capital after allowing for maximum plausible losses, the smarter resolution might involve a recapitalization using funds from the government or a stability fund, without bail-in (other than perhaps contractual bail-in), rather than risk losing many bank customers through a forced bail-in.

Bail-in can also create a risk of cross-defaults in other parts of a financial conglomerate of which the bank is part, thereby compounding an already complex situation.

These risks suggest to me that bail-in options need to be considered with caution. Bail-in may be a potentially useful tool in some situations – such as an isolated bank distress situation where private sector solutions are unavailable and where the impact of a bail-in is not expected to adversely affect other banks. However, it remains questionable whether bail-in is an efficacious means of addressing multiple bank distress or the distress of systemically important banks.

In this context, I would argue that current international thinking in some quarters too readily dismisses the case for bank resolutions that are partially or fully funded through the taxpayer. In some situations, I believe that a taxpayer-funded resolution may be the only viable or potentially the most cost-effective means of resolving a systemically important bank distress. Taxpayer-funded resolutions do not necessarily need to involve losses for the taxpayer; in some situations, they may actually result in a positive economic return for the taxpayer, as has been demonstrated in some taxpayer-funded bail-outs. A well-designed resolution package involving taxpayer assistance has the potential to resolve a distress event with much less adverse impact on liquidity, market confidence, contagion and credit availability than other forms of resolution.

For sure, taxpayer-funded resolutions entail moral hazard. However, moral hazard risks can be managed by ensuring that any taxpayer assistance is appropriately priced, that existing capital and subordinated debt holders bear all losses ahead of the taxpayer and that the board and senior management face appropriate consequences for their part in contributing to the bank's distress. The moral hazard risks can be addressed – at least to some extent – by the smart design of the resolution arrangements.

I therefore think it is a mistake to dismiss the option of taxpayer-assisted resolutions. In my assessment, bank crisis resolutions involving taxpayer funding or risk take-outs will always be an option in the toolbox and may well be the smartest resolution option in some situations, provided that the resolution package is appropriately designed and implemented.

Cross-border bank crisis resolution

David Mayes rightly notes that cross-border crisis resolution presents major challenges and needs to be addressed as part of the response to the global financial crisis. Banks are increasingly operating across national borders, either through subsidiaries or branches (and often via both mechanisms). As we saw in the financial crisis of 2007/8, cross-border banks present major challenges for effective resolution. Despite the efforts made by various national authorities and pan-national bodies, such as the European Union, to facilitate close coordination of cross-border financial distress events, there was a tendency in the recent financial crisis for countries to act primarily in their own interests; MOUs designed to facilitate cross-border cooperation and coordination did not appear to be conspicuously effective.

To some extent, we are at a cross-road on this issue. In the absence of mechanisms to facilitate effective cross-border resolution, there is a risk that home and host jurisdictions may move towards arrangements that require banks to operate as subsidiaries rather than as branches in host jurisdictions. There is a further risk that the authorities in home and host jurisdictions may require subsidiaries to be fully self-contained to enable them to operate on a stand-alone basis without parent bank support. There is a risk that home supervisors may impose ever stricter rules on parent banks to limit their exposure to their foreign subsidiaries.

These measures would be consistent with an autarkic response to the problem – that is, where bank distress is resolved in each jurisdiction on a stand-alone basis. In that sense, they may well provide an effective means of dealing with cross-border distress, but at a cost. Taken to the extreme, an autarkic approach would impose severe efficiency costs on the global, regional and national banking systems, reducing markedly the scope for risk diversification and management, increasing operating costs, increasing funding costs in host jurisdictions and reducing the scope for lending, particularly in the host jurisdictions. On the face of it, an autarkic approach does not strike me as an intelligent, cost-effective response to the cross-border issue.

In my assessment, the wiser path is one that recognizes that banks, and other financial institutions, such as insurers, will increasingly operate across borders, and that the benefits this brings generally far outweigh the costs and risks. What is needed is a framework that facilitates effective cross-border resolution in a manner than resolves the distress on a group-wide basis, minimizes the impact on all affected jurisdictions and apportions the burden of any rescue costs fairly across the relevant jurisdictions.

The Financial Stability Board and Basel Committee have provided helpful guidance on these issues, and many jurisdictions, notably the European Union, are undertaking considerable work in the area. Closer to home, Australia and New Zealand have taken a number of steps to promote a coordinated approach to trans-Tasman banking system distress, including the enactment of legislation in both countries requiring the authorities to have regard to, and seek to avoid adverse impact on, the stability of financial systems in both countries in responding to bank distress. Building on this legislation, the Australian and New Zealand authorities have a close working relationship and a framework for addressing cross-border distress in a manner that seeks to maintain the stability of both countries' financial systems.

The development of effective cross-border crisis resolution arrangements involves a complex array of elements; there is no easy solution. It involves not only addressing complex technical issues, but also seeking an appropriate balance between competing national interests. It requires national authorities to look beyond the short-term national interest and the temptations of an expedient response to a crisis, to the longer-term benefits that effective cross-border resolution arrangements can bring.

An effective cross-border resolution framework is likely to require a number of elements, including:

- statutory obligations on the national authorities in each jurisdiction to seek to minimize adverse systemic impacts on other affected jurisdictions;
- a broadly compatible set of crisis resolution powers across the jurisdiction to enable a coordinated approach to occur;
- a framework, such as a MOU, that sets out agreed procedures and processes to encourage cooperation and coordination in each stage of responding to distress;
- the development of close working relationships at all levels between the relevant agencies across the jurisdictions; and
- the development and periodic testing of cross-border crisis resolution plans.

Ultimately, effective cross-border resolution arrangements may require mechanisms to facilitate burden sharing on an agreed basis between home and host jurisdictions. A framework for mutual recognition of resolution powers, enabling one authority to manage the resolution process across the relevant jurisdictions, is also ultimately desirable. However, these are clearly sensitive issues. Progress in these areas is likely to take considerable time.

Conclusion

The global financial crisis imposed severe costs on many economies; costs that, in some cases, will leave an economic imprint for many years. However, the crisis also focused much-needed attention on the importance of financial stability and the policies and processes needed to promote and maintain it. It has highlighted many lessons for us all on the importance of effective financial distress management. The task now is for us to get the balance right in responding to future financial distress; to find solutions that strike a sensible balance between financial system stability and financial system efficiency.

7 Efficiency, stability, and integrity in the financial sector

The role of governance and regulation

Geoffrey Wood

There are two ways for governments to get organizations to do what they think is in the public interest. One is telling them what to do. This can mean prescribing the outcome, prescribing the process, or even both together. These are forms of regulation. The other is explicitly to recognize that organizations are run by people, not by automata waiting passively to be told what to do. That recognition suggests that rather than simply issuing instructions one should organize incentive structures such that these rational individuals, out of their own self-interest, do what the government wishes. The latter course can best be described as governance. The aim of this chapter is to contrast regulation and governance. First, brief definitions of regulation and of governance are proposed. Then three examples, from different areas of finance, are considered, and it is suggested on the basis of these that in general governance is better than regulation in two ways. First, it is more likely to achieve the desired result. Second, it is likely to be effective for longer.

Having set out examples which suggest this conclusion, an analytical framework is sketched out which suggests that claim, based on examples, is likely to hold in general. The discussion is then briefly related to the distinction between common law and civil law. After that, the chapter concludes with some suggestions for further work.

Definitions

An excellent definition of regulation, one which covers its role in all areas of life, was provided by that most eminent of scholars of it, George Stigler, in 1975. Regulation, he wrote, is '…the exercise of coercive government power'. It is, in other words, telling people what to do and punishing them in some way if they do not perform as instructed.

Now, there is a problem with this definition. Stated baldly, it is somewhat too wide. It seems to imply that any legal rule is regulation, so that a libertarian who wants state enforcement of contracts would be said to be in favour of regulation. But it does help capture the difference which is at the heart of the argument of this chapter. Regulation tells people what to do, while governance involves setting up structures, inside or outside organizations, so as to make it desirable for the organizations *in the best service of their own interests* to do what is thought also to be in the public interest. They may be told how to organize but after that they are left to themselves; state-imposed governance is a particular type of regulation, one which focuses on structures rather than on either processes or outcomes.

Examples of regulation and of governance are helpful at this point. The setting of speed limits on roads, enforced by supervision and punished by one of a range of penalties, is an example of regulation. The repeal of the Bubble Act in 1825 is an example of governance from English financial history – it provided a framework to facilitate still further large-scale investment in risky projects and, thus, to facilitate a faster stage of industrialization.

So much for definitions of regulation and governance.

The three examples by use of which regulation and governance will be contrasted are as follows:

1 The regulation of capital ratios for banks under the Basel accord.
2 The regulation of investment trusts.
3 The regulation of accounting standards.

These are taken in turn.

Capital ratios

Banks are frequently contrasted with other types of firms because of the interdependence between them. There is interdependence between many types of firms, not just between banks. Take a currently topical example. Should a retailer, such as Marks and Spencer, be taken over, there can be little doubt that its relationships with its suppliers, and no doubt to a possibly considerable extent its suppliers themselves, would be changed. Or suppose Marks and Spencer were to fail (that word 'fail' is for the moment used loosely; the need for greater clarity is set out in the appendix to this chapter). That would affect its suppliers – adversely; and its competitors favourably.

And it is really in that last that the crucial difference between banks and other types of firms emerges. When a bank fails (again still using the term loosely), there is an immediate *and adverse* effect on its competitors. This adverse effect comes through three channels. The first is that, certainly if the bank is large, there is some turmoil in financial markets. Second, to the extent that other banks had contracts with the failed bank, these contracts are at the least frozen. Even if most of the money eventually comes back, it may come back slowly. (Continental Illinois eventually paid out over 90 cents in the dollar but that took place over several years.) And third, confidence in banks generally is weakened, and this loss of confidence can lead to a 'flight to quality', which, in the last resort, can become a flight to liquidity requiring central bank assistance.

In summary, the interdependence between banks is different in kind from that between other types of firms. Now, that of itself does not justify interest in them by government. But what *does* seem to justify that interest is the important role of banks in the economy. They transmit monetary policy (they are certainly one of the channels) and they transmit funds from lenders to borrowers. Both of these are important functions.

This has led, surprisingly recently in the case of some countries, to governments (or central banks) imposing regulations on how much capital banks should hold. This is currently set by the Basel Committee on Banking Supervision.[1]

The fundamental difference between Basel 2 and its predecessor is that required capital ratios are related to risk in a much more complicated way. Thus, the more risky a bank's portfolio (of assets) the higher is the capital required. This seems eminently sensible. It is what prudent banks would do without prompting. This is no doubt exactly the viewpoint that led to such widespread support for the principle of Basel 2. But supporting Basel 2 because it follows principles that prudent banks would choose involves a misconception.

First, assessing relative risks in a continually changing market, with rapid financial innovation, is not easy. Assessments are likely to be wrong and to change frequently. Indeed, there are some who argued that Basel 2 was wrong already before it started, in that insufficient allowance was made for the risk diversification produced by investing across a wide range of countries and activities (e.g. Repullo and Suarez, 2004). Second, the attempt at greater accuracy inevitably involves greater complexity. Third, although there is reliance on banks' *internal* risk assessments, Basel 2 actually suggests quite strongly how such assessments be made. This has two difficulties associated with it. First, we can certainly not be sure we know the right model; and second, it may encourage herding, all banks responding to the same stimulus in the same way.

Fourth, there was widespread agreement that Basel 2 would produce 'procyclicality' – increased bank lending in booms and reduced in slumps – since risks in general fall in booms and rise in slumps. The disagreement that exists over this issue is only over how big the effect will be.

Now, all these criticisms are generally accepted at least to some degree. There is however a more fundamental point that has only recently been more generally appreciated. Banks hold capital to use: they run it down as a result of negative shocks and build it up as a result of positive ones. In contrast, regulatory capital sets a floor below which capital is not allowed to fall. *Regulatory capital is not for using.*

Does this mean that banks should be left to choose their own capital? They certainly were in the past; and some systems, notably the UK, proved singularly robust.[2] Now, this is important. It is undoubtedly correct that regulators are concerned primarily about the above-discussed 'external effects' of bank failures, while banks are concerned to survive to earn future profits. But despite this apparent difference of interest (note that it is difference, not conflict: both regulators and banks want banks to survive) in the past, banks, it seems highly likely, took heed of *both* issues. One cannot of course infer this from the ratios they held (even if one can get the data). But one can infer it from actions banks took to monitor other banks and to protect themselves from failures by others. See in evidence clearing houses, the famous Suffolk Banking System in the US, and note return arrangements in Scotland under free banking. Why can we not rely on self-interest now? The answer, it may be argued, is that the governance structure within banks has changed. In the periods just considered, banks, although sometimes quite large, were smaller than now and, very important, in much more concentrated ownership. Further, those who managed the banks usually had a large amount of their wealth in the bank.

So why not reform 'governance'? Why not require bank management to hold their wealth, in increasing proportions as they become more senior, in the bank's equity? This would start to produce the alliance of desired outcome with incentive that we saw in the past.

Unfortunately it cannot be denied that there is a problem with relying on that alone. Banks nowadays often operate across many jurisdictions. Some bank failures are so significant relative to the size of the economy (e.g. in Finland in the 1990s) that recapitalization is required. (That recapitalization is *not* the same as a bail-out.) Often such recapitalization requires at least some taxpayer funds, and governments and regulators understandably want to minimize these costs, at least for their own citizens. Hence, to prevent squabbling, delay, and economic problems following major international bank failures, a simple course could be adopted. To ensure a minimum amount of capital, the principles of the US FDICIA Act could be used to supplement governance.

A basic level of capital is set. But it is *not* a minimum. Rather, a move below it requires a series of prescribed actions, quasi automatic penalties such as not paying dividends or bonuses, and the requirement to raise more capital in a prescribed period.

In sum, because of the international nature of banks, governance reform alone is probably not a satisfactory substitute for Basel 2 but, in conjunction with some simple capital rules (a basic form of regulation), it is.

In addition, of course, it is important that investors and, if possible, depositors, understand the risk management procedures being applied. They could then do what they wished in the light of the understanding. This could increase pressure on management by helping enforce market discipline.

Let us now move on to our second example.

Investment trust regulation

The FSA in the UK has recently proposed a set of changes to the rules governing investment trusts. These new rules were the consequence of a particular problem. To understand them, therefore, it is necessary first to describe the background to that problem, and then the problem itself.

The UK stock market had, by late 2000, witnessed a remarkable bull run that had lasted for almost ten years, starting in the early 1990s. The FTSE All Share Index stood at 960 in October 1990. By September 2000, it had reached 3,266, an increase of some 240 per cent.

What about the people who were 'creating' all of this wealth, the management and executives of the companies? Many of these managers, or the relevant boards of directors, decided to introduce remuneration packages linked to the share price of the company. We now had an additional element in the spiralling process. Management who were previously focused on delivering to shareholders sustainable, high-quality earnings focused instead on strategies aimed at boosting share prices in the short term, thus increasing both their own remuneration and the value of shareholders' funds. (These remuneration arrangements, by failing to distinguish between company performance and market performance, were themselves surely a failure of corporate governance.)

In 2000, the market hesitated, stopped altogether, and then dived. The magnitude and longevity of the fall took most by surprise. Thousands of people who had lost money on their savings, their pensions, and their endowment policies looked to ways of making good their losses. It was often asserted that they were either not told of the risks involved or did not understand the risks when they had been mentioned.

Mis-selling became the single most important issue facing both the FSA and the investment management industry. The claims of mis-selling of endowment and pension products are well documented. There are similarities with the possible mis-selling of split capital investment trusts ('splits'; i.e. of trusts with different classes of shares, usually one getting the capital gain and the others dividends). In the case of splits, some products were sold as low risk. There were allegations that a small number of people had deliberately orchestrated a situation whereby, through a series of cross holdings, the share prices of some trusts had been artificially maintained.

Before turning to the response of the regulators, it is useful to set out a timetable of relevant events (Table 7.1).

The FSA's initial response

Following its own investigations, comment from independent analysts, and increasing interest in the financial press, the FSA decided to gather information on

Table 7.1 Timetable of events

Bull market	1990–9
Technology bubble	1998–2000
Major expansion of splits	1998–2001
Bear market starts	2000
Concerns mounting	2001
FSA discussion paper	December 2001
Treasury Committee agreed to talk to the FSA	April 2002
FSA update report	May 2002
Shareholder complaints	May 2002
Guernsey Financial Authority letter	July 2002
Treasury Committee took oral evidence	July/October 2002
FSA consultation paper	January 2003
Responses to the consultation paper	April 2003
FSA guidelines	Late 2003

113 Split Capital Closed End Funds at the end of September 2001. The FSA then issued a discussion paper in December 2001 and a policy statement in May 2002.

Following discussions with a number of investment trust practitioners, the FSA produced a consultation paper in January 2003, in which it laid out what it saw as the main causes of the problems within the investment trust area and what it saw as the abuses perpetrated. These were as follows:

- gearing
- cross holdings
- ineffectual boards
- dominant investment managers.

Some of the proposals received a sharp critical response. The FSA perhaps inadvertently and unnecessarily provoked some of this. For in their preliminary discussions with the industry, the FSA had raised hackles by implying that the proposed changes were not really for discussion. But there were also rather more fundamental reasons for the objections of the investment trust sector.

All investment trusts were, in varying degrees, affected by at least some of the proposed changes. Some of the major issues were as follows. Gearing can enhance the returns to shareholders when managed effectively; artificially restricting gearing may not inevitably be in the interests of shareholders. Preventing investment trusts from investing in other investment trusts could, far from reducing the market risk to shareholders, actually increase the risk; a means of risk diversification would no longer be available to the investing trust. Proposed changes to the eligibility of certain directors to remain on the board and the total exclusion of a representative from the investment manager being a director were regarded by some as inconsistent with the European Law on Human Rights, and would certainly lead to a reduction of industry-experienced directors being available.

These regulations were, however, aimed at a particular set of recent problems. But the events surrounding the splits crisis were not unprecedented and will surely occur again in the future. Buoyant markets and bull market expectations produced an environment that encouraged over-optimism and downplayed risk. There were three forces that then produced the crisis in the split trust sector.

The first force was a financial one. A sustained bull market from 1990–9 led to both individual investors and professional advisors being lulled into a false sense of security. The severe bear market of 2000–2, when the UK markets plummeted, tested both pension schemes and equity-based savings schemes more generally, as well as the firms that supplied these products to the public.

The second force was a political one. The UK's government (along with most other western governments) was eager to free itself from the responsibility it had earlier taken up eagerly, of providing an aging population with pensions. The aim was to pass this responsibility onto the private sector but with safeguards and a policing system. In the UK, the FSA had the role of providing both of these.

The third was the greatly increased willingness of individual investors to complain and to demand financial redress. The extent to which these complaints were justified is beside the point. The willingness to complain was enough to produce political pressure for a quick and clear-cut response.

These three forces combined to create a highly vocal, and to an extent, litigious population with a newly formed statutory body specifically designed (inter alia) to protect people. The response by the FSA to the splits crisis could well have been different had the FSA been in existence for a number of years before the market fall. By then, the FSA's ability to monitor and react would have been more developed. In particular, it might well have had an opportunity to remind directors of investment trusts of their responsibilities. Directors should ensure: that managements do not undertake self-serving actions – for example, buying shares in one trust in the expectation of that trust in turn buying some of their shares; that the risks of gearing are fully understood by the managers and explained to the shareholders (who then have the choice of selling their shares if they are unhappy with the increased risk); and that any advertising literature issued on behalf of the trust is accurate.[3] All these *already existing* responsibilities clearly implied that directors should ensure their organizations maintain good governance. Had directors paid greater heed to that, the splits crisis, if it happened at all, would have been very much smaller.

As it is, the response, more and tighter regulation, deals with a particular set of problems but does nothing to prevent different problems developing in the future (and creates some new problems). This is in contrast with insisting on good governance, which would have maintained in place the kind of framework which could have kept better aligned the interests of shareholders and management. Again, as in the capital regulation of banks, governance rather than regulation could produce a more flexible and therefore more durable outcome.

Accountants and accountancy

Now we come to our third example from the area of finance.

The two examples discussed so far have in common a feature not so far remarked on in this chapter; there was, or was thought to be, a problem for which no existing remedy existed, so new regulations had to be introduced. Accountancy, the third area examined, shares that feature.

British (and North American) accounting both derive from the same tradition. The original purpose – and still probably the primary purpose – of company accounts is as follows: 'in law the object of annual accounts is to assist shareholders in exercising control of the company by enabling them to judge how its affairs have been conducted' (*Caparo Industries* plc v. *Dickman and others*, House of Lords, 8 February 1980, Lord Jaunay).

Such accounting originated from the practice of 'accounting for ventures' – for discrete operations, such as a voyage to the Indies – and evolved into accounting for the stewardship of going concerns. In the first, the returns, if any, were divided among the shareholders at the conclusion of the venture. Going concern accounting required regular measurement of profit to determine how much a company could distribute to the 'shareholders' without diminishing its capital. These dividends might equal profits if there were no retention of profit in the business.

The one-year accounting period is a convention around which other conventions have evolved – annual tax payments, for example. There are arguments for a longer accounting period or periods (Myddleton, 2004) but the accounting period is now so intertwined with other aspects of life that change would be difficult. But be that as it may, what matters for our purposes is that the annual accounting period emerged originally as a convention, just as accounting emerged from accounting for stewardship of a venture to accounting for that of a going concern.

In 1966, there was a proposal in the US (from the American Accounting Association) to move away from stewardship accounting to accounting for decision making (Myddleton, 2004, p. 36). This was followed up by the US Financial Accounting Standards Board: 'Financial Accounting should provide information that is useful to present and potential investors and creditors and other users in making rational investment, credit and similar decisions' (p. 37). There is thus disagreement about the purpose of accounts and, invariably, as we shall see, disagreement about what kind of regulation of them might be sensible.[4]

For over 50 years, British law has required that company accounts provide a 'true and fair view' of the state of a company's affairs and of its profit or loss for the financial year. Thus, so long as the procedure is revealed, different companies can, depending on the nature of the business, do different things – for writing down old or damaged stock, for allowing for bad debts, for depreciating capital. It is, and this is a point and distinction returned to, a requirement over outputs rather than over inputs or processes.

Formal accounting standards, restricting the use of judgment, started to be discussed in the UK after the 1967 takeover of Associated Electrical Industries by the General Electric Company. (Before then, there had been 'Recommendations on Accounting Principles' – voluntary guidelines on best practice, which often described several possible approaches.) After the takeover, AEI's projected profit of £10 million for the year turned out to be a loss of £4.5 million. (In fact, two-thirds of the turn round was the result of a different judgment about the prospective outcome of long-term contracts.) But what was laid down was still not a set of standards; rather it was a basic framework from which departures were expected to be disclosed and explained. They were not a code of rigid rules. The over-riding requirement remained to give a 'true and fair view'.

International accounting standards have emerged in the last 30 years. There are two basic templates: International Financial Reporting Standards (IFRS) and US Generally Accepted Accounting Principles (GAAP). The differences can be summarized as follows. IFRS are more principle-based standards than detailed prescriptions. Under it, 'true and fair' is the over-riding rule. Alternative treatments are allowed rather than a single one being prescribed.

US accounting is more authoritarian. This, Myddleton (2004) suggests, is a result of the much greater influence there of government agencies over the subject. As a result, '[i]n the USA "presenting fairly" requires absolute compliance with US GAAP even if it might lead to a misleading view. There is no provision in law or practice for any equivalent of the UK's "true or fair override".'

What can be said about the positions? What are the arguments for and against imposing a common set of rules?

First, the 'for'. Six arguments for accounting standards are as follows. They prevent dishonesty by preparers of accounts. Auditors can lack independence. Investors may be damaged without standards. Accounting decisions can be complex. Uniformity in words and layout is helpful. Standards will facilitate cross-company comparisons.

Now, how strong are these arguments? All have encountered criticism. It *pays* insiders to provide information to outsiders. Auditors' incomes depend in the long run on their honesty. So long as accounts provide a clear account of stewardship, they can give no further guidance. Complex tasks can often differ from one another; this can require different solutions. As to uniformity, a sufficient degree tends to evolve. To quote, by way of an example, a development in a related area, '[p]rospectuses in the UK (fell) voluntarily into a reasonably uniform format because users liked it that way' (Myddleton, 2004, p. 91). Regulation could freeze practice when evolution is desired.[5]

As well as these 'negative' arguments against imposed standards, there are 'positive' ones. They can stifle or even forbid independent judgment. They can reduce competition in ideas, and restrict evolution. They may legitimize bad accounting; and they can mislead by raising expectations unduly. On the first, they can lead to '...an approach [which] implies that unless the rules explicitly forbid it, anything goes' (Myddleton, 2004, p. 99). In a voluntary regime, views on the treatment of difficult issues can evolve slowly; disclosure of the method is what matters. And finally, people can be confused by the clear implication that the presentation of accounts has no grey areas. Everything is not black or white; but compulsory standards imply that it is.

In his study of accounting, Myddleton (2004) describes the members of the Accounting Standards Boards as 'revolutionaries'. Table 7.2 (from his book) summarizes his arguments for saying this.

Table 7.2 Orthodox versus revolutionary accounting

	Orthodox		*Revolutionary*
Purpose	Stewardship	v	Decision-usefulness
Audience	Existing shareholders	v	Existing and potential investors
Source of legitimacy	General acceptance	v	Compulsory standards
Basis of measurement	Historical cost	v	Current value

Source: Myddleton (2004).

He goes on to say, '[i]n each case the ASB shuns the orthodox opinion…'. He is on balance against these compulsory standards, making points such as the following. The absence of standards seems to have been no worse for investors than is their presence; most improvements in accounting came before standards and, after standards, were produced independently of them; and, in addition, he questions whether a board established to set standards could ever decide that the right thing to do was to do nothing.

But be all that as it may, as with the previous examples (capital standards in banking and the regulation of investment trusts), it is clear that governance has for a long time done a good job – governance in this present context being a situation where auditors who prepare and check company accounts prosper by being independent and honest, and providing information helpful to the users of the accounts.

At least in those three areas, governance appears to trump regulation. One cannot generalize simply from three cases. But in fact there is a well-developed body of analysis, neglected in this area, which is helpful in exploring the issues further and considering whether the argument is generalizable.

A neglected approach

So far it has been maintained in three cases that detailed prescription of processes will not necessarily produce desired outcomes. Even if they do produce such outcomes initially, they are unlikely to do so in the long term, when circumstances change (that includes people finding their way round the regulation). What can be done, apart from continually changing the regulations?

The alternative, implied by the above discussion, is to consider what kind of behaviour is desired and then put in place the appropriate 'governance' within the firm so as to promote that behaviour. In the three cases examined, the behaviour desired is respectively: to avoid becoming insolvent; to behave as if the manager of the investment trust had the same objectives as the holders of shares in the trust; and to provide accounts which, so far as the data permit, allow an accurate appraisal of the financial performance of a firm over the time period covered by the accounts.

We can, in other words, specify the objective. Can we design contracts to deliver these objectives?

Contract design has in fact received a good deal of attention over the years from economists. It is usually handled under the heading of 'The Principal–Agent Problem', the nomenclature invented by Ross (1973). The 'principal' is the person who wants something done; the 'agent' is the person employed to do it.

The 'problem', as I show, can arise for a variety of reasons. A little background from the history of economics is helpful in showing both the difficulties and the solutions.

Adam Smith touched on the subject in some detail. This he did at several points. For example:

> the work done by slaves, though it appears to cost only their maintenance, is in the end the dearest of any. A person who can acquire no property, can have no interest but to eat as much, and labour as little as possible.
>
> (Smith, 1776, Book 1, Chapter 8)

But his most detailed, and best known, discussion arises in the context of his explanation for the decline of agriculture in Europe after the fall of the Roman Empire. The system was one where the land was worked by 'metayers': 'The Landlord furnished them with the seed, cattle, and instruments of husbandry. The produce was divided equally between the proprietor and the farmer' (Book 3, Chapter 2). Now, what was the problem? Smith identified two problems – there would be underinvestment and there would be misuse of resources.

> It could never, however, be the interest even of this last species of cultivators (the metayers) to lay out, in the further improvement of the land, any part of the little stock they might save from their own share of the produce, because the lord, who laid out nothing, was to get one-half of whatever it produced … It might be the interest of metayer to make the land produce as much as could be brought out of it by means of the stock furnished by the proprietor; but it could never be in his interest to mix any part of his own with it. In France … the proprietors complain that their metayers take every opportunity of employing the master's cattle rather in carriage than in cultivation; because in the one case they get the whole profits for themselves, in the other they share them with their landlords.
>
> (Smith, 1776, Book 3, Chapter 2, p. 367)

Contract design has appeared in various contexts over the years, both before that famous discussion and after it. Hume (1740) seems to have been the first to state the free rider problem.

> Two neighbours may agree to drain a meadow, which they possess in common; because it is easy for them to know each other's mind; and each must perceive that the immediate consequence of his failing in his part is the abandoning the whole project. But it is very difficult, and indeed impossible, that a thousand persons shou'd agree in any such action; it being difficult for them to concert so complicated a design, and still more difficult for them to execute it; while each seeks a pretext to free himself of the trouble and expence, and wou'd lay the whole burden on others.
>
> (Hume, 1740, p. 538)

This was followed up in nineteenth-century discussions of public finance – on the 'benefit approach' and the 'ability to pay approach' to taxation. Various writers, notably Pantaleoni and de Viti de Marco, advocated the benefit approach. Wicksell (1896) pointed out what became known subsequently as the free rider problem with this approach.

> If the individual is to spend his money for private and public uses so that his satisfaction is maximized he will obviously pay nothing whatsoever for public purposes.... Whether he pays much or little will affect the scope of public service so slightly, that for all practical purposes, he himself will not notice it at all. Of course, if everyone were to do the same, the State will soon cease to function.
>
> (Wicksell, 1896, p. 81)

In other words, it can be advantageous to the individual to conceal preference. That, too, is a problem for contract design.

This 'voting' problem has been tackled by various authors: Borda, Bowen, and Vickrey are the best known.

Borda (1781) showed he was aware of the problem – but, as he acknowledged, his 'solution' was a purely academic one: 'My scheme is intended only for honest men.'

Bowen (1943) proposed a sequential voting procedure but one which depended on myopia. Each voter voted according to his time preferences at each stage – but only because the voter did not look beyond that stage. Vickrey (1960) was led to the conjecture that there is no way of aggregating individual preferences by voting that cannot be distorted by strategic behaviour. (A formal proof of this was provided by Gibbard in 1973.)

The problem of monopoly regulation has also been recognized as essentially one of contract design. This was done by Loeb and Marget (1979), who recognized that (as with the voting problem above) the difficulty is lack of information. The regulator, in advance of setting the regulation, knows less about costs (and possibly demand) than does the regulated firm.

The problem of concealment (or non-disclosure) of course also lies behind the problem of moral hazard that has been recognized for centuries in insurance. A number of economists have grappled with how to design contracts for this – see, for example, Arrow (1963), Pauly (1974), and Grossman and Hart (1983).

The same problem inhibits price discrimination. This was discussed in the context of infrastructure provision by Dupuit (1844).

> The best of all tariffs would be the one which would make pay those which use a way of communication a price proportional to the utility they derive from using this service.... I do not have to say that I do not believe in the possible application of this voluntary tariff; it would meet an insurmountable obstacle in the universal dishonesty of passants, but it is the kind of tariff one must try to approach by a compulsory tariff.
>
> (Dupuit, 1844, p. 223)

It arises too in economic planning. Hayek and Robbins had both pointed out the difficulty of such an activity – a market was needed before the information a planner needed would be disclosed. (As late as 1967, Lange did not acknowledge this point.)

> Were I to rewrite my essay today my task would be much simpler. My answer to Hayek and Robbins would be: so what's the trouble? Let us put the simultaneous equations on an electronic computer and we shall obtain the solution in less than a second. The market process with its cumbersome tatonnements appears old fashioned.
>
> (Lange, 1967, p. 158)

If we stand back to see the problems of contract design that economists have grappled with since Hume and Smith, what do we find?

We see first why the subject temporarily (for at least a hundred years) vanished from view.

In a large economy, with many buyers and many sellers and no entry barriers (such as natural monopoly) to a particular activity, the problems vanish. Rational individual behaviour translates into profit maximization for firms' owners. This leads to cost minimization, and hence to productive efficiency. Similarly, consumers facing exogenous prices have the appropriate incentives for utility maximization.

But of course that treated the firm as a 'black box'. *How* did the owners of firms align the interests of the various members of the firm (workers, managers) with profit maximization? The moment that question returned to view, we came to the issue of contract design. The extensive and often complex literature touched on above, which has examined contract design problems, faces such difficulties and sometimes reaches impasses because of three main types of information problem – adverse selection, moral hazard, and non-verifiability. The first is when the agent has private knowledge (about cost or valuation) that is not available to the principal. The second is when the agent can take action (of a type the principal would not wish) unknown to the principal. The third is when both principal and agent have the same information after the event, but no third party can observe it – so even after the event the information cannot be used for contract enforcement in, for example, a court of law.

Now, do these three issues arise in the examples with which this chapter opens?

Relevance in the examples

Consider the three examples – banking system stability, appropriate information disclosure and behaviour towards investors, and accountants and auditors producing 'accounts of stewardship' which are fit for that purpose.

Banking sector instability can be said to be all too visible. The kind of behaviour that was problematic in the 'splits crisis' can certainly be seen after the event, at least in part. Risk disclosure, for example, can be objectively reviewed *ex post*. Similarly, the results of faulty audits reveal themselves – not necessarily immediately but in due course. In all three cases, there is *ex post* visibility, which can be verified by a third party. So one of our problems is not present. What about adverse selection and moral hazard?

Neither of these is relevant. For in the case under review, we are concerned only with observable outcomes *after* the event and not at all with what goes on *inside* the firms; we can also observe the outcomes. What goes on inside these firms is of course of concern for their owners, and there may be problems of contract design there. But that is no concern of ours. We need specify only that the contracts have characteristics which, regardless of their other features, will provide what the authorities regard as desirable.

An example shows how this might be done. My friend and colleague Charles Goodhart has proposed (I think partly in jest but am not sure) that the chairman of any bank which gets into difficulties should be put in the stocks outside the Bank of England and then, as was traditional with those placed in the stocks, be pelted with rotten fruit. This, he suggests, would sharpen their attention to their respective bank's stability. He is, I am sure, right. But I am not persuaded that any prospective British government would adopt that measure.

Another course, much more plausible, is however prompted by the proposal. The proposal was designed to make senior management focus on stability. This could also be done by insisting that contracts do not grant options with no risk of loss and that management has to place its wealth (the more senior they are, the higher the proportion) in the bank's stock and that stock be held, untradeable, by trustees until, say, five years after retirement of the respective manager (and that any contract designed to offset the risk be unenforceable at law). And, if it were so wished, to sharpen incentives also for the owners, double or even triple liability for each shareholder could be reintroduced.

In other words, the nature of the contract design problem allows relatively straightforward solutions – not necessarily optimal, whatever that is thought to mean in this context – but certainly one free of the problem of the regulator continually chasing the regulated. Similar suggestions can be made for investment trusts and accounting. One has, indeed, already been implied for investment trusts – rigorously enforce the existing body of company law and in particular that part of it governing the conduct of directors. Governance can do a better job than regulation in these areas, provided we are willing to intervene in that part of the firm rather than be equally intrusive (at the least) in other parts.

Now, where does that lead in general? What general lessons can be drawn?

General conclusion

Regulation has invariably led to attempts to circumvent it. Accordingly, it is surely worth considering an approach which aligns the interests of the regulated with the regulators, rather than the latter simply telling the former what to do. There is extensive work by economists on contract design. It is worth attempting to draw on that. This claim is surely reinforced by the work of lawyers – notably Richard Posner – showing how judicial interpretations under common law tend to evolve towards economically efficient outcomes. Law, a form of governance, has worked. Why not try it again?

As the economic literature discussed above has shown, there can sometimes be substantial problems with attempting to do so. But so long as there is public concern only with observable outcomes, governance can at least in principle replace regulation. It should certainly replace regulation as the first resort of governments seeking to influence the behaviour of firms. It will be more durable in its effects, and relying on it, and thus focusing on outcomes rather than processes, will ensure that the regulated firms seek the most economically efficient way of doing what the government wants. We would thus be exploiting the most fundamental of all economic insights, one stated by Adam Smith and reiterated by Hayek in his famous 'The Use of Knowledge in Society'.[6] Each individual knows more about his own situation, interests, and desires than any outside observer can. This insight has (with the exception of the work of Stephen Littlechild) been neglected in the field of regulation. Ending this neglect might well prove productive.

Appendix: defining 'fail'

Sometimes when economists use the word 'fail', a definition of exactly what is meant is unnecessary. An example of this would be the phrase '...a wave of bank failures swept the southern states of the USA'. That phrase, from the discussion of the consequences of the failure of Cauldwell and Co. of Nashville, is taken from Friedman and Schwartz's *A Monetary History of the United States*.[7] In that context, further definition is unnecessary, for what was relevant was that such a wave followed from a surge in the demand for cash (instead of bank deposits) following the closure of an important bank and unchecked could have continued still further, because of that same surge in demand. In the context, it was immaterial how much capital bank shareholders eventually got back, for the concern was not with them but with depositors. But for shareholders and creditors other than depositors, the meaning of fail is crucial. Several issues have to be clarified. How much of their funds did they eventually get back? When did they get it? When did they know they would get something back? When did they know how much they would get back? The answers to these questions are surely likely to affect their behaviour. But answers are seldom provided. Rather it is simply assumed that the word 'fail' has an unambiguous meaning, and subsequent behaviour is then deduced.

There is also discussion of the consequences of a big bank failing and what the monetary and perhaps fiscal authorities should do about this failure. This, aside from neglecting the above issues, also ignores an important fact. Banks, the overnight failure of which would disturb the whole banking system, and perhaps the financial system more generally, rarely fail overnight. Indeed, no example exists in British banking history and, in the US, the case of LTCM (not a bank in any case) is arguable. Rather they decline slowly. From Britain, consider the now defunct Midland Bank. In the 1930s (just after it opened its magnificent head office in Poultry, just across the road from the Bank of England), it was the biggest bank in the world. It steadily declined, suffered the ignominy of receiving a takeover bid from its advertising agency, and was eventually taken over by HSBC. That process took some 50 years. In the US, the failure of Continental Illinois, though often described as an overnight collapse, actually was not. Many of its counterparty banks and other financial institutions had noticed the increased riskiness of its lending, and had reduced or eliminated their exposure to it before the collapse came. To summarize, the word 'fail' should be used carefully.

Notes

1 The current regime, labelled Basel 2 as it was the second major agreement, was shown to be seriously wanting by the financial crisis and is being replaced (not surprisingly by Basel 3).
2 This was the case even before the mid-twentieth century, by which time UK banks were a well-capitalized and well-diversified cartel.
3 As set out in the Companies Acts.
4 As an aside, it is worth observing that there appears to be little evidence that company accounts are good at predicting future profits – except of course when they provide evidence of fraudulent or incompetent stewardship (Benston, 1969).
5 Some have argued that, on those grounds, common law is a superior basis for commerce to Roman law.
6 *American Economic Review*, vol. 35, no. 4. pp. 519–30, September 1945.
7 Princeton University Press, 1963.

References

Arrow, K. (1963) 'Research in management controls: a critical synthesis', in C. Bonini, R. Jaecliche, and H. Wagner (eds), *Management Controls: New Directions in Basic Research*, pp. 317–27, New York: McGraw-Hill.

Benston, G.J. (1969) 'The effectiveness and effects of the SEC's accounting disclosure requirements', in H. Manne (ed.), *Economic Policy and the Regulation of Corporate Securities*, Washington, DC: AEI.

Borda, J.C. de (1781) *Mémoire sur les Elections au Scrutin*, Histoire de l'Academie Royale des Sciences, Paris: Imprimerie Royale.

Bowen, H. (1943) 'The interpretation of voting in the allocation of economic resources', *Quarterly Journal of Economics*, 58: 27–48.

Dupuit, J. (1844) 'De la mesure de l'utilité des travaux publics', *Annales des Ponts et Chaussées*, Paris: Scientifiques et Medicales Elsevier.

Gibbard, A. (1973) 'Manipulation of voting schemes: a general result', *Econometrica*, 41(4): 587–601.

Grossman, S. and Hart, O. (1983) 'An analysis of the principal-agent problem'. *Econometrica*, 51: 7–45.

Hume, D. (1740) *Treatise of Human Nature*, Oxford: Oxford University Press.

Lange, O. (1967) 'The computer and the market', in C.H. Feinstein (ed.), *Socialism, Capitalism, and Economic Growth: Essays Presented to M. Dobb*, Cambridge: Cambridge University Press.

Loeb, M. and Marget, W. (1979) 'A decentralised method of utility regulation', *Journal of Law and Economics*, 22: 399–404.

Myddleton, D. (2004) *Unshackling Accounts*, London: IEA.

Pauly, M.V. (1974) 'Over insurance and public provision of insurance: the roles of moral hazard and adverse selection', *Quarterly Journal of Economics*, 88: 44–62.

Repullo, R. and Suarez, J. (2004) 'Loan Pricing under Basel capital requirements', mimeo, July, CEMFI, Madrid.

Ross, S. (1973) 'The economic theory of agency; the principle's problem', *American Economic Review*, G3: 134–39.

Smith, A. (1776) *The Wealth of Nations*, New York: The Modern History.

Stigler, G.J. (1975) *The Citizen and the State*, Chicago: University of Chicago Press.

Vickrey, W. (1960) 'Utility, strategy and social decision rules', *Quarterly Journal of Economics*, 74: 507–35.

Wicksell, K. (1896) *Finanztheoretische Untersuchungen*, Jena: Gustav Fischer.

8 The impact of the global financial crisis on financial policy

Grant Spencer

In this chapter, I consider New Zealand's financial policy response to the global financial crisis. My focus is on permanent changes to policy following the crisis, rather than the initial short-term emergency responses. I cover financial policies overseen by the Reserve Bank, namely monetary policy, liquidity management, and the prudential supervision of banks and non-banks.

Monetary policy

In New Zealand, monetary policy focuses on the maintenance of price stability. This alone provides no guarantee of economic stability or financial stability. However, the experience in New Zealand and overseas suggests that maintaining price stability over the medium term is the best and most worthwhile contribution monetary policy can make to achieving broader economic and financial stability.

Our inflation targeting framework served us well during the financial crisis and helped guide sensible policy responses. Immediately prior to the crisis, monetary policy in New Zealand had been relatively restrictive with the Reserve Bank increasing the Official Cash Rate (OCR) between 2004 and 2007 in response to elevated inflation pressures associated with a booming housing market. As the global crisis emerged and deepened, we responded by reducing the OCR aggressively. The OCR was cut during 2008 and early 2009 from a high of 8.25 per cent to just 2.5 per cent. These reductions were appropriate, despite high headline rates of inflation at the time due to record high oil prices. The policy easing was consistent with an outlook for rapidly diminishing inflation pressures as the global and domestic economies turned sharply downwards.

Going forward, medium-term price stability will remain the primary objective of monetary policy. However, we expect that monetary policy will have more bite over the next few years than it has had for many years, for a number of reasons:

- First, following the crisis, our banks now face a higher cost of funds. It is now more expensive for them to borrow offshore, which in turn has seen them compete more aggressively for funds raised in the domestic retail deposit market. We currently estimate that the spread of the banks' average cost of funds over the OCR is some 150 basis points higher than prior to the crisis. This state of affairs is likely to persist for some time. It means that, for any given OCR, the rates the banks charge their customers for lending will be higher than before.

- Second, the evidence to date suggests that, following the global crisis, households and businesses are considerably less willing to take on new debt. Credit growth remains very subdued. We believe that this diminished appetite for debt will remain for some time as people and companies work to gradually strengthen their financial positions.
- Third, unlike the situation over much of the past 20 years, New Zealand is now facing an upward sloping yield curve – longer-term interest rates are higher than short-term rates. This means that fixed-rate mortgages are now more expensive than floating or very short-term fixed-rate mortgages. This has seen many borrowers shift back to floating rates over the past two years. As a result, as we move the OCR higher, it is likely to have more 'bite' than it did previously.

Liquidity management

As the global financial crisis (GFC) broke, a key policy response from the Reserve Bank was the expansion of liquidity facilities that we provide to banks and other financial institutions, including a broadening of acceptable collateral instruments. This expansion of facilities was needed to ensure that the financial system remained liquid and that institutions could continue to make payments as required without creating undue stress in the interbank market. In particular, as the banks' access to global markets became very restricted in late 2008/early 2009, the Reserve Bank provided access to term funding secured over mortgage-backed securities. The banks also increased their use of parent funding during this period.

With the crisis behind us, we have been reconsidering the appropriate role and scope of the Reserve Bank's liquidity facilities. The crisis has demonstrated the value of liquidity support for fundamentally sound institutions in the face of systemic market disruptions. While it is important that institutions provide for their own liquidity in the first instance, it is clear that central bank liquidity facilities are an essential backstop at times when shocks to confidence cause market liquidity to dry up. Key requirements for central bank facilities are that: their pricing encourages a return to normal market trading; they are targeted at system liquidity, not individual institutions; and they are fully collateralized.

In light of the GFC experience and the Bank's broader mandate to promote the efficiency of the financial system, we intend in the future to adopt a somewhat broader approach to liquidity management than was the case prior to the crisis. The range of securities that we accept as collateral will be wider than in the past in order to help support liquidity in a number of key financial markets. Such markets include: the NZ dollar, bank bills, NZ government securities, and local authority/SOE stock. In addition, access to the Bank's overnight facility will be extended to major NZ dollar settlement systems.

Prudential policy: banks

Turning to prudential policy, the global financial crisis has prompted a major review of policy internationally. In New Zealand, the financial crisis highlighted shortcomings in the banks' management of funding and liquidity rather than credit losses of the sort seen in the major economies. A heavy reliance on short-term foreign borrowing by the NZ banks meant they were vulnerable to the sort of liquidity shock experienced in late 2008/early 2009. While the banks' funding shortfall was met through parent funding and the Reserve Bank's expanded liquidity facilities, the experience underlined the need for banks to lengthen the maturity of their liabilities relative to assets, in order to reduce their vulnerability to such shocks.

To address these issues, the Reserve Bank introduced a new prudential liquidity policy for banks in April 2010. This policy requires that the banks hold sufficient eligible liquid assets to meet one-week and one-month liquidity mismatch ratio requirements. In addition, the banks must meet a Core Funding Ratio requirement of at least 65 per cent. Core funding consists of customer deposits (weighted by size) and market funding of one year or greater to maturity. The Core Funding Ratio requirement will rise to 75 per cent by mid-2012. The banks have already made good progress in lifting their Core Funding Ratios to be well in excess of the 65 per cent minimum requirement.

Internationally, the moves to strengthen banking regulation are being led by the Basel Committee on Banking Supervision (BCBS), made up of banking supervisors from the major economies and convened by the Bank for International Settlements (BIS). The BCBS developed a number of proposals under the broad 'Basel 3' label, which were agreed at the upcoming G20 meeting in November 2010. The proposals focused on strengthening banks' minimum capital and liquidity requirements. These include higher Tier 1 capital requirements, a greater emphasis on common equity in Tier 1 capital, and a leverage ratio to act as a backstop to the risk-weighted capital regime. Other proposals include more explicit liquidity requirements (similar to those described above for New Zealand), arrangements for greater international coordination of supervision, and revisions to international financial accounting standards. The crisis has shown that existing accounting standards are problematic for financial institutions in a number of areas, such as mark-to-market asset valuations and provisioning rules for loan losses.

Another area to receive attention under Basel 3 is the possible use of macro-prudential policy adjustments to help counter pro-cyclical behaviour in financial systems. The BCBS has proposed that banks be required to build up additional capital buffers at times of rapid credit growth that could then be drawn down in times of stress. The intention of the instrument would be to lessen the impact on the economy when the boom turns to bust as well as possibly constraining excessive credit growth. A number of central banks, including the RBNZ, are also looking at other macro-prudential tools that could possibly be used to help limit the extremities of the credit cycle. The challenge here is to find instruments that will actually work without imposing major efficiency costs on the financial system.

Prudential policy: non-banks

New Zealand's non-bank deposit-taking sector comprises a number of different institutional types. The savings institutions (building societies, credit unions, and the PSIS [a cooperative]) have generally weathered the crisis well. The finance company sector, on the other hand, has faced considerable upheaval over the period since 2006, with only about a third of the companies in early 2006 now remaining active. While the global financial crisis added to the difficulties faced by the finance companies, the sector's issues have been largely home-grown as a result of poor lending decisions, particularly with respect to property development lending, and inadequate capital support. While the Crown retail deposit guarantee scheme has provided some liquidity protection for the sector, allowing time for the sounder institutions to rebuild investor confidence, the companies that have been unable to recapitalize or restructure have ultimately been forced to exit the industry.

An amendment to the Reserve Bank Act in late 2008 saw the Reserve Bank become the new prudential regulator of the non-bank deposit-taking sector, with trustees remaining the front-line supervisors. Since then, the Reserve Bank has been developing a new regulatory framework and phasing in the new prudential requirements. Key elements include mandatory credit ratings, connected lending limits, an 8 per cent minimum capital requirement, and fit and proper tests for senior managers and directors. While these reforms are clearly too late to avert the negative consequences of earlier finance company practices, the overall aim is to raise safety standards in the sector so that the remaining players are more resilient to future business cycles.

Conclusion

The global financial crisis had major effects on the NZ financial system and economy. It prompted responses across the full range of Reserve Bank policies, including monetary policy, liquidity management, and prudential policies. Many of these responses were short term in nature but there have also been important long-term policy consequences. Indeed, in the prudential policy area, there is significant policy change yet to come from the strengthening of international standards under the 'Basel 3' initiative. Most of the permanent policy changes undertaken by the Reserve Bank have related to liquidity: requiring banks to protect themselves better against liquidity shocks; and recognizing a somewhat broader role for the Reserve Bank in supporting financial system liquidity in times of stress. This should not be surprising given that the dominant transmission channel for the global financial crisis was an unprecedented reduction in global financial system liquidity.

9 Creating policy stigmas in financial governance

The International Monetary Fund and capital controls

Jeffrey M. Chwieroth

Policy stigmas are an important aspect of financial governance. Their prescriptions serve both to regulate behaviour and to identify what counts as 'good' financial governance. Conformity with stigmas is thus an important part of signalling 'good' financial citizenship. This chapter explores the source, significance, and shortcomings of one particular policy stigma, that which has been attached to capital controls. Focusing on the International Monetary Fund, it examines empirically how the degree of approval fixed to controls has varied considerably across time and space and within the IMF itself. It analyses the origin and impact of this stigma as well as the potential costs and risks it raises.

The financial crisis that originated in developed economies in summer 2007 and that intensified and spread following the collapse of Lehman Brothers in September 2008 led to a destabilizing sharp, but temporary, reversal of capital inflows to emerging markets. Yet with many emerging markets now decoupling from the slow recovery in developed countries, capital inflows, attracted by significant interest-rate differentials, soon returned in abundance. Notwithstanding the benefits of these flows, many emerging markets are concerned that the recent surge could cause problems for their economies in terms of exchange rate volatility and financial instability. As a result, some governments have taken action to restrict capital flows.

But in imposing these restrictions, many governments have tended to be timid in their actions, taking great effort to present them as small in magnitude, market-based in orientation, and temporary in duration, while eschewing more intrusive and permanent measures that could be necessary for the restrictions to be effective. One important reason for this behavioural tendency is the perception of a stigma attached to use of capital controls. Policy stigmas are an important, but understudied, aspect of financial governance. This chapter seeks to strengthen our understanding of stigmas by exploring their impact on the use of capital controls. It provides an analysis of one source of this stigma, the International Monetary Fund (IMF), and the significance that variation in this stigma has had on policymaking.

The chapter also addresses some shortcomings of stigmas. When a policy is stigmatized, it generates significant costs, actual or perceived, on the government that implements it. These costs in turn place severe limits on the policy autonomy of governments. In some cases, this constraint may prove beneficial, imposing discipline on policies that are clearly suboptimal from the standpoint of economic theory and aggregate welfare. Yet rarely are stigmas derived from a theoretical consensus that provides a singular truth about optimal policy. By raising the actual or perceived costs of a particular policy, stigmas may unintentionally encourage governments to pursue alternative policy choices that, while seemingly optimal given the constraints imposed by the stigma, may generate unanticipated suboptimal outcomes more severe than those that would have developed had the stigmatized policy been pursued. From a political economy standpoint, stigmas are also often associated with varying distributional consequences that are nonetheless cloaked behind the rhetoric of optimality.

Policy stigmas in financial governance: source, significance, and shortcomings

A policy stigma is severe social disapproval of a particular course of action that is perceived to be against prevailing standards of behaviour. Within the field of international political economy, policy stigmas are understood to result from constitutive and regulative norms (Abdelal *et al.*, 2010). Regulative norms specify the boundaries of legitimate practice and thus order and constrain behaviour and, in doing so, constitute what counts as legitimate behaviour for actors with particular identities. For instance, the statement 'Governments practising "good" financial governance do not use capital controls' contains both a regulative and a constitutive element in that it places constraints on the range of legitimate social action and links it to an actor with a particular identity.

Policy stigmas exist in all areas of world politics but they are likely to be particularly influential in finance because of the importance of confidence and credibility. Policies that are deemed illegitimate or lacking credibility cannot be sustained because of the response of market actors to such policies. Since policies require market confidence to in order to work, policy stigmas can have an overwhelming influence on the ability of governments to set policy. These stigmas, regardless of their truth value, define the possible and the feasible.

Stigmas define the meaning fixed to particular policies, shaping the way that actors interpret them. In game theoretic language, stigmas define the range of actions that an audience will view favourably, thereby constructing and sustaining credibility and confidence. By sending a negative signal, governments that implement stigmatized policies expect to trigger an adverse market reaction. Nicely summarizing the constraints that stigmas can impose, Kirshner (2003) observes:

> The astonishing result of this [stigmas] is that in a hypothetical menu of five economic policies, each of which was plausible from the standpoint of economy theory, if three were *perceived* to be illegitimate, they would not in fact be sustainable, *solely for that reason*.
>
> (p. 13, emphasis in original)

Policy stigmas vary across time and space. What may be illegitimate for one type of actor ('developed countries') may not be illegitimate for another ('developing countries'). Moreover, a policy choice stigmatized at one particular moment may have been perfectly legitimate at another moment. For instance, whereas in the early post-war era the use of capital controls during a crisis was conventional wisdom, by the mid-1980s such actions had become seen as sending a negative signal to market actors. Liberalizing controls during a crisis, on the other hand, was argued as necessary to send a positive signal to markets and to restore confidence (Bartolini and Drazen, 1997). Policies, like fashion, are thus subject to fads. But what is fashionable at one moment can later become passé. To paraphrase Keynes, what was once defined as orthodoxy often later becomes redefined as a heresy.

International organizations play an important role in fixing meanings, thus constituting the legitimate boundaries of policymaking (Barnett and Finnemore, 2004). In the area of financial governance, the IMF has been a key player in this regard. Through the authority delegated to it by its member states and its command of specialized knowledge, the IMF commands a degree of deference to its pronouncements on what counts as legitimate policy practice. The institutional tools available to the IMF – conditional lending, surveillance, and its coordinating role with official creditors and private market actors – make it a highly influential actor in particular settings.

Notwithstanding recent events in the euro area, most developed countries seem to have 'graduated' from a history of serial default (Reinhart and Rogoff, 2008), which means they typically can borrow extensively in their own currencies and depend less on the IMF to provide them with a seal of approval. Historically, emerging markets and developing countries tend not to enjoy this luxury and thus often depend on the IMF to inspire and sustain market confidence.[1] Conditional lending and surveillance provide the IMF with two important in-house levers to encourage governments to avoid policies that it stigmatizes.

Equally significant is the coordinating role the IMF plays for official creditors and financial market actors. Progress in debt rescheduling via the Paris Club and the Highly Indebted Poor Countries Initiative is tied to IMF approval, as was progress for many Eastern European countries in their accession negotiations with the European Union (EU). Access for countries such as Greece to the newly created EU stabilization fund also partly depends on IMF approval. Private creditors and investors also often take their cues from the IMF. Although evidence on the magnitude and composition of the 'catalytic' effect from the IMF seal of approval is mixed, there is much more definitive evidence suggesting the presence of 'paralytic' effect from IMF disapproval (Edwards, 2005). In other words, financial market actors do not necessarily flock to countries meeting IMF approval but they do tend to flee from countries meeting its disapproval.

Member states are an important influence on the policy beliefs of international organizations (IOs). Their preferences set the 'outer structural constraint' in which the organization operates (Woods, 2006). Yet because IOs, like the IMF, have significant autonomy, it is necessary to explore intra-organizational processes to understand the policy beliefs they espouse.

The policy beliefs the IMF espouses, like those of any organization, are linked to the beliefs that prevail within the profession from which it recruits (Chwieroth, 2010). Professions are major agents in the construction of policy beliefs, and because the IMF primarily recruits from the economics profession and maintains close links to it, this means many of the organization's beliefs originate from the academic community. Technical knowledge and normative conceptualizations originating from the economics profession offer the staff a lens through which to develop shared diagnoses and policy prescriptions. Fads and fashions in the economics profession can thus have an important influence on the content of the policy stigmas put forth by the Fund.

Organizational beliefs also change via experience through processes of adaptation and learning. Adaptation involves a change in beliefs about the desirability or possibility of using a given policy instrument or instrument setting without any corresponding change in beliefs about the desirability of a particular goal to which the instruments and settings are directed. It can entail changes in organizational language, structures, and symbols, and small modifications of behaviour but the organization's general goals and assumptions remain intact. Learning, on the other hand, involves a comprehensive change in beliefs about the possibility or desirability of a given goal. Organizational language, structures, and symbols are fundamentally altered.

Pre-existing beliefs impose an important constraint on the process of updating beliefs, channelling the lessons that emerge and raising barriers to change. Pre-existing beliefs will tend to engender a confirmation bias in updating, thereby narrowing the kind of information that is considered relevant and filtering this information in such a manner as to match these beliefs. Consequently, when organizational staff encounter outcomes that fail to match up with their expectations, they tend to adapt rather than learn. Change through experience tends to be gradual rather than revolutionary; the exception being times of perceived crisis. In fact, learning is so cognitively difficult that it typically requires a realignment of personnel that enables alternative beliefs to be brought to bear on experience.

Change also comes through the strategic efforts of 'norm entrepreneurs' within an organization. These actors operate from within organizations to change the meaning fixed to particular policies or events and to re-frame and construct what is feasible and legitimate. The success of these entrepreneurs typically depends on their ability to frame new initiatives so that they resonate with pre-existing organizational principles and practices.

In addition to understanding some of the sources and significance of stigmas, it is worth highlighting some of their potential shortcomings. Since economic theory rarely provides a definitive answer as to the optimal policy in every context, there will almost always remain a range of policy choices that are feasible or legitimate. Yet stigmas can skew the ways in which actors understand and react to problems, creating a powerful constraint on policymaking. By raising the actual or perceived costs of a particular policy, stigmas may unintentionally encourage governments to pursue alternative policy choices that, while seemingly optimal given the choice set constrained by the stigma, may entail costs and risks that are more severe than those that would have developed had the stigmatized policy been pursued. As a result, stigmas can unintentionally lead to unanticipated suboptimal outcomes.

From a political economy perspective, it is important to note that, while the aggregate consequences across the range of feasible policy choices may be similar, it is almost certainly the case that they vary in terms of their distributional consequences, despite typically being cloaked under the veil of efficiency and optimality. Policy stigmas are likely to introduce asymmetric costs and benefits to various countries and actors within and across economies. This is particularly problematic because policy stigmas, even those based on sound economic logic, necessarily limit the degree of 'policy space' available to governments, thus artificially privileging some interests over others.[2] Desirable policy will often vary across economies depending on their social priorities and levels of development (Rodrik, 2009). The risk from policy stigmas is that they can become too general and uniform, thus rendering them unsuitable for particular local needs and contexts.

Finally, the effort to stigmatize policies runs the risk of converging on a belief system that provides a poor quality template. It should be noted that this line of argument does not suggest an orientation of 'anything goes'. Rather, the argument is that economic theory often identifies a broader range of plausible policy options than stigmas permit and that such stigmas can end up generating significant risks and negative consequences. Ultimately, as the experience of the IMF in the decade after the Asian financial crisis illustrates, these risks and consequences can feed into resentment and backlash on the part of some actors towards the organization promoting the stigma.

The following sections illustrate these arguments about stigmas by examining historical variation in the legitimacy the IMF fixed to capital controls.

Capital controlled: a creation without stigmas

At the end of the Second World War, collectively shared Keynesian beliefs produced widespread support in the 1940s and 1950s for the view that unfettered capital mobility – particularly for short-term flows – was undesirable and that controls were essential. Rather than being stigmatized, capital controls were the norm. Within the IMF, this norm had two bases of support (Chwieroth, 2010, Chapter 4).

First, the IMF membership supported the legitimacy of controls. The United States, though it decided not to rely on controls and viewed them more sceptically than most of the IMF membership, generally accommodated their use. Other members of the IMF lent greater support, with a number of governments, particularly in Western Europe, fearing the disruptive effects of speculative capital flows.

From within the IMF, the staff also provided a second important base of support for controls. Recruitment patterns proved to be a key influence on the staff approach. In the 1930s and 1940s, Keynesian-minded economists played an important role in helping to construct capital controls as a legitimate policy instrument. Some scholars suggest that support for controls was based on the belief that they were necessary to maintain exchange rate commitments and policy autonomy (Helleiner, 1994). Yet, among most economists, support for controls – particularly in the 1940s and 1950s – went deeper than reconciling elements of what would become the Mundell-Fleming model; it also rested on an understanding of market behaviour that suggested unfettered capital mobility was undesirable in itself.

This understanding of market behaviour rested on Keynes's fundamental insight that market behaviour was not simply a rational reaction to an efficient use of information regarding fundamentals. Instead, for Keynes, market behaviour was plagued by a pervasive uncertainty that limited the ability of investors to make use of information efficiently. Constrained by uncertainty, incompletely informed investors came to rely on conventions to help them surmise what other actors might do. Prices were seen not as representing the 'true value' of a financial asset but rather what investors thought others believed it was worth, each of whom was assigning value from the same point of view. But conventions could become self-reinforcing and come to take on a life of their own, leaving governments subject to wide swings in market sentiment that were often unrelated to fundamentals. A system based on unfettered capital mobility was thus seen as prone to manias, crashes, and panics.

In more contemporary parlance, Keynes and his followers were united by the view that factors intrinsic to the operation of markets limit the extent to which actors use information efficiently; the result often being myopia, herding, momentum, and rationing, which manifests itself in capital inflow 'bonanzas' followed by abrupt and 'sudden stops' and reversals. Because these factors are intrinsic to the operation of markets and are difficult, if not impossible, to eliminate, controls were legitimated as an essential and permanent policy instrument.

Through their participation in the Bretton Woods delegations and the professionalization of their graduate students, Keynesian economists helped define the range of policy options that could be entertained by the Fund staff. When the staff members came to draw on their training to diagnose economic problems and to form policy judgments, the Keynesian content of this training helped ensure that the legitimacy of controls would be upheld, even when it later contradicted with the preferences of powerful member states. Many staff members recruited in the 1940s and 1950s would serve in senior positions until the 1980s.

The norm of capital control was formally institutionalized in the IMF's Articles of Agreement at the Bretton Woods Conference. As opposed to long-term flows – which were seen as 'productive' and 'legitimate' – short-term flows were seen as necessitating control. The Fund's Articles explicitly gave member states the right to use controls and formal policy encouraged the use of controls, rather than IMF resources, to manage capital outflows, empowering the Fund to request governments employ controls and to declare them ineligible for IMF financing if they refused.

Despite widespread endorsement of the norm of capital control, there were developments in the early post-war period that foreshadowed the eventual stigmatization of capital controls. During a brief interval, 1945–7, the United States sought to promote a return to neoclassical orthodoxy with Keynesian advocates losing favour within the new Truman administration and members of the private financial community emerging in prominent policymaking positions. Two significant events occurred during this interval: the failed attempt at sterling convertibility and an IMF board decision on the use of the organization's resources (Chwieroth, 2010, Chapter 4).

Delegates to the Bretton Woods Conference had sought to endow the IMF with the authority to mandate the use of cooperative capital controls to help strengthen their effectiveness. Although opposition from the private financial community succeeded in watering down this provision in the Articles, there remained an expectation that governments would offer their cooperation upon request. But when Britain and Western Europe, faced with massive capital flight to the US, turned to it for assistance, they found this expectation to be proven erroneous. Instead, the US insisted that countries faced with capital flight adjust their policies. The US refusal dealt a fatal blow to the expectation that cooperative controls would be a norm in financial governance.

A second key event was a 1946 IMF board decision, implemented at US insistence, which ruled out the use of IMF resources to finance capital account crises. The decision ensured that IMF resources could not be employed to support countries with ineffective capital controls. By restricting governments from using IMF resources to finance capital account crises and refusing to implement cooperative controls, the US placed the burden on countries to adjust.

However, the deepening of the crisis in Europe and the onset of the Cold War led to an end of this brief interval and fostered a change of views within the US. Reversing their earlier position, US officials came to accommodate official financing as a support mechanism for ineffective controls. This financing took the form of the Marshall Plan.

After this brief interval, the US became more accommodative, even encouraging, of the use of capital controls abroad. Perhaps the high point of this orientation was US support for a 1956 IMF board decision that reaffirmed that governments could employ controls 'for any reason' and 'without approval of the Fund' (as cited in Chwieroth, 2010, p. 114). This decision deepened the formal legitimacy of capital controls as a policy instrument.

The limits and hollowness of Keynesianism in the 1960s

The 1960s were a decade of significant transition in the norms of financial governance emanating from academic economists. Monetarism would emerge as a formidable challenger to Keynesianism but it was the development of the neoclassical synthesis that would have a far greater impact at this time. Proponents of the neoclassical synthesis sought to adapt Keynes's insights so that they could fit within the broad confines of neoclassical orthodoxy. Like Keynes, they rejected the neoclassical assumption that prices adjust instantaneously to clear markets; instead, arguing that it was possible for the economy to reach an equilibrium characterized by excess supply or insufficient demand. In such circumstances, government intervention was necessary.

But rather than point to conventions to account for investment volatility, as Keynes had, proponents of the neoclassical synthesis pointed to short-run market imperfections, such as price and wage rigidities. Cast aside was the emphasis on uncertainty; replacing it was a focus on market errors that prevent actors from forming their expectations efficiently only in the short run. This theoretical department induced what Best (2005) calls the 'hollowing out' of Keynesianism.[3]

Although proponents of the neoclassical synthesis and monetarism disagreed over the desirability and efficacy of government intervention, they shared remarkably similar views about market behaviour. While the former focused on short-run market errors and the latter on lags and adaptive expectations, both shared an underlying faith in market rationality. The invisible hand of the market could become paralysed in the short run, described by Keynes, but in the long run it behaved as neoclassicals suggested.

For proponents of the neoclassical synthesis, their understanding of market behaviour suggested that, while markets could be left unfettered in the long run, in the short run there was a case for intervention. This view inspired a series of 'second-best' arguments that suggested that a government facing one clear distortion or market error could, in principle, improve welfare by introducing capital controls. However, because intervention was legitimate only so long as the distortion or market error paralysed markets in the short run, it would necessarily be a *temporary*, rather than a *permanent*, measure and markets would be left unfettered in the long run. Permanent intervention would in the long run entail significant administrative costs, generate increasing distortions, and invite evasion and corruption. Monetarists went even further, claiming that all controls were counterproductive and making the case for floating exchange rates.

The emergence of this new understanding of market behaviour undermined the Keynesian standard of behaviour that controls should be an essential and permanent feature of financial governance. Adherents to the neoclassical synthesis, such as Tobin, treated speculative capital flows as something that could and should be managed via market-oriented measures, such as taxes and tax-like instruments.

This view is therefore quite similar in an important respect to arguments for floating exchange rates. Neither approach seeks to *eliminate* speculation, as Keynes had, but rather seeks only to keep it within certain limits and transfer some of the costs to investors who engage in it. From a Keynesian perspective, the Tobin tax and similar proposals fail to confront the far more pervasive problems of uncertainty and convention-driven market behaviour. Taxes, tax-like instruments, and floating exchange rates increase the costs of international financial transactions but leave them otherwise unfettered. The emergence of the neoclassical synthesis, as well as monetarism, meant that beginning in the early

1960s few academic economists doubted the *long-run* desirability of liberalizing capital controls.

At this time, the US, reflecting the rise to advocates of the neoclassical synthesis to prominent policymaking positions, and West Germany became important advocates of greater freedom for capital movements. They in turn lent crucial support to an initiative from IMF managing director Per Jacobsson that would authorize the Fund to finance disruptive capital outflows (Chwieroth, 2010, Chapter 5). Although France and Canada opposed the proposal, they could not prevent the initiative from being approved. Advocates of authorizing the IMF to finance capital account crises saw it as a means to encourage greater freedom for capital movements because it would enable governments to avoid the use of capital controls. The US thus began to back away from its early post-war accommodation of controls and now came to support official financing, not as a means of buttressing ineffective controls but rather as a means of encouraging liberalization.

The Fund staff's views also evidence some change during this period. With the change in preferences of some leading member states, there was now greater space for the staff to consider alternatives to Keynesianism. During this period, the staff became less wedded to Keynesian prescriptions for implementing or tightening controls to deal with capital flow surges; instead they placed greater emphasis on the need for adjusting policies and for drawing on official financing so as to refrain from using controls.

Although the staff were surely aware of the academic developments surveyed earlier, their new, comparatively greater emphasis on adjustment and financing was not due to the emergence of the neoclassical synthesis and monetarism. On the contrary, while the staff did modify their proclivity for advocating controls to respond to disruptive capital flows, they retained a Keynesian understanding of market behaviour. Staff reports at the time continued to offer concerns about investor decisions governed by conventions; 'especially as speculation tends to feed upon itself' and can 'force a country into devaluation when it is not in a state of fundamental disequilibrium' (as cited in Chwieroth, 2010, p. 129). Moreover, the staff told the IMF board that their informal approach would be to favour the use of controls over adjustment.

Instead of having new beliefs transmitted to them from the academic community, the staff adapted their beliefs in light of the experiences of the 1960s. The staff viewed the gradual liberalization of controls in the 1950s and 1960s as beneficial in promoting trade and development, as well as easing the adjustment process in some countries. Country experiences with utilizing unilateral controls also suggested to the staff that they were increasingly ineffective.

In this period and later on, existing organizational principles and practices shaped the staff's receptivity to adapting their beliefs. An important factor behind the staff's receptivity to greater emphasis on adjustment as opposed to controls was the way this adaptation fitted with the Fund's approach to balance-of-payments adjustment. This approach, known as the Polak model, directed the staff's attention to deficit country policies as the source of instability and obscured the influence of external factors such as convention-driven investor behaviour. The lesson that controls were increasingly ineffective also resonated with the Polak approach, which implied that measures that failed to address underlying payments imbalances, such as controls, would at best produce only a short-term improvement in the balance of payments.

Adaptation and the way that these adaptations fit with existing organizational principles and processes thus overturned previous beliefs that prioritized the use of controls to manage balance-of-payments pressures. But the experiences of the 1960s did not lead the staff to adopt the belief that unfettered capital mobility was desirable in itself. The Fund's personnel configuration of Keynesian-minded economists made the organization largely unreceptive to the possibility that liberalizing all capital flows was desirable, even though some leading member states – particularly the US and West Germany – were advocating such a view. As a result, the staff members adapted their existing beliefs to the perceived limits of Keynesianism but failed to learn new ones that identified complete capital freedom as a desirable goal.

To be sure, capital controls were not yet stigmatized as a policy instrument but the beliefs underpinning their legitimacy were notably different from those of the early post-war era. Rather than being seen as an essential and permanent solution to the problem of pervasive uncertainty, they were now cast as, at best, a temporary response to the limited difficulties posed by disruptive capital flows. The erosion of support for controls was clearly under way.

Academic stigmatization and international monetary reform

The emergence of new classical economics based on rational expectations, efficient markets theory, and real business cycle (RBC) theory resulted in the academic stigmatization of capital controls. These new beliefs, which cast market actors as rational and efficient in the use of 'all available information', resemble many of the same principles of neoclassical orthodoxy that Keynes had challenged. Market actors not only perfectly understand the complex workings of the economy, they also are aware of the statistical distributions of all the shocks that can potentially hit the economy. In this world, there is no uncertainty, only risk. Systematic mistakes by market actors, such as asset bubbles or excesses, self-fulfilling crises, short-run market errors, and lags, are impossible since all actors know the workings of the economy.

These and other insights were later formalized in Dynamic Stochastic General Equilibrium (DSGE) models, which became the new bedrock of macroeconomics. Macroeconomists also resurrected the law of Ricardian equivalence, which suggested, contrary to Keynes, that fiscal policy could not affect output. RBC theorists further added to the stigmatization of government intervention through arguments that explained long-term growth and cyclical movements as a function of productivity shocks rather than fluctuations in aggregate demand. In the new field of financial economics, the efficient markets hypothesis suggested that since financial markets are 'efficient' in employing all available information in determining asset prices, prices reflected the true state of the economy based on fundamentals and actors could be left to make Pareto-efficient decisions based on unfettered trade in financial assets and to supervise themselves with self-regulation.

A new broad continuum of beliefs, labelled *Neoliberal*, emerged, which ranged from the neoclassical synthesis to monetarism to new classical economics. Although proponents of each of these schools of thought offer different views on the desirability and efficacy of government intervention and the behaviour of market actors, Neoliberals, as I define them, all draw to some extent on neoclassical-informed assumptions and models and share the view that unfettered capital mobility is desirable in the *long run.*

To be sure, there remained considerable debate among economists. Some economists, drawing on second-best arguments, highlighted that capital controls could be welfare-improving in the presence of other distortions. But these same economists also generally only sought to demonstrate that controls could theoretically improve welfare. In practice, these economists argued it was better to remove the existing distortion by adjusting policies rather than introducing a new distortion.

Yet some economists, the New Keynesians, who see themselves as the intellectual successors of the neoclassical synthesis, remained sceptical of arguments that removed any scope for the use of controls. Like the neoclassical synthesis, New Keynesian understandings of market behaviour are premised on the assumption that market actors employ information efficiently in the long run but not in the short run, where market errors could justify government intervention. But the New Keynesians, like their intellectual predecessors, focused largely on introducing Keynesian flavours to an otherwise neoclassical recipe. Introducing wage and price rigidities into a neoclassical model populated by rational and efficient market actors had little to do with the Keynesian emphasis on uncertainty and convention-driven behaviour (Skidelsky, 2009). Indeed, until the late 1990s, the difference that remained among most economists tended to be one of degree rather than kind. Debates persisted within the profession over sequencing and temporary controls, but few questioned the long-run desirability of freeing capital movements. As Tirole (2002, p. ix) observes: '[A] wide consensus had emerged among economists, capital account liberalization – allowing capital to move freely in and out of countries without restrictions – was unambiguously good.' In short, academic economists had come to stigmatize capital controls.

With some key advocates of these new beliefs ascending to key policymaking position in the Nixon administration, their emergence had an immediate impact on the Fund's formal rules. Yet at least initially they did not affect the staff's informal approach, nor did it produce a corresponding stigmatization in financial governance. Indeed, on the eve of the US closure of the gold window in 1971, one observer (Krause, 1971, p. 536) noted, 'Capital movements have been progressively liberalized by most countries, but actions which tend to restrict capital movements do not elicit cries of outrage.' In fact, European and Japanese officials, and the IMF management and staff, would not abandon their support for controls for some time, which pitted them against the US, who now for the first time pressed for their removal.

Acting as a 'norm leader', the US insisted on changes to formal IMF rules so that they seemingly directed the staff to encourage liberalization, at least in circumstances where controls impeded balance-of-payments adjustment (Chwieroth, 2010, Chapter 6). One modest change, made at US insistence, was that the Fund's Articles now stated that one of the essential purposes of the international monetary system was to promote freedom for capital movements. But disagreements among the Fund's membership ensured that this revision did not undermine a government's right to use controls and that it fell short of developing a code of conduct on their use, which the US had favoured.

Although the IMF's leading member state had become increasingly hostile to capital controls, the staff did not demonstrate much change. This was largely due to the fact that collectively shared beliefs within the Fund continued to view controls as a legitimate policy instrument. In the context of the reform negotiations, most staff members initially favoured controls to support the fixed exchange rate system. But even after the move to generalized floating in 1974 – which is commonly depicted as a crucial turning point in lessening concerns about capital mobility – most staff continued to envision controls as one of several means that governments should use to maintain 'normal zones' for their exchange rate. Moreover, staff support for controls also led them rarely to implement special consultations, which the US had insisted upon, with a government if controls were introduced for balance-of-payments reasons. Thus, although the US had become increasingly hostile to controls, and had succeeded in changing the IMF's formal rules, the organization had yet to stigmatize them.

Towards a general but uneven stigmatization

The 1980s and 1990s was a period of significant change to the IMF staff's informal approach (Chwieroth, 2010, Chapter 7). It was a period when most of the IMF's leading member states, including Japan and members of the European Union, came to accept the desirability of freeing capital flows and completed the process of dismantling their own controls. Although the staff recognized the emergence of this new ideational climate among the member states, encouragement for advocating liberalization or stigmatizing controls was not pushed on them. Without a legal mandate or active influence from member states or IMF management, the staff discarded their attachment to earlier beliefs that legitimized controls as essential policy instruments, and replaced it with beliefs that spanned the full continuum of Neoliberal beliefs described earlier. A new informal approach emerged that identified freeing capital flows as desirable, at least in the long run, but interestingly, until the mid-1990s, there was no change in the Fund's formal rules.

Rather than emphasizing uncertainty and convention-driven behaviour, as the staff did in the early post-war years, increasingly in the 1980s the staff saw market actors as rationally responding to an efficient reading of fundamentals.

Beginning in the mid-1980s and continuing until the Asian financial crisis, the general informal orientation of the staff was to emphasize the cost of capital controls and the benefits of liberalization, while underemphasizing the risks and vulnerabilities associated with openness. Initially, the staff concentrated on the efficiency gains from capital account openness and the need to attract foreign investment as the principal rationales for liberalization. Over time, the staff increasingly stigmatized controls as essential instruments of macroeconomic planning. Whereas for much of the post-war era the staff had lent legitimacy to traditional arguments for controls (i.e. that controls could increase domestic investment and tax revenue, support financial interventionism and macroeconomic planning, permit greater monetary policy independence and manage balance-of-payments pressures), the general orientation of the staff for much of the 1980s and 1990s was to stigmatize controls as harmful for economic performance, generating severe distortions, delaying policy adjustment, and sending negative signals to market actors.

With respect to capital flight, which was a major disruptive influence on Latin American economies during the debt crisis, rather than seeing it as early post-war IMF staff had (as a principal 'cause' of the problem facing economies), the staff from the mid-1980s onwards understood capital flight to be a 'symptom' of poor fundamentals. With this shift in the meaning fixed to capital flight, the IMF began emphasizing policy adjustment rather than the imposition or intensification of controls on outflows. In fact, in cases where controls were seen as ineffective because of extensive capital flight or use of parallel foreign exchange markets, some staff pressed for liberalization. By the mid-1990s, some staff had been encouraging liberalization informally, though not uniformly or indiscriminately, for nearly a decade.

These new beliefs led the staff to downplay the potential risks of capital flow volatility and to overlook the potential usefulness of 'supply-side' regulatory measures aimed at market actors based in the financial centres of developed countries; a prescription consistent with an alternative interpretation, more closely aligned with Keynesian beliefs and often advocated by emerging markets and developing countries, that stresses factors intrinsic to the operation of international capital markets as contributing to financial instability. Tighter regulation of market actors, for instance, through internationally coordinated tightening of capital requirements to limit herding behaviour (Dobson and Hufbauer, 2001), could have proven useful in reducing the negative externalities that emanated from the financial centres of developed countries. But the staff eschewed such regulatory measures; instead, often welcoming supply-side liberalization as beneficial for providing emerging markets and developing countries greater access to international capital markets.

It has often been said that the IMF's stigmatization of controls resulted from management acquiescence to pressure from the US, who in turn were shaped by demands from the private financial sector. But the evidence does not support this portrayal (Chwieroth, 2010, Chapter 7). IMF management did little to encourage the staff to shift their views. Michel Camdessus, managing director from 1987 to

2001, emerged in the mid-1990s as a strong supporter of giving the IMF the authority to promote liberalization and jurisdiction over the capital accounts of its members (Abdelal, 2007). But no specific intellectual or operational guidance was forthcoming from Camdessus or First Deputy Managing Director Stanley Fischer until after the staff had already shifted their views.

Without any strong indication that management favoured a particular orientation, it is difficult to conclude that it drove staff behaviour. To be sure, once management signalled its preferences, various organizational incentives played a role. But these incentives were largely limited to reinforcing the shift that had come 'from within' rather than initiating any significant shift 'from above'.

The US was also not the primary determinant of the change in the staff's orientation. Beginning in the 1980s, the US saw greater freedom for capital movements as in its long-term interest and sought to promote it in specific bilateral settings, such as Japan, South Korea, and Taiwan. But the issue was not viewed as a top priority or one on which to expend resources within the Fund. It was only in the mid-1990s that the US Treasury began to make a big push for the staff to encourage liberalization. In short, though the Fund's new orientation benefitted long-term US interests, it was not a direct result of them.

In the early 1990s, after most controls had been dismantled within Europe, some governments became strong advocates for greater freedom for capital movements, which in turn lessened the degree of preference heterogeneity among the G7. Yet, importantly, this new preference configuration did not emerge until after the staff's general orientation had shifted. This new preference configuration may have helped reinforced the staff orientation but it was not the source of it. It should also be noted that, despite US and European support for greater freedom for capital movements, the IMF board could never reach a consensus on the legitimacy of controls and thus failed to issue any directives on the issue until 1995.

With respect to the private financial sector, it is clear that they exerted little influence on the staff's orientation. First, the staff failed to consult the private financial sector on this issue and thus it had little opportunity to make its views known. Second, if the staff had engaged in such outreach, it would have heard that the private financial sector was generally cautious in its support for greater capital freedom, viewing it as desirable in principle but with its enthusiasm tempered by an awareness of the risks and vulnerabilities that can accompany premature liberalization.

Without firm directives or formal rules from management or member states, and in the context of preference heterogeneity among IMF members, the staff were provided with significant autonomy to develop their orientation independently. This autonomy permitted the staff to rely on their own judgment and initiative to determine whether liberalization should be encouraged informally in a given case.

Professionalization and administrative recruitment were two critical factors shaping the staff's new orientation. Beginning in the mid-1980s, the substantial group of individuals who had served as members of staff since the 1940s and

1950s began to retire in large numbers. These retiring staff, which because of their Keynesian training and the experiences of the 1930s were more inclined to view controls as legitimate, were subsequently replaced primarily by 'Neoliberal-trained' economists who had joined the staff in the 1960s and early 1970s. This personnel realignment helped overturn long-standing beliefs and associated practices that had legitimated capital controls. Without this personnel realignment in the 1980s, the Fund's stigmatization of controls therefore would have been, in all likelihood, delayed, more incremental, and less coherent than it was.

In the 1980s and 1990s, in addition to the role of new recruits replacing retiring staff members, learning via country experiences helped alter the orientation of the Fund. The transition to capital account openness – particularly among EU countries – was seen by many staff members as critical in demonstrating the desirability of liberalization. Other staff pointed to the case of Indonesia as an example of the benefits of liberalization for emerging markets and developing countries. Staff research studies also provided evidence that disconfirmed for many staff the validity of traditional arguments for controls.

These experiences and evidence helped foster among the staff a comprehensive reappraisal of organizational goals. Old organizational ideologies, norms, language, and routines were largely discarded, and new ones took their place. Rather than adapting through simply adding new agendas or policy instruments to existing organizational practice, the staff experienced a deeper shift in their beliefs about desirable goals. By helping to create an internal ideational configuration that made it more acceptable within the Fund to analyse controls from a more critical perspective, the personnel alignment of the 1980s played an important part in creating an environment conducive for learning. In the absence of this realignment, the cognitive difficulties associated with learning likely would have limited the extent to which it occurred.

Although it is difficult to assess the precise impact of the IMF's general, but uneven, stigmatization, there is much evidence to suggest that it was significant. Notably the IMF was legally prohibited from requiring capital account liberalization as a formal condition for loans and thus it could not insist that governments liberalize in the same manner it could for other policies. Processes of social approval and disapproval thus became an important influence.

Some governments initiated liberalization in the context of loan programmes in order to ingratiate with IMF officials and gain their material and symbolic support and/or to provide political cover against their domestic opponents (Woods, 2006; Mukherjee and Singer, 2010).[4] Others drew on the expertise of the IMF through its technical assistance missions, which in many cases offered advice encouraging greater liberalization (Chwieroth, 2010, pp. 171–3). IMF surveillance missions routinely encouraged governments to liberalize, serving as a 'cheerleader' that provided technical and normative support to reformers (Independent Evaluation Office, 2005). Along with credit rating agencies, the IMF's stigmatization served to heighten the reputational costs imposed by financial market actors on countries that used or introduced controls (Abdelal, 2007). As a result, in contrast to the early post-war era, rather than intensifying or introducing restrictions during a crisis, governments in the mid-1980s began to liberalize them (Haggard and Maxfield, 1996, p. 37). In short, controls became perceived as a negative signal by financial market actors.

Critics of the Fund have wrongly accused it of having uniformly promoted liberalization in a 'one size fits all' fashion (Stiglitz, 2002). Yet careful examination of the evidence reveals that, beneath the surface of the Fund's general orientation to support greater freedom for capital flows, lurked considerable internal debate over how governments should proceed towards this goal. The staff did not agree on whether to proceed rapidly or slowly, nor on whether to proceed with various preconditions or allowances for the introduction of temporary controls. Within the halls of the IMF, these debates over interpreting and applying the emerging norm of freedom for capital movements took the form of a struggle between 'gradualists' and supporters of a 'big bang'.

Gradualists emphasized sequencing (i.e. ensuring that certain supporting policies and institutions were in place before additional liberalizing measures were undertaken), while big-bang proponents argued for a rapid move to liberalization without regard to sequencing. Although both groups generally stigmatized the use of administrative controls (i.e. outright prohibitions or quantitative limits) and restrictions on capital outflows, particularly when they were introduced during a crisis, this consensus did not extend to the issue of sequencing or to the use of temporary market-based controls on capital inflows. The Fund thus promoted a general but uneven stigmatization of capital controls. As a result, though the staff collectively shared a belief in the long-run desirability of greater freedom for capital flows, their views were not monolithic and they often offered conflicting analyses and recommendations on how to proceed towards it.

This internal debate was very much a reflection of a similar intellectual battle occurring within the economics profession. While professionalization and administrative recruitment fostered a shift in the general orientation of the Fund, it also created subcultures within the organization, as new recruits brought contrasting beliefs associated with unsettled debates within the economics profession. Intra-disciplinary debates about sequencing and allowances for selective capital controls provided an ideational basis for internal bureaucratic struggles within the IMF.

The gradualist position developed first. Informed by the neoclassical synthesis/New Keynesian understanding of market behaviour, it viewed liberalization as desirable in the long run but viewed selective controls as often necessary to remove distortions or correct short-run market errors. Gradualists, for instance, saw the differential speed of adjustment for goods and asset markets as reason for sequencing reforms. The gradualist position was also partly a reaction to a financial crisis in Chile in the early 1980s, which some staff attributed to the government's decision to liberalize in the absence of critical supporting policies and institutions, such as robust prudential financial regulations.

Drawing on standard second-best arguments for intervention, much of the initial gradualist sympathy for temporary controls was that they could insulate weak and poorly regulated financial systems from capital flow volatility.

Controls would provide policymakers the breathing space necessary to implement, but not avoid, policy adjustments needed to strengthen their financial systems and prudential regulations. In a few countries, the staff pointed to problems posed by weak banking systems (Poland in 1992 and the Czech Republic in 1993) or inadequate prudential regulations (Thailand in 1992 and Mexico in 1993) as suggesting a need to slow down the pace of liberalization or to tighten regulations.

But most of the staff failed to appreciate fully the need for sequencing. Instead, from the late 1980s until the mid-1990s, advocates of the big bang eclipsed the gradualists. Internal advocates or 'norm entrepreneurs', such as Manuel Guitian, a high-ranking staff member, were quite successful in promoting this view within the IMF. Guitian and other big-bang supporters sought to discredit gradualist arguments, claiming that the ineffectiveness of controls made sequencing irrelevant and that gradualism was a recipe for vested interests to maintain the permanence of controls. Big-bang supporters also downplayed the importance of constructing robust prudential regulations prior to liberalizing. Instead, they argued the best route to robust prudential regulations was to liberalize, as it would permit market discipline to operate and ensure that government stepped up their efforts to enhance the regulatory framework.

The overlap between big-bang arguments and organizational principles aided the advocacy of big-bang proponents. During and after the 1980s debt crisis, the organization as a whole was receptive to market-based measures that permitted developing countries greater access to capital flows. As a result, the Fund was often biased towards any liberalization, regardless of its sequence, as better than no liberalization at all. Big-bang advocacy was also resonated with the general enthusiasm at the end of the Cold War for 'shock therapy' approaches to market reform. The big-bang approach was thus in many ways an extension of the shock therapy approach to non-transition economies, though it was also employed by some staff in Eastern Europe and the former Soviet Union as well. Arguments for sequencing based on second-best reasoning also did not fit well in an organization with a culture that prioritized 'first-best' policy prescriptions.

The ascendance of the big-bang approach was also facilitated by the way the IMF was organized. Until 1992, organizational expertise and responsibility for monetary systems and exchange restrictions were kept in separate departments. Although staff in both departments were aware of the links between domestic financial and international financial liberalization, because organizational expertise and responsibility for monetary systems and exchange restrictions was kept separate until 1992, there was no strong organizational capacity to explore systematically how domestic financial and international financial liberalization might be coordinated. When organizational expertise and responsibility for monetary systems and exchange restrictions was finally merged, it took some time for the staff in the new department to develop any specific conclusions about sequencing.

Despite their differences of view, gradualists and big-bang advocates were united in their opposition to controls on outflows, a view that had started to emerge in the 1960s, when the staff found controls to be an inappropriate substitute for adjusting policies in response to balance-of-payments pressures; that solidified in the early 1990s, when the staff observed that the intensification of controls on outflows by some governments failed to prevent the collapse of their exchange rate commitments during the European Exchange Rate Mechanism crisis.

Support for any kind of administrative control that prohibited or limited particular transactions also all but evaporated. But temporary market-based controls on inflows proved much more controversial. At the centre of the debate was the use of such measures in Chile in the early-to-late 1990s. Big-bang supporters attacked the measures as prolonging unsound policies, creating severe distortions, and failing to substitute for adjusting policies that were driving capital surges. Their initial evaluations suggested the effectiveness of Chile's controls would prove short-lived, forcing the introduction of additional restrictions to maintain the same level of control and thus introducing further distortions. Initial empirical studies of the controls by big-bang supporters pointed to evidence that the Chilean controls did not appear to slow down the volume of capital flows, permit greater monetary independence, or prevent real exchange rate appreciation.

However, gradualists within the Fund saw the measures as providing a legitimate way of insulating Chile's underdeveloped and poorly regulated domestic financial system from capital flow volatility. Some prominent academic economists (Eichengreen and Wyplosz, 1996) also began to make similar arguments. But this prescription did not fit well with the framing offered by the big-bang supporters or with the organization's cultural emphasis on first-best policy prescriptions. As a result, influential gradualists developed a strategy to frame such measures not as a substitute for adjustment but as 'prudential measures' to safeguard the domestic financial system.

Big-bang supporters initially proved resistant to this framing but the crisis in Mexico in 1994–5 offered gradualists an opportunity. The 'twin' currency and banking crisis in Mexico provided a vivid demonstration for many within the Fund of the need to coordinate financial sector development, prudential supervision, and capital account liberalization. Although most within the IMF, including management, attributed the crisis to unsustainable macroeconomic policies in the context of a fixed exchange rate, gradualists were able to convince some staff members that Mexico's rapid privatization of the banking system and liberalization of the capital account had contributed to the crisis and that Chile's relative stability during this period was due in part to its controls.

In the aftermath of the Mexican crisis, there was greater awareness of the risks of inadequate sequencing, enhanced receptivity to arguments stressing a need for prudential regulation, and heightened sympathy for temporary market-based controls. The Mexican crisis also helped the gradualists to undermine the big-bang framing of the Chilean controls. As a result, the staff for the first time turned their attention towards evidence suggesting the controls had lengthened the maturity structure of inflows, thus minimizing vulnerabilities to the domestic financial sector. Although the general orientation of the Fund was to stigmatize controls on outflows and any type of administrative restriction, and to view temporary market-based controls on inflows as distortionary, waning in effectiveness over time, and as a poor substitute for policy adjustment, there was now increased sympathy for justifying such measures on prudential grounds and on a temporary basis.

In the immediate aftermath of the Mexican crisis, staff responsible for the organization's relations with Brazil, the Czech Republic, Hungary, Slovenia, and Thailand accommodated temporary market-based controls on prudential grounds. But a big division had opened up within the organization at all levels, even management, where Fischer appeared more open than Camdessus to the use of temporary market-based controls. In various countries, such as Chile, Romania, Russia, and South Korea, big-bang supporters continued to advocate liberalization enthusiastically. Interestingly, in some countries, the staff from various departments within the Fund clashed in the advice they offered directly to country officials. Far from offering a 'one-size-fits-all' policy template, in the words of one high-ranking IMF staff member, 'one side of the house was stepping on the accelerator, while the other side was applying the brake' (quoted in Chwieroth, 2010, p. 197).

Nonetheless, because big-bang advocates tended to be the most vocal and do most of the writing about the topic, the Fund became widely perceived as in favour of rapid liberalization. To be sure, the orientation of the Fund created a general stigma on the use of controls. But this stigma was uneven and became increasingly so after the Mexican peso crisis. In spite of this unevenness, the perception on the part of key actors that it was uniform likely created many of the effects associated with stigmas that were outlined earlier.

Failed formal stigmatization and reconsideration of informal stigmas

The latter half of the 1990s witnessed within the Fund both the high-water mark and demise of enthusiasm for greater freedom for capital movements. It was a period in which an attempt was made to align formal IMF rules with the general, though uneven, informal stigmatization of the Fund staff. An initiative emerged that sought to amend the IMF Articles to give the Fund the formal mandate to promote liberalization as well as fuller jurisdiction over the capital account policies of its members. In granting the Fund fuller jurisdiction over the capital account, the initiative would have prohibited governments from imposing virtually all types of controls without Fund approval and would have committed governments to liberalizing existing controls. In short, the amendment would have formally stigmatized capital controls. The amendment also would have enabled the IMF, for the first time in its history, to include capital account liberalization as a condition for accessing its financial resources.

IMF management and European governments embraced the proposal enthusiastically, but US officials, while supporting the principle of greater freedom for capital movements, offered weaker support (Abdelal, 2007; Chwieroth, 2010, Chapter 8). The amendment also faced opposition from developing countries who wanted to retain the autonomy to impose controls in crisis situations without IMF approval. They were also concerned that the IMF staff would become overly enthusiastic in advocating liberalization. Breaking from the norm of G7 consensus, Canada also opposed the initiative, stressing a need for greater understanding about preconditions and sequencing as well as legal aspects of amending the Articles before moving ahead.

Still, despite these divisions, the IMF board did manage, in 1995, to offer its first operational guidance to the staff, directing them to cover capital account issues more fully and to strengthen their work in encouraging and supporting liberalization. This directive buttressed the general orientation of the staff, but failed to settle the debate between gradualists and big-bang supporters. Between April and October 1997, efforts to amend the Articles reached their peak. Consensus on the amendment, however, proved elusive.

The initial financial turmoil in Thailand in July did little to dampen enthusiasm for the proposed amendment. Indeed, at the Fund's September meetings, the commitment to the initiative was reaffirmed. However, the subsequent spread and intensification of the crisis and growing criticism of the Fund's response undermined support.

While proponents of the amendment sought to represent the crisis as market actors rationally imposing discipline, though perhaps excessively, on economies characterized by policy and institutional deficiencies, a growing number of opponents were emboldened to advocate a rival view that pointed to 'herding behaviour' and 'contagion' among incompletely informed market actors whose excessive pessimism had triggered instability even in the presence of sound fundamentals. From this rival perspective, the crisis undermined the case for liberalization and thus the proposal to give the Fund the authority to promote it. Equally significant for the downfall of the initiative was the threat from some influential members of the US Congress to withhold their support for US contributions for the pending IMF quota increase if the Treasury continued to support the amendment. The US Treasury subsequently withdrew its modest support rather than jeopardize a key priority. The initiative was then suspended indefinitely.

Inside the Fund, the staff initially attributed the crisis to policy and institutional failures, legitimating policy adjustment and structural reform, rather than controls on outflows, as the legitimate response. Not surprisingly, the US Treasury and IMF management offered a similar perspective. Thus, when Malaysia imposed controls on outflows in 1998 to deal with contagion from the crisis, it was subjected to severe criticism.

What is particularly noteworthy about this interpretation of the crisis is not the 'causes' it identifies, but rather the ones it fails to identify. In focusing exclusively on causes, this particular narrative obscured the impact of incompletely informed market actors driven by conventions towards 'herding behaviour'. In other words, it failed to highlight the more pervasive market failures associated with Keynesian views.

An alternative crisis narrative, reflecting a mixture of Keynesian and New Keynesian understandings, emerged that pointed to factors intrinsic to the operation of international capital markets that make them inherently volatile and prone to herding behaviour. In this alternative Keynesian-inspired view, the crisis was more an international financial panic than the result of policy and institutional errors (Sachs, 1997; Stiglitz, 1998). By the autumn of 1998, the climate of opinion among academic economists had clearly shifted towards a genuine reappraisal of pre-crisis beliefs.

Academic economists began to devote greater attention to factors intrinsic to the operation of capital markets that could trigger herding behaviour and market panic (Bhagwati, 1998). In applying this perspective, many academic economists, like some members of the IMF board, pointed to China and India as examples of countries that had maintained controls and therefore managed to escape the worst effects of the crisis. A number of academic economists also offered their support for restraints on capital mobility, with some – most notably Krugman (1998) – even offering support for controls on outflows.

Inside the Fund, a similar reappraisal of prevailing beliefs took place due to adaptation as well as advocacy of this alternative, Keynesian-inspired view by some influential staff members. Internal advocates of the Keynesian-inspired view renewed the organization's attention to problems of asymmetric information and domestic distortions that create the possibility for 'sharp investor reactions [that] can give rise to unpredictable market movements and, in the extreme, financial crises' (Eichengreen and Mussa, 1998, p. 2) The conclusion of an influential report testifies to the significant lessening of the stigma attached to controls:

> To the extent that the problem is information asymmetries that are intrinsic to the operation of financial markets, that cannot realistically be removed, and that give rise to significant systemic risks, *this creates an argument for the permanent application of policies designed to influence the volume of certain types of financial transactions*. If these policies are operationalized through the use of taxes and taxlike instruments that make their effect felt by altering relative prices, rather than through the use of administrative controls, there is no reason why they should be viewed as incompatible with the still-desirable goal of capital account liberalization.
>
> (Eichengreen and Mussa, 1998, p. 30, emphasis added)

A few points should be noted about this conclusion. First, it suggests a remarkable revival of Keynesian-inspired understanding of market behaviour and standards of policy behaviour; factors intrinsic to markets, not fundamentals, are identified as possibly responsible for capital flow volatility, and permanent, as opposed to temporary, controls are seen as possibly essential. But the similarities to Keynesian views should not be overstated. The report's proposal is limited to market-based controls on inflows and strictly rules out the use of administrative measures. More significant is the fact that the staff team that authored the influential report still clearly retained a belief in the long-run desirability of liberalization.

Significantly, this belief in the long-run desirability of greater capital freedom channelled how the reassessment of beliefs within the Fund played out. Rather than implicating capital account openness per se as responsible for the crisis, prevailing beliefs led the staff to identify poorly sequenced liberalization, such as South Korea's decision to liberalize short-term but restrict long-term inflows, as a principal culprit. This interpretation undermined virtually all support for the big-bang approach but did not induce reconsideration of the long-run desirability of greater capital freedom. The demise of support for the big-bang approach also translated into stronger and broader support within the IMF for temporary market-based controls on inflows.

The stigma the IMF attached to controls on outflows also lessened somewhat, partly as a result of advocacy within the Fund for the alternative Keynesian-inspired view and partly as a result of the Malaysian experience. In line with its initial interpretation of the crisis, the Fund staff had expected Malaysia's controls to prove ineffective, harmful to growth, and damaging to Malaysia's reputation by sending a negative signal to global financial markets. But when these expectations were not fully met, a number of staff members reconsidered their earlier beliefs. By 1999, the staff had become much more accommodating of Malaysia's decision and had concluded that they had been effective in creating temporary 'breathing room' that government officials used to adjust policies. Some IMF officials now concede that the decision may have been the appropriate one. But the jury remains out as to whether the controls functioned as intended.

Nevertheless, the ultimate significance of the Malaysian experience was to challenge prevailing beliefs within the Fund, which had unequivocally stigmatized the use of controls on outflows during a crisis. The experience demonstrated for many inside the Fund and the economics profession that controls on outflows could prove effective in crisis situations, if only under a limited set of conditions. Although the general orientation of the staff was in principle opposed to controls on outflows and much more sympathetic, even supportive, of controls on inflows, they became much more accommodating of their selective use in the wake of the Malaysian experience.

In the decade between the Asian financial crisis and the financial crisis of 2007–9, the staff elaborated and refined the gradualist consensus that had emerged (Chwieroth, 2010, Chapter 9). Although they did not dispute the long-run desirability of capital account liberalization, in the aftermath of the Asian financial crisis they became much more cautious in encouraging it and attached much greater legitimacy to selective limitations on capital mobility. Controls were tentatively and conditionally accepted as legitimate policy instruments in select circumstances, and even then most staff tended to offer strong reservations. Still, this did not prevent the staff from accommodating or even encouraging their use in certain circumstances, especially in contexts where liberalization threatened to expose countries with weak and poorly regulated financial systems to greater risk. The academic literature on capital controls in the decade that followed the Asian financial crisis, as well as the importance that many academic economists and the Fund began to place on institutions as a critical determinant of economic performance, reinforced the emphasis on gradualism.

Norm continuity was also apparent in the Fund's continued emphasis on poor fundamentals and institutions as the primary cause of financial instability and in its insistence on policy adjustment and structural reform. The tacit presumption of the IMF and the G7 was that the primary source of financial instability lay in emerging markets. Market actors, most of whom are based in financial centres in developed economies, were relieved of most of the blame for financial instability and were not subject to tighter regulation. On the contrary, faith in markets led the G7, and the US and the UK in particular, over the next decade to assign to market actors an increasingly significant role in the regulation and supervision of financial markets.

The IMF and the G7 sought to correct errors and deficiencies in crisis-afflicted economies by encouraging them to adopt various international financial standards and codes, most of which were informed by the interests and experiences of G7 countries, and in particular the Anglo-American regulatory approach, and virtually excluded emerging markets and developing economies from much input into their design. To be sure, the Fund developed an increasingly sophisticated understanding and appreciation of factors intrinsic to the operation of international capital markets that can trigger financial instability but the IMF showed little willingness to entertain regulatory measures aimed at reducing negative externalities emanating from the financial sectors of developed countries.

One reason for this was the preferences of leading member states, most prominently the US and the UK, which opposed more intrusive regulation of their financial sectors. Although emerging market officials, particularly in East Asia, objected to the predominant interpretation of the IMF and G7, they lacked adequate representation or influence within the IMF and standard-setting bodies to affect significant change in the policy discourse. In addition to the preferences of leading member states, the beliefs of the IMF staff also still prioritized their attention towards fundamentals and institutions in emerging markets; the tacit presumption being that the main risks to systemic stability lay there. Finally, the IMF lacked the institutional tools to provide equivalent leverage over developed economies.

It is important to highlight the consequences and risks; that is, the shortcomings associated with this continuity in norms. First, some emerging market officials perceived these norms as introducing asymmetric costs and benefits skewed in favour of developed countries and the interests of their financial sectors. Many emerging market officials also resented being encouraged to adopt standards and codes developed in bodies in which they had little or no input and which they perceived as inappropriate for their economies. Many of these officials also drew the lesson that measures needed to be taken to minimize their vulnerability to global financial markets and to the IMF.

In theory, capital controls could have provided one option. By limiting short-term flows and excessive risk taking, restraints on capital flows could have been used to reduce the likelihood of financial crisis and thus the probability of borrowing from the IMF. Yet the stigma attached to controls raised the actual and perceived costs of their use and heightened the appeal of reserve accumulation as an alternative insurance mechanism. Self-insurance via reserve accumulation, while seemingly optimal given the stigma attached to controls, has subsequently helped to generate some unintentional and unanticipated suboptimal outcomes that could have potentially been avoided had the stigma been lifted.

Precautionary reserve accumulation is, of course, beneficial. Reserves can be used unconditionally to meet any external financing need, thus freeing up 'policy space', and they can help prevent crises through the signalling associated with the ability to meet short-term obligations and stem sharp depreciation of the currency. Reserves can also be used to minimize the need for costly adjustments during a crisis.

Yet reserve accumulation is not without costs and risks. Large reserve accumulation has significant opportunity costs in terms of foregone consumption and investment for the accumulating countries, particularly for emerging markets and developing countries with high returns to capital and many unsatisfied social needs (Rodrik, 2006). Moreover, if the counterpart of reserve accumulation is that many governments pursue export-oriented growth and current account surpluses, an aggregate systemic deflationary impact may emerge should the rest of the world be no longer willing to incur balance-of-payments deficits (IMF, 2010e).

Since governments have largely concentrated their reserve holdings in the government debt of few countries, this raises additional possible costs and risks. Large and sustained accumulation may over time undermine confidence in the reserve currency through debt sustainability concerns. These concerns could escalate to the point of creating conditions for a rapid switch out of a specific reserve asset with large and disruptive exchange rate and wealth effects and possibly implications for financial stability. Such concerns have generated a long-running debate speculating on whether the US dollar could collapse. Large and sustained accumulation, by depressing interest rates in the reserve issuing economy, may also foster excessive risk taking and volatile capital flows. Indeed, some observers draw such a link between the global macroeconomic imbalances that emerged after the Asian financial crisis and the recent financial crisis that originated in the US (Brender and Pisani, 2010). Finally, reserve accumulation concentrated in a select few currencies exposes the entire international monetary system to shocks arising in the reserve issuing economies.

Although the stigma attached to controls was not the sole motivation for reserve accumulation following the Asian financial crisis, it certainly played a role in heightening its appeal as a way to minimize vulnerability to global financial markets and the IMF. The actual and perceived costs of imposing controls induced governments to search for alternative insurance mechanisms with reserve accumulation seemingly being the optimal strategy. Yet reserve accumulation, while offering some benefits, also creates costs and risks that underscore the potential shortcomings associated with stigmas; that is, that they rarely produce optimal outcomes despite often being cloaked in such language.

In fact, within the Fund, there is growing recognition of such potential shortcomings. As part of the on-going clarification of its views (see below), some within the IMF have suggested that greater use and acceptance of capital controls within an agreed multilateral framework could play an important part in managing capital flow volatility and thus potentially lessen a key motivation for reserve accumulation and the build-up of global macroeconomic imbalances (IMF, 2010e). Removing the stigma attached to controls, in other words, could lessen one key motivation for reserve accumulation by freeing up policy space for alternative insurance mechanisms.

Clarifying stigmas in the post-crisis era

The financial crisis of 2007–9 has generated signs that the norms of financial governance are changing. The norm of self-regulation, upon which much of the Anglo-American model and international standards and codes has been based, has been seriously undermined. There has been an important ideational shift in the way that financial crises are understood. In contrast to the period following the Asian financial crisis, in the current reform debate there is a strong consensus that the same market actors who over the past decade had been permitted to self-regulate were responsible for triggering the crisis.

The need to minimize negative externalities emanating from the financial sectors of developed economies is now widely accepted. The severity of the crisis, along with the massive taxpayer rescue of the financial system, has generated significant popular backlash against financial institutions and the policy norms they championed. This popular backlash has generated unprecedented political pressure within the US and the UK to tighten financial regulation. The policy response from developed countries also effectively re-wrote orthodoxy on crisis management. Over the past decade, the G7 had lectured crisis-afflicted countries on the need to restore confidence by closing insolvent financial institutions, strengthening fiscal discipline, and raising interest rates. Then, when faced with a crisis in their financial systems, G7 countries pursued precisely the opposite policies.

Interestingly, the IMF, traditionally a preacher of fiscal discipline, was one of the first prominent advocates for governments to embark on Keynesian-style fiscal expansion. It has also called for and supported efforts to expand the perimeter of regulation so as to minimize negative externalities emanating from the financial sectors of developed economies. It has also developed new unconditional and precautionary lending facilities that are meant to provide insurance against crisis. Within the IMF, crises are clearly no longer understood as largely being a 'home-grown' phenomenon; there is now significantly greater recognition of the potential for externally induced crises to spread to otherwise sound economies.

In addition to damage done to Anglo-American intellectual hegemony and leadership, the crisis has also accelerated the gradual shift in financial wealth and geopolitical clout away from the West to new emerging powers. Indeed, there was great symbolism in the decision to convene the G20, rather than the G7, to set the reform agenda and act as the steering committee for the world economy. Despite these important trends, it is still far from clear what, if anything, will replace pre-crisis norms as the new basis for financial governance. The EU has pretentions to exercise greater leadership but problems in its banking system and sovereign debt markets have undermined the attractiveness of its norms. China's performance during the crisis, particularly the ability of its state-managed financial sector to maintain growth, has attracted many admirers. Yet for the time being, China appears more interested in drawing on existing international standards and codes to upgrade its financial sector than in elaborating a new consensus (Walter, 2010). Without a clear focal point for coordination and in the face of significant domestic political pressure, there are increasing signs that governments, from both developed and emerging economies, are willing to stake out unilateral and regionally defined norms of financial governance.

These important ideational and power shifts provided the backdrop for the IMF to clarify its orientation towards capital controls, which had modestly and cautiously lent greater legitimacy to their use since the Asian financial crisis. In the early stages of the recent crisis, some countries, such as Argentina, Iceland, Indonesia, Russia, and Ukraine, imposed controls on outflows as a way of managing contagion from the crisis. The IMF, in line with the more flexible approach pursued since the Malaysian experience, accommodated and lent its tacit approval to these actions, even endorsing those in Iceland and the Ukraine as part of its lending programmes to these countries. However, the IMF has not encouraged others to follow suit.

Some prominent academic economists began calling on the G20 to offer greater support for controls on inflows to be used to protect weak or poorly regulated financial systems (Rodrik and Subramanian, 2008; Buiter, 2008), as well as for controls on outflows to offset sudden stops (Calvo, 2008). But the US and the UK did not initially waver in their commitment to the free flow of capital. To be sure, the crisis did heighten the traditional Franco-German scepticism of free market finance but this scepticism did not yet spill over to Anglo-American officials.

The political atmosphere in developed countries began to shift in autumn 2009. Monetary easing and liquidity support, while helping to save the financial system from collapse, also permitted the financial sector to earn record or near-record profits and bonuses. This outraged the public at a time of rising budget deficits, public debt, and unemployment. Prominent politicians and regulators, such as the head of Britain's financial regulator (Turner, 2009) and the then German finance minister (Steinbruck, 2009), made statements in support of a global tax on financial transactions as one of several possible ways of recouping the cost of the financial rescues and as a way to reduce the size of the financial sector and curb bonuses. But these statements did not command the support of the US or UK Treasuries, though both did express interest in more work being done on how to discourage speculative behaviour and on how banks could make a bigger contribution given their greater reliance on taxpayer support. It was then, at its September 2009 summit, that the G20 instructed the IMF to provide a report that would examine how banks could contribute to paying for the cost of the crisis, with the Tobin tax being identified as one of several options under consideration.

In addition to the popular backlash that characterized the domestic political climate in developed economies, the frame attached to capital controls began to shift. Despite the allowances the IMF had made for controls following the Asian financial crisis, its general orientation was widely perceived to be one that identified controls as market-unfriendly and as imprudent policy. Critics of the Fund argued that, though it had become more accommodative of controls, its orientation was that capital account openness remained fundamentally beneficial and that reaping the benefits placed the burden on governments to adjust their policies and institutions (Subramanian, 2009). This orientation, according to critics, precluded the staff from providing guidance to emerging markets on what to do should governments be unable to undertake these reforms. While this criticism does not fully capture the diversity of views espoused by the IMF, it does point to a more critical gap in the Fund's orientation at the time. In particular, it points to the IMF's failure to engage with important practical questions about how governments should design capital controls should they prove necessary. Critics suggest, not entirely without basis, that had the Fund done so, it would have associated itself with the view that capital account openness could be potentially harmful.

This orientation has started to change, partly because the crisis exposed intellectual deficiencies in the pre-crisis orthodoxy that held markets to be rational and efficient (Financial Services Authority, 2009). This may in turn have opened up space within the Fund for those staff members who have long been sceptical of this orthodoxy to press their arguments more forcefully. Growing interest within the economics profession in the insights of behavioural economists may also have been influential in shaping the Fund's views. Harkening back to Keynes, these economists stress the limitations of market rationality and efficiency and use social, cognitive, and emotional factors to understand how market actors make economic decisions (Akerloff and Shiller, 2009). These insights fit well with the emerging post-crisis consensus within the G20 and the IMF on the need to move towards greater macro-prudential regulation, which seeks in part to deal with how markets, if left unfettered, can create greater systemic risk.

Although not initially framed in this manner, capital controls began to feature in discussions about macro-prudential regulation (Subramanian, 2009; Subramanian and Williamson, 2009). It has become increasingly accepted that controls could form part of the policy arsenal against future crises, especially the build-up of asset bubbles, by helping to counter-cyclically restrict credit growth and leverage caused by capital inflows. From late 2009 to mid-2010, a number of emerging markets, including Brazil, South Korea, and Indonesia, introduced controls to protect their economies from financial instability and to reduce currency volatility.

With their enhanced clout, some emerging market officials have become increasingly emboldened to call on the IMF and the G20 to provide greater support for the use of capital controls (Subbarao, 2010). Reserve accumulation and stronger policy frameworks and fundamentals have provided many emerging markets increasingly with the capacity to chart a course independent of IMF influence. As a result, the IMF management and staff may have been partly motivated to respond to these calls from emerging market officials as a way of currying their political support, particularly at a time when the Fund is seeking to boost its financial resources in part by drawing on additional contributions from some large reserve-holding countries.

An important political obstacle to lending greater support to controls was removed when the stance of the British government eventually shifted. Faced with significant domestic political pressures and polls predicting defeat in an approaching election, the Labour government subsequently did a U-turn and provided some backing for such calls made by emerging market officials. In November 2009, then Prime Minister Gordon Brown surprised his G20 colleagues by raising the possibility of a Tobin tax as a way to help banks pay for the insurance they received from taxpayers (HM Treasury, 2009). Having spent more than a decade defending the City of London's 'light-touch regulation' from intrusive Franco-German initiatives, the approaching British election and the public outrage on banker bonuses and the costs of the financial rescue probably led Brown to cultivate a tougher image.[5] Yet the US Treasury remained steadfastly opposed.

In early 2010, the IMF elaborated its orientation. Although an IMF (2010c) report to the G20 did not support the Tobin tax as a means of inducing the financial sector to pay for the taxpayer support it receives, the staff did release another well-publicized report (Ostry *et al.*, 2010) that clarified the circumstances under which controls on inflows would form a legitimate part of the policy toolkit.[6] The report identified controls as one of several legitimate tools that policymakers could deploy to moderate over-heating of their economies. Free-flowing capital can threaten emerging economies because surges of inflows can create shocks, causing currencies to appreciate rapidly and asset prices to soar, the report argued. There were thus important macro-prudential considerations that supported the use of controls on inflows in some specific instances; that is, when the economy is operating near potential, the level of reserves is adequate, the exchange rate is not undervalued, and if the flows are likely to be transitory. But the report argued the circumstances under which controls were likely to prove effective were limited, and their effectiveness would likely prove to be mainly on the composition of flows rather than on the aggregate volume.

In line with the macro-prudential framing fixed to controls, the report uncovered evidence that controls that reduced risky liability structures had been useful in reducing fragility during the recent crisis. It added that countries where extensive controls had been in place, such as China and India, experienced better growth trajectories during the recent crisis. Reflecting greater scepticism that capital flows are the result of rational and efficient market actors, the report also highlighted concerns about herding behaviour, bouts of excessive optimism and pessimism, and the possibility of collateral damage from asset bubbles and busts, even when the flows are fundamentally sound.

Finally, the report offered an interesting analysis of the multilateral dimensions of capital controls. On the one hand, it warns that widespread use could undermine the benefits of financial integration and divert capital to countries less able to absorb it. Widespread use could also frustrate needed rebalancing of global demand, especially if they were implemented in economies with undervalued currencies as a means to resist appreciation. On the other hand, as indicated earlier, by curtailing short-term flows and risky liability structures, controls could limit the demand for reserves and thus contribute to reducing global imbalances. Such considerations led the staff to suggest developing a code of conduct governing the use of controls, something that the Fund has been considering as part of its on-going mandate review.

In fact, as part of this review, some have raised the idea again of once again revising the IMF's Articles to provide it with a new mandate to oversee the capital account policies of its members (IMF, 2010a, 2010b). As part of its mandate review, the IMF is also considering strengthening surveillance so as to help members design and implement controls, ensuring that negative spillovers are avoided and that broader goals are taken into account. Despite this recent shift, the perception of a stigma still remains. Emerging markets still generally fear that the use of controls will send a negative signal and harm their reputations with official and market actors. The IMF managing director also recently made clear that controls should only be used to combat temporary surges and must not become permanent (Oliver, 2010). Surges of a long-term nature would indicate, according to the IMF managing director, indicate the need for adjusting policies and institutions.

In spite of opposition from the US and doubts from the IMF, European leaders continue to press for consideration of a global tax on financial transactions as a way of dampening speculation and providing resources for future financial rescues. The recent crisis in Greece and across the euro area has only served to heighten traditional European scepticism about speculation and free market finance. The new intellectual climate, continued popular outrage at excesses in the financial sector, and the Obama administration's newfound willingness to contemplate radical financial reforms promise to make the issue one of significant debate in the months to come.

In terms of significance, it is clear that the evolution of the Fund's position following the Asian financial crisis and its recent clarification has opened up greater policy space for emerging markets that have the capacity to chart a policy course independent of IMF influence. Most of these recent actions to curtail capital flows have received a muted reaction from global financial markets and credit rating agencies. Yet it would be somewhat of a stretch to claim, as some have, that 'the stigma on capital controls [is] gone' (Rodrik, 2010). It is perhaps more accurate to state that the stigma has been lifted on the use of capital controls for those economies facing a very precise set of conditions. In that sense, the recent crisis has simply formalized the unevenness of the stigma that has persisted since the mid-1980s, and at best added greater reinforcement to its uneven nature. One key task now facing policymakers is to confront the shortcomings that remain from it.

Conclusion

Policy stigmas are an important aspect of financial governance. The behavioural prescriptions contained in stigmas constitute and regulate issues, interests, communities, and modes of action in international finance. The behavioural prescriptions embodied in stigmas are regulative, but also constitutive because understandings of what counts as 'good' or 'legitimate' financial governance are brought to life through those behavioural prescriptions. Stigmas play an essential role in signalling, and establishing and maintaining reputations for 'good' behaviour. Understanding the source, significance, and shortcomings of these stigmas is vital to strengthening our knowledge of governing the financial sector.

This chapter looks at the source, significance, and shortcomings of one particular policy stigma, that which has been attached to capital controls. Focusing on the IMF, it traces empirically how the degree of approval attached to their use has varied considerably across time and space and within the organization itself. In the early post-war era, capital controls were endorsed and failed to elicit any cries of outrage, but then gradually over time it became increasingly frowned upon for developed countries to employ them. From the mid-1980s onward, the IMF began to introduce this stigma as a universal requirement, though it did so in an uneven and selective fashion. Since the Asian financial crisis, the stigma attached to controls has become more uneven and, to some extent, this unevenness has been formalized. Changes in the IMF's orientation have been driven not just by shifts in the power and preferences of member states but also by the evolving makeup, beliefs, debates, and strategic efforts of its staff.

The stigma attached to controls has not been without its shortcomings. There is much evidence to suggest it skewed the way the IMF reacted to problems, processed information, and formulated responses. To its credit, the IMF has shown it can adapt and learn but this has depended more on the presence of a severe crisis rather than through routine institutionalized channels. Much of the more comprehensive reassessment of organizational goals has depended on generational change within the Fund driven by personnel realignment.

This suggests a somewhat pessimistic reading of the potential for organizational change. Organizations like the Fund appear locked into particular world views or cultures to which they remain wedded for prolonged periods. The important policy question that comes from this observation is how can we force organizations like the Fund to consider all policy options when needed? Put differently, how can we avoid group-think in policy? Such considerations suggest a need for the IMF to do more to strengthen the culture and practice of learning within the organization.

Critics of the Fund maintain that the stigma that remains attached to controls continues to restrict 'policy space' for emerging markets. If correct, then the risk is that, despite its recent clarification, the Fund's orientation on capital controls could feed into its long-standing legitimacy problems with emerging markets. This line of reasoning suggests another important argument as to why the IMF should work to design a set of best practices for implementing controls, perhaps as part of its on-going mandate review. If the IMF was to pursue such a course of action, it could go a long way in convincing many emerging markets and developing countries, who perceive the Fund's support for capital account liberalization to reflect the beliefs of developed countries and the interests of their financial sector, that it is representing and taking into account their interests and experiences. It thus could contribute to the on-going efforts to address its legitimacy problems. Finally, to the extent that the stigma has contributed to the build-up of global macroeconomic imbalances, if the IMF began work on designing a multilateral framework for the use of controls, it could help to minimize the appeal as well as the costs and risks of reserve accumulation.

Notes

1 This distinction between developed countries, on the one hand, and emerging market and developing countries, on the other, is in a state of flux. The recent rapid increase in public debt and the deterioration of the fiscal positions that followed the financial crisis of 2007–9 has significantly increased the perception of sovereign risk for some developed countries. Conversely, some emerging market countries, particularly those that had improved policy fundamentals and reduced vulnerabilities in the pre-crisis period, are generally better placed and likely to experience significantly better public debt and fiscal positions than most developed countries in the near future. Consequently, their 'debt intolerance' may have decreased. In addition, many emerging markets have made significant efforts in the past decade to improve their ability to borrow in their own currencies, thus partly tackling the problem of 'original sin'.

2 *Artificial* here means not derived from any singular economic truth.

3 See also Leijonhufvud (1968).

4 One staff report (Ishii and Habermeier, 2002, p.9) finds that, since 1978, approximately '43% of IMF financial stabilization programs have influenced recipient countries to liberalize their capital account'.

5 The Labour government subsequently lost the election in May 2010. At the time of writing, it is unclear the extent to which the current Conservative–Liberal Democrat coalition supports such measures.

6 See also IMF (2010d).

References

Abdelal, R. (2007) *Capital Rules: The Construction of Global Finance*, Harvard: Harvard University Press.

Abdelal, R., Blyth, M., and Parsons, C. (eds) (2010) *Constructing the International Economy*, Ithaca: Cornell University Press.

Akerlof, G.A. and Shiller, R.J. (2009) *Animal Spirits: How Human Psychology Drives the Economy, and Why It Matters for Global Capitalism*, Princeton: Princeton University Press.

Barnett, M. and Finnemore, M. (2004) *Rules for the World: International Organizations in Global Politics*, Ithaca, NY: Cornell University Press.

Bartolini, L. and Drazen, A. (1997) 'Capital account liberalization as a signal', *American Economic Review*, 87(1): 138–54.

Best, J. (2005) *The Limits of Transparency: Ambiguity and the History of International Finance*, Ithaca: Cornell University Press.

Bhagwati, J. (1998) 'The capital myth: the difference between trade in widgets and dollars', *Foreign Affairs*, 77(3): 7–12.

Brender, A. and Pisani, F. (2010) *Global Imbalances and the Collapse of Globalized Finance*, Brussels: Centre for European Policy Studies.

Buiter, W.H. (2008) 'Some suggestions for the G20 on November 15th', in B. Eichengreen and R. Baldwin (eds), *What G20 Leaders Must Do to Stabilise Our Economy and Fix the Financial System*, pp. 17–20, London: VoxEU.org Publication.

Calvo, G. (2008) 'The new Bretton Woods agreement', in B. Eichengreen and R. Baldwin (eds), *What G20 Leaders Must Do to Stabilise Our Economy and Fix the Financial System*, pp. 53–55, London: VoxEU.org Publication.

Chwieroth, J.M. (2010) *Capital Ideas: The IMF and the Rise of Financial Liberalization*, Princeton: Princeton University Press.

Dobson, W. and Hufbauer, G. (2001) *World Capital Markets: Challenge to the G-10*, Washington, DC: Institute for International Economics.

Edwards, M.S. (2005) 'Is non-compliance costly? Investor responses to IMF program failures', *Social Science Quarterly*, 84(4): 857–73.

Eichengreen, B. and Mussa, M. (1998) *Capital Account Liberalization: Theoretical and Practical Aspects*, IMF Occasional Paper No. 172. Washington, DC: IMF.

Eichengreen, B. and Wyplosz, C. (1996) 'Taxing international financial transactions to enhance the operation of the international monetary system', in M. ul Haq, I. Kaul, and I. Grunberg (eds), *The Tobin Tax: Coping with Financial Volatility*, pp. 15–41, Oxford: Oxford University Press.

Financial Services Authority (2009) *The Turner Review: A Regulatory Response to the Global Banking Crisis*, London: Financial Services Authority.

Haggard, S. and Maxfield, S. (1996) 'The political economy of financial internationalization in the developing world', *International Organization*, 50(1): 35–68.

Helleiner, E. (1994) *States and the Reemergence of Global Finance: From Bretton Woods to the 1990s*, Ithaca: Cornell University Press.

HM Treasury (2009) *Risk, Reward and Responsibility: The Financial Sector and Society*, London: HM Treasury.

Independent Evaluation Office of the International Monetary Fund (2005) *The IMF's Approach to Capital Account Liberalization*, Washington, DC: IMF.

International Monetary Fund (2010a) *The Fund's Mandate – An Overview*, Washington, DC: IMF.

International Monetary Fund (2010b) *The Fund's Mandate – The Legal Framework*, Washington, DC: IMF.

International Monetary Fund (2010c) *A Fair and Substantial Contribution by the Financial Sector: Final Report to the G-20*, Washington, DC: IMF.

International Monetary Fund (2010d) *Global Financial Stability Report*, April edition, Washington, DC: IMF.

International Monetary Fund (2010e) *Reserve Accumulation and International Monetary Stability*, Washington, DC: IMF.

Ishii, S. and Habermeier, K. (2002) *Capital Account Liberalization and Financial Sector Stability*, IMF Occasional Paper No. 211, Washington, DC: IMF.

Kirshner, J. (2003) 'The inescapable politics of money', in J. Kirshner (ed.), *Monetary Orders: Ambiguous Economics, Ubiquitous Politics*, pp. 3–24, Ithaca: Cornell University Press.

Krause, L. (1971) 'Private international finance', *International Organization*, 25(3): 523–40.

Krugman, P. (1998) 'Saving Asia: it's time to get radical', *Fortune*, 138(5): 74–80.

Leijonhufvud, A. (1968) *On Keynesian Economics and the Economics of Keynes: A Study in Monetary Theory*, New York: Oxford University Press.

Mukherjee, B. and Singer, D.A. (2010) 'International institutions and domestic compensation: the IMF and the politics of capital account liberalization', *American Journal of Political Science*, 54(1): 45–60.

Oliver, C. (2010) 'IMF warns on emerging market currency controls', *Financial Times*, 11 July.

Ostry, J.D., Ghosh, A.R., Habermeier, K., Chamon, M., Qureshi, M.S., and Reinhardt, D.B.S. (2009) *Capital Inflows: The Role of Controls*, IMF Staff Position Note SPN/10/04, Washington, DC: IMF.

Reinhart, C.M. and Rogoff, K.S. (2008) *This Time is Different: Eight Centuries of Financial Folly*, Princeton: Princeton University Press.

Rodrik, D. (2006) 'The social cost of foreign exchange reserves', *International Economic Journal*, 20(3): 253–66.

Rodrik, D. (2009) 'A plan B for global finance', *The Economist*, 14 March.

Rodrik, D. (2010) 'The end of an era in finance', *Project Syndicate*, 11 March, available at www.project-syndicate.org/commentary/rodrik41/English (last accessed 30 September 2010).

Rodrik, D. and Subramanian, A. (2008) 'We must curb international flows of capital', *Financial Times*, 25 February.

Sachs, J. (1997) 'Power unto itself', *Financial Times*, 11 December.

Skidelsky, R. (2009) *Keynes: The Return of the Master*, London: Allen Lane.

Steinbruck, P. (2009) 'Tax trades to share the costs of the crisis', *Financial Times*, 24 September.

Stiglitz, J. (1998) 'What caused Asia's crash? Bad private sector decisions', *Wall Street Journal*, 4 February.

Stiglitz, J. (2002) *Globalization and its Discontents*, New York: W.W. Norton.

Subbarao, D. (2010) 'Volatility in capital flows: some perspectives', comments at the High-level Conference on The International Monetary System, Swiss National Bank/IMF, Zurich, Switzerland, 11 May.

Subramanian, A. (2009) 'The IMF beyond Istanbul', *Business Standard*, 30 September.

Subramanian, A. and Williamson, J. (2009) 'The Fund should help Brazil to tackle capital inflows', *Financial Times*, 25 October.

Tirole, J. (2002) *Financial Crises, Liquidity and the International Monetary System*, Princeton: Princeton University Press.

Turner, A. (2009) 'How to tame global finance', *Prospect*, Issue 162, 27 August.

Walter, A. (2010) 'Chinese attitudes towards global financial regulatory co-operation: revisionist or status quo?', in E. Helleiner, S. Pagliari, and H. Zimmerman (eds), *Global Finance in Crisis: The Politics of International Regulatory Change*, pp. 153–69, London: Routledge.

Woods, N. (2006) *The Globalizers: The IMF, the World Bank, and their Borrowers*. Ithaca, NY: Cornell University Press.

10 Missing the red flag

Gillian G.H. Garcia

The chapter examines the material loss reviews conducted by the inspectors general of the four federal banking agencies to find the causes of the 111 banks and thrifts that failed in the United States with material losses to the Federal Deposit Insurance corporation (FDIC)'s Deposit Insurance Fund during the period 2007–9. The analysis concludes that these institutions failed for reasons long recognized to be causes of bank failure: weak management, fast growth, reliance on volatile sources of funding, inaccurate accounting that exaggerated earnings and capital, concentrated assets, particularly assets involving commercial real estate and construction, acquisition, and development loans. The chapter also examines deficiencies in the supervisors' implementation of the prompt corrective action provisions of the FDIC Improvement Act. It concludes by asking why prompt corrective action (PCA) failed to achieve its goals and suggesting changes, including macro-prudential oversight, that might improve supervisory achievements in the future.

There were few bank failures in the United States in the early 2000s but, by the end of November 2010, the FDIC's web site reported that there had been 314 failures and 13 assistance transactions since the end of 2007.[1] The cost to the FDIC and the country has been great. The FDIC's Annual Reports for 2008 and 2009 show that the balance of the Deposit Insurance Fund (DIF) fell from positive \$52.4 billion at the end of 2007 to \$17.3 billion a year later and to negative \$20.9 billion at the end of 2009. This was not supposed to happen.

In the 1980s and early 1990s, more than 2,900 commercial banks and savings institutions failed in the United States (Government Accountability Office (GAO), 2007). The S&L debacle alone is estimated to have cost taxpayers \$150 billion in 1990 dollars (FDIC, 1998). At the time, Congress considered that the federal banking regulators (the Office of the Comptroller of the Currency [OCC], the Federal Reserve, the Federal Deposit Insurance Corporation [FDIC], and the Office of Thrift Supervision [OTS]) had failed their discretionary duties 'to take timely and forceful action to address the causes of the failures and prevent losses to the deposit insurance fund and taxpayers' (GAO, 2007, p. 1). Politicians declared 'never again!' and, to put their resolve into effect, in December 1991, they enacted the FDIC Improvement Act (FDICIA), which mandated that federal prudential supervisors take remedial actions under the Act's prompt corrective action (PCA) provisions.

Evidently, these provisions have not prevented banks from failing with substantial losses since 2007. The chapter asks why bank regulation and supervision failed to prevent these unfortunate events. The first section examines PCA's capital provisions and its non-capital requirements. It also describes FDICIA's mandate that the inspectors general (IGs) of each federal banking agency conduct in-depth reviews of bank and thrift failures that cause material losses to the Deposit Insurance Fund (DIF). The next section analyses the material loss reviews (MLRs) that IGs have released for banks that failed in 2007, 2008, and 2009. Then, after observing that prompt corrective action has not achieved the lawmakers' 'never-again' intentions, the following section debates what went wrong. The chapter concludes by offering some suggestions to allow PCA to achieve the goals that were set out for it in 1991 and, in doing so, it examines recent proposals to initiate macro-prudential oversight.

Prompt corrective action provisions

Congress hoped that, using PCA, prudential supervisors would successfully encourage bankers to remedy their bank's problems before it failed. Moreover, if failure became unavoidable, supervisors were to resolve (close, place into receivership, and have the FDIC sell or liquidate) the troubled institution before it became book-value insolvent. These measures were intended to strengthen the banking industry and to minimize losses to the DIF. Bank and thrift failures during the financial crisis of 2007–9 have shown that PCA has not achieved its meritorious objectives. See Figure 10.1 (and also Table 10.2).

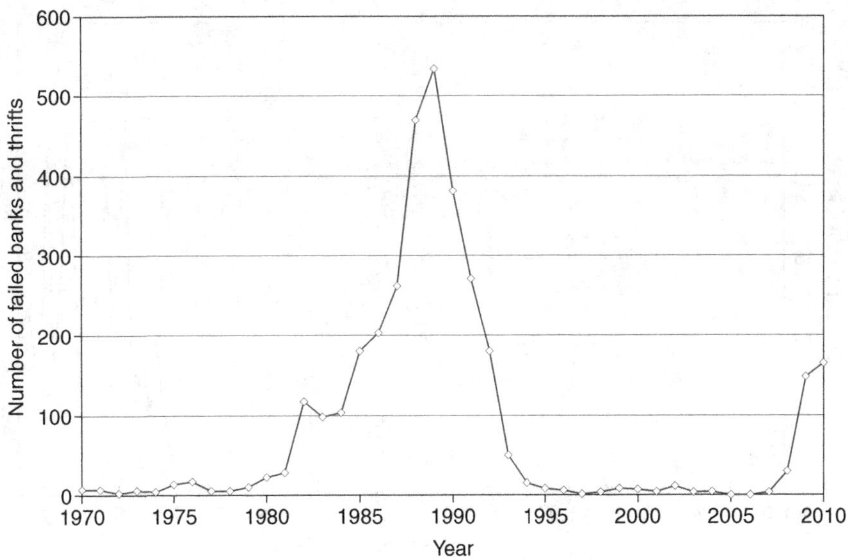

Figure 10.1 Number of failed banks and thrifts: 1970–2010 (source: Data from FDIC Historical Statistics at www2.fdic.gov/hsob/index.asp).

By November 19, 2010, 149 banks and thrifts had failed during the year – just above the number that met their demise in the whole of 2009. Evidently, the spate of bank and thrift failures in the US is not over. It is not even clear that the recent decrease in the number of monthly failures can be sustained. (See Figure 10.2.)

In December 2008, the FDIC adopted a restoration plan to return the fund eventually to its designated minimum of 1.15 per cent of insured deposits. The agency subsequently amended and stiffened the plan when staff estimated that the DIF would incur $100 billion in losses between 2009 and 2013 (Murton, 2010).[2] The FDIC charged banks higher premiums and imposed special assessments in 2009 and 2010 so that banks prepaid their insurance premiums. (For example, they prepaid $46 billion in December 2009.) The Dodd-Frank Wall Street Reform and Consumer Protection Act relaxed some of the previous restraints on DIF funding in July 2010 and the FDIC now aims to achieve a legislated higher target ratio of 1.35 per cent by 2020 (Murton and Edwards, 2010).

PCA's capital provisions

The prompt corrective action provisions, embodied in Sections 38 and 39 of the Federal Deposit Insurance Act, are some of FDICIA's most important reforms. They require supervisors to classify banks and thrifts into five categories (well-capitalized, adequately capitalized, undercapitalized, significantly undercapitalized, and critically undercapitalized) according to a leverage limit (the ratio of tangible equity capital to total assets) and one or more risk-based capital

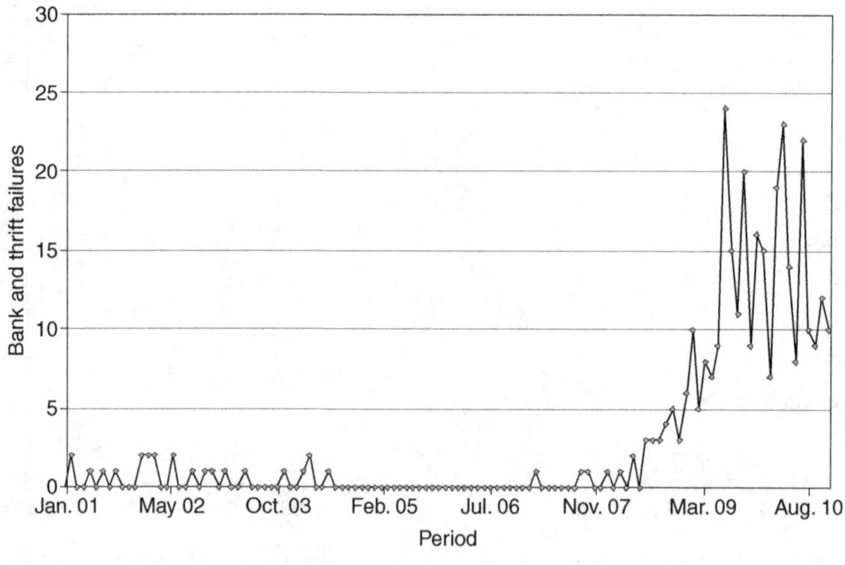

Figure 10.2 Bank and thrift failures: monthly 2001–10 (source: FDIC, Failures and Assistance Transactions, December 2010).

measures. FDICIA charged the four banking regulators with implementing the legislation's capital measures – they did so by using three ratios: (1) total capital to risk-based assets, (2) tier 1 capital to risk-based assets, and (3) the leverage ratio. See Table 10.1.

Banks rated well-capitalized could follow their own business plans with less supervisory restraint than others. The legislation specified that increasingly stringent restrictions be applied to a bank as its condition and its capital ratios deteriorated. The graduated steps aimed to improve regulators' ability to identify and promptly address banks' deficiencies before they became irredeemable. Crucially, the legislation determined that a bank became critically undercapitalized when its ratio of tangible equity to total assets fell to or below 2 per cent. Then (barring exceptional circumstances) it was to be placed into receivership within 90 days. By resolving a troubled bank before it became book-value insolvent, legislators aimed to minimize losses to the deposit insurance funds.[3]

Non-capital measures

Regulators in the US have long held broad discretion to discipline errant institutions. This authority was reiterated and strengthened in FDICIA. Recognizing that capital is a lagging indicator of an institution's condition, Section 38 allowed regulators to take non-capital remedial measures, such as removing officers and directors and downgrading an institution's capital class. Section 38(g), for example, allows supervisors to reclassify or downgrade an institution's capital category by one step if they determine, after notice and an opportunity for a hearing, that an institution is in unsafe and unsound condition or is engaging in unsafe and unsound practices. Downgrading from well to adequately capitalized would have denied an institution the right to garner brokered deposits without an

Table 10.1 PCA's capital categories

Capital category	*Total risk-based capital*[a]	*Tier 1 risk-based capital*	*Leverage ratio*[b]
Well-capitalized	10% or more and	6% or more and	5% or more
Adequately capitalized	8% or more and	4% or more and	4% or more
Undercapitalized	Less than 8% or	Less than 4% or	Less than 4%
Significantly undercapitalized	Less than 6% or	Less than 3% or	Less than 3%
Critically undercapitalized	Tangible equity capital is 2% or less regardless of its other capital ratios		

Source: GAO (2007).

Notes

a The ratio of tier 1 plus tier 2 capital to risk-weighted assets, where tier 1 capital is primarily equity capital and tier 2 capital includes also subordinated debt, loan loss reserves, and certain other instruments.

b The leverage ratio is tangible equity divided by average total assets, where tangible equity is core capital plus outstanding perpetual preferred stock minus all intangible assets, except certain purchased mortgage servicing rights.

FDIC waiver. Troubled institutions often rely on brokered deposits to avoid illiquidity. Under Section 38(f)(2)(F) regulators can also require improvements in management by dismissing officers and directors who are unable to strengthen their undercapitalized institution's ability to become adequately capitalized materially.

Section 39 required regulators to specify three safety and soundness standards related to non-capital criteria – standards that encompassed: (1) operations and management; (2) compensation; and (3) asset quality, earnings, and stock valuations. Section 39 could be implemented by regulations or guidelines and allowed supervisors to take action, such as requiring the speedy submission of a remedial plan, if an institution failed to meet one or more of these standards. The FDIC's Risk Management (RM) Manual and Formal and Informal Actions Procedures (FIAP) Manual implement Section 39's provisions. For example, the FIAP Manual allows supervisors to take action against a non-problem institution 'in which inadequate practices and policies could result in a material loss to the institution or management has not responded effectively to prior criticism'. As the analysis in the next section reveals, the non-capital provisions would have allowed regulators to take action against almost all of the failure-causing problems that the MLRs have revealed. But these provisions were rarely used.

Material loss reviews

As enacted in 1991, Section 38(k) of FDICIA required the Office of the Inspector General (OIG) of each federal banking agency to conduct a written material loss review of an institution that it supervised if it failed and caused a loss to the DIF that exceeded the greater of $25 million or 2 per cent of the failed institution's total assets at the time the FDIC was appointed receiver. MLRs were to examine the causes of the bank or thrift's failure and the adequacy of its supervisory oversight, including the implementation of the PCA provisions, and to make recommendations for preventing any such loss in the future.

Despite FDICIA's non-capital provisions, the FDIC's MLRs frequently noted that 'PCA did not require action until the institution was at serious risk of failure'. (See, for example, p. 3 of the FDIC OIG's [2010] MLR for Westsound Bank.) None of the OIG's reviews examined supervisors' use of PCA's discretionary powers. In fact, with the exception of 12 MLRs by the FDIC's OIG, the reviews did not even acknowledge the existence of non-capital provisions. Instead, in assessing each agency's implementation of PCA, the reviews focused almost solely on the execution of its capital measures. In fact, GAO (2007, p. 6) noted that '[A]ll four regulators agreed that, by design, PCA is *not* a tool that can be used upon early recognition of a bank or thrift's troubled status.' Nevertheless, '[R]egulators made limited use of the non-capital supervisory actions under sections 38 and 39.' Instead, they often relied on moral suasion to encourage institutions to make improvements or to obtain the resignation of ineffective officers and directors. GAO found that supervisors only occasionally used the non-capital provisions to take actions that could have provided discipline that was intermediate between persuasion and informal or formal enforcement actions.

FDICIA's MLR provisions were amended by the Dodd-Frank Wall Street Reform and Consumer Protection Act (Financial Reform Act) of 21 July 2010. The FDIC OIG's web site (www.fdicoig.gov/mlr.shtml) reveals that the Act amended section 38(k) 'by increasing the MLR threshold from $25 million to $200 million for losses that occur in the period January 1, 2010 through December 31, 2011'. The Financial Reform Act called, however, for the OIG to 'perform in-depth reviews of failures when the associated losses are not material but they involve unusual circumstances'. 'This provision precludes us from continuing the current analysis of MLRs for banks that failed after 2009 because the comparisons would not be equivalent.

PCA in action

The US banking industry revived as the 1990s progressed and the economy recovered from the 1991 recession. As Figure 10.1 shows, the numbers of failures receded. Moreover, the industry was profitable until the financial crisis broke and, as Figure 10.2 shows, failures were rare in the early 2000s. GAO (2007) reports that the number of undercapitalized institutions fell from 1,235 in 1992 to 14 in 2005, while the percentage of well-capitalized banks increased from 94 per cent in 1992 to 99 per cent in 2005. Thus almost all of the industry was subjected to minimum supervisory restrictions during the decade leading up to the crisis. If the regulators identified unreasonable risks, FDICIA's capital provisions would not offer them an opportunity to apply corrective measures. They would need to employ other deterrents, such as the non-capital provisions or their longstanding discretionary powers, to excessive risk taking.

It is not clear to what extent the PCA provisions contributed to the improvement in the banking industry and the DIF during the late 1990s and early 2000s. In fact, there were early doubts about its likely effectiveness. Carnell (1993) and Horvitz (1995), for example, opined that regulators would be unwilling to forgo their supervisory discretion in order to implement FDICIA's rules. Moreover, Eisenbeis and Wall (2002) and Kaufman (2004) noted that losses on the few banks or thrifts that failed in the first ten years after FDICIA's passage were greater than might have been expected. These failed institutions were supposed to have been closed before they reached book-value insolvency. Nevertheless, GAO (2007) found that IGs considered that supervisors had applied PCA's capital provisions correctly in 12 of 14 cases they examined. The OTS did not utilize PCA appropriately, however, in the failure of Superior Bank, FSB of Illinois, in 2001. In addition, GAO found that regulators made limited use of Section 38's non-capital provisions because they preferred to use moral suasion or other means. For example, the OCC used the reclassification power only twice between 1992 and 2005. While regulators stated that the power to dismiss officers and/or directors could be useful, it was not much used – in fact, it was never used by OTS or the Federal Reserve supervisors during that time period.

Material loss reviews in the recent crisis

By October 2010, the IGs for the FDIC and the Federal Reserve had published reviews for the banks that failed with material losses in the period 2007 to 2009. Their reviews are summarized in Table 10.3. In the early years, the Federal Reserve's IG conducted cursory reviews that contained less analysis than those conducted by the other three IGs. This situation changed, however, in 2010 when the Fed began to conduct more thorough reviews.

The OIGs have been placed under pressure by the large number of banks and thrifts that failed in 2009 and 2010 with material losses. The FDIC coped with its overload by hiring one of the major accounting firms, KPMG, to conduct six of the reviews that it has published in 2010. The Treasury Department's OIG fell behind in conducting the reviews, which Section 131(k)(3) of FDICIA requires to be made available expeditiously or within six months of two ambiguous events. The FDIC interpreted the requirement to mean within six months of failure but the Treasury's OIG interpreted the Act differently. By the time the Reform Act was passed in July 2010, the last full MLR that Treasury's OIG released was for a bank that failed in August 2009 and for a thrift that failed in July 2009. Once the Act was passed, Treasury ceased to conduct reviews of banks that failed after that date unless they were projected to have caused $200 million or more in losses to the DIF. Moreover, so far, neither OCC nor OTS has found any special circumstances that warranted a review in greater depth. Hence it is not possible to analyse the MLRs for all of the banks and thrifts that failed in 2009. Comparable reviews are not available for banks that failed in the second half of 2009 and were supervised by the OCC or the OTS. The actions of three of the OIGs suggests a distinct lack of enthusiasm for complying the FDICIA's material loss review provisions; only the FDIC's OIG has consistently met the spirit of the Act.

Table 10.2 presents data on the number of institutions, the value of their deposits, the number of failures, the number of failures that caused material losses to the FDIC, and the estimated losses in dollars and percentage of assets for banks supervised by each of the four banking regulators. In the period 2007 to 2009, 95 of the more than 5,000 banks supervised by the FDIC failed; 67 had material losses of $17.1 billion, which averaged 21.7 per cent of their assets. Of over 850 institutions supervised by the Federal Reserve, 19 failed and 17 had material losses that totalled $3.5 billion, or 25.6 per cent of their assets. For the OCC, 38 of the more than 1,500 banks it supervised failed; 11 had material losses of $2.8 billion, or 19.9 per cent of their assets. Of the roughly 800 thrifts supervised by the OTS, 29 failed and 16 had material losses of $18.5 billion, or 20.4 per cent of their assets. The MLR figures for the OCC and the OTS are incomplete because they ceased conducting reviews for institutions that failed in the second half of 2009, unless they each incurred losses in excess of $200 million.

Table 10.3 examines proxy measures for the capital, assets, management, earnings, and liquidity (CAMEL) classification system.[4] It provides a strong picture of the causes of bank failure. Of the 111 MLRs, 105 blamed concentrated assets. Concentrations on commercial real estate, and acquisition and development loans were citied especially often. Risky home mortgages or mortgage-backed securities were far less often seen as the cause of these reviewed failures.[5] A large number (42) of the failures occurred in banks that had been newly chartered within the past ten years. Moreover, 64 banks and thrifts – some old-established institutions – had changed their charter and/or their business plan during the 2000s, when Whalen (2010) claimed that bankers developed preference for a state charter rather than a national charter. Ninety-nine of the failed institutions experienced fast asset growth; 93 had a weak board; 94 had inadequate risk controls; and 72 relied on volatile sources of funding, especially brokered deposits and Federal Home Loan Bank advances. In 2008, the Federal Reserve placed much of the blame for its material loss failures on the state of the economy. By 2010, all of the IGs listed the bad economy as an important contributing factor in many of the material loss failures.

These indicators have long been recognized as precursors of failure. As Chris Adam, commenting on the chapter, has observed, these dangers are 'known knowns'. Yet they were not acted upon. Because new banks are recognized to be subject to an increased risk of failure, regulators have supervised de novo banks carefully during their initial three years of operations. Clearly oversight of new banks and thrifts was needed over a longer period and the FDIC has now extended the period of concentrated oversight to seven years – even that may well not be long enough. The OCC was concerned about over concentration in real estate in 1980 when the author was a visiting scholar at this agency. The US Government Accountability Office (GAO) and the US Congress recognized the dangers of fast growth and brokered deposits during the S&L debacle. Lindgren *et al.* (1996) examined the causes of bank failure in financial crises around the world and staff of the International Monetary Fund warned countries in East Asia and elsewhere about the dangers of fast growth; volatile funding sources; weak management; inadequate risk controls, underwriting and credit administration; phony accounting; and concentration in real estate assets before and during the financial crisis there in the mid-to-late 1990s. Staff at the FDIC and the OCC warned about the propensity of de novo banks to concentrate their assets in risky real estate (De Young and Hasan, 1998; De Young, 2003; Yom, 2005). Yet agency IGs found that these various conditions were important factors in almost all of the 111 institutions that failed with material losses in 2007–9. Examining why this happened takes us to the MLRs' analysis of supervisors' actions.

Inspector generals' analyses of supervision

One of FDICIA's provisions required onsite inspections to be held annually. Although this objective was not achieved for all institutions, the average time between inspections fell from 609 days in 1986 to 373 in 1992 and the cycle for most inspections ranged between 12 and 18 months. Thus supervisors should not have been blind-sided when institutions deteriorated, especially as banks and

Table 10.2 Failures and material losses: 2007–9[a]

	FDIC	*Fed*	*OCC*	*OTS*	*Total*
2009					
Number of institutions[b]	5,039	858	1,505	773	8,175
Their deposits (billion)[b]	\$1,733	\$962	\$4,142	\$713	\$7,550
Number failed or assisted[c]	78	18	30	22	148
Number of ML reviews[d]	56	16	10	11	93
Assets of ML institutions (million)	\$67,365	\$13,496	\$12,075	\$17,035	\$109,971
Estimated material losses (million)[d]	\$13,722	\$3,446	\$2,603	\$5,478	\$25,249
Percentage loss	20.4	25.5	21.6	32.2	23.0
2008					
Number of institutions[b]	5,163	874	1,515	809	8,361
Their deposits (billion) [b]	\$1,642	\$857	\$3,597	\$923	\$7,019
Number failed or assisted[c]	15	1	8	6	30
Number of ML reviews[d]	11	1	1	4	17
Assets of ML institutions (million)[d]	\$11,349	\$229	\$2,100	\$48,600	\$62,278
Estimated material losses (million)[d]	\$3,354	\$72	\$214	\$12,900	\$16,540
Percentage loss	29.6	31.4	10.2	26.5	26.6

2007					
Number of institutions[b]	5,215	888	1,676	815	8,594
Their deposits (billion) [b]	$1,645	$831	$3,274	$945	$6,695
Number failed or assisted[c]	2	0	0	1	3
Number of ML reviews[d]	0	0	0	1	1
Assets of ML institutions (million)[d]	0	0	0	$25,000	$25,000
Estimated material losses (million)[d]	0	0	0	$108	$108
Percentage loss	0	0	0	0.4	0.4
2007–9[a]					
Number failed or assisted: total	95	19	38	29	181
Number of MLRs	67	17	11	16	111
Assets of ML institutions (million)	$78,714	$13,725	$14,175	$90,635	$197,249
Estimated material losses (million)	$17,076	$3,518	$2,817	$18,486	$41,897
Material losses as percentage of assets	21.7	25.6	19.9	20.4	21.2

Notes

a Data to December 31, 2009.

b Numbers and deposits of institutions are taken from FDIC Summary of Deposit data for National Totals by Charter Class for June of each year. FDIC data include FDIC-supervised savings banks. OTS data include federally chartered and OTS-supervised savings associations, available at www.fdic.gov.

c Data are taken from the FDIC's Historical Statistics (2009) on Failures and Assistance Transactions, which include cases of assistance under a systemic risk determination, available at www.fdic.gov.

d Author's analysis of material loss reviews by the FDIC, the Federal Reserve, the OCC, and the OTS, published by the end of October 2010. Only for banks that failed up to August 2009. Only for thrifts that failed up to July 2009.

Table 10.3 Factors contributing to material failure with material losses

Factor contributing to failure	*2009*				*2008*				*2007*	*Total 2007–9*
	FDIC	*Fed*	*OCC*	*OTS*	*FDIC*	*Fed*	*OCC*	*OTS*	*OTS*	
Structure										
Number of MLRs	56	16	10	11	11	1	1	4	1	***111***
One-bank holding company	45	n.a.	6	7	8	1	1	4	1	***73***
New charter	27	3	1	3	6	0	0	2	0	***42***
Recent change in charter or business plan	34	3	9	4	8	1	1	4	0	***64***
Capital										
Inadequate ALLL	41	6	7	3	9	1	1	4	1	***73***
Assets										
Fast growth	49	14	9	10	11	0	1	4	1	***99***
Had concentrated assets	53	16	10	8	11	1	1	4	1	***105***
Concentration on risky home mortgages	4	3	3	3	4	0	0	3	0	***20***
Concentrated on acquisition, development, construction loans	46	12	4	5	11	1	9	1	0	***89***
Concentration on commercial real estate	48	16	9	7	6	9	1	1	0	***97***
Concentration on MBS	4	1	2	2	0	0	0	2	1	***12***

Management										
Dominant individual(s)	18	1	6	2	6	0	0	1	0	***34***
Weak board and senior management	50	13	9	3	11	1	1	4	1	***93***
Inadequate risk controls	49	13	9	5	11	1	1	4	1	***94***
Lax underwriting and credit administration	44	8	9	7	11	1	1	4	1	***86***
Risky incentive compensation schemes	10	1	3	1	4	0	1	1	1	***22***
Ignored supervisory concerns	35	7	5	3	10	1	0	4	1	***66***
Violated laws and/or regulations	34	4	4	2	8	0	1	1	0	***54***
Earnings										
Accounting malfeasance	23	1	6	4	9	0	1	3	1	***48***
Misused interest reserves	19	3	5	2	8	0	0	1	0	***38***
Losses due to the weak economy	5	16	0	1	n.a.	1	n.a.	n.a.	n.a.	*n.a.*
Liquidity										
Relied on volatile sources of funding	39	9	7	2	9	1	1	3	1	***72***
Heavy use of brokered deposits	36	9	7	2	9	1	1	3	1	***69***
Relied on Federal Home Loan Bank advances	27	7	4	2	11	1	1	2	0	***55***
Relied on high-rate deposits	11	4	3	1	n.a.	n.a.	n.a.	n.a.	n.a.	*n.a.*

Source: Author's analysis of material loss reviews.

Note
n.a. means not available.

thrifts are required to report extensive data to their supervisor and the FDIC in their call reports each quarter. These and other data are analysed in off-site analysis.

As reported in Table 10.4, one of the IGs' common complaints was that supervision of the failed banks had been slow and ineffective. In half of the MLRs, IGs found that supervisors failed to follow up to ensure that their recommendations were implemented. In 69 MLRs, IGs observed that institutions were allowed to ignore supervisory expressions of concern and that existing laws and regulations were not enforced in 41 cases. Examiners' work papers were weak in 31 of the MLRs.

In three-quarters of the MLRs, IGs judged that supervisors had correctly implemented FDICIA's provisions. As mentioned above, they considered only FDICIA's capital provisions. In the reports it issued in 2010, however, one inspector general – the Federal Reserve's – criticized Federal Reserve supervisors for *not* effectively implementing the PCA provisions in 13 of its 16 more recent reviews.

Why were the risks ignored?

One can understand why a single examiner could be lenient with a bank that was highly profitable in the early years of the decade and would confine criticism to recommending that management improve its risk controls. But the examiner was likely to take even that minimum action only if the bank's concentration sharply exceeded its peer group's holding of commercial real estate or reliance on volatile funds. Peer group analysis appears to have been pervasive and to have allowed over concentrations to develop within the industry. No one seemed concerned that the industry as a whole was becoming dependent on real estate and volatile funding. Moreover, almost half of the MLR banks appeared to have been allowed to continue operating while violating laws and or regulations. It appears that it was hard for one examiner in isolation to discipline a profitable and apparently well-capitalized bank. It also appeared to have been hard to apply discipline even if that bank was abusing interest reserves, making inadequate provision for losses, or employing accounting dodges to over-estimate its net income and capital.

It is possible to understand that it was hard for an individual examiner to lean against the prevailing profitable wind. But I wonder why no senior supervisory manager or agency leader questioned whether it was possible for so many of the banks to continue to be profitable in what was clearly perceived at the time, as I have been informed in conversations with supervisory staff, to have been a bubble situation.

Academics have suggested a number of explanations or supervisory actions that fail to protect taxpayers' interests. They are discussed in Garcia (2010). As I worked on this chapter, I held conversations with staff at the regulatory agencies in order to obtain their assessment of what went wrong. The talks revealed the following explanations. First, examiner personalities make them loners. They

Table 10.4 Material losses and supervisory errors

	2009				*2008*				*2007*	*Total 2007–9*
	FDIC	*Fed*	*OCC*	*OTS*	*FDIC*	*Fed*	*OCC*	*OTS*	*OTS*	
Number of MLRs	56	16	10	11	11	1	1	4	1	***111***
New institutions	27	3	1	3	6	1	0	2	0	***43***
Recent change in charter or business	34	8	6	3	2	0	1	1	1	***56***
Supervision										
PCA done right	50	3	10	5	10	1	1	2	0	***82***
Supervision slow and ineffective	50	16	8	5	11	1	1	4	1	***97***
Failed to follow up	17	11	6	5	11	1	1	4	1	***57***
Bank allowed to ignore supervisors	37	6	7	3	9	1	1	4	1	***69***
Guidelines ignored	30	6	7	3	9	1	1	4	1	***62***
Failed to enforce laws/regulations	14	1	6	1	10	4	1	3	1	***41***
Weak work papers	5	1	6	9	5	0	1	4	0	***31***
Enforcement actions										
Informal	63	10	0	4	8	3	0	9	0	***97***
Formal	55	26	12	9	15	1	2	6	1	***127***

Source: Author's analysis of material loss reviews.

conduct their inspections and file their reports away, without discussing their work with their fellow examiners or bringing their findings to the attention of their senior managers. Second, examiners individually knew that there was a real estate bubble. Third, examiners did not make strong representations about the bubble to their managers because they knew they would not get a sympathetic hearing. Fourth, some agency heads did not wish to address the bubble problem because they were being influenced by the politicians to whose committees they reported. It was easier for agency managers to ignore the bubble because they knew that both the Democratic and the Republican Administrations wanted to encourage economic growth, favoured housing as a target of national policy, and wanted to extend home ownership to lower-income households. But the MLRs revealed that many of the failures reviewed were caused by commercial, not residential, real estate, although many ADC loans financed the early stages of home construction.

Consequently, the fifth explanation becomes important for explaining what went wrong. It asserts that the politicians to whom the regulatory agencies report were being advised by the powerful finance and real estate industries to let the country ride the then-profitable real estate wave. The real estate and banking industries are influential in every US state and virtually every congressional district. Sixth, politicians were sympathetic to these industries' concerns because they were dependent on their contributions to their re-election campaigns. Sadly, that is the analysis presented by staff from the regulatory agencies whose opinion I sought. This interpretation is consistent with the findings in the special report on backdating capital contributions by the United States Department of Treasury's Inspector General (2009a). The Treasury's OIG found that the Office of Thrift Supervision had allowed a number of thrift institutions that subsequently failed with large losses to the DIF to backdate capital contributions. The losses at one of these thrifts, IndyMac, were particularly costly to the DIF (Treasury OIG, 2009b). Such backdating allowed the thrifts to maintain their well-capitalized status and thus continue to avoid PCA discipline and in particular to remain liquid by relying on brokered deposits for funding, without risking the rejection of their request to the FDIC for a waiver from this FDICIA provision. In some instances, the Treasury's special backdating report states that the OTS actually required thrifts to backdate the receipt of capital from their holding company, thus thwarting PCA discipline.

There is perhaps another reason why the country's and the regulatory agencies' leaders did not take stronger measures to restrain the risky behaviour that they observed. Maybe they truly believed that 'this time is different' (Reinhart and Rogoff, 2009). Maybe they did not restrain bank risk taking because doing so would have meant pricking the bubble, which was contrary to Federal Reserve policy at the time. Fed policy was – and maybe still is – to let a bubble run its course and clean up the financial mess afterwards by lowering interest rates to aid the recovery – in the 'Greenspan put'. Maybe policymakers really believed that increasing productivity and greater prosperity meant that real estate valuations were based on fundamentals and did not reflect a bubble. Maybe they judged that during 'the Great Moderation', they had conquered financial crises and could successfully prevent/combat future recessions. Maybe such hubris prevented needed restraint.

Potential corrections to strengthen PCA

Prompt corrective action is a noble idea worthy of adoption in other countries, as Mayes *et al.* (2008) and Nieto and Wall (2007) advocate. It is therefore important to remove the barriers that prevent it from achieving its objectives. The analysis above suggests several local corrections could be made to the supervisory system in the US. Such improvement includes (1) placing less reliance on peer review analysis; (2) conducting intensive oversight of de novo institutions for ten years, instead of three or seven years; and (3) making greater use of FDICIA's non-capital provisions and of informal enforcement actions. It also suggests that supervisors should keep their examination reports in a computerized, centralized location and that they conduct research on them to build an overall picture of the industry's trends and exposures to undue risk. Agency research departments could also conduct macro-prudential research and build closer contacts with supervisors to encourage supervisory departments to act on the results of their research. Together with supervisory departments, agency research departments could hold supervisory and research seminars across all of the banking agencies to form an independent inter-agency supervisory position on the state of the banking industry and the risks that it faces.

None of these local 'fixes' is likely to make sufficient improvement, however, if the agency's climate is unreceptive to securing effective oversight of each individual institution – oversight that is undertaken in the context of industry trends and the risks that these pose for the industry, and the nation, as a whole. The analysis presented in the previous section is discouraging in this regard because it suggests that obtaining an effective supervisory system that serves the interests of the country as a whole, its workers, and taxpayers will not be easy. The US political system would need to become less dependent on money. The US has tried on several previous occasions in the past to reform its campaign finance laws, without great success. The US has also tried to insulate the regulatory system from political influence but it seems to have failed in the years leading up to the recent financial crisis. This is a sobering thought. Whereas FDICIA sought to mandate supervisors to take remedial action and sought to reduce their discretion to act, or not act, the 2010 Reform Act has taken the opposite approach. It has left implementation of its reforms to massive rule-making by the regulatory agencies. We must hope that the regulators make and implement those rules in the interests of the country at large and that this brings greater stability and prosperity not just to the US but to the global economy.

Building a national, even an international, picture of the risks facing the financial services industry and measures to address these risks requires inter-agency cooperation. It would be an important element in initiating the macro-prudential oversight that the G20, the International Monetary Fund, and the European

Union are currently championing to reduce the chances and severity of future financial crises. But supervisors of international banks are concerned not to lose a bank's headquarters and its subsidiaries to other countries. In the US, supervisors are also concerned not to alienate those they oversee so much so that they change their charters and their federal supervisor. As long as supervisors face such competitive concerns, they are likely to moderate the discipline they exert in order to attract or retain the banks they oversee, and macro-prudential oversight will be correspondingly weakened. Thus, macro-prudential oversight may alleviate some industry weaknesses but the author does not expect it to be a panacea that will relieve the world of future financial crises. Can we expect macro-prudential oversight to prevail over hubris?

Notes

1 See www2.fdic.gov/hsob/index.asp.
2 The DIF's loss estimates were subsequently reduced as banks' capital improved as they reduced their provisions for losses.
3 Banks and thrifts were separately insured until the Bank Insurance Fund and the Savings Association Insurance Fund were combined into the Bank Insurance Fund in 2005.
4 There is no proxy in the paper for systemic risk in the CAMELS classification system.
5 Cole and White (2010) have made similar findings. Mortgages and, especially, mortgage-backed securities and their derivatives are believed to be more of a problem at the major banks and thrifts that were merged with assistance or otherwise rescued rather than being allowed to fail. Acquisition, development, and construction loans often financed the beginning phase of house construction.

References

Carnell, R.S. (1993) 'The culture of ad hoc discretion', in G. Kaufman and R. Litan (eds), *FDICIA One Year Later*, Washington, DC: The Brookings Institution.

Cole, R.A. and White, L.J. (2010) 'Déjà vu all over again: the causes of US commercial bank failures this time around', paper presented at the conference on Finance and Sustainable Growth, the 10th annual conference sponsored by the FDIC and the Journal of Financial Services Research, October.

De Young, R. (2003) 'De novo bank exit', *Journal of Money, Credit and Banking*, 35(5): 711–28.

De Young, R. and Hasan, H. (1998) 'The performance of de novo commercial banks: a profit-efficiency approach', *Journal of Banking and Finance*, 22(4): 566–87.

Eisenbeis, R. and Wall, L. (2002) 'The major supervisory initiatives post FDICIA: are they based on the goals of PCA? Should they be?', in G. Kaufman (ed.), *Prompt Corrective Action in Banking: 10 Years Later*, Greenwich, CT: JAI Press.

FDIC (1998) *The FDIC and RTC Experience: Managing the Crisis*, Washington, DC: Federal Deposit Insurance Corporation.

FDIC (2010) 'Material loss review for Westsound Bank', *Report No. MLR-10–0005*, December.

FDIC (n.d) *Formal and Informal Procedures Manual*, available at www.fdic.gov.

FDIC Division of Supervision and Consumer Protection (n.d.) *Risk Management Manual.*

Garcia, G.G.H. (2010) 'Failing prompt corrective action', *Journal of Banking Regulation*, 11(3): 171–90.

Horvitz, P.M. (1995) 'Banking regulation as a solution to financial fragility', *Journal of Financial Services Research*, December: 369–80.

Kaufman, G. (2004) 'FDIC losses in bank failures: has FDICIA made a difference?', *Economic Perspectives*, Federal Reserve Bank of Chicago, third quarter, pp. 13–25.

Lindgren, C.-J., Garcia, G., and Saal, M.L. (1996) *Bank Soundness and Macroeconomic Policy*, Washington, DC: International Monetary Fund.

Mayes, D., Nieto, M., and Wall, L. (2008) 'Multiple safety net regulators and agency problems in the EU: is prompt corrective action partly the solution?', *Journal of Financial Stability*, 4(3): 223–57.

Murton, A.J. (2010) 'Memorandum to the board of directors', June 8, FDIC, Washington, DC.

Murton, A.J. and Edwards, B.D. (2010) 'Memorandum to the board of directors', October 14, FDIC, Washington, DC.

Nieto, M.J. and Wall, L. (2007) 'Preconditions for a successful implementation of supervisors' prompt corrective action: is there a case for a banking standard in the European Union?', *Bank of Spain Working Paper*, no. 0702.

Reinhart, C.M. and Rogoff, K.S. (2009) *This Time is Different: Eight Centuries of Financial Folly*, Princeton, Princeton University Press.

United States Department of the Treasury (2009a) *Audit Report: Safety and Soundness: OTS Involvement with Backdated Capital Contributions by Thrifts*, OIG-09–037, May 21.

United States Department of the Treasury (2009b) *Safety and Soundness: Material Loss Review of IndyMac Bank, FSB*, OIG-09–032, available at www.treasury.gov/about/organizational-structure/ig/Documents/oig09032.pdf (accessed 21 December 2009).

United States Government Accountability Office (2007) *Deposit Insurance: Assessment of Regulators' Use of Prompt Corrective Action Provisions and FDIC's New Deposit Insurance System*, GAO-07–242, February.

Whalen G.W. (2010) 'Why do de novo banks choose a national charter?' *OCC Economics Working Paper*, no. 2010–2.

Yom, C. (2005) 'Recently chartered banks' vulnerability to real estate crises', *FDIC Banking Review*, July, 17(2): 1–15.

11 Time for a paradigm shift in thinking

Jane Diplock

By the end of the last century, our conceptualization of the finance sector regulation was looking out-dated. This century has seen a shift in thinking that stresses the importance of a more networked view, a shift accelerated by the perceived causes of, and fall out from, the global financial crisis. It has also seen greater focus on corporate governance. The International Organization of Securities Commissions is at the forefront of this new international thinking, which suggests more effective ways of encouraging and regulating markets. There are important implications for the New Zealand financial sector reform.

The title of this chapter might at first glance sound somewhat remote. It suggests a big picture that, while academically interesting, might seem to have little to do with the everyday realities of the business conducted by boards and individual directors. I hope, however, to build a bridge between that bigger conceptual picture and on-the-ground, day-to-day business decision making; to share my understanding of the essential link between the international regulatory landscape and the domestic scene.

I begin by sketching my perspective on the crisis, its causes and lessons and go on to explain the new thinking replacing the old orthodoxy, and what the implications of this new thinking are – not just on a world-scale but for individual boards and their directors, shareholders and the wider community at home.

I begin and end, however, with the importance of corporate governance.

The importance of corporate governance

Governance is the codification of sound ethical standards. It covers every aspect of how a company behaves. As a general principle, every decision a company makes and every initiative it institutes must be soundly based not just in the pragmatics of profit but in high ethical standards. It prevents, as one astute observer has put it, self-interest getting out of hand. Self-interest may be rational, but it can sometimes endanger the system as a whole. The purpose of corporate governance standards is to influence the drivers of market players' behaviour, to encourage greater transparency, reduction of conflicts of interest and a focus on the interests of investors and other stakeholders. That is why I believe corporate governance to be one of the biggest challenges the post-financial crisis world faces.

Those yet to wake up to the new reality might think that an over-statement. To them, corporate governance is the icing on the cake. Certainly not the cake itself, let alone the bread and butter, of doing business. Surely, they would argue, what investors need is for their investment to grow. Surely, in the hard-nosed business of growing investments, it is financial survival that matters. Though it might *look* good to pay some attention to *how* you do business, it is *what* you do that finally counts. It is the financial bottom line that matters.

I believe this view to be, at best, limited; at worst, a serious risk to the health of international securities markets and the global economy. Which means it is a serious risk to us all. As a regulator, I am keenly interested in encouraging and, where necessary, enforcing good corporate governance, not merely in the cause of pursuing virtue for its own sake but because it is a vital plank in investor protection. Investor protection enhances investor confidence and, without investor confidence, markets stagnate or decline. This affects the real economy and benefits no one. Now, more than ever, investors need the assurance that issuers have robust corporate governance principles in place and that these are being fully disclosed.

Earlier chapters discuss the lessons of the financial crisis. That particular elephant will be in the room for some time to come and we ignore it at our peril.

The crisis was the result of a number of factors coming together to form a time bomb that exploded in the heart of the financial world. One of them was the macroeconomic fiscal imbalances that prompted domestic policies fostering undisciplined credit.

Other contributing factors were reliance on the continuous growth of asset prices; opaque markets, which developed toxic, over-valued products that failed to reflect concomitant risk; lack of transparency; inadequate infrastructure; investor greed that sought yield without attending to due diligence; and markets reflecting perceived rather than true value.

These are apparently disparate factors. Yet, seen from this distance, we can, I think, discern a common thread – poor corporate governance.

The old orthodoxy

Before the global financial crisis, many believed that, when it came to market behaviour, self-interest was a regulator rather than a risk. The notion of corporate governance as little more than window-dressing was the orthodoxy of those pre-crisis years. Those who held to this view did so with such conviction that, in making a powerful case for leaving ethics, morality and sustainability out of business, they paradoxically ended up claiming the moral high ground. Those who argued against it, or even expressed reservations, were too often dismissed as sad, sentimental, old-fashioned and slightly eccentric.

Many – possibly most – of those who held to this view honestly believed that to put naked entrepreneurial zeal into practice was to do their best for shareholders. To some extent, they were right. Certainly, entrepreneurial zeal is vital. Too many, however, were deluded by the mistaken idea that they had to choose between being *good* and being *profitable.* Too many believed it was an either/or situation. That good governance was an optional add-on rather than an essential operating principle – a luxury rather than a necessity. It took the global financial crisis to teach them that this was not so.

The lessons of the crisis

I see the three major lessons of the crisis as being:

- that markets matter
- that global markets are vitally interconnected
- that governance and sustainability matter.

Markets matter

The crisis overturned the widespread belief that, so long as institutions such as banks were regulated, markets would look after themselves. We thought that the self-interest that drove markets meant they would self-regulate, while continuing to deliver sustained economic growth and welfare. The crisis put paid to this belief. The self-interested behaviour that led to the crisis arose in market conduct and infrastructure and the risks were transmitted through the markets.

Most informed observers, policymakers, investors and regulators – including former US Federal Reserve chairman Alan Greenspan – now agree that the orthodox faith in market discipline to regulate markets was misplaced.

What has supplanted this mistaken idea is the insight that the overall health of markets relies on the health of all their nodes and linkages, and the capital flows between them. The new concept of systemic risk recognizes that financial stability is as much the concern of securities markets regulators as it is of prudential supervisors. Regulation of markets *and* regulation of systemically important institutions are the virtuous twins of financial stability. Both must be in place if we are to avoid further crises.

Global markets are vitally interconnected

One of the most painful revelations of the crisis was that national borders can no longer stand in the way of capital flows. Securities markets are highly interconnected because technology has made them global. Money moves around the world with the click of a mouse. Before the crisis, few New Zealand investors and market participants would have imagined that the mis-selling of a mortgage product to an unemployed person in the suburbs of Chicago could impact on their economic futures and that of those around them. Yet it could and it did. We discovered, to our dismay, that disruption in one market was capable of causing major disruptions in other, apparently remote, markets. This is an insight we ignore from now on at our peril.

A number of writers in the financial area have noted that language and, in particular, metaphor tend to shape not only our thoughts but our actions, and that some metaphors are distinctly more useful than others in providing us with tools to manage our world. In 2003, Richard B. Wagener wrote that:

> Financial system metaphors tend to remain grounded in 17th century physics and 19th century biology. They rarely incorporate the integral visions of 20th century quantum physics or ecology, and more recently the internet. The result is 'machines' rather than ecosystems.[1]

Although attitudes have moved on somewhat in the last seven years, and particularly since the crisis, this view still has a considerable hold on many in the financial world.

A much more useful way to conceptualize the nature of international transactions and relationships in the twenty-first century has been elucidated by Bank of England Executive Director of Financial Stability Andrew Haldane.[2] He draws an analogy between the complex adapted network – 'a cat's cradle of interconnections' – of financial markets and other complex network systems. He points out the parallels between the degradation of ecosystems, the spread of epidemics and the disintegration of the financial system. Each element is essentially a branch of the same network family tree. This model emphasizes not fixed, separate elements but the interconnections between them, and the potential for what happens in one part to affect others, even those that are apparently remote.

There is a fascinating and productive parallel here between the ecological perspective, which stresses the interconnectedness of all life on earth, and this new perspective on capital markets, which stresses networks. The new network thinking emphasizes dynamic activity rather than static structure. It implies a system whose components are constantly interacting and these require the tending and encouragement more appropriate to an organism than to a machine.

I believe that looking at the global financial system as a network will provide us with new ways of understanding, assessing and coping with systemic risk. It may also enable us to understand the inter-linkages between commodities markets, energy markets, carbon markets and the broader financial markets. Abandoning our old institution-by-institution approach and looking instead at the capital flows between them will give rise to regulatory tools that will help us manage these risks far better than we have in the past.

Governance and sustainability matter

The crisis taught us the hard way that good governance is necessary for a stable securities market. John Bogle, one of my colleagues on the international Financial Crisis Advisory Group,[3] has emphasized the role of self-interest. John, as the founder and former CEO of Vanguard Group of Mutual Funds in the US, is no mere ivory-tower idealist. He has wittily – and accurately – referred to the global financial crisis as 'a crisis of ethic proportions', a phrase that immediately brings to mind the importance of governance. This ethical crisis was prompted by what he identifies as a 'sea-change in capitalism'. He says the sea-change occurred when giant companies began to be governed not by their owners but by agents, and certain public corporation managers began putting their own interests ahead of the interests of the company's owners.

I think he is right. I think this change led inevitably to such practices as profligate lending by US mortgage brokers, who expected risks to be sold on; to conflicts of interest at the heart of advising on – then rating – complex securitized products; to excessive remuneration. Individuals acting rationally in their own short-term self-interest brought the international financial system to its knees. Clearly such practices were unsustainable in the longer term. They demonstrated extremely poor governance and understanding of the drivers for a sustainable business.

These drivers of short-term behaviour led directly to unethical outcomes. They ran contrary to good corporate governance and were the cause of the collapses and major investor losses that characterized the crisis; resulting in a worldwide loss of investor confidence in markets. Such practices, and the attitudes that justified them, added up to an eventual overwhelming by unregulated market forces of traditional, centuries-old standards of conduct.

IOSCO's perspective

The new 'ecological' perspective on markets I have outlined makes it clear that it is no longer enough to adopt a narrow, national approach. What happens in one part of the financial market network is likely to have implications for others. In the twenty-first century, all matters relating to markets and their governance, regulation, financial reporting, accounting and auditing must be globally oriented. The International Organization of Securities Commissions (IOSCO), whose executive committee I have the honour of chairing, is at the forefront of this new understanding. It is the recognized standard setter for the world's securities markets. It exists to promote global financial stability by means of agreement on, and application of, consistent standards across the world's financial markets. Where those standards fail to be met, it aims to enable effective enforcement across jurisdictions. This level of international cooperation gives transgressors fewer places to hide.

IOSCO's 119 jurisdictional members regulate more than 95 per cent of the world's securities markets. Most are independently constituted government regulators. Essential to its goals and methods are the three premises I outlined earlier:

- that market stability is crucial to economic health
- that markets are global
- that good market conduct is crucial to market stability.

IOSCO considers corporate governance to be the key to capital market integrity and stability, and its work has always focused on addressing risks to investor protection and on the fair and efficient functioning of financial markets. It has established a research function to analyse risks across markets. This will focus on risk assessment and project management support and, in particular, produce risk outlooks, exploratory analysis, impact assessments and data analysis. Several recently published IOSCO reports address specific aspects of market behaviour that potentially constitute systemic risks, including conflicts of interest, due diligence practices, ownership structures and other drivers of behaviour. These reports required examination of the current boundaries of regulated activity, extending the reach of regulation, in some cases beyond its traditional scope. They address alternative approaches regulators might take and encourage greater transparency in markets.

The New Zealand situation

The last two decades have seen New Zealand move from a fairly light-handed regulatory regime to one drawing close to international best practice. In 2003, our financial sector was thoroughly reviewed by the IMF and World Bank under the FSAP programme. The aim here, as elsewhere, was to uncover vulnerabilities in our regulatory framework.

The report on New Zealand was basically positive. However, it did identify a gap in our regulatory framework relating to financial intermediaries, which meant a potential for mis-selling. The financial advisor industry reforms now being put into effect are a direct outcome of that assessment seven years ago. They will close this regulatory gap by professionalizing the industry and thereby giving investors more protection.

The limits of regulation

The finance company collapses of recent years harshly revealed the limitations of New Zealand's regulatory framework. The collapses were entirely a home-grown phenomenon. We cannot blame them on overseas factors beyond our control. However, we can – and must – recognize that this country was also caught up in the spirit of the times. The collapses were not merely bad luck. Quite often – as subsequent Securities Commission investigations have shown – they were precipitated by a negligent or, in some cases, fraudulent failure to act on the part of directors. A failure to do what was required to protect investors and – finally and ironically – to protect the companies themselves. I have been widely quoted as saying that the finance company collapses occurred in a regulatory desert. I stand by that statement.

Two points need to be made here. The first is that the Commission did not and could not prevent companies from failing. We worked towards a more level playing field for investors but there will always be an element of risk in securities market participation.

Second, there was nothing the Commission could have done to prevent the finance companies from failing. Given the dictates of our founding Act, our role was limited to ensuring risks were properly disclosed in prospectuses, investment statements and so on, so investors could assess their individual risk in light of the offered return. Once offers were allotted, our role ceased. Trustees had oversight of the product and the behaviour of directors throughout the product's life. We had no other part to play. Regulators are not freelance crusaders but creatures of statute. They can do no more than operate within their remit and, if that appears to be too limited, ask for more powers. This we did, and I will come back to the regulatory changes currently in the wings and being implemented. With the creation of the new Financial Markets Authority (FMA) in May 2011, the position has changed. The FMA has stronger powers. Had these been available earlier, the problems posed by the finance company sector could have been reduced.

Failures of governance

Our work has shown again and again that most corporate failures and breaches of securities law are at least partly attributable to what is at some point a failure of governance. This certainly proved true in the case of the failed finance companies. We have seen failures to ensure accurate disclosure and financial reporting, particularly in relation to related-party lending and/or asset quality. We have seen poorly capitalized companies without any liquidity buffer against a downturn. We have seen heroic valuations in a declining market.

There have been instances of too few directors, or even sole directors, on boards, as well as periods when boards included no independent directors at all. In some cases, independent directors failed to ensure they were adequately informed, or took insufficient interest in the business. Directors are, of course, entitled to receive and rely on expert advice but they should not do so blindly. They need to assess valuations and other external reports critically and exercise common sense and good judgment. We have seen ineffective audit committees or none at all. We have seen poor or inadequate auditing of companies. We have seen poor handling of business growth or expansion and evidence of failure to recognize or act on warning signs in a timely manner.

Back in 2004, the Securities Commission published nine principles of corporate governance. These are applicable at every level – from the small investor and company director, through to large businesses, politicians, regulators and regulatory bodies. The Commission itself regularly reported against these principles, as well as monitoring companies' performance against them. Encouraging and, where necessary, enforcing sound governance is a vital plank in investor protection and, therefore, market health. In New Zealand, as in other jurisdictions, complying with the law is the minimum requirement. Rather, we urged all market participants to aim for best practice and a good number of them do.

Enforceable directors' duties

I believe it is essential that the FMA has the power to investigate whether directors are acting appropriately and, where it can be shown they are not, for such directors to face enforcement consequences. The Ministry's Securities Act review discussion document released in mid-2010 draws no conclusions on whether directors' duties should be enforceable but it does acknowledge that current legislation has resulted in 'under-enforcement'. Legislation governing directors' behaviour exists but it is the responsibility of companies to enforce it. This is useless. This gap continues to leave the Commission almost powerless to act against companies accused of financial misappropriation until it is too late to protect investors.

It is a particular anomaly given the situation in Australia, where charges can be laid against directors for recklessness and dishonesty. In 2005, for instance, after the collapse of HIH Insurance, its former director was sentenced to four-and-a-half years in jail. Australia also allows the initiation of civil actions by investors. It makes no sense that directors can behave differently on either side of the Tasman. The Institute of Directors has indicated support for regulations to deter reckless behaviour and acknowledged the scope for a degree of enforcement. The sticking point is likely to be what this degree should be.

One argument against enforceable duties is that it will make good independent directors even harder to find than they are now. However, in other countries where directors' duties are appropriately enforceable, there has been no diminution in the numbers of people willing to become directors.

Gender balance on boards is another issue being addressed around the world. Studies have shown that companies with more women on their boards are more successful than those with fewer. Smart companies are now aware it makes good business sense to appoint more women. I agree that directors are not always responsible for shareholder losses and company failures. Poor business models and changes in economic circumstances can and should bring about the collapse of some businesses. However, as I have pointed out, Commission investigations have repeatedly shown that poor governance often is to blame. I believe directors need to be held more accountable for their responsibility to shareholders and for good corporate governance.

Regulatory changes

Two related and important changes are in progress: the Securities Act review and the new super-regulator, the Financial Markets Authority. A new Securities Act came into force in 2012 and the government consulted on its 200-page discussion document of the prior legislation. It replaced the Securities Act 1978 and the Securities Markets Act 1988, as well as amending other relevant legislation.

The discussion paper looked at the types of financial products regulated, exemptions for offers to specific classes of investors, disclosure documents and collective investment schemes. The final chapters discuss a range of matters, including possible public enforcement of director duties. The review raises the prospect of significant change to enforcement powers, which might allow regulators to investigate companies proactively in the future. It is, inevitably, a delicate exercise, involving striking a balance between open markets and prudent stewardship of investors' money. As I said before, we cannot regulate away market risk but we must do what we can to build a framework that makes those risks more transparent.

The new super-regulator – the Financial Markets Authority (FMA) – was established in May 2011. This is an independent Crown entity, consolidating powers and functions currently fragmented across the Securities Commission, the Registrar of Companies, the Government Actuary and NZX. It will enforce the law relating to securities, financial reporting and companies, as it applies to financial services and securities markets. It will also regulate and oversee trustees, auditors, financial advisors and financial service providers, including people who offer investments. Even in its first month, it was able to take enforcement actions that were not possible before.

The Securities Act review and the FMA are most welcome signs of progress. They will do a great deal to restore the confidence of investors in our financial markets. If, as I believe, company failures often occur because of gaps in our regulatory framework, these moves will shore up those gaps and make a recurrence less likely.

Conclusion

My key message is the vital connection between day-to-day business decision making and the health of global markets, and between personal responsibility and worldwide trends. Various jurisdictions will always enshrine corporate governance in various guises – in company law, in principles, in guidance – but I believe we will increasingly see global standards formalized as we explore the potential for curbing dangerous excesses. Just as countries are no longer economic islands, so individual actions must be seen as – and shaped by – a global awareness. The ecological model of the finance world is now far more appropriate than the old structural model.

Understanding the global financial system as a network provides a timely and useful analytical tool. It encourages us to be aware of and identify systemic risks in markets and to look at regulation that will manage these risks at every level. Imagine how an environmentalist would laugh if you suggested that what separate countries and individuals do or do not do was nobody else's business. We should be similarly derisive about the same notion applied to securities market regulation, corporate governance, sustainability and directors' duties.

We must train ourselves to think globally and act locally and to expect no less of others. Not merely, as I said at the outset, for the sake of virtue alone but because good governance is good business. Good governance builds financially, environmentally and socially sustainable businesses, and these are the businesses that investors increasingly look to invest in. Change can be difficult. It demands something of us personally: imagination; effort; adjustments in our everyday behaviour. Old habits must be broken. However, this process is already underway. The paradigm is *already* shifting. Some will have the will and courage to embrace it; others will need more time, more persuasion; others still will require coercion. I invite the reader to be among those at the forefront of change.

Notes

1 'Financial metaphors: mechanic, organic or…?', *Financial Advisor*, March 2003, available at www.financialadvisormagazine.com/component/content/article/686.html?issue=31&magazineid=1&itemid=27id%3d1%26itemid%3d27/.
2 *Rethinking the Financial Network*, speech delivered April 2009, available at www.bankofengland.co.uk/publications/speeches/2009/speech386.pdf.
3 This group reports to international accounting standards setters and informs the G20 group of finance ministers and central bank governors of its progress.

12 Cultural considerations for prudential supervisors[1]

Charles Littrell

This chapter takes a personal and non-academic approach to outlining several cultural characteristics that are relevant to prudential supervision. I define 'culture' mainly on two axes:

1 What is most important to a given group; and
2 How priorities have changed in the past 30 or so years.

The different industries within the financial services sector view the world through somewhat different perspectives. Understanding (while not necessarily agreeing with) these perspectives helps prudential supervisors become more effective.

This chapter focuses upon industry trends roughly matching my professional career, which commenced in the early 1980s and has mainly focused upon banking, albeit with significant excursions into the insurance and pension industries. I expect that readers of similar vintage will see much they recognize in this document but such readers will very likely disagree with some of my observations and conclusions. Cultural observations are necessarily subject to differences in interpretation.

Prudential supervisors carry out two core tasks: identifying emerging risks among their regulated flocks, and responding as early and as effectively as possible to these risks. Better understanding industry cultures will assist in both these tasks. Risks tend to emerge from cultural 'blind spots' within an industry and effective responses may sometimes be hindered by the industry's culture.

In this chapter, I look at five industries: banking, investment banking, life insurance, general insurance and superannuation. I have deliberately omitted funds management because this industry is seldom prudentially supervised. I also address two professions: auditors and actuaries, both with important ties to prudential supervision.

Banking

Banking has been characterized and often damaged by four cultural characteristics: size mania, dislike of the core business, changing views on the value of capital soundness and changing definitions of what is moral.

Banking is a remarkably risky business, which typically presents itself, and more worryingly thinks of itself, as a remarkably stable business. Banks are typically highly levered, structurally illiquid and exposed to economic adversity over which they have no control. Historically, they are also prone to fads and myopias which lead to lending booms followed by busts and consequent bank failures. Those of a masochistic bent in my line of work can profitably review Reinhart and Rogoff[2] for a reminder that boom/bust/failure patterns have existed since modern banks and economies were created.

Although substantial banks can fail for reasons other than bad lending,[3] poor credit quality is the main bank killer. Poor credit quality is closely associated with insufficiently controlled balance sheet growth. Historically, this growth was concentrated in the loan portfolio but in the last few crises was accompanied by growth in derivatives and other products which, although not loans, still carry credit risk.

Size mania

From time immemorial to about 1990, depending upon the country in question, large banks cared a great deal about their asset size relative to their competitors. In the post-war era of heavily regulated banking, where it was fairly difficult to make a bad loan, competing on asset size made sense. When banks were deregulated from the 1980s, unfortunately, a focus on asset size leadership became deadly dangerous. The most notable example in Australasia was the Bank of New South Wales's (latterly Westpac's) determination to remain the largest bank through the 1980s, which lead to Westpac's near-crippling losses in the early 1990s. This was far from a uniquely Australasian problem: perhaps most famously, Bank of America's late-1970s determination to stay larger than Citibank contributed to serious financial difficulties at BoA. These difficulties ultimately weakened what was the world's largest bank sufficiently to facilitate its acquisition by a North Carolina-based regional bank.

Although a weakness for growth remains a major prudential problem in banking, the world's more competent bankers now understand that becoming the largest bank by assets is neither admirable nor even sensible. To revert to the Westpac example, that bank's management in the late 1990s and early 2000s explicitly rejected any strategy of restoring its former primacy and limited growth. This is one reason why that bank performed relatively well during the global financial crisis (GFC).

Here we have a case of most bankers learning from horrid example and the mania to be number one in asset size has at least for the moment ceased its grip on the banking industry. Prudential regulators are well aware of the risks associated with growth and, in any sensible regime, including in Australia, the banks out-growing their peers receive considerably more attention simply due to the fact of their rapid growth.

Dislike of the core business

Let us now move on to the 'cultural cringe' of commercial bankers in comparison to investment bankers. Into the 1980s at least, commercial bankers in many countries envied investment bankers for their apparent sophistication, high returns on capital and much higher average compensation. When commercial banks were deregulated, it was common to see them seek to grow their investment banking divisions, often through acquisitions of second tier investment banks. 'One day we will be just like Lehman Brothers or Bear Stearns' was the aspiration. In the 2008 crisis, this aspiration was too often achieved, as commercial banks lost appalling sums of money in the same fashion as their investment banking cousins.

The investment banking cultural cringe was part of a larger move to universal or 'bancassurance' business models, in which financial conglomerates formed to offer all financial products to all customers. It would be fair to say that the global history of such business models is poor, in shareholder value and prudential terms. The Benelux experience during the recent crisis is a case in point, and one must wonder whether Citigroup's losses would have been lessened had that organization's senior management and board not attempted such a broad span of financial services industries. Then there is the inverse example of AIG, where a large and very valuable insurance company came unstuck by its foray into offering credit derivatives.

The Australian experience is perhaps better than average, in that the four major banking groups have also become major life insurance and funds management groups, without suffering undue financial stress. One can argue whether or not shareholders have done well from this strategy but overall the outcomes seem to have been reasonable. Since 1980, bankers have become less attracted to lending money and taking deposits and more attracted to other financial services. This trend has somewhat reversed in the past two years, on the deposit front at any rate, as the value of stable funding has become more apparent. In the 1980s, lending was perceived to be an unattractive business in many developed economies. It was (and is) highly regulated, capital intensive, often over-competitive and with much larger potential losses than potential gains. This combination is dangerous in any industry; see the US airlines for a leading example.

In Australasia, bank lending is also capital intensive and highly regulated but perhaps less competitive than is the case in the US and Europe. From the early 1980s deregulation, the story in our part of the world has been the more or less steady growth of the larger bank share of lending and financial services. From the mid-1990s to around 2005 we may have benefitted from a prudential sweet spot, in which non-bank competition was sufficient to put pressure on the banks to improve their productivity and reduce their margins but not so much pressure that the banks started making overly risky loans at less than sustainable margins. Post the GFC, we are faced with a world where non-bank lenders are at least temporarily impaired and it is not clear where competitive pressure will be sourced against the banking oligopoly. This is a problem of efficiency, which I expect most readers will agree is better than a problem of many large, failed banks.

In this sense, we are left with a paradox. The commercial banker inferiority complex since the 1980s led the global industry into investment banking and bancassurance, too often with very adverse prudential outcomes. In Australasia, at least since the early 1990s, the major banks have been happier to focus upon their core businesses, while expanding into life insurance and funds management, and the results have generally been positive. One reason for the difference has been that Australian banks lost their appetite for global investment banking, after their problems of the early 1990s. By the middle of this decade, Australian banks had among the lowest exposures of the world's major banks to proprietary trading and investment businesses. What was perceived as a strategic weakness five years ago is now a decided strength.

In prudential terms, the lesson seems reasonably clear: worry when a banker loves non-bank businesses more than the core lending and deposit-taking business. Banks can too easily fail in their core business but on the global example can more easily fail when they stray from their core, particularly where this involves taking more proprietary trading and investment risks.

Changing views on capital soundness

As for capital, those with longer memories will recall that the world's banks generally responded to the 1988 Basel I introduction by increasing their capital ratios and bragging about their sound capital positions. This was a particularly fortunate outcome in Australia, as capital increases in the late 1980s essentially pre-funded loan losses in the early 1990s.

The trend to bragging about capital soundness lasted until around 1995, at which point the trend reversed to bragging about capital 'efficiency'. 'Maintaining a maximally efficient capital position' sounds much better than 'minimizing equity and maximizing leverage' but they are close to the same thing.

Why did this trend not lead to insufficient capital and bank failures in Australia? The answers are far from clear and doubtless multiple but one clear answer is the fact that Australian banks rapidly grew leverage against sound assets, not against bad assets. The fact that Australian banks could grow rapidly without taking undue risks was a combination of good luck and good management. The fact that APRA was pushing back hard against uncontrolled growth and over-leverage for the five years leading to the global financial crisis probably helped but was not the major factor in Australia avoiding GFC-related bank failures.

Changing views on morality

Finally, the banker's self-conception of morality has changed in the past few decades. Where the banker of 1980 would recognize a moral duty to depositors, the community, shareholders, the firm itself and employees, by around 2000 this was reduced to 'shareholder value above all' in official communications and, perhaps, 'maximizing executive option payouts' in practice. From a prudential regulator's viewpoint, the absence of self-imposed moral duty to depositors is a particular worry. The banker of 1980 would have agreed that he had a moral duty to ensure that depositor funds were safe. This duty is a pale shadow of its former self in 2010; 'depositors are just another supplier' might better match the position for many modern bankers. The global rush by banks to issue covered bonds, which effectively subordinate depositors, is one manifestation of the trend towards depositors as just another supplier.

What are the implications of these cultural trends for prudential supervisors? They are reasonably obvious:

- Bankers must be watched closely for signs of growth mania. Any banker bragging about asset growth or league table positions is automatically suspect.
- Bankers seeking to grow outside banking are probably taking more risks than might be initially apparent. This particularly applies where the growth has no basis in the bank's traditional customers. Products such as AAA-rated but ultimately toxic collateralized debt obligations (CDOs) might have been met with more effective scepticism had bankers and regulators better realized that they were chasing and allowing growth that had nothing to do with real customers.
- Ideally bankers have permanently rediscovered the joys of a sound capital base. But it is more likely that bankers and institutional equity investors will shortly wish to re-start the leveraging ('capital efficiency') merry-go-round. Regulators will need to maintain their obstinacy on this point in the face of a world that increasingly loses the memories of 2008.
- In the absence of banker moral commitment to depositor safety, one implication is that prudential supervisors will need to intervene more or less constantly, but hopefully mildly and effectively, to keep banks and bankers within a tolerable (to depositors, not shareholders) risk profile.

Investment banking

'Investment banking' means different activities to different people. From the 1930s to around 1980, investment banking focused upon matching debt and equity issuers with investors, typically through an underwriting process. To undertake this business, investment bankers needed to become experts in what drives investors, issuers and markets. Developing this expertise required and contributed to expertise in making markets via trading desks.

In hindsight, it is a tragedy that the league table was a central element in the investment banking culture. The annual attempt to move up the debt and equity underwriting league tables contributed to continued price cutting in the underwriting business, particularly for high-quality bond underwriting, to the point where these businesses may not have been paying their way.

From about the mid-1980s, investment bankers increasingly realized that they could make more money from their market expertise directly on a trading floor than they could from renting this expertise by underwriting capital issues. From the 1990s, they extended this realization from trading to proprietary investment more generally.

By converting from acting as an underwriter to a trader and a proprietary investor, investment banks made a lot more money but took a lot more risks. Ultimately, they kept most of the money but laid off the risks on society, particularly in the US but also in Europe.[4]

As this transition took place, investment bankers lost their moorings on conflict of interest. The investment banker of 1980 was expert at balancing between three conflicting interests: the firm, the issuers and the investors. Clearly an investment bank existed to make money but a successful underwriter needs to balance investor and issuer interests too. There is always the temptation to maximize the profits from one transaction but with the constraint that becoming too greedy will lose clients for future transactions.

Accordingly, 'the client comes first' was not only the asserted but more or less a plausible position in many investment banking firms, at least away from the trading floors. This was not due to altruism but due to the recognized need to keep a stable of potential issuers and investors happily doing business with the firm.

By the current decade, some lip service was still paid to 'the client comes first' but in the major firms, it was really 'our proprietary trading and investment profits come first'. By 2005, the major investment banks did not need clients; they only needed counterparties.

From a prudential regulator's viewpoint, it is best to avoid characterizing investment banks as a group. Some boutique firms specialize in providing advice, and 'the client comes first' is still a credible aspect of such a culture. But these firms typically do not require prudential supervision because they do not need a large balance sheet. Firms which invest and trade, as well as underwrite, need prudential supervision, and underwriting nowadays tends to be the least of these activities.

A wise prudential supervisor, faced with an investment bank heavy with proprietary trading and investment, will realize that it is up against a difficult supervisory proposition. Culturally, investment bankers are very intelligent but not necessarily very wise. An abundance of intelligence tends to lead to an abundance of profits in good times. But a paucity of wisdom means that greed and hubris can overwhelm caution, in an environment changing so rapidly that regulators will have difficulty keeping up.

Life insurance

Life insurers display a near-schizophrenic culture due to a joint reliance upon actuaries and commissioned sales forces.

In my experience, life insurance executives are strongly committed to meeting the valid financial claims made upon them. The idea that a life company would be unable to pay a death or disability claim or meet annuity obligations, most relevantly, is not merely a financial but a moral failing. This aspect of the culture clearly gives prudential regulators great comfort.

On the other hand, most life insurance companies are mainly investment managers. In Australia, for example, 90 per cent of the life industry's balance sheet represents money invested in superannuation funds.

Under the relevant Australian legislation,[5] life companies are required to look after the interests of policy holders in priority to shareholder interests. It would be fair to say that Australian life companies as investment managers ensure that the products they offer are very safe, in the sense that all promises will be honoured, but not necessarily very good, in the sense of value for money.

The combination of safe products with unattractive returns derives from a cultural dichotomy: the joint reliance upon actuaries and commissioned sales forces.

Life companies rely heavily upon actuaries, both internal and external. There is a great deal of respect for actuaries and their advice tends to be followed closely.

At the same time, most life companies have traditionally relied upon commissioned sales forces. 'Life insurance is sold, not bought' is a common catchcry. Sales forces require sales managers. It would be fair to observe that the typical sales manager personality differs greatly from the typical actuarial personality.

Accordingly, a wise prudential supervisor will pay close attention to the balance of power in a life company between actuaries and sales managers. Is the company dominated by actuaries or by sales managers, or (ideally) is there a balance between the two? A sales-dominated company will tend to focus upon growth and take more risks than are comfortable in the process. An actuary-dominated company will take fewer and hopefully better controlled risks but may become moribund over time. The best result is a life company with creative tension between the sales and actuarial executives.

In the Australian case, there have been some prudential issues with life companies over the years but Australian policy holders and annuitants have enjoyed a good record of having their promises met.

General insurance

Traditionally, life companies and general insurance companies have greatly varying cultures, which may be one reason why, at least in Australia, combined companies have not done particularly well.

General insurance companies traditionally differ in their culture from life insurance companies for at least three reasons:

- Claims are negotiable.
- They are sales-dominated.
- They rely heavily upon reinsurers.

These differences are generally negative in prudential terms but over the past decade the general insurance industry has re-invented itself as a more mature and safer industry. Accordingly, some of these differences are fading.

It is a striking characteristic of many financial services consumers that they would not dream of robbing or defrauding a bank, or of making a fake death claim to a life insurance company, but they are perfectly comfortable making an inflated or unjustified claim on a general insurance company.[6] Accordingly, where a bank and a depositor seldom argue about how much the bank owes the depositor, a general insurance company views a claim as merely the first step in a negotiation.[7] The fact that claims are negotiable, particularly the larger and more complicated claims, has tended to drive a certain elasticity of approach in the general insurance industry.

Unlike life insurance companies, actuaries have historically played a limited role in general insurance. Where a prudential supervisor looks to a life company balanced between actuaries and sales managers, prior to the last decade general insurance companies had no such balance and have been traditionally sales driven.

Finally, reinsurance is useful for life companies but critical for general insurance companies. Without reinsurance, every general insurance company in the world would need to hold capital for all the catastrophes that could happen locally. Reinsurance pooling of risk makes the industry much more capital efficient and (when well managed) safer. It would be fair to assert, however, that the traditional relationship between the primary insurers and the reinsurers was based upon highly personal and somewhat informal agreements, with litigation resulting from time to time when disagreements arose.

The combination of a negotiable approach to claims, a sales-driven culture and critical but less formal reinsurance arrangements produced an industry that was, until this decade, highly unsatisfactory in prudential terms. The industry was driven by an underwriting cycle featuring periods where insurance was written at highly unprofitable rates to maintain market share. The subsequent losses then led to large (doubling or more) premium increases, which led to large profits and the next round of unwise new entrants.

Poor documentation greatly exacerbated the prudential problems associated with the underwriting cycle. Very large insurance and reinsurance contracts were written on so-called cover notes, which often lacked follow-up documentation.[8] Major reinsurance contracts were often left unsigned and were less than precise in specifying coverage.

These trends culminated in a large shake-out in the global insurance industry in the late 1990s and early in the 2000s. HIH was the most notable Australian example but many insurance companies around the world failed, suffered severe impairment or were revealed to have engaged in deceptive or inappropriate activity.

The Australian public sector's response to these failures was greatly strengthened legislation, regulation and supervision, at a point when the industry also realized that it needed to improve. Reviewing some of the changes APRA required in 2003 and 2004, from a 2010 perspective, demonstrates just how far the industry had to progress:

- We required general insurance companies to secure actuarial sign-offs on their claims projections.
- We required these companies to execute contracts for reinsurance properly, rather than leave them unsigned.
- We imposed a new prudential regime that is similar in approach to the banking prudential regime.

Curiously, there was material opposition from the industry to the first two points, which today are accepted as obvious necessities.

In addition to financial failures, the general insurance industry of ten years ago displayed a flexible attitude towards probity. This was most starkly reflected in the use of so-called financial reinsurance contracts, which were claimed to provide capital but which in many cases were simply vehicles for deceptive accounting. After a great deal of enforcement activity against local and offshore firms and their officers, the industry seems to have cleaned up its approach to proper accounting for liabilities and capital.

The general insurance industry of 2010 looks much better in financial and cultural terms than the industry of 1999. Among other things, there is much more pricing discipline and, hopefully, this will hold, mitigating destructive underwriting cycles. There is more actuarial and professional risk manager input to balance the industry's sales-driven tendencies. And there is a general increase in professionalism, including professional practice in documenting important transactions and contracts.

Given the generally satisfactory state of affairs in the general insurance industry, the main cultural task for the prudential regulator is to be on the watch for reversion to past poor practices. Both regulators and the industry have better tools in place to monitor reckless pricing and sloppy operations, however, so it is to be hoped that the improvements of the past decade are permanent.

Superannuation

In Australia and many other countries, superannuation/pension arrangements rely upon trusts rather than company structures.[9] The trustees are held to higher than corporate standards in their dealing with fund members.

Conflict of interest is the defining cultural issue in superannuation. Trustees control member money for decades and have a great deal of freedom in how the fund is operated, and in how the money is invested.

APRA has for many years conducted considerable research and statistical effort into understanding trustee behaviour. All this work indicates that we are not dealing with one industry in cultural terms, but two:[10]

- the *for-profit* sector, which originated mainly with life insurance companies and banks; and

- the *not-for-profit* sector, which originated with corporate superannuation plans but is now dominated by multi-employer public sector and industry funds.

The for-profit superannuation sector, as with life insurance policies, offers a product which is relatively high on safety but with poor returns. Given that the great majority of new money flowing into Australian superannuation is defined contribution rather than defined benefit, poor returns materially impair a member's post-retirement lifestyle prospects.

On the safety front, for example, APRA supervisors have uncovered incorrect unit pricing at a number of retail funds and the corporate owners of these funds have refunded over half a billion dollars (including costs) to fund members. At the same time, however, these funds on average earn about 2 per cent less per annum than their not-for-profit equivalents. APRA's research and statistics suggest that most of this difference arises from fund expenses, with some differences arising from investment returns.

For-profit trustees and trustee directors are conflicted between the need to earn profits for the corporation sponsoring the fund and the need to act in the member interest. Our research indicates that this conflict is largely resolved in favour of shareholders rather than fund members. Not-for-profit funds can be conflicted, for example, by the desire to direct funds to the employing industry, but such conflicts are relatively rare and limited. APRA's statistics indicate that there are some poorly performing not-for-profit funds and this poor performance is frequently associated with poor governance. Any league table of medium- or longer-term returns in the Australian superannuation industry, however, is typically dominated at the top by not-for-profit funds and at the bottom by for-profit funds.

It is also striking that the directors of not-for-profit funds usually have their own superannuation invested in the funds and often their families are invested in the funds as well. The converse does not apply: for-profit trustee directors and their families seldom invest in their funds under trusteeship.

APRA's statutory tools in superannuation are less powerful than those for banking and insurance. The Australian Government is currently considering new arrangements for the industry, including an uplift of APRA's powers and responsibilities to match our other industries. Should APRA receive an expanded mandate in superannuation, we will need to think more deeply about the core cultural issues flowing from conflicts of interest in this industry.

Auditors

'Where were the auditors?' is a traditional catch-cry associated with financial scandals. This was highlighted, for example, in the Enron scandal, which contributed to the demise of Arthur Andersen. It has been striking that, from 2007 to 2009, one seldom if ever heard, 'where were the auditors?' It was as if the world had given up on auditors being able to detect and respond effectively to impending failures among their clients. If so, the world's collective opinion is remarkably accurate.

Returning once again to 1980, at that point auditors took great pride not only in their professional competence but in the value of their opinions. Through the next three decades, however, audit opinions have largely lost their value, in the sense that a person could rely upon them. This has arisen for at least three reasons.

First, competition drove down audit fees, in the same way investment banker spreads on underwriting and banker spreads on corporate lending dropped. This led auditors into other businesses, notably consulting. The growth of non-audit relative to audit fees is a well-documented issue, and led to clear conflicts of interest. Second, increasingly expensive litigation meant that a large audit firm could not afford to make a mistake with a large client, lest the resultant civil or possibly criminal litigation drive the whole firm out of business. Finally, through the decade and resulting from Sarbanes–Oxley and similar measures, bad accounting and auditing has become a criminal matter, greatly lifting the personal risk of an incorrect audit opinion.

We are living in a world where it would not only be unwise commercially but potentially catastrophic personally for auditors to give firm opinions. Accordingly, a culture of risk minimization has in a remarkably brief period grown to dominate the audit profession. From the prudential regulator's viewpoint, this change is understandable but unwelcome. Audit opinions have little prudential value, if firms and individual auditors effectively insulate themselves from the consequences of an incorrect opinion. The matter is further complicated by statutory and regulatory reliance sometimes placed upon auditors, for example, in certifying the accuracy of statistical reporting, or in opining on a regulated entity's compliance with prudential standards.

Over the past decade, APRA has evolved from material reliance upon auditors, to selective reliance. We consider an audit opinion valuable on strictly objective matters, such as statistical return accuracy. We also value the professional competence of auditors, when they are not providing conflicted opinions. For the core traditional product of an annual audit opinion, however, APRA does not place much prudential reliance.

I emphasize that none of the above is meant to denigrate auditor probity or competence. Audit firms and auditors are living in a world where one mistake can mean firm bankruptcy and personal impoverishment or imprisonment. In such a world, risk avoidance must dominate the culture. If a modern opinion says, in effect, 'you can't rely upon this opinion', then a wise prudential regulator will in fact not rely upon that opinion.

Actuaries

There are many similarities between auditors and actuaries, in that they traditionally provide professional opinions which may have statutory consequences. So far, the actuaries have not retreated as far down the risk minimization path as have the auditors. This may be because a large firm has yet to be brought undone by litigation, in which case it is only a matter of time before actuarial opinions become less useful.

I observe, in what is hopefully a long period before this result, that Australia's actuarial culture is far more sensitive to individual professional reputation than seems to be the case with auditors. This may arise in part because the actuarial profession is very much smaller than the audit profession and an actuary must guard his or her personal reputation in a consequently smaller and better informed field. There is also the consideration that the traditional role of actuaries in life insurance and defined benefit superannuation gives them some statutory underpinnings that are less available to auditors.

In any event, actuarial culture is similar to audit culture in that professional competence is highly valued and peer view is highly valued but, as noted above, different in that extreme risk avoidance is not yet present. Accordingly, APRA tends to place more prudential value on actuarial opinions than upon audit opinions, while maintaining appropriate scepticism. In-house actuaries are obviously conflicted, even if professional, and external actuaries face financial conflicts similar to auditors.

Cultural responses in the prudential regulator

Modern prudential regulators are more principles driven and more proactive than our predecessors of the 1980s. We try to shape our culture accordingly. When engaging across our regulated institutions and their professional advisors, prudential regulators should remain mindful that differing cultural settings may require differing prudential approaches.

Bankers tend to be cooperative on technical risk-management issues, but at the margin will remain too fond of growth and leverage. They are also suckers for acquisitions and new lines of business, which work out badly more often than we would like. Accordingly, bank prudential supervisors should be suspicious of high growth, particularly suspicious of growth in new businesses, and guard against higher leverage in the various forms this can take. If bankers and regulators are both doing their jobs properly, there should be constant engagement and probably disagreement at the margin on the appropriate rate and form of growth.

Investment banking has moved into an unhealthy space where making money from information advantages drives the business, without any mooring in customer benefit. Prudential regulators in this area must remain mindful that investment bankers will head rapidly in any direction that looks profitable and they may not be able to control the resultant rapid and risky growth.

Sound life insurance companies balance their risk manager/actuarial personality with their sales manager personality and prudential supervisors must be on the lookout for lack of such balance. The general insurance business has pleasingly matured in the past decade and prudential supervisors must remain vigilant that the bad old ways of an uncontrolled underwriting cycle and sloppy business practices do not return.

In the superannuation or pensions business, conflict of interest is inherent and drives trustee behaviour. Prudential supervisors who are empowered to do so must identify and respond effectively to these conflicts.

While at one point auditors and actuaries provided strong professional and sometimes statutory support to prudential supervisors, those days are largely passed for auditors and may pass for actuaries. Accordingly, prudential supervisors will not unduly rely upon these professional opinions but will value them within the context they are provided.

In closing, I acknowledge that the above discussion is necessarily general, and there are a great many exceptions to the patterns I have asserted for each industry. It nonetheless remains the case that the cultural look and feel of each industry and supporting profession differs. Prudential supervisors can improve their performance by understanding and responding appropriately to these differences.

Notes

1 The views expressed in this chapter are personal and do not necessarily reflect the views of the Australian Prudential Regulation Authority (APRA).
2 C. Reinhart and K. Rogoff, *This Time Is Different: A Panoramic View of Eight Centuries of Financial Crises*, 2008, Cambridge MA: MIT Press.
3 BCCI, Barings and Riggs National Bank come to mind over the past two decades.
4 For a useful synopsis, see A.R. Sorkin, *Too Big To Fail: The Inside Story of How Wall Street and Washington Fought to Save the Financial System – and Themselves*, 2009, New York: Viking.
5 *Life Insurance Act* (1995), in our case.
6 One of the major Australian general insurance company executives notes that, during the first year flat-screen televisions were sold in Australia, his company received more claims for stolen flat-screen TVs than the total of such units sold in the country!
7 I hasten to add that the great majority of claims are paid in full and quickly, but a substantial minority require 'adjustment'.
8 For example, there was a great deal of litigation associated with the 11 September 2001 World Trade Center destruction: at issue was whether or not the event was single, with a $6 billion liability, or multiple, with a $12 billion liability. The relevant documents offered surprisingly little guidance on this rather essential issue.
9 In Australia, the relevant legislation is the *Superannuation Industry (Supervision) Act 1993*.
10 This chapter does not consider personal or self-managed superannuation funds, which are a third category.

13 Firm stability and system stability

The regulatory delusion[1]

Geoffrey Wood with Ali Kabiri

> Critical to the contestability of any market are the conditions for entry and exit. Restricting entry limits competition and fosters firms' ability to build and maintain dominant positions. Restricting exit also undermines competition. If unsuccessful firms are not allowed to fail that may distort pricing and so weaken the viability of firms that would otherwise be successful.
>
> (Thomas F. Huertas, Director, Banking Sector, Financial Services Authority, 20 June 2008)

When the regulators examine the grocery business in the UK, they are invariably concerned with competition. Is one firm or another too dominant? Is it treating customers appropriately? How is it treating its suppliers and its small competitors? In short, 'is the industry competitive?' is always, in one form or another, the question that is being asked. Concern is often prompted by the (entirely inappropriate) test of market share. A question that is never asked is how robust a particular individual firm is.

To anyone familiar with regulation in the financial sector, that is distinctly odd. A question always in regulators' minds there is 'how stable is the firm?'.[2] Why is that not asked of firms in the grocery sector? Banking services are important but so, after all, is the supply of food. Yet the regulators never worry about what would happen if, to take a wildly implausible example, Tesco, the largest grocery chain in the UK, were to fail overnight.

Why is that question not asked? The answer is surely in two parts. First, and very important for the failing firm's suppliers and employees, there is for such firms a well-established and well-tested insolvency regime. That regime has for many years worked well in the sense of enabling orderly winding up or selling on of insolvent businesses and has done so within a time period which in most cases has no doubt been irritating but seldom literally intolerable. Second, there is no fear that a vacuum would be left by such insolvency. To continue with our example, if Tesco were to fail, far from there being a dearth of groceries, within hours, Sainsbury's, Morrisons and the other main competitors would be fighting vigorously over this new market opportunity.

Accordingly, then, the analogy of the grocery business with the banking business would imply that, if we have a suitable bankruptcy code and easy entry and exit for banking, regulators need no longer concern themselves with individual firms. For the *effective* industry would no longer be the total of the firms currently in it but rather the total of actual members plus potential entrants.

The aim of this chapter is to consider whether that is an appropriate way to think about banking, or if banking can be changed so that it becomes the appropriate way. For if it can, the problems facing the regulators, and much more important those facing the economy, would be not only different from what they are at present but also much more tractable and a major barrier to effective market discipline would be removed.

To address this, two matters particularly need to be considered. These are, first, barriers to entry and, second, the insolvency code. They are considered in that order.

Barriers to entry

What are these barriers? The term originated in the industrial economics literature of the immediate post-Second World War period. Many industrial economists of that period were concerned to explain data apparently inconsistent with the competitive model and resorted to monopoly as an explanation. The particular phenomenon that troubled many was the *persistence* of higher rates of return in some industries than in others. Why, they asked, did new entry not eliminate this?[3]

The answer given was that there were barriers to entry. But there was no unanimous definition of these barriers. The three best known are those of Bain (1968), Stigler (1968), and Ferguson (1974).

Bain (1968) wrote that the existence of such barriers was demonstrated, and their size measured, by '...the extent to which established firms can elevate their selling prices above the minimal average costs of production and distribution ... without inducing potential entrants to enter the industry'[4] (p. 252). Ferguson (1974) defines barriers as '...factors that make entry unprofitable while permitting established firms to set prices above *marginal* cost, and to persistently earn monopoly return' (p. 10; Ferguson's italics). For Stigler (1968), barriers were '...a cost of production (at some or every rate of output) which must be borne by a firm which seeks to enter an industry but is not borne by firms already in the industry' (p. 67).

These definitions differ in their implications. For Bain and Ferguson, economies of scale could be a barrier, while for Stigler they could not be, so long as the same production technology was available to all. And there are other differences. But what they have in common is that different possibilities may face insiders and outsiders. And that is exactly why they miss something important in the present discussion. Consider the availability of licences to operate as a taxi driver. In London, these are in perfectly elastic supply with regard to the price at which they are sold, for the only requirement is to pass a test.[5] But suppose there were a restricted supply of such licences and in the first instance they had to be bought from the local authority at a market-determined price, although they could subsequently be traded. In this case, outsiders and insiders would all face the same costs, and bidding for the licences would eliminate monopoly profits, but there would still be a barrier to entry, created in this case by the restriction on the supply of licences.

Because they neglect such legally imposed entry barriers, these commonly used approaches to the study of barriers to entry are not helpful in the study of a regulated industry. Indeed, in the particular case of banking, they suffer from two crucial weaknesses. The first is that identified by the taxi licence example. Lott (1987) has pointed out that if licences are not tradable then the possibility for monopoly profit exists. For example, financial sector regulators may impose an unpriced entry condition, such as the requirement that senior management be 'fit and proper' for their posts. This may be relevant for the consumer protection aspect of regulation, but only indirectly for the stability aspect. Discussion of it is therefore deferred for the moment.

The other matter the industrial economics notions of barriers completely neglect is speed of entry. If our concern is with a stable industry supply curve (recognizing that only perfectly competitive industries have supply curves but making use of the concept nonetheless by use of the assumption that the demand curve is stable), then what matters is that, if a firm in the industry gets into difficulties and fails, a new entrant can speedily take over its business and take its place. For that, it must be possible for the new firm to enter rapidly and, equally important, for the failed firm to leave rapidly.

These are taken in turn.

Rapid entry

Why can new firms not enter banking rapidly? Why, if bank A fails, can bank B not come in overnight and start trading? The reasons are several and, to an extent, involve the bankruptcy code. But before discussing that code, we must consider the matters of *familiarity*, *the clearing house* and *the regulator*.

It is plain that people prefer to deal with familiar names. A well-known demonstration of this is the notorious difficulty with which foreign banks enter a country and start business there. Numerous studies have attested to this, noting in particular the years of low, possibly negative, profits that must be faced, particularly through the number of 'lemon customers' these firms acquire in their initial years (Hoggarth *et al*., 1998).

This can be circumvented but the only obviously successful way is to take over an existing firm and gradually gain acceptance of the new name and business practices through slow development of the previously well-known company. A notable example of this in the UK was the takeover in November 2004 by Santander of the Abbey Bank. The latter was initially branded jointly with Santander and only after some years was the Abbey name dropped. This was possible because, while Abbey was certainly not doing particularly well at the time of the takeover, it certainly had not failed, so a leisurely approach could be followed. A subsequent consequence of the establishment of Santander's name in Britain was that when later (in 2009) Santander took over a failed bank, it could start using its own name immediately when running the business.

It also appears to be possible for firms with a reputation in one area to transfer that reputation to another. Sainsbury's was a well-established grocer when it moved into banking. Tesco is following the same route, as is John Lewis on a much smaller scale, at least at the moment. But even that route can face a difficulty. There must be no possibility of exclusion from the clearing house by its existing users. This has implications for the ownership of the clearing house. Having it owned solely by its users presents tremendous opportunities for delay. A preferable ownership structure would be a free-standing regulated monopoly, regulation being of the same model as that used for the UK's regulated utilities. Ownership by the state might seem attractive at first glance but, apart from all the inefficiency such ownership usually brings, there must be no question of political influence over entry to the clearing house. Even the fear of it could deter potential entrants – entrants such as Santander might well fear implicit protectionism. The regulated monopoly would have as part of its monopoly right the duty not to 'unreasonably exclude' new entrants. Tests of unreasonableness could be laid down in advance but no doubt these would have to be examined in the courts.

And finally in this section comes the regulator. If it is easy to exit banking, then the gatekeeper role of the regulator is much simplified. Regulators need not greatly concern themselves with the competence of the potential new management. What would mainly matter would be the honesty of that management. For if they were fraudulent, this would be very troublesome, at the least, for their customers and issues of compensation could arise, thus inviting ad hoc political support for hard cases – and such support of course rewards becoming a hard case.

All these changes would be close to pointless, however, if struggling firms did not leave the industry but were, if they really got into difficulties, supported by the taxpayer through his agent, the government. Recent practice has been to support such firms. Can that be stopped? To answer that, it is useful to look at a particularly well-documented example of support for a failing bank.

The support of Northern Rock

When at the end of 2007 Northern Rock got into difficulties, the Authorities (the term for the collective of the Bank of England, the FSA, and the Treasury) did not follow the traditional, well-tested, and shown to be robust, nineteenth-century approach.[6] They could have considered whether the troubled institution was of sufficient importance that its failure would have damaged the reputation of London, as they did in the case of Barings in 1890, and if it failed that test it would have been allowed to sink or swim and liquidity provided to the rest of the banking sector as needed to calm any subsequent panic.

Northern Rock was not allowed to sink or swim. There was a determined attempt to keep the institution going, or to find a rescuer for it. This can certainly not be justified by the size or reputation of Northern Rock. It was not a particularly large institution and even its greatest admirer would not claim that it was a bank of international renown similar to that of Barings in 1890, one whose failure, even if orderly, might fundamentally damage the reputation of London. Why, then, did the Authorities act as they did?

A range of factors probably influenced the decision. First and most obviously is that the problem came as a shock, and one to previously untested regulatory and money market regimes. Then there are some factors about which it is possible at this time only to speculate, although more data may become available in the future when archives are opened (if written records of discussions were kept).

Gordon Brown had just become Prime Minister. Opinion polls suggested that there had been a subsequent sharp leap in the popularity of the ruling Labour government and there was much speculation that an election would be called. Closing a bank (or nationalizing it) would probably have done little good for the government's prospects of victory. A second consideration is that such action might not have reflected well, at least in the popular press, on the 'Tripartite Arrangements' (see Milne and Wood, 2009) for financial stability, arrangements that had been put in place when Gordon Brown was Chancellor of the Exchequer. Third, Northern Rock was headquartered in an area where unemployment was above the national average. The political background was not favourable for the sink or swim option.

There were, however, also good economic reasons why the traditional course was not followed.

There was, first, a technical aspect of the Bank's money market operations and then, more fundamentally, the nature of interbank linkages. These latter made it extremely difficult to subject a commercial bank to a normal corporate insolvency procedure. And finally, the nature of retail bank deposits in the twenty-first century differed from that in the nineteenth, and in a way which made even orderly closures of a bank difficult both politically and economically.

A discussion of money market operations would take us a little away from the main line of analysis; it can therefore be found in the appendix to this chapter.

The nature and extent of interbank linkages create a problem with the 'sink or swim' option in the following way. When Northern Rock got into difficulties, there was no separate legal framework for handling bank insolvency; it would have been subject to the normal law of corporate insolvency. Its transactions, its assets, and its liabilities would be frozen. A court-appointed liquidator would try, avoiding a 'fire sale', to dispose of the assets at the best possible price, taking quite possibly some time to do so in order to minimize the loss for creditors. This would of course cause problems for a modern banking system, as it could leave many transactions uncompleted for months or even years.[7]

Northern Rock's failure highlighted the absence in the UK of any regime for handling bank insolvency, such as was available in some other countries. Such a regime would provide a mechanism for maintaining critical banking services and ensuring an orderly resolution of bank assets and liabilities.

Finally on the reasons for the Authorities' actions, when 'sink or swim' was the course of action, retail depositors differed in two ways from their modern-day counterparts. They were more prosperous than the average citizen and they did not rely to the same extent on bank transactions for day-to-day living – banking services were not as crucial to functioning in nineteenth-century society as they are now. In Britain today, the politicians, who make the ultimate decision over bank closure, could not tolerate bank customers, especially poor ones, losing both money and access to banking services. Indeed, aside from any questions of protecting savings, loss of access to banking services would impede economic efficiency in many ways, by, for example, forcing reliance on cash and unwarrantedly destroying credit ratings.

Britain does have a deposit insurance scheme supposedly intended to deal with these things but, despite changes since Northern Rock, it remains significantly defective. There are no practical arrangements for ensuring that insured depositors are paid out in any reasonably short time frame; they could, and very likely would, have to wait months for the money that is due to them. Deposits therefore have to be transferred to another institution if there is to be continuity, or the bank has to continue operating as a bridge bank.

Freedom to exit

What can be done to replace the need to preserve firms by easily allowed and readily tolerated freedom to exit?

Much has already been done in the UK. It is now possible to take a bank away from its shareholders and management while it is still solvent and keep it running so that all who transact with it can continue doing so. The bank can then be sold on, in an orderly way, in whole or in parts, to buyers who will keep it running and restore it to financial health. The proceeds from the sale are used to settle the bank's debts, and anything left goes to the shareholders.[8]

Such a facility, which has existed for some years in the US, was proposed in the UK by the Treasury Select Committee of the House of Commons and the proposal was implemented in the Banking Act (2009). The procedure has, indeed, already been successfully used to carry out the closure of the Dunfermline Building Society in 2009.

Does anything else need to be done?

The answer to that question is in two parts. First, if banks are to be capable of being closed while still solvent, their capital must be monitored and not just by their management – for in distress there would be, at the least, a desire to be optimistic. Such monitoring would, however, increase rather than reduce freedom of exit; for the regulators would surely be aware of the opprobrium they would incur if they exercised forbearance which turned out to be unjustified. But some banks would be, by virtue of their size or their complexity or interdependencies with the rest of the system, hard to handle in such a manner without extensive advance planning. Here the concept of the 'living will' comes in.

Regulators should prepare for failure. They should do that because it is almost certain that something will go wrong at some time and because the consequence of lack of preparedness when Northern Rock got into difficulties was a nearly disastrous bank run. This preparation should have two parts. The regulators should regularly plan what they are going to do in the event of a big bank needing help and, because each bank will be somewhat different, there should be a plan for every bank and these plans should be regularly updated. These plans, one for each bank, would be based on each bank's 'living will'.

The living will

The Governor of the Bank of England has recently urged that banks be required to draw up 'living wills'. The Treasury Select Committee of the House of Commons has also recommended the idea. What are these wills? Why are they desirable?

The term 'living will' comes from a development in English law relating to individuals and their well-being. When an individual dies, if he or she leaves a will which is legal, then whatever property left on death is disposed of according to the testator's wishes, subject to taxes and any challenges from parties who think they were entitled to a bequest (or a bigger bequest). A 'living will' does very much the same thing, but for an individual who, although incapacitated, is not dead. The 'will' appoints 'attorneys', who can take decisions for the individual who can no longer do so, either according to instructions given in the 'living will' or, if discretion has been given, according to what they think best for the individual. These decisions can appertain either to medical treatment (including its withdrawal or withholding) or to financial matters, or both.

The idea is then that banks draw up an analogous document. Why has this idea taken hold, and what would the document do?

Earlier problems

To continue with the analogy, when a company is declared bankrupt, it has its affairs wound up under the bankruptcy code. This is analogous to the will of a person, except that every company has the same will; the order in which creditors are paid off and the proportions, if apportioning is necessary, are prescribed in law. This normally works well, giving a degree of certainty to commercial transactions by letting people know the risks they are exposed to if things go wrong with a company with which they are dealing. Changes were made to it over the years but there was no questioning of whether it was an appropriate procedure for all kinds of company.

Then, in 2007, the banking system got into difficulties. In Britain, this showed first in the struggles of Northern Rock, the mortgage lender. This bank was eventually nationalized. But no one wished the only feasible response to a bank's being close to insolvency being to nationalize it. As described above, a special insolvency regime for banks was quickly put in place and that regime has already been used successfully. Why then is there call for a 'living will' for banks? Given that banks can now have orderly funerals promptly conducted under this new legislation, why should they bother with 'living wills'?

The existing legislation applies in principle to all commercial banks and building societies. It does not however cover investment banks, even in principle, and while it does in principle cover large, complex, international banks, there are, and surely correctly, doubts about whether it could be applied to them.

There are doubts about the applicability of the current prompt closure procedure to investment banks simply because these banks are not deposit-taking institutions but rather institutions which arrange deals and act as counterparties in complex transactions. A very important aspect of the latter is shown by their role in structured products, such as the fairly widely sold 'guaranteed equity return' funds. These guarantee a minimum return from a portfolio in return for there being a cap on returns from the portfolio. The closure of Lehman's (in September 2008) cast a good number of these products into jeopardy. Orderly closure along the lines of prompt corrective action would not help much here, nor would it help with, for example, holdings of credit default swaps.

International banks, because they have assets and liabilities in many countries, can if they face an emergency capital shortage call on many countries – which could mean that no country felt responsible. And large banks could, quite simply, be beyond the capacity of the liquidators to understand and wind down in a reasonable period of time.

These are the problems 'living wills' are designed to deal with.

What the wills would do

Essentially, they would tell an outsider how the bank worked. Of particular importance, they would clearly assign different assets and liabilities to different subdivisions of the bank. They would provide an accessible list of counterparties, and their associated transactions. They would clearly describe provisioning and write-off procedures that had been adopted in particular cases and were adopted as general rules. In short, just as a person's living will lays out what should be done when he or she can no longer do it for themselves, so would a bank's living will provide all the information needed for someone to intervene when it was in trouble and to run it down (or otherwise dispose of it) in a prompt and orderly manner. The 'will' would need updating from time to time, but frequency of updating should depend not primarily on the passage of time but on the frequency of occurrence of material changes to the bank's structure or portfolio.[9]

These living wills would thus be important in two ways. First, they would ensure that when some institution, however large or complex, got into difficulties, it could be handled without major and harmful spillover effects. That in itself is a good argument for living wills. Second, and associated with that, these wills would make future crises less likely; for they would ensure that no bank was ever again 'too big to fail'. The 'brooding presence' (to quote Lee Bucheit[10]) of the risk of failure would once again make bankers act in a prudent way. Further, ensuring that no bank ever again was 'too big to fail' would make market discipline effective and the so-far fruitless search for effective methods of regulatory discipline otiose.

Consumer protection?

When transacting in financial products, consumers generally receive protection additional to that they receive when buying other types of good. The case for their doing so has been questioned. George Benston (2004), for example, argued strongly against it. It is unnecessary to enter that argument here. But it is worthwhile to consider, if we take for granted that consumers require additional protection in this area, how this protection should be provided if the arguments above on the role of the regulator insofar as stability goes are accepted.

The new model regulator would be concerned not with the stability of individual firms but with the stability of the industry and would aim to achieve this by ensuring easy entry and exit in banking. The latter would conflict with consumer protection. For however readily new entrants replace departing firms, it is hard to imagine that the process would be entirely free of inconvenience for the consumers directly involved. There would thus be a conflict if one regulator were charged both with consumer protection and with the protection of system stability. The first responsibility would lead to seeking the protection of existing firms, while the latter would be concerned to ensure a speedy exit at the first sign of trouble. This tension would be exacerbated by inevitable political pressures. Consumers are regularly and frequently complaining, either directly to the regulator or through their political representatives, that one financial institution or another has treated them badly. They seldom write in to complain that an institution is endangering financial stability. Resources and attention would therefore be focused on only one aspect of the regulator's duties.

The case for what has become known as the 'twin peaks approach' – that is to say, separating maintenance of stability from consumer protection – is, on the arguments immediately above, already a strong one. Recognizing that stability-focused regulators should be concerned with the industry not the firm strengthens the case.

A digression in the history of economic thought

At the start of this chapter, it was observed that, because economics has tended to focus on a particular notion of competition, the arguments of this chapter have not been as widely applied to financial regulation as they should have been.

The most common definition of competition used, implicitly or explicitly, by economists, is that of atomistic competition. In this view, there is competition in a market when there is a large number of firms, each producing at the least-cost point of its long-run average cost curve, and with, even temporarily, no pricing power. This is a notion particularly convenient in a general equilibrium model. But it is not the only notion of competition.

William Baumol, along with several co-authors, has developed the notion of contestable markets. This is summarized and placed in the context of prior work in Baumol (1982). His key points are that a 'perfectly contestable market' is 'characterized by optimal behaviour yet applies to the full range of industrial structures…' (p. 2). That and, particularly important, '…oligopolistic structure and behaviour are freed entirely from their previous dependence on the conjectural variations of incumbents, and, instead, are generally determined … by the pressure of potential competition to which Bain directed our attention so tellingly' (p. 2). And third, that there is not a '…rough continuum, in terms of industrial performance, ranging from unregulated pure monopoly as the pessimal arrangement to perfect competition as the ideal…' (p. 2). He cites Bain (1956) as his most notable predecessor but also notes the arguments of Fama and Laffer (1972) that even two firms can be enough to guarantee optimality.

In fact, the idea that the threat of entry affects behaviour extends much further back in the history of economics. A notable example is the use that Alfred Marshall made of the 'trees of the forest' analogy, to explain how firms died and were replaced, or even crowded out before death, by thriving new enterprises:

> but here we may read a lesson from the young trees of the forest as they struggle upwards through the benumbing shade of their older rivals. Many succumb on the way and few survive: those few become stronger every year, they get a larger share of the light and air with every increase of their height, and at last in their turn they tower above their neighbours and seem as though they would grow on forever … but they do not. One tree will last longer in full vigour and attain a greater size than another: but sooner or later age tells on them all. Though the taller ones have better access to light and air than their rivals, they gradually lose vitality: and one after another they give their place to others.
>
> (Marshall, 1890, pp. 315–16)

The above passage on the 'trees in the forest' which, in the first five editions, had gone on '…as with the growth of trees, so it is with the growth of businesses' was changed in the sixth edition (1910) to read 'as with the growth of trees, so it was with the growth of businesses as a general rule before the great recent development of vast joint-stock companies' (p. 316). But Marshall still believed that his hypothesis of the life cycle held '…in many industries and trades'. He also added the qualification that, while the joint-stock firm might grow in size, it would not obtain increased internal economies as it grew.

A further change was made in the eighth edition of 1920; if conditions in an industry were such that new firms could quickly master the economies of scale, then it would be likely that the established firms would be 'supplanted quickly by still younger firms with yet newer methods' (Marshall, 1920, pp. 286–7)

Schumpeter's (1942) perennial gale of creative destruction surely invites invocation at this point, perhaps even to suggesting that the gale can help thin out the forest and allow new enterprises to emerge.

In short, the idea of competition that emerged not from the formal Walrasian analysis but from the less formal Marshallian and Austrian approaches is helpful in guiding regulatory policy. The formal approach, in contrast, despite its numerous uses, has tended to encourage regulators, or at least many of the economists who advise them, to look in the wrong direction.

Conclusions

There is much concern among regulators to ensure the stability of banks. Liquidity requirements and capital requirements are to be raised and regulation is, we are told, to be tightened (whatever that means) and made more intrusive. The argument of this chapter is that focus on the stability of the individual firm is misguided. Rather, focus should be on the stability of the industry. Key to that is not the stability of individual members of the industry but rather free entry to and exit from the industry. Promoting that should be concern of regulation. This also implies that regulators concerned with banking stability should not also have the responsibility of consumer protection. This is, however, merely reinforcing an existing and well-supported argument. The key point of this chapter is that industry stability matters for banking and firm stability does not.

Appendix

The system of money market operations used by the Bank of England lets the commercial banks choose their own level of cash reserves according to what they expect to need in the month ahead. If they get this forecast wrong, they can earn interest on the surplus, or borrow more through the standing facility. The problem is with the latter. Borrowing more, at the 'penalty' rate above the basic one, is seen as revealing a mistake by the bank doing the borrowing. There was therefore no way of the Bank of England supplying additional liquidity through the standing facility, either directly to Northern Rock or via other banks that in turn lent to Northern Rock, even if offered good and normally acceptable collateral, without its action being interpreted as a signal that the borrowing bank had in some way blundered; so use of the standing facility erodes access to funding from the markets and reduces rather than increases available liquidity.

Under the money market system in use when the classic Lender of Last Resort system developed, the discount houses (see Milne and Wood, 2009) were continually transacting with the Bank, on frequent occasions borrowing more than once a day. Hence there was nothing abnormal in such borrowing, and nothing to give rise to alarm. But even had such a system been in place, it would not have been enough to prevent Northern Rock defaulting on short-term obligations. Northern Rock had such a large funding shortfall that it would not have had anything like enough eligible collateral (such as government bonds) to use for this borrowing.

Notes

1 An earlier version of this chapter was delivered at the Seelye Distinguished Lecture at the University of Auckland on 22 September 2010.
2 They are also in the UK and many but not all other jurisdictions concerned with how the firms treat their customers. That is for the moment a side issue; it is examined subsequently.
3 In fact, the observation is not in general inconsistent with competition. The theory predicts the equalization of marginal returns but what is generally observed is accounting, that is to say, average, returns. Average returns equal marginal only if all factors of production are in perfectly elastic supply.
4 It should be remarked that this is not a definition like the others; it gives the consequences of a barrier, rather than saying what the barrier is.
5 As it takes different people different amounts of time to learn to pass the test, the existence of the test allows rents on ability to be earned.
6 Detailed description and analysis of the Northern Rock episode can be found in Milne and Wood (2009).
7 In an insolvency, REPO borrowing (financing through an initial sale of a security and its later repurchase at a slightly higher price) is closed out, in a similar way to OTC derivative transactions, but unsecured borrowing, such as Northern Rock relied on because it lacked eligible collateral for REPO finance, must be left finally to be resolved through the insolvency procedure.
8 For banks for which that can be done, the choice of capital ratio could be left to the management of the institutions concerned; they would simply be told that if it went below some fairly arbitrary number they would be expropriated.
9 This of course reminds us that however well-designed rules are, use of judgment is inescapable.
10 'The sanction that capitalism imposes on imprudence, incompetence, sometimes just bad luck, is failure. It is the brooding presence of that sanction that keeps managers on their toes, that keeps them acting in a prudent way' (Lee Bucheit, Cleary Gottlieb Steen & Hamilton LLP, to the House of Lords Economic Affairs Committee, 2009).

References

Bain, J.S. (1956) *Barriers to New Competition*, Cambridge, MA: Harvard University Press.

Bain, J.S. (1968) *Industrial Organisation*, Chichester: John Wiley and Sons.

Baumol, W. (1982) 'Contestable markets: an uprising in the theory of industrial structure', *American Economic Review*, 72(1): 1–15.

Benston, G.J. (2004) Henry Thornton lecture, City University, London.

Fama, E. and Laffer, A. (1972) 'The number of firms and competition', *American Economic Review*, 62(4): 670–4.

Ferguson, J.M. (1974) *Advertising and Competition: Theory, Measurement, Fact*, Cambridge: Ballinger.

Hoggarth, G., Milne, A., and Wood, G. (1998) 'Alternative routes to banking stability', *Bank of England Financial Stability Review*, 5: 55–68.

Lott, J.R. (1987) 'Licensing and non-transferable rents', *American Economic Review*, 77(3): 453–5.
Marshall, A. (1890) *Principles of Economics*, 1st ed., London: Macmillan.
Marshall, A. (1910) *Principles of Economics*, 6th ed., London: Macmillan.
Marshall, A. (1920) *Principles of Economics*, 8th ed., London: Macmillan.
Milne, A. and Wood, G. (2009) 'Shattered on the Rock? British financial stability from 1866 to 2007', *Journal of Banking Regulation*, 10(2): 89–127.
Schumpeter, J.A. (1942) *Capitalism, Socialism and Democracy*, New York: Harper Bros.
Stigler, G. (1968) 'Barriers to entry, economies of scale and firm size', in *The Organisation of Industry*, Homewood IL: RD Irwin.

14 Surviving the next financial crisis[1]

David G. Mayes

The last few years have illustrated very clearly how ordinary people with only limited savings can lose them through unfortunate investment. No one wants to see such stories again. However, it is widely argued that New Zealanders save too little for their future and, when they do save, they appear to put a disproportionate amount in the housing market and less than most other developed countries in the equity market.[2] It may well reduce the rate of return that people obtain on average but it may also slow the rate of growth of the economy.

In this chapter, I address how the financial risks society faces can be better managed in the future and some of the more distressing losses avoided. My theme, therefore, is how to prepare for and manage future financial crises better. This implies that I regard the occasional occurrence of financial crises as inevitable and I explain why I think that is the case. There is also plenty we can do to reduce the chance of crises as well and I refer to that. However, to my mind, the important steps are to ensure that the costs of any crises that do occur are limited and manageable. Beyond a certain point, the costs of crisis avoidance may exceed that from manageable crises. The costs of crisis avoidance occur every year but the costs of crises themselves only materialize if there is indeed a crisis. Indeed such crises can actually be catalysts for change. That said, many countries clearly devoted too little resources to crisis avoidance this time around and, to some extent, we have been lucky on this occasion. New Zealand has fortunately not had to find out how well it could survive a more major shock. Countries such as the UK who thought they had an excellent setup, developed over more than a century, found they were very wrong.

The worst crises affect everybody very noticeably but in many cases only part of the population really suffers – those who have invested in enterprises that fail, those who lose their jobs, those who have negative equity in their houses and have to sell them. Much of the cost may be hidden because it will fall on future taxpayers. If we look at the impact of the present crisis – for many countries, although significant, it is not out of line with some other downturns in the post-war period. For some of the transition countries, declines in GDP by around 20 per cent, which would be truly shocking in advanced countries, are smaller than the declines they experienced 20 years ago and, where growth rates have been rapid, may have less damaging effects. For others, it is a major event. Countries will therefore react differently. If they have got away lightly by comparison, the temptation to do little is much greater.

Finland provides a lot of interesting evidence as a result of having had a financial crisis already in the early 1990s – one which had a worse impact on GDP than the Great Crash of 1929. It is relatively unlikely that Finland would have had the economic success of recent years without the crisis. Up till then Finland had experienced a continuing cycle of inflation and devaluation. Problems of limited competitiveness had been addressed by a steady expansion in the size of the public sector but the point of unsustainability had been reached. Deregulation was taking place, albeit rather reluctantly, and the likely outlook was a process of slower growth and slow attrition of public benefits as the fiscal arithmetic failed to add up. As it was, the enforced dramatic change from the crisis got the country back onto sustainability and made the unpleasant cuts in benefits and public spending politically acceptable as the alternative was worse. The political window for radical change to overcome longstanding problems tends not to be wide and it is easy not to take advantage of it.

I am not of course advocating welcoming crises as a means of enabling rapid change but moderate crises can shake out the inefficient that otherwise persist through vested interests and give opportunities for the innovative. If one is unlucky enough to have a crisis, in my view, it is important to make it work for you, rather than simply cause enduring or irreparable harm, even if avoiding the crisis altogether would have been better. We have just such an opportunity now. People are shocked by how much what seemed to be a stable and beneficial financial system could suddenly collapse and harm them. Many of the necessary changes have already been made but the appetite for further action as the economy picks up is likely to shrink.

My remarks are in two parts, first addressing how we might structure the financial system in order to reduce the impact and occurrence of crises and second how as individuals and enterprises it is possible to organize ourselves so as to reduce the impact should a crisis occur.

How crises occur

Let me begin by substantiating my remarks about the inevitability of crises. More than ten years ago, the Bank of Finland decided that it needed to make the lessons of the Nordic crises better known across the EU as many of its new partners seemed very complacent. (Finland joined the EU in 1995, along with Sweden and Austria.) These lessons had three components:

- Try to avoid making the same mistakes that we did, which led to a crisis.
- Evaluate which methods of crisis resolution seem to work best.
- Prepare in good times for the next crisis as you cannot do so when it comes.

The first step in the research to back up this campaign was to assess how the Nordic crises had come about. There were of course plenty of existing studies so this was mainly an exercise in bringing them together. My suggestion (Mayes *et al.*, 2001) was that there were seven causes, but with the benefit of seeing the present crisis this analysis can be simplified. These were:

1 a major regulatory change that opens both buyers and sellers to new opportunities and risks of which they have little experience;
2 a period of rapid economic growth;
3 a rapid rise in asset prices;
4 a weak framework for supervision;
5 a tax regime that encourages borrowing;
6 unsustainable macroeconomic policies;
7 a substantial adverse shock.

That all sounds rather familiar in terms of the present crisis, yet it was all able to happen – again. If we look at the lessons from the Asian crises that followed only five years later, again one would have seen some similar factors. So, writing seven years before the present crisis, we were able to explore a number of scenarios for future crises, one of which emanated from the US as a result of excessive growth in asset prices. None of this implies any unusual foresight. It is simply that it is possible to envisage collective mistakes. When you look back at them, it seems impossible to understand why people could not spot the unsustainability and act earlier, thereby avoiding the crisis. Sometimes the people who do see the problem do not have the power to act. On other occasions, they feel that they will be smart enough to exit before the crash happens. Take the Argentinean crisis, for example. A clear year beforehand, at the annual Royal Economic Society conference, there was no debate about whether Argentina was going to face a crisis. The question was simply was it going to devalue or default, or both? Spreads were so large on their debt that no country could afford to pay them for long. Yet it took the year before the problem was resolved. Acting a year earlier would have reduced the losses.

Clearly we cannot spell out what will lead to the next crisis and agree on it or it will not happen, but some combination of the seven factors I set out as underlying the Nordic crises will do. All that we require for a crisis is a sudden change of view over future prospects. Those who are highly geared will have to unwind their positions dramatically as markets freeze up in the short run, worried about who it is who is going to be making the losses. Tom Sargent (2001) in the US expressed this very simply when he suggested that it was only human nature to think that we might be able to do better in the future. Hence, if we have a period when we start to do better, people will readily believe that there has been an underlying change and that better performance will be possible indefinitely. The longer that continues, the more people believe it and the more the success feeds on itself. Recent explanations include the impact of information technology, or the higher quality of macroeconomic management or the improvement in regulation permitting greater competition and innovation – the list goes on. The longer the improved performance continues, the greater the gap from the underlying reality and the more unpleasant the ultimate adjustment.

Each of us has our own scenarios where continuing success must come to an end. Take the example of China. The only drawback is that China's rapid growth has already continued longer than most outsiders thought possible. Some day there must be a limit to the degree to which China can take market share from others, although it is increasingly being sustained by its own demand. The question is when and whether the slowdown will be orderly. If we think back to the 1980s when similar concerns were expressed about Japan, the parallel is clear. But anyone who withdraws from the Chinese market too early is going to lose a major opportunity, so it will not happen and any over-extension will no doubt be fuelled by the Chinese authorities, who will be naturally unwilling to see the process slow down. The later the adjustment takes place, the bigger China will be and hence the greater the spillover effects.

This is a long build-up to a simple point. It is inevitable that we cannot predict the next problem but we can structure ourselves so that the impact is something we can absorb. So let me move on first to what can be done at the economy-wide level.

Structuring the system

In the present crisis, we have seen three major forces that have contributed to the size of losses. The first is that action has been slow, the second is that we did not have the tools to resolve many financial problems without recourse to the taxpayer and the third was that the safety net was inadequate. All of these can be addressed and to an extent are being addressed. Let me take them in turn.

Acting early enough

I have already made it clear that it is inherent in crises that we do not manage to head them off. My concern here is simply to try to make them more limited in scale. This requires three main things:

- good information;
- a well-integrated structure to manage crises quickly, coherently and without contradiction;
- the powers and ability to act swiftly and effectively.

Addressing the first means that we must ensure that we have good analytical tools and staff and hence give ourselves the best opportunity of identifying problems early. If such a system is to work well, it is inevitable that we will have a number of false alarms, but the occasional unnecessary bank examination is a small price to pay. Spending a few million dollars each year to avoid losing 20 or 30 per cent of GDP unnecessarily – that is the cost of a typical crisis according to Hoggarth *et al.* (2002) – is a good bargain.

The major lesson we have learnt is that traditional supervisory schemes that concentrate on making sure that each individual financial institution is run prudentially are not enough. We need to look at system-wide problems as well. New Zealand is actually rather well placed to do that as the Reserve Bank, which like all central banks tends to look at the broader picture, is also the supervisor. In general, however, such advance warning, while straightforward in theory, is difficult to achieve in practice. As a result, other countries have set up macro-prudential authorities to address this risk directly.

In my opinion, there is little to be gained from setting up a new authority in New Zealand but there is an argument for the RBNZ to be given macro-prudential tools so it can act on any threats that it sees. One of the problems that central banks face is that they have only one main tool, which is using short-term interest rates to manage future inflation. They cannot use that same tool to achieve the twin goals of price and financial stability unless they happen to coincide. There is debate about what the second tool should be but the consensus is that it should be something that affects risk taking directly, say, the loan-to-income ratio or the loan-to-value ratio. Any tool that imposes harsher restraints when more risk taking appears to be taking off will suffice. Such a tool needs to take into account procyclical pressures over and above the concern for inflation. The simplest such pressure is asset prices.

In one sense, what is being asked for is a 'joined-up' approach to financial regulation, which ensures that problems do not slip through the gap between agencies. Of course, alert regulators will point out gaps to government. New Zealand's new regulator, the Financial Markets Authority (FMA), will tend to fill such gaps. The RBNZ has picked up responsibility for finance companies and for insurance but some players in the financial system may be left behind. Indeed a natural reaction would be to set up new financial initiatives which exploit such gaps.

In the new regime, it will be essential for the FMA and the RBNZ to have a close working relationship and that both relate clearly to government. Here there is a potential problem as both Treasury and the Ministry of Economic Development (MED) have a responsibility. In small countries, it is usually fairly easy for authorities to work together but, to do this, crisis preparation needs to have been extensive. Crucially, some particular entity needs to be in charge and ensure that the various organizations deliver the same message. It is impossible to cover every eventuality in advance and the participants have to be able to decide sensibly on the spot. Experience from simulations as well as real crises shows the opportunity for the inexperienced to make serious errors is enormous. The first actions of the FMA will be on trying to design a system that will work well in normal times. Crisis concerns will come second. Thus, even with good intentions, a fully-fledged system will take years to develop. Even so it is necessary to be ready in the short run. We do not unfortunately know whether the consequences of the present crises are fully played out yet and a fourth round of shocks is still possible. If these turned out to be in Asia and Australia was heavily affected, it will not be pleasant for New Zealand either.

However, even if some agency is taking responsibility for all facets of the financial system, this does that mean that it will act promptly. Ending a period of rapid growth that turns out to have been sustainable will be a career-ending move. There is hence a tendency to forebear. This can best be offset by triggers that compel action unless a good case can be made. In the US, this is known as prompt corrective action (PCA) (Mayes *et al.*, 2008). There are some difficulties translating these ideas to other jurisdictions but the principle is simple. As a financial institution starts to breach the buffers for prudential behaviour, the authorities should institute progressively more vigorous requirements to turn the institution round, ultimately resolving it before losses mount. (In the US, a bank must be closed within 90 days if the leverage ratio falls below 2 per cent.) Others argue that the leverage ratio is too crude or that this permits the bank to decline too far before closure. In any event, a declining bank needs to be identified before it becomes insolvent if problems are to be manageable.

What we have learnt from the crisis – or perhaps had reaffirmed – is that triggers based on a bank's capital often do not give adequate early warning. Other supervisory information is needed, although this may be publicly available. Both Northern Rock and HBOS in the UK, which had to be rescued, were identifiable, simply from the decline in their share price, which fell more than 25 per cent three months before intervention by the Bank of England (Mayes and Wood, 2008). Clearly the smart money knew already. Even if supervisors are not so well informed they can see that. In Norway, for example, an Extraordinary General Meeting has to be called if a bank's share price falls more than 25 per cent between Annual General Meetings. Taking steps to address it must be on the agenda. The UK authorities themselves admitted that there had been serious deficiencies in their supervision (FSA, 2008) and that simply tightening up their procedures, without the need for new legislation, would reduce the chance of repeating the errors.

There is no PCA requirement in New Zealand and the RBNZ operates on a much more discretionary basis. What New Zealand does have is the ability to act early and effectively by establishing Statutory Management and resolving a bank immediately if it becomes insolvent. While small banks will simply be closed, larger banks may be subject to 'Bank Creditor Recapitalization' (since relabelled Open Bank Resolution), which entails an overnight rapid assessment of the extent of the problem, a writing down of claims on the bank so that it is sufficiently recapitalized to continue operating and a reopening with a guarantee against further losses without any material break. PCA is as much deterrence as it is action. Banks will want to act of their own volition in advance of the regulator's intervention as this will increase the chance of the shareholders saving at least something and more of those involved saving their jobs. The speed and inevitability of intervention under PCA will push banks into action well before the crisis looms.

In the modern world, the cause of a crisis is quite likely to be in another country and with the modern globalized financial environment it is very difficult for any country to address the problems on its own. The most obvious case is cross-border banks. The problem may occur in someone else's jurisdiction. Moreover the means of solving it may also lie there. In such a case, a country just has to live with the consequences. This is why New Zealand has insisted not just that all its major banks be locally capitalized and incorporated, even if they are foreign-owned, but that they are capable of operating on their own at a day's notice should the parent or any other major supplier fail. Fortunately we do not know if these arrangements work. Some aspects of this arrangement are innovative so it will not be clear until it is tried how well it may work. I discuss some of these aspects later.

In the EU, no such easy solution is available as a bank licensed in another member state can operate a branch without restriction. Moreover, supervision of that branch is the responsibility of the home country. The host country may not be well informed about problems in advance nor have the legal power to handle the problem should it occur. This caused some serious problems and it has not yet been resolved. This takes me neatly on to my next topic.

Having the tools to resolve problems without recourse to the taxpayer

I have already noted the importance of prompt action in the early stages of bank problems, in trying to find a private sector solution, either through the bank itself or through others stepping in. However, the same promptness needs to apply when this fails and the authorities themselves need to step in. Many countries, New Zealand included, cannot step in until the bank is insolvent. Elsewhere, to minimize losses, the authorities can, or indeed in some cases must, step in earlier once capital has fallen to unacceptable levels and no viable rescue package seems available. While the timing of stepping in is important, what is much more essential is the power to act. A clean and swift transition is required. The resolution of Fortis in Belgium and the Netherlands was hampered by a string of court actions by disgruntled shareholders. The decision needs to be final and the recourse should be only for ex post compensation if the courts find it is justified.

In the modern world, it is not viable to keep people away from access to their bank accounts for all but trivial periods of time. They will soon start to default on key payments or run out of cash as people operate typically on very small balances. In New Zealand, the plan is to avoid any material loss of access for large banks by resolving them overnight. If a small bank is closed, then the problem is rather different. Depositors would not normally regain access to their accounts for quite some time. This does not work and was being addressed in Australia before the crisis. The resolution of a bank has to involve some means of maintaining access to accounts. In the US, where bank closures are a relatively frequent occurrence – there have been some every week since October 2008 and over 400 since the crisis started – three methods are used. The norm is that the deposits will be transferred to another bank. Usually all the existing computer software and bank branches will be used but sometimes the transfer is such that all the facilities are available virtually immediately through the acquiring bank's own branches and internet system. There may be some initial delays and inconvenience until the practicalities of the transfer are complete and everyone has access codes and cheque books, etc., but that will probably be accepted.

In just a few cases where it has not been possible to set this up in time, the bank or at least the relevant parts of it will be taken into what is effectively temporary public ownership, known as a 'bridge bank', until it can be sold, or the depositors will be sent cheques, which they can pay into another bank of their choice and open an account there.

Being able to do this requires very considerable prepositioning. It must be possible to identify each person's deposits at the end of each day. The computer systems must be well enough known that overnight any adjustments can be made, such as transforming the codes to the new bank and sorting out which deposits are eligible. The acquirer has had to have time to perform due diligence so that bids can be made and the authorities can accept the best bid. In the US, they have three months to do this, while in the UK, as a result of experience, they reckon this can be completed within two months. The actual switchover is then quite quick. The Bank of England estimated two hours in the case of the Dunfermline Building Society, where the deposits were switched to the Nationwide. If this is done in the middle of the night, the inconvenience to depositors will be trivial.

However, to do this the authorities need adequate powers and the organization to do it. In the case of the UK, it is the Bank of England and in the US it is the Federal Deposit Insurance Corporation in most cases. Technically, it is the Reserve Bank in New Zealand but the processes are not all in place. The main reason is simply that no part of the public sector has a direct financial responsibility for deposits as they are not insured. In most countries, as soon as a bank fails or has its licence withdrawn, the deposit insurer is responsible for ensuring that people can get at their insured deposits. Larger deposits beyond normal transactions deposits can wait and be sorted out as part of the insolvency process.

Deposit insurance is thus one area where the New Zealand system is clearly deficient. Most countries regard deposit insurance as an essential part of the toolkit but New Zealand does not. There are some good reasons for the current stance, one of which is that all the major banks have an implicit guarantee from the Australian government that they will not fail and Kiwibank, with government ownership, can also expect to be bailed out. Deposit insurance is therefore largely redundant. Failures in the remaining banks would not be likely to have systemic consequences. There are some problems in free-riding the Australian system, not so much for New Zealand as for Australia. If we assume it is going to be the taxpayer who bails out one of the large four banks, the Australian government on behalf of the Australian taxpayer will be somewhat aggrieved that they have to foot the bill for the whole group, including New Zealand. It is only if the problem lay primarily in New Zealand that there would be a difference. In theory, the Australian parent could walk away. However, it is usually thought that the loss of reputation would be so great, even though two of the banks are trading under a different brand name and one has a subsidiary with a different name, that the parent would fear for its survival and hence bail out the subsidiary. Hence under present circumstances there would be pressure for New Zealand to provide some compensation for the losses. This runs heavily against the philosophy there, which is very much that the burden for bank failure should be placed on those who knowingly took the risks and not on the rest of society, which did not realize it had such a contingent liability. Deposit insurance would go a long way to avoiding this.

However, unfortunately, one of the major changes to emerge from the crisis is the attitude to deposit insurance. Before the crisis, all OECD economies except Australia and New Zealand had deposit insurance. In most countries, such insurance was compulsory but limited so that it covered the large majority of people's retail balances completely. To give two examples, in the EU, the minimum coverage per depositor per bank was of the order of €20,000, while in the UK it was more than twice as large. In the case of Northern Rock, that level covered around 95 per cent of depositors completely and over 90 per cent of deposits. Now deposit insurance has become much more comprehensive. In the EU, the lower limit is €100,000. New Zealand introduced insurance temporarily with the high coverage limit of $1 million per account holder per bank. Before that, depositors could expect to take a haircut upon a failure as they can again now. Australia reviewed its current limit of $1 million in October 2011 and has reduced the limit to $250,000 – but this is still higher than in the EU.

Deposit insurance normally has two purposes. The first is to make sure that people who cannot reasonably be expected to form a clear judgment about the strength of bank and are ill able to afford substantial losses do not lose. Put differently – the well-informed get out early, leaving the less informed to bear the brunt of the losses. Depositors are junior unsecured creditors – Australia has domestic depositor preference, so there the position is not so threatening. The second is to avoid financial instability.

The crisis has confused thinking. Deposit insurance is really intended for the occasional failure of bank in normal times – that is, when the rest of the banking system is healthy. Having these large sums insured makes the scheme potentially more expensive. Perhaps some opportunity for voluntary insurance of large deposits could be arranged. With limited insurance designed to cover non-crisis times, the levy on banks would not have to be large and would only be topped up as deposits increased. Indeed depending upon how the NZ Bankers Association, if they were to run the scheme, chose to organize it, the banks' deposits with the scheme might remain part of their capital. It would also act as an incentive for people to spread their risks. The state cannot totally step away from such a scheme as it is always possible that the claims on the scheme might exhaust it. Until such time as the fund can be replenished, it needs to have the guaranteed right to borrow from the government, so credibility is maintained. Such funds need not be large. If the insurance limit were $50,000, for example, people could have up to $250,000 covered if they spread their deposits across the main banks. Not many people have more in the bank than that. In any case, one would not expect the entire banking system to fail.

I mentioned in passing a second issue, namely the difference in treatment of large and small banks. There is no threat to systemic stability from closing a small bank but if a large bank closes this may disrupt the entire financial system.

It is therefore necessary to employ some resolution technique that will allow the vital operations of the bank to continue, while extinguishing the rights of existing shareholders and recapitalizing. New Zealand does have a route for this, unlike most countries. For others, typically it has been necessary for the taxpayer to bail out the bank because there are no such tools available. As a result, the pressure in other countries has been either to reduce the bank to a size that can be handled or to seek special routes to recapitalization. The phenomenon has been variously described as 'Too Big To Fail' or 'Too Complex To Resolve'. However, in the worst cases, as in Iceland, the authorities did not have the resources to bail out the bank and a major systemic crisis erupted. I labelled this 'Too Big to Save' in my 2004 discussion of the Icelandic problem (Mayes, 2004a) – more than four years before it happened – and in Sigurðsson (2004) the structure of the problem is set out in detail.

As mentioned earlier, the powers to transfer assets and liabilities, form a bridge bank, nationalize and compel the residual organization to provide vital services are likely to be sufficient. These are summarized neatly in the UK Banking Act 2009. It is a matter of the resolution authority being clear that it can exercise these powers in respect of all banks within the time available. For large banks, this requires preparation, variously referred to as a 'living will' or 'funeral plans'. In their book *Too Big To Fail*, Gary Stern and Ron Feldman argue that for any banking licence to be approved the subject banks must convince the authorities that they are not too complex to fail. It is more difficult to impose this on existing banks but it appears that the political will to do so may well exist in Europe. New Zealand thinks it is the case already but in Australia they have decided that the taxpayer will pay – something which makes a joint scheme across the two countries very difficult.

In many respects, we should not really be facing these circumstances at all. If markets work well then banks that are being poorly managed should either be restructured through shareholder pressure or be taken over by others who believe they can run them more efficiently. Unfortunately the second mechanism does not work well, which means that one of the main forces for market discipline is impaired. The New Zealand banking system is already concentrated to the point that a merger between any of the main four players would be unwelcome, both domestically and in Australia. Indeed the demise of the National Bank of New Zealand as a separately owned entity was not greeted with enthusiasm from the point of view of promoting competition. Ideally it would have been purchased by a third party and not an existing participant. It is not that New Zealand has a unique problem. It was the purchase of ABN-AMRO, a very sound but underperforming bank, by a consortium led by the Royal Bank of Scotland that led to a sizeable part of the crisis in the UK and the Netherlands. The consortium simply had to pay too much for the purchase and became overleveraged. Sizeable banks are very difficult to purchase, even in distressed circumstances. Lloyds Bank TSB in the UK was able to acquire HBOS in the early stages of the crisis, when it became distressed, but the result was that the enlarged Lloyds Bank Group itself had to go to the government for funding.

We could go in two directions to tackle this issue. One would be to break up the large banks until they were small enough to be reasonable purchase targets. The second is to make it easier and less disruptive to restructure and recapitalize any banks that do fail.

The first option of breaking up would be politically difficult and hugely unpopular with the banks themselves. However, it appears from the Independent Commission on Banking, that the UK is contemplating such an approach. It is in any case irrelevant in New Zealand as the large banks are small by international standards. We have however seen that there is scope for very specific market entry, as is the case with Kiwibank. I am not in general in favour of state-owned banks, as there is no obvious reason why governments should be better at running banks than the private sector and quite a lot why they should not. However, Andrianova *et al.* (2010) have shown that if you take all other things which affect bank performance into account, such as the regulatory environment, the extent of competition and so on, then state banks do seem to be associated with a benefit for the economy, so perhaps the question is rather more open than most people thought, if they can be run at arm's length.

In any case, there is strong pressure round the world to consider whether 'narrow' banks should be created as these could provide a safe haven for depositors. In their extreme, such narrow banks are just transaction banks, rather like the post office in many countries. They charge you for the services they provide and do not offer much in the way of interest on accounts as the forms in which they can on-lend your funds to others are severely restricted, such as the holding of government paper. It is possible to broaden the scope somewhat to include lending on residential mortgages – in effect, a building society with expanded services and a banking licence – or enter other low-risk markets. The UK is currently exploring a more drastic division, requiring retail banks to stay out of investment banking, as was the case in the US until the repeal of the Glass-Steagall Act.

The jury is very much out on this topic as some banks have considerably improved their profitability by being broad banks. Offering people a choice between narrow and broad banks is one thing but banning broad banks is very much another. Breaking banks up because they are too complex to handle in the case of a crisis is also a different issue from simply banning broad banks. The Bank of England advocated the former, although even there the question is whether inability to handle the complex organization is something that the regulator rather than the bank should work on. In practice, it is a combination. As I mentioned earlier, it is important not to damage a sound banking model simply because there have been regulatory failures and some egregious examples of poor products and poor risk management. Some of course argue that the banking model is itself impaired and that a significant shift in ethical standards is required.

However, I want to focus simply on what can be done to make the resolution of banks less costly and disruptive. The simplest element is to ensure that recapitalization can be triggered automatically once crucial thresholds are breached.

The most straightforward of these is to have contingent capital. This can take a number of forms but one that has already been used successfully is the ability to switch some debt into equity. Debt needs to be repaid but equity does not. It has now been realized in the new Basel Committee agreement on capital requirements that only equity acts as a real buffer. If any other capital is used to manage a difficulty, it will constitute a default and hence trigger close-out clauses and a full-blown failure.[3] There are some examples where this ability to implement a debt for equity has been applied to subordinated debt (Denmark, for instance) but this could easily be extended to more senior debt, as Lloyds has illustrated in the UK, by issuing what are known as coco bonds – contingent-convertible bonds that become equity if core capital drops below the regulatory limits. The trigger for such a conversion from debt to equity could be of two sorts – a problem with the particular firm and a problem in the financial system as a whole.

Some writers on this topic have suggested (Squam Lake Group, 2009) that such conversions should only be forced if the financial system as a whole is under threat and that an independent agency would make this judgment. Otherwise if a bank fails it would simply be allowed to go into insolvency and the conversion would not be triggered. The reason is two-fold. The first is that this could otherwise be a way of protecting the existing shareholders from the consequences of their actions. Normally when a bank fails the existing shareholders are wiped out first and only then do the junior debtors have to bear a loss. This would need to apply in this case, even if the bank has some residual value, in which case the shareholders would need to be recompensed up to the extent of that value – which could be independently assessed. The second is that it is simply unnecessary if there is no systemic threat. As Huertas (2010) has pointed out, existing shareholders will find their holdings heavily diluted by the issue of new equity to the debt holders. So the result will be close to the priority in an insolvency and very unlikely to make anyone worse off than had an insolvency been applied.

There are other types of contingent capital, some of which take the form of insurance, whereby a third party agrees to provide capital under specific circumstances. The danger with this insurance is that, in the event of substantial claims, it may not be possible to honour the contract – especially if it occurs at a time of crisis when the providers themselves may be under stress. With a convertible bond, the bank already has the money; it is simply relieved of the obligation to pay it back. No one has to find new capital. Clearly this will have an impact on the cash flow of the lender and may affect the collateral value of the holding. However, the chance that this will lead to knock-on failures is likely to be lower.

A similar approach can be used for variable capital buffers or provisioning. The need for extra capital or provisions could be generated either by the growth of the firm or by the growth of the economy as a whole, or indeed by the growth of asset prices. Spain uses the individual bank's performance to generate the extra requirements, while Columbia and Peru use GDP. For these rules which apply to normal times, when the bank simply needs to take more precautions, the

Spanish approach sounds the more relevant, but when the question is what to do on failure the answer is rather more open, although I am inclined to opt for systemic risk being required as the trigger. Nevertheless, the Lloyds bonds were issued on the open market without any intervention by the authorities. So if they feel that this is a good route to recapitalization and so do the purchasers of the bonds, then it is very hard to think of a reason why they should not use it. (Incidentally, it will give a price for the default risk.) Of course, if such bonds are widely used, it may be that it will be difficult to find adequate numbers of lenders at a viable price.

Having an adequate safety net

One of the most cited problems in handling crises is what is known as moral hazard. Any facet of the system that can be construed as helping people in the event of difficulty can act as a disincentive for them to take avoiding action. Thus if I am fully insured against damage to my car, irrespective of who is responsible, I may take less care in how I drive or park, or where I leave my car. This is something we clearly wish to avoid in banking. We want banks and other financial institutions to exercise the same care as they would if they have to bear all the consequences. But we have seen what has happened on this occasion – large banks in difficulty have been bailed out. How will this affect moral hazard? My guess is not at all, as this was the expectation beforehand. The same is true under deposit insurance. People expected not to lose their deposits beforehand and this has turned out to be true. In any case, they did not exercise market discipline over their banks to any noticeable effect. It is just not realistic to suggest that people read about the relative performance of their banks and move their deposits accordingly. They would do if there was a serious threat to a bank but then it would be too late and this would result in a general run.

To handle a crisis, one needs a balance between what people can be realistically expected to do for themselves in the way of insurance and what society needs to provide in order to spread the shock sufficiently over the country as a whole and over time. In the previous section, I discussed how we can try to make sure that the need to involve other people is as small as possible. I have already discussed the case of deposit insurance. A purely industry-financed scheme can cover the whole of all ordinary people's bank accounts against the failure of small banks and the failure of a large bank when the rest of the system is healthy.[4] In a crisis, this is no longer true. Much more extensive guarantees may be required. They can only be offered by the state on behalf of the taxpayer. But as on this occasion, the expectation is that there will be no actual need to pay out, except perhaps in the form of a temporary loan to the deposit insurer until such time as it can be recapitalized by the surviving banks. This can go horribly wrong, as the Irish Government has discovered. They thought in issuing a blanket guarantee for bank creditors in September 2008 that they were only likely to be liable for a few billion euro, not a sum that threatened the solvency of the country and required a bail-out from the EU and the IMF.

The position changes if the authorities decide that the only route to resolution is nationalization or if they feel obliged to indulge in some form of TARP (Troubled Asset Repurchase Program) scheme – whether it is a general scheme or a 'bad bank'. 'Bad banks' or asset management companies (AMCs) are often set up as a means of separating a troubled bank into a healthy 'good bank' by stripping out all the impaired assets and placing them in the residual, 'bad bank'. Someone has to pay enough to purchase the bad assets in order to recapitalize the good bank, although this could be done by the creditors rather than the taxpayer. This too is controversial. In the Nordic crisis, Finland and Sweden used bad banks, whereas Norway did not. The Norwegians argue that it is better to invest in the bank as a whole, as management of impaired assets can be much more flexible if one is a bank with a continuing business rather than an AMC which will terminate when the last bad loan is resolved (Moe *et al.*, 2004).

Most of the safety net relates not to financial institutions but to the tax and benefit system and, as such, lies largely outside what I want to cover. However, following the recent review of the welfare system in New Zealand it should be possible to insulate people better against future crises. The system is relatively complicated and there has been a lot of change elsewhere, particularly in Europe. For example, most countries these days feel that the pension system should have three pillars to it. The first is a state-based scheme that protects those that cannot protect themselves and provides what society regards as the minimum acceptable level of benefit through general taxation. The second pillar provides personal pensions as the result of employment, with both employers and employees having to make contributions, while the third pillar is voluntary but with incentives encouraging people to save more. This is the sort of structure in New Zealand, although until Kiwisaver there was not much encouragement of greater saving.

In Australia, they feel that there has to be a greater element of compulsion, with a 9 per cent compulsory scheme, which is set to rise to 12 per cent. But then their basic benefit coverage is not so extensive. Of course pensions are only a small part of the scheme, which extends to health care education, unemployment and a range of publicly provided services, such as libraries, parks and supported social activities. Countries have found interesting ways to provide incentives for people to have wider insurance against adverse circumstances. One of these is to take the three-pillar system I described much further and to enable considerable flexibility with the second pillar so that it can handle unemployment, disability and ill-health as well. This has been of particular interest to the new member states of the EU who, with the collapse of the former Soviet Union, found that the basis for their social welfare system had been swept away and needed to start again without any accumulated funds (Mayes and Mustaffa, 2010). Thus, in such a scheme, if I lost my job in a crisis, I could draw on my pension funds to some extent if I wished. In the same way, if I had an injury which reduced my earning capability, I might wish to take some of my benefits earlier, perhaps for retraining, over and above the schemes which are publicly provided. With ACC, the Accident Compensation Commission, New Zealand has a rather different structure to its insurance, with a comprehensive, compulsory, no-blame, low-cost, state-run insurance system for all injuries.

The key issue is where the balance should lie between encouraging people to make provision and forcing them to do so, as ACC does. Either way round, the progressive reduction in savings rates of recent decades needs to come to an end. It is an interesting tribute to how urbanized New Zealand has become. Farmers are only too aware that that their incomes may vary widely – prices can vary sharply from one year to the next and so can yields. If they do not make adequate provision in good years and are mortgaged up to the hilt, they do not survive the bad years. Most people now rely on a much more stable environment.

Currently New Zealand finances this negative saving by borrowing abroad, primarily through the banking system. There is a limit to how far this can continue, which will be reflected initially in an increase in the cost of funds as foreign lenders begin to worry if they will be paid back and then in the danger of sudden stops to lending altogether, including refinancing.[5] Such sudden stops trigger a major financial crisis if adequate buffers are not in place – historically, foreign exchange crises are much more common than banking crises. One great advantage of the present floating exchange rate system is that New Zealand is much less vulnerable to foreign exchange crises than it was in the past under the fixed exchange rates. But at some point, even with a floating rate, a country becomes vulnerable again because such a large proportion of financing can be cut off by decisions made outside the country. (Of course if there were a currency union with Australia, this particular problem would fall to much lower levels.) On the whole, this is not a problem for the individual. People do not borrow overseas directly but through banks, so New Zealand is not like Poland and some other central and Eastern European countries, where people have mortgages in foreign currencies but no foreign currency income. Here the problem falls on the domestic (but foreign-owned) banks.

There are some areas of the safety net I have not mentioned because systems worked. Central banks were able to be the Lender of Last Resort to markets and get financial institutions through the period of non-functioning markets. However, it looks as if quantitative easing was not as successful as hoped in reducing real interest rates, as the Japanese found in their crisis. We are yet to see how elegantly the main central banks can exit from this exceptional position. As with fiscal policy, the objective is to ease back carefully so that the process of recovery is not impaired. It is a delicate balance between being too rapid and tipping the economy back into recession and being too slow and allowing inflation to take off.

The wholesale guarantees have enabled banks to tap financial markets; indeed in Australia there is some suggestion that they have been a subsidy for the investment banks, rather than a facility for which the taxpayer has been adequately compensated. In the UK, it appears that the extraordinary measures by the Bank of England have been profitable and hence the taxpayer will gain by the process. Whether they will gain from the government's purchase of bank shares is still to be revealed.

My point here, however, is simply to make it clear that I am focusing on what has not worked well and could do with improving. It is not a balanced assessment of how this crisis has been handled round the world. Many stabilizers have worked well and prevented even worse losses. Even in New Zealand and Australia, it is easy to envisage how the Reserve Bank or the government could have said or done something that would have made the crisis a lot worse in the short run. As far as I can see, their performance since the crisis broke has been well judged and, even with hindsight, the changes in actions that would be made are second order. This is, however, not true of the pre-crisis preparations, where no doubt the New Zealand authorities wished they had implemented the comprehensive supervisory regime for non-bank financial institutions through the Reserve Bank and the Financial Markets Authority from the outset of the new regulatory regime in 1996.

Reducing the impact of crises

In theory, the financial system should act as a shock absorber for problems in the real economy. It offers a ready opportunity to spread risks widely across society and across time. We can amass the resources to handle a crisis in advance and we can spread paying for the crisis over subsequent years. Thus debt should be below long-run sustainable levels after a long period of growth without crises. This New Zealand had, but countries such as Greece did not. Even the UK, which had promoted prudent fiscal policy, was running a structural deficit in good times when the crisis struck and has hence paid a substantial price as it had relatively little slack (Mayes, 2010).

Part of the reason the system acted as a shock amplifier and not a shock absorber on this occasion was a matter of faulty design of the system. Having capital buffers based on ratings meant that the required capital varied countercyclically. In good times, ratings are higher and hence capital requirements are lower. When the economy collapses, ratings fall and banks need to raise new capital to compensate exactly at the time that it is most difficult to do and when capital is being eroded because of losses. The problem is thus made much worse; banks have to shrink lending and hence push more firms into insolvency, setting up a vicious circle of needing to sell assets at a discount in an impaired market.

Why, you ask, was it not foreseen? Well, it was. People drew attention to the problem in the planning stage of the Basel 2 agreement in the discussions and the results were published – one of the articles (Peura and Jokivuolle, 2004) actually won an award. I, among others, also advocated some solutions for the problem based on measures known as dynamic provisioning and dynamic loan-to-value ratios employed in Spain and Hong Kong, for example (Mayes, 2004b). In the latter case, the faster asset prices rise, the smaller the proportion of the increase that can be used as collateral, as the chance of a fall in prices increases. These warnings and suggestions were ignored. When you are a small country, there is only so much you can do to affect international agreements. New Zealand, which is not a member of the EU, can set its own standards, providing they exceed those required in international agreements. However, attempts to do this in Finland may have contributed to pushing the largest bank into Swedish control and the second largest into Danish control. In New Zealand, the banks cannot get out of the local regulatory control, although if the Trans-Tasman arrangement comes into full operation, it will end up with a single regime with Australia, which would no doubt largely reflect Australian and not New Zealand standards.

The new Basel 3 rules have largely been developed. As expected from Basel 2, the focus is primarily on increasing regulatory capital. The basic cushion is now largely common equity, which can actually be run down without the bank failing. To this is added a larger margin for systemically important banks and the option for counter-cyclical capital. Moreover, plans are in place to encourage contingent capital – debt which can be converted into equity in the event of a crisis. The Reserve Bank of New Zealand has been sensible in tackling liquidity first, ahead of Basel, as in most respects liquidity is more important than capital. If a bank runs out of liquidity, it cannot pay its bills today. If its capital falls below regulatory limits, it means that the bank may not be able to pay its bills at some stage in the future. Undercapitalized banks sometimes struggle on for years and sometimes do get recapitalized. Illiquid banks fail. The new liquidity rules buy time. Even if people will not lend any new money, a bank has some time to put a restructuring in place, possibly with the help of the authorities, if they have adequate liquidity. It is noticeable that the Basel Committee recognized this importance and tried to have a matching agreement on liquidity in the 1980s but sadly this proved too difficult. This time around, liquidity buffers have been added, as has a minimum leverage ratio.

Clearly we can address much of the problem of financial stability and the ability to weather future crises by concentrating on organizing the lower-risk business sensibly and enabling it to handle very considerable shocks. However, the real concern lies with the higher-risk business. Higher-risk lending plays an essential part in economic development and welfare. If priced appropriately and managed, it can be profitable but it will always be subject to swings and correlated losses. Hence lenders have to be in a position to absorb such losses. Hence this is not a wise area for most retail investors, even though the potential returns may seem attractive.

One issue which New Zealand faces is trying to replace the failed finance company sector. The remaining institutions have a choice. They can become more conservative and turn themselves into banks, providing they can meet the conditions, and be supervised to a high standard by the Reserve Bank. Or they can remain in the less supervised, higher-risk sector, although even there the level of supervision has increased. There is a clear problem. There is a market for higher-risk capital for property investment and innovative ideas but this has to be provided by people who can absorb major losses. Such lending should be profitable as the returns on the successful ventures should more than cover the losses on the failures. In the property sector, there will always be failures from time to time, especially when the market turns down. Lenders need to be large institutions to cope with this. Small institutions find such projects give them excess exposure to specific borrowers.[6] Similarly, in venture capital, it makes much more sense for much of the capital to come from institutions, rather than individuals. Some of the problem is simply that New Zealand is a small market and it is difficult to develop the necessary institutions. Many of the projects have become large compared to the lenders. It is endemic in the property sector that development costs are underestimated and hence the lender is faced with a dilemma. If they do not advance even more, the project may fail and they will lose. If they do increase their advance, then if the project fails the lender will fail along with it. Creating such institutions, except perhaps as bank subsidiaries, is very difficult. Here again we return to the broad versus narrow bank argument. Such higher-risk subsidiaries might fail. If the parent does not intervene, then this may harm the banking business as reputation will suffer. If they do intervene and save the subsidiary, then there will be an immediate hit to bank capital. It is not an easy decision.

Finland faced the same problem in the 1960s, but there the Bank of Finland had a slightly wider remit, as it had a duty to ensure that all the necessary financial instruments and institutions were in place to enable Finnish firms to compete on an equal basis. The Bank thus set up a smart card company, helped develop the stock exchange and in the present context set up a major venture capital firm, Sitra.[7] As soon as the institutions got operating properly, the Bank could withdraw. As a result, there is a much greater supply of venture capital in Finland than New Zealand from large institutions.

The problem is that these sorts of finance are provided at the fringe and the size of those involved in financing it can be very small. Such higher-risk activities are not usually suitable for retail investors. People need to be very clear about the problems they are taking on and put together a balanced portfolio. For the retail investor, that can only be done through a fund. The dilemma in the search for stability is that this sector remains small. If the boundary is pushed out too far, this lending is discouraged and, insofar as it does take place, it may be through even more obscure direct relationships that will be difficult to monitor and police. The same applies to hedge funds. It is better to regulate them lightly, while trying to bar access to small retail investors, so that one can have some idea of what is going on, than to drive them offshore. They are helpful in addressing higher-risk issues as long as they are restricted to people who can afford the risk. As Svein Gjedrem, the former Governor of the Bank of Norway, put it:

> Hedge funds provide opportunities for rich people to take high risks and make high returns – most people think that is OK; hedge funds provide opportunities for rich people to take high risks and make high losses – most people think that is even more OK.

Most of my remarks have been directed at trying to design the financial system and its regulation in such a way that it is better able to withstand shocks, rather than suggesting how individuals might structure their own finances to weather such a storm. Most of the precepts for good financial management are well known. It is sensible to have a cushion for times of disadvantage, particularly for retirement. It is often a mistake to put everything in the same place. Pay off your mortgage first. Take advantage of subsidized offers, such as Kiwisaver. Be cautious about risky investments until you have quite a substantial portfolio and so on. But I guess perhaps one of the most important is understand the importance of advice and the interests of the people who would like to advise you.

It is extremely difficult to regulate advisors. New Zealand is steadily improving the position but it will never be perfect. All of the main banks and investment analysts find they need to employ substantial teams in order to offer their advice to clients. They need a whole range of country and industry specialists to build a picture of where investment opportunities seem likely to go in the future. There are rating agencies that try to give an independent view of the riskiness of products and organizations' debt. One feature of the crisis has been to reveal how big the mistakes are that rating agencies can make and the consequences these mistakes can have. Reform of rating agencies is therefore under way. One major side of this is to consider the incentives.

Although rating agencies are independent, they work for the seller. Working for the buyer is too difficult to organize. In the past, most of their payment has been up front so they do not lose on a particular contract if their judgment is at fault. Their reputation will however be affected in a competitive world. A further problem is that they also give advice to issuers about how to structure products. There are some clear conflicts here and the World Shadow Financial Regulatory Committee set out how these might be addressed when it met in 2010. It has not addressed the issue of advice but here again the same problems apply. If an advisor gets all their income up front, they have no incentive to worry about what happens subsequently to the product they have 'sold'. It is where their income comes from a continuing relationship with the client that the interests of the client and the interests of the advisor are likely to be better aligned. If the focus is on the short term, a problem that has also bedevilled executive remuneration in the finance industry, then the market is likely to be more volatile and the chance of crises and their size greater. As Bruce Sheppard remarked in Chapter 2, one should perhaps ask what proportion of their personal wealth an advisor has in the product they are promoting.

All these issues are being worked on and I cannot hope to address them effectively here. I merely recall some of the main conclusions I have drawn. There are eight of them.

1 The frequency and costs of crises will be reduced if there are effective mechanisms in place for handling them quickly and assigning the losses to those who knowingly took the risks in a preassigned priority.

   - New Zealand has this through the Reserve Bank Act 1989 but the procedures are untried (fortunately).

2 Detecting risks early and acting on them promptly before insolvency is essential for minimizing the losses.

- Some form of mandatory prompt corrective action might assist in encouraging banks themselves to act before they are forced.

3 To avoid retail bank runs in times of uncertainty, people need to be guaranteed virtually uninterrupted access to their accounts and explicit insurance of ordinary deposits is required.

- Where banks do not continue to trade, this involves considerable prepositioning to be able to move deposits from one provider to another seamlessly.
- There are also good equity reasons for protecting deposits, rather than letting ordinary people take the first hit (after the shareholders).

4 The problem of 'Too Big To Fail' and 'Too Big To Save' must be addressed, by:

- having structures that can be handled – living wills
- prepositioning
- liquidity buffers that offer enough time to be ready or solve the problem before failure
- contingent capital to provide automatic, immediate recapitalization outside (frozen) markets.

5 For major crises, the government will still have to stand ready to provide guarantees for institutions and insurance funds and the central bank to provide liquidity for markets.

6 In the same way that banks are being forced to have larger buffers against risk, so most people should take the lesson from this crisis that they need to take greater precautions against future risks. An important part of that buffer needs to be in liquid, high-quality assets.

- Trying to sell a house or other less liquid asset in a crisis where markets are seriously distressed may be impossible at a reasonable price.

7 The Reserve Bank's requirements for liquidity buffers are a welcome step.

8 The market for higher-risk projects and innovation needs to get working again following the demise of the finance company sector.

- Venture capital is very limited.
- There are serious risks in having small organizations finance large risks.

I end with one remark in case I have given the impression that this crisis is somehow special and simply the result of unscrupulous people in the US being prepared to offer NINJA (no income, no job or assets) mortgages and to trade in exotic products where you can insure yourself against risks you do not have.

The deposit insurance agencies are required to undertake what is known as material loss reviews if there are serious losses. There have of course been plenty of them in the last couple of years. As explained by Gillian Garcia in Chapter 10, the sad feature of them is that most of the bank failures in the US that were investigated were, to a large extent, caused by typical problems – exposure to related parties, large unhedged exposures, too great a concentration on the non-residential property market, too great a dependence on wholesale funding, inappropriate persons in positions of authority, etc. If the authorities had simply responded to the normal warning signals, then some of the problems could have been avoided. It is inherent in crises that the warning signals are for some reason ignored or explained away or that significant activities lie outside control, as in the case of the investment banks in the US. Carmen Reinhart and Ken Rogoff (2009) have written an excellent book called *This Time is Different*. It covers a huge range of crises over the last 150 years and some stretching as far back as the thirteenth century. Watch out for those words – they are accompanied by a flashing sign which reads 'Fasten Your Seatbelt'.

Notes

1 An earlier version of this chapter was presented in the Dean's Distinguished Speaker Series on 22 June 2010.
2 The Governor of the Reserve Bank has emphasized the problems this saving behaviour may lead to (Bollard, 2010).
3 Under the international guidelines for prudent banking laid down by the Basel Committee on Banking Supervision, which is part of the Bank for International Settlements, all banks have to hold at least 8 per cent of their 'risk-weighted' assets in the form of Tier 1 and Tier 2 capital, where Tier 1 capital is essentially common stock and reserves, while Tier 2 capital includes a wider range of reserves and subordinated debt. The idea of Tier 1 capital is that it can be used to offset losses without any payments taking place. Once subordinated debt is included, then someone who is owed money is not paid back. At this stage, the bank is insolvent. Hence in recent negotiations the importance and size of Tier 1 capital and other contingent instruments that can be used to offset losses without reaching insolvency are being increased. The Basel Committee has issued two sets of rules in this regard, the first in 1988 and the second, which was only just coming into force in 2008 as the crisis broke. These are already being revised. The first two are labelled Basel 1 and Basel 2 and the new agreement, Basel 3.
4 It is debatable who actually pays for a bank-financed scheme. Clearly in part it will be depositors but it may also be other customers and possibly shareholders, according to where the bank chooses to place the cost.
5 The New Zealand Treasury and Reserve Bank organized a conference on this topic on 23–24 June 2011. The papers are available at www.treasury.govt.nz/publications/research-policy/conferences-workshops/macroeconomicimbalances.
6 There are some ways around this, such as the issue of property bonds, but the risk still needs to be diversified across people who can afford to bear it. One of the difficulties which contributed to the collapse of some finance companies was that they structured their property loans so that no payments had to be made until the development was completed, thus providing no cash flow.
7 www.sitra.fi/en/how-does-sitra-operate.

References

Andrianova, S., Demetriades, P. and Shortland, A. (2010) 'Is government ownership of banks really harmful to growth?', *DIW Discussion Paper*, no. 987.

Bollard, A. (2010) *Address to the Wellington Chamber of Commerce*, June 14, available at www.rbnz.govt.nz/news/2010/4040739.html.

FSA (2008) *The Supervision of Northern Rock: A Lessons Learned Review*, Internal Audit Department, March.

Hoggarth, G., Reis, R. and Saporta, V. (2002) 'Cost of bank instability: some empirical evidence', *Journal of Financial Stability*, 26(5): 825–56.

Huertas, T. (2010) 'The road to better resolution: from bail-out to bail-in', revised version of a paper delivered to the conference on 'The Euro Area and the Financial Crisis', National Bank of Slovakia, 6 September.

Mayes, D.G. (2004a) 'Comments on "Interaction of monetary and financial stability in a small open economy – the case of Iceland"', SUERF seminar in Iceland, Reykjavik, 4 June.

Mayes, D.G. (2004b) 'Getting the best out of Basel II for the European Banking System', in R Ayadi and A Resti, *The New Basel Capital Accord and the Future of the European Financial System*, pp. 64–70, Brussels: CEPS, April.

Mayes, D.G. (2010) 'Case Study 4 – United Kingdom', in *Regulatory Reform for Recovery: Lessons from Implementation during Crises*, pp. 181–254, Paris: OECD.

Mayes, D.G. and Mustaffa, Z. (2010) 'Social models in the enlarged EU', *RECON Working Paper*, 2010/20.

Mayes, D.G. and Wood, G.E. (2008) 'Lessons from the Northern Rock episode', *Economie Internationale*, 114: 5–27.

Mayes, D.G., Halme, L. and Liuksila, A. (2001) *Improving Banking Supervision*, Basingstoke: Palgrave.

Mayes, D.G., Nieto, M.N. and Wall, L. (2008) 'Multiple safety net regulators and agency problems in the EU: is prompt corrective action partly the solution?', *Journal of Financial Stability*, 4(3): 232–57.

Moe, T.G., Solheim, J.A. and Vale, B. (2004) *The Norwegian Banking Crisis*, Occasional Paper 33, Oslo: Norges Bank.

Peura, S. and Jokivuolle, E. (2004). 'Simulation based stress tests of banks' regulatory capital adequacy', *Journal of Banking and Finance*, 28(8): 1801–24.

Reinhart, C.M. and Rogoff, K.S. (2009) *This Time is Different: Eight Centuries of Financial Folly*, Princeton: Princeton University Press.

Sargent, T. (2001) *The Conquest of American Inflation*, Princeton: Princeton University Press.

Sigurðsson, J. (2004) 'Small countries, large multi-country banks: a challenge to supervisors – the example of the Nordic-Baltic area', in D. Mayes and A. Liuksila (eds), *Who Pays for Bank Insolvency?*, pp. 142–63, Basingstoke: Palgrave-Macmillan.

Squam Lake Group (2009) *Improving Resolution Options for Systemically Relevant Financial Institutions*, Squam Lake Working Group on Financial Regulation, available at www.squamlakegroup.org/images/Squam%20Lake%20Resolution%20Options%20Oct%2026%20Final.pdf (accessed 14 June 2010).

Stern, G. and Feldman, R. (2004) *Too Big to Fail: the Hazards of Bank Bailouts*, Washington, DC: Brookings Institution.

Index

Page numbers in ***italics*** denote tables, those in **bold** denote figures.

9781138799479